History of Universities

VOLUME VIII
1989

History of Universities

VOLUME VIII
1989

Oxford University Press
1989

History of Universities is published annually as a single volume.

Editor:
Laurence Brockliss (Magdalen College, Oxford).

Assistant Editor:
Mark Curthoys (Nuffield College, Oxford).

Bibliography Editor:
John Fletcher (University of Aston in Birmingham).

Editorial Board:
P. Denley (Westfield College, London)
W. Frijhoff (Erasmus Universiteit, Rotterdam)
N. Hammerstein (University of Frankfurt)
D. Julia (Centre de recherches historiques, EHESS, Paris)
J. K. McConica (St Michael's College, Toronto University)
N. G. Siraisi (Hunter College, New York)

Papers for publication in History of Universities as well as
books for review should be sent to the editor, Dr. L. W. B. Brockliss,
Magdalen College, Oxford, OX1 4AU, United Kingdom.

A leaflet 'Notes to OUP Authors' is available on request from the editor.

Details of subscription rates and terms are available from
Oxford Journals Subscription Department, Walton Street,
Oxford, OX2 6DP, United Kingdom.

© Oxford University Press 1989

British Library Cataloguing in Publication Data
(data available)
ISBN 0 19 822724–8

Library of Congress Cataloguing Publication Data
(data available)

Typeset by Latimer Trend and Company Ltd, Plymouth
Printed in Great Britain by
Biddles Ltd, Guildford and King's Lynn.

Contents

Articles

Research in Progress

Conference Reports

Essay Review

Book Reviews

Bibliography

The Medical Faculty at Early Fourteenth-Century Lérida

Michael McVaugh and Luis García Ballester

Much has been written about the fourteenth-century medical faculties of the west-Mediterranean universities, Montpellier and Lérida, despite the scarcity of textual evidence from this period. Montpellier's published *cartularium* provides us with the material for a general survey of institutional developments during the century, but it has little to say about how general rules were translated into academic practice.[1] The Leridan documentation, which has not yet all been drawn together nor indeed published, has to do almost entirely with the century's first and last decades and, like Montpellier's, deals with the school's organization and structure, though in less detail.[2] It is difficult to identify (much less talk knowledgeably about) individual masters or students at Montpellier, and virtually impossible to do so at Lérida. Thus it is doubly fortunate that a document has come to light in the archive of the cathedral of Lérida that provides us with new information bearing on the situation at Montpellier as well as at Lérida.

The document, dated 1344, is a license to exercise the mastership in medicine in the *studium generale* of Lérida. It is found, in two somewhat different versions, in the notarial manual of Ferrer Sobrepena for 1334–44; the first version was modified by a number of marginal additions, and the notary seems eventually to have decided to rewrite the whole document, omitting the detailed list of witnesses included in the first version. We publish below the license in both versions, for reasons that will become apparent; it seems to show that Arnau ça Riera (Arnaldus de Riaria), a disciple of master Jean (Johannes) Maseti, received training in medicine at Montpellier and that now, after further years of practice, he has been given private and public examination and been found 'sufficiens et idoneus' to exercise the office of *magister in medicina* in the *studium generale* of Lérida and elsewhere.

The Leridan *studium* was founded in 1300 by Jaume II of Aragon, who explicitly named medicine as one of the subjects to be taught there, along with canon and civil law and the liberal arts, 'so that our folk need not pursue them in foreign lands.'[3] The first master to teach medicine at Lérida was Guillem Gaubert de Béziers, who lectured there intermittently from 1301 until 1304.[4] His teaching was regularly interrupted by summonses to attend the royal family in Valencia or Jaca or Barcelona, and the Leridan *pahers* (the town councillors) who had hired him found his repeated departures irritating; in February 1304 Jaume II had to insist that the *pahers* continue to pay Guillem his salary, despite his absence from Lérida on a medical errand to Montpellier for the king.[5] Later that year dissension closed the *studium*, and Guillem left for good. It reopened in 1310, and the councillors wrote the next year to Pere Gavet (in July) and then to Bernat de Bonahora (at the beginning of October) in an attempt to reinstitute medical education, but there is no evidence that either responded to this call;[6] only in 1315 does Pere Gavet appear in the documentation as a teacher in Lérida, and by 1318 (after a dispute over his unpaid salary) he had left for Barcelona.[7]

We have testimony to the presence of only three other masters in medicine at the school before 1350. Pere Colom lectured there in 1323–4, and appears to have been alone, for he was forced to wait until masters Joan Amell and Pere Gavet could travel to Lérida before he could be examined for his final degree. Again King Jaume had to intercede with the *pahers* and command that they continue to pay Colom his salary (on the grounds that his failure actually to receive his degree was no fault of his)—Jaume's interest in and support of academic medicine is evident throughout his reign.[8] Bertran de la Torre was being paid to lecture in surgery at Lérida at the time of his death, *c*. 1330, and Jaume's son and successor, Alfons IV, nominated Guillem of Avignon to replace him, but there is no evidence that Guillem ever came to Lérida.[9] Finally, Jacme d'Agramunt was master of medicine at the school in 1348.[10] There is no reason to believe that any of the other figures sometimes assigned to the medical faculty—for example, Henricus Theutonicus, Joan de Sist, Rigo de Frisce, Jacme de Brindisi—ever taught at Lérida;[11] one who has been so assigned, 'mestre Anglons', may not even have been a physician.[12]

Even these few data suggest that payment of the medical master was a recurrent problem at Lérida. When the school was founded in 1300 the king had granted the municipal officers the right to appoint its masters, but this privilege had aroused the jealousy of the bishop and chapter and helped bring about the temporary closure of the *studium* in 1305.[13] Five years later the school reopened when the town conceded the right of appointment to the bishop and agreed to contribute 2500 *sous*[14] annually towards the salaries of the masters for ten years if the bishop would do the same; but tensions persisted between the town and the see, and in September 1313 King Jaume intervened, imposing a new arrangement that endured for the remainder of the century. Under its terms the right of appointment was returned to the town, and the bishop and chapter were required to contribute 3000 *sous* annually towards salaries; moreover, the *magister medicine* selected by the city was singled out to receive a canon's portion from the chapter.[15] It is not unlikely that in return for this unique supplement the physician was now expected to provide medical care to the chapter as well as teach in the school; contracts of this sort, providing a physician with a salary and a canon's portion in exchange for medical services to the chapter, are known from other cathedral towns in fourteenth-century Cataluña.[16] At Lérida, of course, the medical master received his salary from the town rather than from the chapter, and it may be that the *pahers* paid it so grudgingly—and at a lower rate than that enjoyed by the doctors of law[17]—because they felt that in these new circumstances he should primarily be a charge upon the cathedral.

Our information about the administration and the rest of the faculty of the *studium* is equally scanty for the first half of the fourteenth century.[18] Ramón Gaya Massot was able to identify only a handful of Lérida's rectors (who served one-year terms) in the years before 1350.[19] As for the masters, a charter of 1328 indicates that at that moment only seven were being paid by the town to teach: two in civil law, two in canon law, one in medicine, one in grammar (a second grammatical master was dependent upon the cathedral), and one in logic and philosophy.[20] Slightly more than a century later, to be sure, the faculty had grown noticeably. By 1447 there were two masters of medicine at Lérida (Francesc Queralt and Joan Pena), and this not only met the requirements set out in the new regulations of that year but had also been the practice of the school 'for as long as anyone can remember';[21] the two joined with four masters in canon law and three in civil law to make up the school's senior faculty. At what point the masters' numbers thus increased has so far been left to the imagination, for no documents about the day-to-day activities of the university in this period have hitherto been found. Arnau's medical license seems now to suggest that this growth had already taken place by 1344. Significantly, the list of masters whom we find as witnesses to the act includes the same numbers in the same fields as those required by the curriculum of 1447: two medical masters (Jacme d'Agramunt and 'Waltero de Wrobruge Anglico'), together with four in canon law (Guglielmo Arnaldi of Padua, Guillem de Noguer, García Romeo, and Ramón Frisci) and three in civil law (Pere Despens, Guillem Servet, and Pericon Despens). The newly discovered license gives us not only an indication of the university's early growth but also a sign that medicine remained a relatively unimportant faculty. The continuing dominance of legal studies already in this first half-century of the school's existence is further confirmed by contemporary notarial records of the selling, pledging, and loaning of books, in which works on *decretales* and, to a lesser extent, on civil law predominate.[22]

Some of the particular individuals who witnessed the license are of special interest. Of the two medical masters, one, Jacme d'Agramunt, has been a figure of interest since 1909, when a manuscript of his *Regiment de preservació de pestilència* was discovered in the parish archive at Verdú (40 kilometers east of Lérida). This work has subsequently attracted much attention as the only academic medical work known to have been composed in Catalan during the first half of the fourteenth century; its colophon explains that 'ffo acabat aquest tractat en l'an de [1348] per Maestre Jacme d'Agramont, maestre en arts e en medicina en lo [derrer] an de la sua lectura' at the *studium* of Lérida.[23] Opinions have differed as to whether 'tercer' or 'derrer' should be read here, and hitherto there has been no independent documentation of the teaching of Jacme at Lérida,[24] but our license now provides this evidence, and makes it virtually certain that the colophon reads 'derrer': if Jacme was already lecturing at Lérida in 1343–4 (the school year ran from October to June), 1347–8 would have been at least his fifth year as a teacher there.[25] The second medical master, Walter de Wrobruge (= Roborough in Devonshire?), is otherwise unknown, but it is enormously intriguing to find an Englishman in this Catalan faculty—as well, apparently, as a Paduan and a Castilian. Pere Despens, one of the three *legum doctores* who witnessed the license, had apparently taught at the school since 1338, though at first his service as royal counsellor took him away from Lérida so much that he was forced to pay a substitute to lecture for him.[26] Pere ça Vench, the canon of Vic who appears as rector of the school for 1343–4, was unknown to Gaya Massot.

Guillem de Bellvis, named here as Lérida's chancellor, had held the office since 1329 but by November 1344 would be dead and replaced by Guillem Ramón de Montcada; the fact that he was not physically present at the act of licensing may or may not foreshadow his imminent death.[27]

The license seems also to shed light on the licensing procedures of Lérida and Montpellier, but on examination its confusing language and the apparent contradictions between its two forms raise new problems. The first version speaks of Arnau ça Riera as a bachelor in medicine who has been recommended by his master Jean Maseti and has been publicly and privately examined at Lérida. It also makes reference to a document notarized at Montpellier in March 1329, without making clear what the document contained; the reference appears to have been added as an afterthought, to be inserted into the body of the license, but the most likely place for it to have been inserted would seem to make it record the granting of a master's insignia to Arnau—fifteen years before the Lérida master's license was issued.[28] The second, reworked, version implies that the document of 1329 certified Arnau's study at Montpellier (presumably as *bacallarius*); and that Jean Maseti presented him to the faculty at Lérida and, after he had passed the doctoral examinations, personally conferred the signs of mastership upon him there. We cannot be sure which, if either, version—the earlier text, full of emendations and insertions, or the subsequent, more carefully written one— accurately represents the contents of the notary's statement. Was the Lérida examination a confirmation of a license Arnau had already achieved at Montpellier without actually incepting, fifteen years before, or did it mark his final arrival at the master's level?

The situation is further confused by what we know about Jean Maseti, for there were two people by this name at Montpellier in the first half of the fourteenth century. One was master of medicine in 1313 but seems no longer to have been teaching in 1335, for he was not on the list of Montpellier masters given in a charter of that year.[29] Another was merely 'bacallarius de medicina' in 1332, and was presumably the former's son; whether he ever received the

master's degree is unknown.[30] Only the father could have supervised
Arnau's studies in the years before 1329; the son could have
presented Arnau personally in 1344, but we would have to assume
that the son had gone on to take his degree as *magister* and that
Arnau had somewhere established a professional relationship with
him.

What we know of Arnau's career in the decade before 1345 makes
the latter assumption seem implausible. The ça Riera family of
Gerona produced successful physicians and surgeons throughout
the fourteenth century, and Arnau was the son of Berenguer ça
Riera (d. 1310), surgeon to Jaume II.[31] Arnau appears as *fisicus et
cirurgicus Gerunde* in May 1331, but by October 1334 he was in the
service of Alfons IV, who granted him 1000 *sous* yearly on the
royal revenues from Barcelona in March 1335. He continued to treat
the king during much of that year (administering *onguens e
empastres* to his patient in October), although he was apparently not
present at the king's death in January 1336. From 1336 to 1341 (and
perhaps beyond) he acted as physician and surgeon to Alfons's son
and successor, Pere IV, who, praising Arnau as 'peritum in medicinali scientia', increased his stipend to 4000 *sous* and allowed him
to collect it from royal revenues in Gerona. In the spring of 1344, at
about the time he received his license at Lérida, he collected nearly
240 pounds from the treasury—due him for salary, clothing allowance, a horse, and 'diverses rahons'.[32] Nowhere in these many
documentary references is he alluded to as 'professor' or 'magister in
medicina', even though such titles were ordinarily insisted upon by
those who held them, and we thus cannot feel confident that he had
completed his degree requirements at Montpellier in the 1320s, but
the unusual phrase in which King Pere emphasized Arnau's learning
was certainly evoked by his formal medical training. Once he had
incepted at Lérida, however, Arnau insisted upon his new title; the
epitaph composed at his death in May 1348 speaks of him as having
been 'magister in medicina'.[33]

It does not help resolve our problem—is Arnau's license primarily
describing events at Montpellier in the 1320s or those at Lérida in
the 1340s?—to compare the details of the license with what we know
of graduation ceremonies at these two schools. The statutes of the
medical faculty of Montpellier, dating from 1340, suggest that the
normal sequence for the promotion of a bachelor was 'in examine
publico in scolis faciendo, . . . in privato, . . . in aula episcopali, . . . in

adepcione magistratus.' The candidate began by responding in the classroom to the questioning of each master in the faculty. Next he presented himself secretly, armed with two 12-pound candles for light, at an *examen privatum* or *rigorosum*, where he swore to his qualifications (length of study, legitimacy of birth), promised to fulfil the requirements of all new masters, and was passed (*receptum*) if he received the support of two-thirds of the masters present. Now, under the aegis of his master, he could be presented to the bishop, who arranged for a committee—an episcopal representative and two medical masters—to give him a public examination in both theory and practice; having been found *sufficiens* by this tribunal, he swore once more to incept, and to lecture for the next two years at Montpellier, whereupon the bishop's representative gave him the 'licenciam accipiendi insignia magistralia, quandocumque vobis placuerit; quibus receptis, damus vobis auctoritatem et licentiam legendi, disputandi, practicandi, ... et omnia alia faciendi.' In the final stage, the actual inception, the university community assembled in formal dress in the church of St. Firmin; the master-to-be swore to observe the privileges of the university, which were read out by the chancellor; his teacher 'accedat juxta cathedram magistrandi et commendet eum'; and, as a new master, he formally defended a *questio* with the others.[34]

We are less well informed with regard to Lérida. No other license from the school is known for the fourteenth century; the earliest that survives is one for a bachelor of canon law dated 1431, and the first medical license (likewise a bachelor's) is from 1585; neither provides useful comparative material.[35] The *ordinations antigues* of 1300 do not define the examination procedure; they merely suggest that at Lérida, as at Montpellier, a candidate first gave a *lectio*, then underwent an *examinatio in privato*, and finally was given an *examinatio publica*.[36] But if Rashdall is right in concluding that these ordinations 'are undoubtedly modelled ... [on] the whole organization and educational system of the University of Bologna,'[37] we can perhaps assume that the examination procedure too was similar. Bolognese practice was very like that revealed by Montpellier's 1340 statutes: a 'rigorous' private examination followed by a public one in which the licentiate delivered an address, was invested by his master with the insignia of his office (the *cathedra*, book, ring, and biretta), and was kissed and blessed.[38]

Our information about practices at Lérida and Montpellier is thus not adequate to let us decide where the events described in Arnau's license took place, for they are consistent with both schools. Indeed, graduation exercises appear to have been sufficiently similar throughout the European universities in this period that, as far as we can tell, the rites described in Arnau's license would fit Paris or Bologna quite as well as they do Montpellier or Lérida.[39]

Hence there remain two ways to interpret the events that preceded our documents, each with its own difficulties. It is possible that Arnau completed his studies at Montpellier by 1329, was presented by his master Jean Maseti (senior) to the faculty there, was examined privately, and was licensed by the bishop, but did not go on to incept at that time—perhaps (as was not at all uncommon in the European university world) because of the considerable expense involved in inception. In 1344, however, financially secure after a decade of service to the kings of Aragon, he incepted at Lérida (perhaps after re-examination)—claiming back payment from the royal treasury in order to pay the costs of graduation. This explanation supposes that the earlier version of Arnau's license ('1' in Appendix II, below) is the more trustworthy, and that it preserves in a series of interpolations the content of a document of 1329 that certified Arnau's fulfilment of a master's requirements at Montpellier. Here, however, it is hard to believe that Arnau could have received the insignia (as stated in those interpolations) before incepting; could the reference to their presentation have been merely anticipatory?

It is also possible that Arnau had fulfilled a bachelor's requirements at Montpellier by 1329 but had not proceeded to the mastership, to which he was presented at Lérida by Jean Maseti (junior). Under this explanation, we would suppose that version '2' of the license was correct, and that it had been rewritten to correspond better to the facts. Here the difficulty is that we can establish no prior relation between Maseti and Arnau. It is not impossible that Maseti could have taken his master's degree at Montpellier and come to Lérida to teach in its school, though the admittedly fragmentary city and episcopal archives give no hint of his presence there; and so long as material does not turn up that conclusively places Arnau in the royal entourage during 1342 and 1343, it is not out of the question that Arnau too was in Lérida, completing his studies, in those years. But we cannot feel confident of this second explanation without some positive evidence on these points, especially since it entails accepting the presence of an unprecedented three masters teaching medicine simultaneously in the Leridan *studium*.

In either case, Arnau's certification demonstrates convincingly the consolidation of Lérida as a medical school that had taken place in the previous twenty years. In 1324 Pere Colom had been the only medical master there, and had been allowed to teach even though he still lacked his final degree; but his situation was unsatisfactory enough from a professional point of view that he left after the city fathers delayed in paying him his salary (like Pere Gavet before him). It seems clear that by 1344 the faculty had attained stability, that it had grown to the size that would remain optimal for a hundred years and more, that its masters were content with their situation there, and that its degrees were not despised by the ambitious—which Arnau ça Riera certainly was.

A further tantalizing hint that the faculty was maturing intellectually is the insertion into version '2' of Arnau's license of four references to medicine as a *scientia*.[40] At the beginning of the fourteenth century there was considerable debate over the nature of medical knowledge, a debate that had definite practical implications. Was medicine merely a mechanical *ars*, with no claim to kinship with speculative philosophy? Was it an art higher in dignity and status, like the liberal arts? Might it not even be *scientia*, true knowledge derived from certain principles? These successive possibilities provided increasingly powerful justification for medical training in an academic setting, entailed increasing social prestige for a university-trained physician, and encouraged the introduction of examinations as a means of controlling access to medical practice. Considerations of this sort may lie behind the discussions at Bologna, starting perhaps as early as the late 1270s, that tended to define medicine as at least to some degree a *scientia*.[41] It is quite likely that the insertions into Arnau's license signal the same emerging consciousness among the Leridan masters that the dignity of their discipline would be enhanced by emphasizing its status as *scientia*, and this is another indication of the medical faculty's growing self-confidence. In the absence of texts and commentaries from the faculty, it is only from clues of this sort that we can hope to reconstruct anything of its intellectual development. Let us hope that other documents may some day appear that will give us insight into the consolidation of the medical faculty at Lérida in these two decades.[42]

Department of History
The University of North Carolina at Chapel Hill
Hamilton Hall
Chapel Hill, N.C. 27599
U.S.A.

REFERENCES

1. *Cartulaire de l'Université de Montpellier*, ed. A. Germain (2 vols.; Montpellier, 1890).
2. Ramón Gaya Massot, 'El "Chartularium universitatis Illerdensis" ', *Miscelánea de trabajos sobre el estudio general de Lérida*, 1 (Lérida, 1949), 9–47.
3. 'Ut nec potissime nostros fideles et subditos pro investigandis scientiis nationes peregrinas expetere nec in alienis ipsos oporteat regionibus mendicare,' Archivo de la Corona de Aragón (henceforth ACA), Cancillería reg. 197, fo. 275. The full text has been published several times: by Prosper de Bofarull, *Colección de documentos inéditos del Archivo de la Corona de Aragón* (Barcelona, 1850), vi, 204–8; by P. Sáinz de Baranda, *España sagrada*, xlvii (Madrid, 1850), 341–3; by Jaime Villanueva, *Viage literario de las iglesias de España* (Madrid, 1851), xvi, 196–8; and by Antoni Rubió y Lluch, *Documents per l'història de la cultura catalana mig-eval* (Barcelona, 1908–21), i. 14–16. General accounts of the early history of the university are available in Heinrich Denifle, *Die Universitäten des Mittelalters bis 1400* (Berlin, 1885; reprinted, Graz, 1956), 499–508; and in Hastings Rashdall, *The Universities of Europe in the Middle Ages*, ed. F. M. Powicke and A. B. Emden (Oxford, 1936), ii. 91–6. Johannes Vincke, *Die Hochschulpolitik der Aragonischen Krone im Mittelalter* (Staatliche Akademie zu Braunsberg, Personal- und Vorlesungs-Verzeichnis, Sommersemester 1942), 17–33, examines closely the king's motives for creating a university and establishing it at Lérida in particular.
4. Biographical information is provided by Ernest Wickersheimer, *Dictionnaire biographique des médecins en France au moyen âge* (Geneva, 1936), [i] 244. Rubió y Lluch, *Documents*, ii. 13–14, publishes a document pertaining to Guillem's career at Lérida, and elsewhere (ibid., ii, p. xxxii) he identifies a few of the many documents bearing on Guillem's service as physician to Jaume II in the years 1303–7. Guillem's pension from the king was long in arrears, however, when he died on 8 December 1322 (ACA, Real Patrimonio, reg. 634, fo. 73).

5. See below, Appendix I, no. 1. Guillem's presence in the city is not attested after September 1304 (ACA, Canc. reg. 294, fo. 224v).

6. Both letters are found in ACA, Canc. reg. 208, fo. 20v. The documentation was summarized by Heinrich Denifle, 'Urkunden zur Geschichte der mittelalterlichen Universitäten', *Archiv für Litteratur- und Kirchengeschichte*, 4 (1888), 252, who erroneously dated the letter to Gavet as of 3 April; it is actually dated 5 July (*iii nonas iulii*). Ramón Gaya Massot published the full text of the document in 'Provisión de cátedras en el estudio de Lérida', *Analecta Sacra Tarraconensia*, 30 (1958), 287, but read the date of the letter to Bonahora as 'secunda kalendis octubris'— in fact, it reads 'Gerunda, kalendas octubris'. We can find no basis for the contention of Josep Lladonosa that Bonahora and Gavet were actually present teaching at Lérida in 1311 (*Noticia histórica sobre el desarollo de la medicina en Lérida* [Lérida, 1974], 70; 'Commentaris i aportacions documentals pera la historia de la medicina de Lleida,' *Anales 1977, Ilustre Colegio Oficial de Médicos de la Provincia de Lérida*, 23).

7. For a survey of Gavet's career, with documentation, see Joseph M. Roca, *L'estudi general de Lleyda* (Barcelona, n.d.), 71–8; and Jorge Rubió Balaguer and Antonio de la Torre y del Cerro, *Documentos para la historia de la Universidad de Barcelona*, i (Barcelona, 1971), 13–14.

8. Two documents bearing on Pere's teaching career are published below in Appendix I, nos. 2–3; the first of them is touched on by Rubió y Lluch, *Documents*, ii, p. lxv, and by Ramón Gaya Massot, 'Las rentas del estudio general de Lérida', *Analecta Sacra Tarraconensia*, 25 (1952), 297. A third document, in ACA, Canc. reg. 413/414, (2) fo. 1, describes Pere as physician to the *infante* Alfons and commands that the *pahers* of Lérida pay him the 900 *sous* still owing him 'pro eo quia legit in dicta civitate in arte medicine'; it is dated 1 July 1327. We do not believe that the 'Petri Colom' included as one of the 'civium Ilerde' in February 1328 (Rubió y Lluch, i. 82) can be identified with the former medical master; on the other hand, the 'magister Petrus Columbus fisicus' of Tortosa who in October 1348 paid his daughter's £150 dowry may well be the same man (Arxiu Històric Provincial de Tarragona, protocolos Tortosa 1122, fo. 5). We have discussed the king's attitude towards medicine in some detail in our Medical Licensing and Learning in Fourteenth-Century Valencia' (American Philosophical Society, in press).

9. Alfons's letter to the *pahers* referring to Bertran's death and nominating Guillem is cited by Gaya Massot, 'Las rentas', 297–8, who does not however reproduce the text, for which see below, Appendix I, no. 4. 'Maestre Bertran de la Torre cirurgich' was present in Lérida to give testimony in February 1325 (Arxiu Municipal de Lleida [henceforth AML], reg. 767, fo. 151bis-v), but was not necessarily teaching in the *studium* then; indeed, a document published by Denifle ('Urkunden',

260) dated 8 August of the same year indicates that the school had recently been closed.

10. Below, nn. 23ff.

11. Josep Lladonosa, *La facultat de medicina de l'antiga universitat de Lleida* (Barcelona, 1969), 9–10, and *Noticia histórica*, 65, citing Rubió y Lluch as his authority. This error derives from a misreading of Rubió y Lluch, *Documents*, ii, p. xxxii, who comments merely 'al costat dels metges catalans, y potser en major nombre encara, trobem els metges estrangers', and is referring generally to physicians whose names appear in the royal archives, not to those present at Lérida: 'Senyalem alguns dels que trobem en les nostres notes: mestre Rolf, anglicus, . . . Enricus Theutonicus, *in medicinali sciencia professori*, al qual concedeix el rey una cavalcadura en abril de 1311. . . . El mes de març de 1296 patí el rey una malaltia a Nàpols, essent assistit per Joan de Sist, Rigo de Frisce i Jaume de Brindis.' In his 'Comentaris i aportacions' (p. 24), Lladonosa compounds the confusion by asserting that these latter three physicians arrived at Lérida after 1327, 'ja mort Jaume II'. Other statements by Lladonosa that we have not been able to substantiate are that Joan Amell 'regía la Facultad de Medicina 1312–1313' (*Noticia histórica*, 70) and that Guillem de Carcassonne shared lecturing responsibilities with Pere Colom in 1326 (*Noticia histórica*, 71; 'Comentaris i aportacions,' 23). On this latter point Lladonosa again cites Rubió y Lluch as his authority when he says that Guillem received a salary of 500 *sous* annually from the *pahers*; but the document to which Rubió is referring (ii, p. xxxii)—ACA, Canc. reg. 426, fo. 50v—merely records a grant to Guillem by the *infanta* Teresia. Elsewhere (*Documents*, ii, pp. lix–lxvi) Rubió provides a sketch of the fourteenth-century *studium* of Lérida together with a list of its masters known to him, all based scrupulously upon archival evidence: the only physicians he names there as having taught at Lérida before 1350 are Guillem de Béziers and Pere Colom (p. lxv).

12. 'El trienni 1341–1344, la facultat de Medicina de Lleida era servida per maesse Anglons' (Josep Lladonosa i Pujol, 'La sanitat i la higienea Lleida entre Arnau de Vilanova i Jacme d'Agramont [segle XIV]', *Anales 1976, Ilustre Colegio Oficial de Médicos de la Provincia de Lérida*, 90; *Noticia histórica*, 72). The references we have found in the Leridan *Llibres de Consell* (AML, reg. 397, fos. 53, 54r–v) do not actually identify 'mestre Anglons' as a physician, but it is not impossible that he was one. A 'magister Thomas Anglici cirurgicus nunc civis Ilerdensis' was placed under royal protection in February 1328 (ACA, Canc. reg. 429, fo. 162v); his house in Lérida was robbed of various things— including 'quendam librum medicine'—in October 1330 (ACA, Canc. reg. 437, fo. 131v; Rubió y Lluch, i. 100). This is probably the same man as the 'maestre Thomas cirurgich de la ciutat' who was required to present a *desuspitatio* in March 1332 (AML, reg. 770, fos. 130v–131v).

In June 1336 Pere IV commanded the *pahers* of Lérida to observe the
rights of 'Magister Thome Anglici cirurgici civis nunc Ilerde' (ACA,
Canc. reg. 586, fo. 192). It seems likely, however, that this 'maestre
Thomas' left Lérida in 1338. In August of that year Master Thomas
'Gallesii', surgeon of Lérida, was given permission by Pere IV to move
to Valencia and practise there (ACA, Canc. reg. 864, fo.
94v), and
indeed the next January we find 'magister Thomas de Angles', surgeon
of Valencia, given permission to carry arms in that city (ACA, cartas
reales, Pere IV, no. 525). In May 1340 an *elongamentum* was granted to
'magistro Thomasii Anglesii cirurgico civitatis Ilerde' (ACA, Canc. reg.
605, fo. 193v), but this may simply reflect that he was still tied to Lérida
by debts even after having moved to Valencia. There is thus some
reason to question whether the 'maestre Anglons' in Lérida in 1344 can
be the same man as the 'mestre Thomas Anglici' of 1328–40. Even if he
were, of course, there would still be no evidence to tie him to the medical
faculty or to the *studium*; the language of the *Llibre de consell* implies at
most some sort of contract with the city.

13. The appointment and support of the Leridan teachers is treated fully by
Gaya Massot, 'Las rentas', 293–338, and 'Provisión de cátedras', 233–
96.

14. In both Aragon and Cataluña the currency system was one where 240
denarii = 20 *solidi* (*sous*) = 1 *libra*—in the two kingdoms it was called,
respectively, currency 'of Jaca' and 'of Barcelona'; in 1310 two *sous*
of Jaca exchanged for three of Barcelona. Lérida was at the time very
much on the frontier between Aragon and Cataluña, and salaries for the
studium were paid in money of Jaca.

15. '... Quod dicti episcopus et capitulum per octo annos continue subse-
quentes solvant et solvere teneantur anno quolibet dicte universitati tria
mille solidos jaccenses ... et dare per dictos annos canonicam porcionem integriter uni magistro medicine quem eadem universitas duxerit
eligendum' (AML, pergaminum 79; published by Sáinz de Baranda,
España sagrada, 351–2).

16. E.g., in April 1305 'magister Albertus fisicus' contracted to serve the
bishop and chapter of Gerona in exchange for a canon's portion and
thirty pounds (600 *sous*) yearly in money of Barcelona (Arxiu Diocesà
de Girona, Notularum 2, fo. 21v).

17. Gaya Massot ('Las rentas', 297) argues for the likelihood of a lower
salary. The unimportance of medicine at Lérida relative to canon and
civil law was made apparent from the start in the *ordinations antigues* of
1300, which commanded students of 'laws and decretals' to pay 10
sous to their masters *pro lectura*, those of medicine only 3. Law
students also had to pay twice as much as medical students to their
masters at the time of their examinations, and were expected to pay
more to the university beadle too (Villanueva, *Viage literario*, xvi. 221,
224). The same hierarchy is reflected a generation later in the fact that

teachers of law were styled *doctor*, while the teacher of medicine was, like the teachers of arts (grammar, logic, and philosophy), merely termed *magister*, 'master' (see below, n. 20). The town had agreed to pay 600 *sous* yearly to Pere Colom to teach, and 400 to Bertran de la Torre (see Appendix I, docs. 2, 4). An indication of the value of such salaries (when paid) can be obtained from Charles Emmanuel Dufourcq, 'Prix et niveaux de vie dans les pays catalans et maghribins à la fin du XIIIᵉ et au début du XIVᵉ siècle', *Le Moyen Age*, 71 (1965), 475–520.

18. Josefina Mateu Ibars, 'Scholares, bacallarii, doctores y magistri del estudio general de Lérida. Contribución a su nómina. Siglos xiv–xv', *Ilerda*, 45 (1984), 175–207, provides a list of students and masters supposed to have been at Lérida in the Middle Ages, but the list has been compiled from sometimes uncritical secondary sources and therefore cannot always be used with confidence.

19. Ramón Gaya Massot, *Cancilleres y rectores del estudio general de Lérida* (Lérida, 1951), 21–4, 45–56.

20. In February 1328 Alfons IV provided that 'universitas proborum hominum civitatis Ilerde debeatur et teneatur salarium . . . dare solvere et asignare quolibet anno duobus doctoribus legum . . . uni qui legat ordinarie et alteri extraordinarie in legibus; item et alteri qui legat decretum et alteri qui legat decretales ordinarie in ipso studio Ilerde; item et uni magistri suficienti qui legat medicinam; item et uni magistri in gramatica preter illum qui iam legit beneficiarius ab eclesia Ilerde; item et uni magistro qui legat logicam et filosofiam in studio memorato . . .' (Rubió y Lluch, *Documents*, i. 83; summarized by Gaya Massot, 'Las rentas', 296–7).

21. 'In dicto studio a tanto tempore quod memoria hominum in contrarium non existit consueverunt ordinarie legere duo . . . magistri prout etiam legunt in medicina seu arte de fisicha in scolis de mane' (Arxiu de la Catedral de Lleida [henceforth ACL], caixa 151, leg. 7156: 'Reformatio studii generalis Ilerdensis'; the document is undated, but refers to Eugenius IV [1431–47] as the reigning pope).

22. See, for example, the documentation in ACL, Manual de Ferrer Sobrepena 1339–42, fos. 55, 59, 73vr, 76, and 1344–6, fos. 25, 28, 76; Manual de Bernardo Urdi 1342–57, fos. 17–18, 46.

23. Joan Veny i Clar (ed.), '*Regiment de preservació de pestilència' de Jacme d'Agramont (s. XIV)* (Tarragona, 1971), 93.

24. Enric Arderiu discovered four references to the wife of Jacme d'Agramunt in the Leridan *Llibre de Consell* of 1350–1 (one of which actually alludes to his book) that seemed to indicate that Jacme was then dead, presumably of the plague (Veny i Clar, '*Regiment*', 23). Further information about master Jacme may be added from the case in the series *Crims* (AML, reg. 776, fos. 82–5, and loose sheet 130v), from October 1351, when he is explicitly spoken of as dead: his wife was Na

Ysabel, they had at least one son, and their house was in the Carrer de Madrona. But this case, too, has nothing to say about his career in the *studium*.

25. To be sure, it is conceivable that Jacme did not lecture continuously during the period 1343–8. A letter of June 1346 published by Denifle ('Urkunden', 261–2) reveals that 'en le studi de la Ciutat de Leyda sa esdevengut algun torp, per lo qual ha cessat la lectura algun temps en lo dit Studi. . . .'

26. ACA, Canc. reg. 602, fo. 107.

27. Hugo de Fenollet, who substituted for Guillem de Bellvis at this examination in February 1344, must have left at the end of the school year, in June, for in October 1344 the councillors of Lérida were complaining that he had not appeared to teach as *legum professor*, although they had invited him to do so (Roca, *L'estudi*, 58–9). Gaya Massot has published (from MS Escorial D. III. 3, 97–8) an undated letter from Pere IV to Hugo urging him to come from Mallorca to teach; Gaya supposed it to have preceded the councillors' complaint and hence to have been written in the summer of 1344 (Gaya Massot, 'El "Chartularium" ', 28–9, 42–3). However, we have found this same letter in ACA, Canc. reg. 873, fo. 219v, dated 11 kal. Oct. 1342 (followed on fo. 220r by a royal safe-conduct for Hugo, which Gaya did not find in the Escorial manuscript). It was evidently this invitation of late 1342 that led to Hugo's presence at Lérida during the next school year, 1343–4.

28. The document is dated 10 March '1328', but in Montpellier at this time the new year began at the feast of the Annunciation, 25 March, so that in modern terms this would be March 1329.

29. The 1313 reference (to 'Johannes Massati') is in *Cartulaire*, i. 229; the document of 1335, listing 13 masters, is ibid., i. 292–3.

30. *Cartulaire*, i. 287.

31. For a discussion of this family, see Enrique Cláudio Girbal, 'Médicos ilustres de la familia Çarriera de Gerona', *Revista de Gerona*, 17 (1892), 65–71; A. Cardoner Planas, 'Los cirujanos ça Riera del siglo XIV', *Medicina Clinica*, 2 (1944), 160–2; and Christian Guilleré, *Diner, poder i societat a la Girona del segle XIV* (Girona, 1984), 83. We hope to join Dr. Guilleré in preparing a full account of this family at a future date.

32. Arnau's career can be partially reconstructed from the following archival sources: Girona, Arxiu Històric Provincial, 5, no. 30, 6 kal. June 1331 (we are indebted to Christian Guilleré for the reference); ACA, Canc. reg. 468, fo. 173v; 536, fo. 42v; 601, fo. 133; 603, fos. 43r–v, 89r–v; 858, fo. 142v; 859, fos. 164r–v, 221–2, 224r–v; 862, fo. 52; 1056, fos. 21–22; 1462, fo. 165v; and ACA, Real Patrimonio, reg. 305, fo. 91; 306, fo. 68; 307, fo. 52v; 322, fos. 118v–119r.

33. Girbal, 'Médicos', 69–70.

34. *Cartulaire*, i. 354–63.

35. Luis Rubio Garcia, 'Los titulos conocidos del estudio general de Lérida', *Miscelánea de trabajos sobre el estudio general de Lérida*, 2 (Lérida, 1950), 185–208.
36. Villanueva, *Viage literario*, xvi. 221.
37. Rashdall, *Universities of Europe*, ii. 94.
38. Ibid., i. 224–9. Professor Luke Demaitre has called our attention to the absence of any reference to the presentation of a ring in Arnau ça Riera's ceremony.
39. For Paris, ibid., i. 458–64.
40. We are grateful to an anonymous referee for having pointed out the interest of this feature.
41. Nancy G. Siraisi, *Taddeo Alderotti and His Pupils* (Princeton, 1981), 120 ff. The situation at Montpellier (from which several of Lérida's early masters seem to have come) has not yet been carefully examined. It might be noted, however, that as early as 1239 anyone wishing to practise medicine in Montpellier was required to undergo an examination by two of the medical masters, and that the document establishing this begins with the assertion that 'in firmamento scienciarum inter liberales artes medicinalis sciencia tanquam luminare majus noscitur prenitere' (*Cartulaire*, i. 185–6).
42. We wish to thank Luke Demaitre and Edith Sylla for their comments upon an earlier version of this paper.

Appendix I

1.

15 February 1304.

Valencia.

Jaume II commands the *pahers* of Lérida to continue to pay master Guillem de Béziers his salary, despite his absence in Montpellier on the king's business, until he either returns to Lérida or sends a *bacallarius* to lecture in his place.
(ACA, Cancilleria, reg. 235, fo. 18)

Fidelibus suis paciariis et probis hominibus civitatis Ilerde. Salutem etc.
Cum nos magistrum Guillelmum de Biterris phisicum nostrum pro quibus-

dam nostris expressis negociis ad nostram curiam duxerimus evocandum, ipsumque ad partes Montispessulani pro quibusdam rebus medicinalibus pro necessitate corporis nostri in presentiarum providerimus transmitendum, et intellexerimus quod vos ipsum absolvere noluistis cum de partibus Ilerde occasione predicta dicessit nisi personaliter rediret ad civitatem Ilerde, vel quod faceret ibidem venire infra certum tempus de Montepessulano unum bachallarium qui in eiusdem absentia lectiones suas continuaret, nosque propter accessum eiusdem ad partes ipsas ipsum valde utilem et fructuosum sanitati nostre disponente domino propterea reputemus, ideo vobis dicimus et mandamus quatenus ipsum donec reversus fuerit vel ad vos miserit bachallarium ipsum de partibus Montispessulani predictis absolvere curetis omnino satisfaciendo sibi salario suo, non obstantibus supradictis, iuxta promissionis per vos sibi facte contincntiam et tenorem. Datum Valencie, idus februarii anno domini m°.ccc°.iii°.

2.

8 November 1324.

Lérida.

Jaume II commands the *pahers* of Lérida to pay master Pere Colom the salary owed him for teaching in the *studium*, since it was through no fault of his that Joan Amell was unable formally to confer the mastership upon him within the agreed-upon time.
(ACA, Cancilleria, reg. 184, fos. 186v–187r).

Jacobus etc. fidelibus suis paciariis civitatis Ilerde ac clavariis studii eiusdem civitatis etc. Ex parte magistri Petri Columbi phisici fuit humiliter expositum coram nobis quod cum ipse plus est quam annus elapsus convenisset cum paciariis et clavariis precessoribus vestris in dicto officio quod ipso actu legente et continue in dicto studio artem medicine, faciente ibidem residentiam personalem, darent et dare anno quolibet tenerentur eidem pro suo salario triginta libras jaccenses, ita tamen quod dictus magister Petrus infra certum tempus deberet recipere magisterium in studio civitatis pretacte; tamen quia dictum magistrum infra tempus per eum premissum recipere non potuit, licet in hoc facerit posse suum, eo quia habere nequivit dilectum phisicum nostrum magistrum Johannem Vernelii [*sic*] sub quo dictum magistrum recipere debebat, tam propter infirmitatem dicti magistri Johannis quam etiam quia nos propter infirmitatem nostram eum necessarium habuimus (ut hoc per literas vobis missas per dictum magistrum Johannem dicitur apparere), vos dictum salarium sibi promissum solvere recusatis, non obstante quod a dicto tempore citra continue legerit in studio predicta; quare suplicavit nobis sibi super hiis de opportuno remedio provideri. Qua suplicatione benigne admissa, vobis dicimus et mandamus quatenus, si est ita, dicto magistro Petro soluatis et solui faciatis salarium per vos debitum eidem (cum quod per eum non stat sibi non debeat inputari); aliter per presentes mandamus vicario et curie prefate civitatis et Palliarensis quod vos ad predicta faciendum compellat fortiter et districte, prout de jure et ratione fuerit faciendum. Datum Ilerde, vi° idus novembris anno domini millesimo ccc° xx° quarto.

3.

8 July 1327.

Barcelona.

Jaume II certifies that Pere Colom is not to be blamed for having failed to take his master's degree within the time agreed upon, and therefore instructs the *pahers* of Lérida to pay Pere the 900 *sous* still owed him for teaching in the *studium* there.

(ACA, Cancillería, reg. 190, fo. 246r–v).

Jacobus etc. fidelibus suis paciariis et clavariis civitatis Ilerde etc. Adiens presentiam nostram fidelis fisicus incliti infantis Alfonsi karissimi primogeniti et generalis procuratoris nostri comitis Urgelli magister Petrus Columbi, nobis exposuit reverenter quod vos difertis sibi solvere nongentos solidos jaccenses ad solvendum sibi restantes ex maiori quantitate per predecessores vestros in dictis officiis sibi dari promissa pro eo quia legit in dicta civitate in arte medicine, ut in quodam publico instrumento inde confecto dicitur contineri, ex eo quod asseritis vobis non constare quod infra tempus in dicto instrumento contentum idem magistrum Petrum curaverit cum effectu requirere fideles nostros magistrum Johannem Amelii fisicum nostrum maiorem et magistrum Petrum Gaveti magistros in medicina per quos examinari et magistrari habebat in studio Ilerdensi quo ad dictum studium accederent ad sibi honorem magisterii impendendum, prout inter dictos predecessores vestros et dictum magistrum Petrum Columbi fuerat in dicto instrumento comprehensum. Idcirco nobis dictus magister Petrus Columbi humiliter supplicavit ut, habita certificacione cum dictis magistris Johanne Amelii et Petro Gaveti de predictis, vos inde deberemus cum nostra littera reddere certiores; quocirca, dicta suplicatione benigne admissa, vos certos facimus per presentes quod ut dicti magister Johannes Amelii et magister Petrus Gaveti in sua fidelitate testificati fuerunt a quibus super predictis certificationem recipi fecimus per fidelem judicem curie nostre Petrum Cima dictus magister Petrus Columbi cum diligentia requisivit eosdem infra tempus in dicto instrumento contentum et etiam ultra per totum annum quod accederent ad dictum studium Ilerde ibidem pro sibi honorem magisterii conferendo, quod ipsi facere non potuerunt legitimis rationibus impediti. Mandamus igitur vobis quatenus tam ex debito justicie quam nostri contemplacione iamdicto magistro Petro Columbi vel cui loco sui voluerit dictam quantitatem peccunie exsolvatis sicut nobis placere cupitis et servire. Datum Barchinone, viii° idus julii anno domini m° ccc° xx° septimo.

4.

17 April [1330].

Barcelona.

Alfons IV instructs the *pahers* of Lérida to pay master Guillem de Avignon the 400 *sous* yearly that they had formerly paid the late master Bertran de la Torre for lecturing on the art of surgery.
(ACA, Cancillería, reg. 438, fo. 114r–v).

Alfonsus etc. fidelibus suis paciariis clavariis et probis hominibus civitatis Ilerde. Salutem etc. Cum pro fideli nostro Guilelmo de Avinione cirurgico penes vos quos scimus circa nostra exequenda beneplacita fore promptos teneamur nostras preces effundere, et intellexerimus quod honorabilis frater Jacobus ordinis Sancte Marie de Mutensia iam penes vos intercessit ut dicto Guilelmo provideritis de illis quadringentis solidis qui consueverunt dari anno quolibet magistro Bertrando de la Torre quondam pro lectura artis cirurgie, idcirco cum predictus magister Bertrandus dies suos finierit, dictusque Guilelmus quem esse intelleximus sufficientem et ydoneum ad lecturam predictam sit paratus in dicta civitate legere ac etiam practicare, vos rogamus intente quatenus obtemperando precibus dicti fratris Jacobi honore nostri et eiusdem fratri Jacobi dicto Guilelmo provideatis de iamdictis quadringentis solidis ut in civitate remaneat supradicta hocque adveniet nobis gratum. Datum Barchinone, 15 kal. madii.

Appendix II

There are three documents that we must consider in trying to reconstruct Arnau ça Riera's medical degree occupying fos. 135r–138v in the notarial manual of Ferrer Sobrepena for 1334–44 in the Arxiu de la Catedral de Lleida. Fo. 135r preserves what appears to be the earliest version of this degree (1), with many marginal and interlinear corrections and brief insertions (the latter enclosed within square brackets in our text below). This version also twice signals the existence of longer interpolations, which are written out on the folio's verso. Of these, the first repeats with only minor modifications a phrase already present in the license. The second and longer one, however, is a significant addition, describing the presentation to Arnau of the insignia of mastership; near its end it contains a symbol indicating yet another interpolation, and then breaks off abruptly just seven words later. After a blank space equivalent to perhaps six more lines of script, the scribe has added a few further lines that certify the Montpellier document on which Arnau's Leridan degree was based. It would seem natural for these last lines to be the interpolation called for in the passage above them, and in fact they would make good sense as such, indicating that the document recognized the granting of the master's insignia to Arnau at Montpellier in 1329; nevertheless, these lines lack the corresponding symbol that would clinch the identification, and the reader is consequently left uncertain as to their relation to the text.

On fo. 136r–v appears a second version of the degree (2), whose first half copies the first part of (1) closely, incorporating many of the marginal and interlinear corrections made to that earlier version (but with some further interlinear corrections of its own). Its second half, however, has been rewritten. The scribe evidently shared our uncertainty about the proper placement of the certifying lines that follow the second interpolation to (1), and eventually chose to insert them into the text at the place where Arnau's medical studies are first mentioned—though (1) gives no reason to think that these lines originally belonged there. Fos. 137r–138r are blank; but fo. 138v contains a few lines (3) that are clearly the first, practice draft of the scribe's attempt to incorporate the certification smoothly into the text at this new spot.

1.

(fo. 135r)

Examinatio et licentia magistri in medicina (et de predictis omnibus ad eternam rey memoriam et predictorum notitiam pleniorem eidem domino Arnaldo mandavimus fieri presens publicum instrumentum per notarium scriptum)

Pateat universis quod nos Hugo de Fenolleto, canonicus Ilerdensis et Gerundensis ac locum tenens [hoc casu] venerabilis et prudentis viri domini

Guilelmi de Pulcro Visu archidiachoni Ilerdensis, vice cancellarii generalis studii Ilerdensis, atendentes quod virtutum meritam sunt bene merentibus tribuenda, ideo dignum non inmerito reputamus ut hii quos propter diutinam et iugem vigiliarum et studiorum instantiam scientie nobilitas[1] predotavit honoris et dignitatis prerogativa letenter et privilegio ga[u]deant speciali ut per continuas laborum[2] amaritudines quas passi fuerunt in studio fructum desideratum[3] reperiant in docendo et ipsorum remunerationis exemplo que minuit vim flagelli alii ad impendendum solertius operam studio attentius inducantur.[4] Insuper etiam attendentes quod honorabilis et discretus vir dominus Arnaldus[5] de Riaria, bacallarius[6] in medicina, diversa litterarum studio decoravit laudabiliter conversando ac fructum presertim medicinalis scientie per quam utiliter tam legendo[7] quam[8] praticando utiliter etiam seminavit, prout fidedignorum relatibus et facti experientia nobis constat, eundem bacuallarium nobis presentatum per venerabilem et discretum virum dominum Jhoanem Maseti,[9] medicine magistrum, ad licentiam magistratus in medicina obtinendam et per nos receptum privatim examinari fecimus, ut est moris. Cumque[10] in prefatu examine intra magistrorum plurimorum ibidem asistentium testimonium deliberatione prehabita pro sufficienti et ydoneo extiterit aprobatus,[11] [nos ipsum ad examinationem publicam admisimus, quo etiam in publice examine eorundem magistrorum testimonio sufficienti reperto,] volentes [eundem] prout rationi congruit de suo labore honorem debitum reportare, eidem domino[12] Arnaldo[13] de Riaria legendi ordinarie disputandi repetendi et omnes alios actus magistrales exercendi qui ad cuiuslibet magistri in medicina officium expectare noscuntur in dicto generali studio Ilerdense et etiam ubique terrarum auctoritate qua fungimur† plenariam potestatem et licentiam [ducimus] concedendam,[14] [15] ipsum [dominum Arnaldum] ad honorem magisterii in medicina nichilominus assumentes.‡

In quorum testimonium sibi presens[16] [publicum instrumentum] sigilli officii cancellarie apensione[17] fecimus comuniri; quod est actum in cathedrali ecclesia Ilerdense iii° idus februarii, anno a nativitate domini M°[18] CCC° XL° quarto, presentibus et [ibidem] assistentibus reverendo in Christo patre domino Jacobo dei gratia episcopo Ilerdense et venerabilibus et prudentibus viris dominis[19] P. ça Vench, Vicense [canonico], rectore dicti generalis studii Ilerdensis; G. A.[i] Patavi, G.° de Noguerio, Garssia Romei, [Raymundo Frisci,] decretorum; Petro Despens,[20] [G°. Servietis,] Pericono Despens, legum doctoribus;[21] Jacobo de Acrimonte, Waltero de Wrobruge Anglico, magistris in medicina; pluribusque aliis canonicis militibus bacallariis[22] [civibus peritis religiosis] scolaribus in jure canonico civili medicina [et artibus, qui ibidem convenerant ad sollempnitatem omnium predictorum[23]]; et aliis tam clericis quam laicis; et testibus ad hec rogatis et specialiter convocatis, discretis viris Michaele Despens, Jacobo de Solerio, canonicis, P. Balaguario de Sobrepena et P. ça Gual, benefficiatis sepefate ecclesie.

(fol. 135v)

† plenariam potestatem et licentiam ducimus concedendam ipsum dominum Arnaldum ad honorem magistri in medicina nichilominus assumentes

‡ Et quoniam ad conssumationem cuiuslibet negotii apetendus est finis laudabilis per quem saltem apareat principium et medium precessisse, ideo dominus Arnaldus de Riaria prelibatus²⁴ a predicto domino Johanne Maseti in [magistrali] cathedra²⁵ existente cathedram magistralem in signum excellentie, librum in signum sapientie, birretam in signum glorie, osculum in signum dilectionis et amicitie, et benedictionem in signum benedictionis eterne, sibi²⁶ non presumendo set seipsum anima et corpore humiliando, petiit iuxta²⁷ morem sollempniter exhiberi; qui quidem dominus Johannes Maseti²⁸ in medicina magister ipsi domino Arnaldo de Riaria tanquam benemerito predicta insignia per eum petita [ibidem] sollempniter²⁹ ministravit. Et de predictis omnibus³⁰

per publicum instrumentum confectum in Montepessulano per³¹ Philipum Gauterii notarium publicum auctoritate regia decima die menssis marcii anno domini M° CCC° XX° VIII°.

1. *corr. ex* nobilitatis
2. *corr. ex* labiorum
3. *corr. ex* desideramus
4. *del.* ideo
5. *del.* ça Riera
6. *corr. ex* baguallarius
7. *del.* inibi
8. *del.* ibi et alibi
9. *corr. ex* Mazeti
10. *del.* examinari
11. *del.* nos ipsum
12. *del.* Galtero de
13. *del.* ça Riera
14. *corr. ex* con***us
15. *del.* per presentes
16. *del.* litteras consessimus
17. *del.* m***tamus duximus
18. M° M° *MS*
19. *del.* locumtenente dicti vicecancellarii
20. *del.* R. Frisci
21. *del.* pluribus aliis
22. *del.* et

23. et artibus . . . predictorum *corr. ex* qui ibidem convenerant ad sollemnitatem omnium predictorum
24. *corr. ex* probatus
25. *del.* ibidem
26. *del.* petiit
27. *del.* moris
28. *del.* in*?* predictus
29. *del.* exhibuit etc.
30. *del.* dominus A[rnald]us prefatus petiit sibi fieri publicum instrumentum ad rey memoriam sempiternam que fuerunt acta
31. *del.* filipum

2.

(fo. 136r–v)

Licentia magistri in medicina

Pateat universis quod nos Hugo de Fenolleto, [legum doctor et] canonicus Ilerdensis et Gerundensis ac locumtenens hoc casu venerabilis ac prudentis viri domini Guilelmi de Pulcro Visu archidiachoni Ilerdensis[1] cancellarii generalis studii Ilerdensis, atendentes quod virtutum merita sunt bene merentibus tribuenda, ideo dignum non inmerito reputamus ut hii quos propter diutinam et iugem vigil[i]arum et studiorum instantiam scientie nobilitas predotavit honoris et dignitatis prerogativa letenter et privilegio gaudeant speciali ut per continuas laborum amaritudines quas passi fuerunt in studio fructum desideratum reperiant in docendo et ipsorum remunerationis exemplo que minuit vim flagelli alii ad inpendendum solertius operam studio atentius inducantur. Insuper etiam attendentes quod honorabilis [et discretus] vir dominus Arnaldus de Riaria, bacallarius in [scientia] medicine, diversa litterarum studia decoravit studendo et laudabiliter conversando specialiter in generali studio Montis pesullani, tam audiendo quam omnes cursos suos [perfecte] legendo [ibidem], prout nobis de predictis per quoddam instrumentum ibi[2] confectum[3] x[a] [die] mensis martii anno domini M°CCC°XXVIII° extitit facta fides, insuper etiam in illis partibus [et in istis multis annis] publice praticando, prout fidedignorum relatibus nobis constat, eundem bacallarium nobis presentatum per venerabilem et discretum virum dominum Jhoannem Maseti [in scientia] medicine magistrum ad licentiam magistratus in[4] [dicta scientia] obtinendam et per nos receptum privatim examinari fecimus, ut est moris. Cumque in preffato examine iuxta magistrorum plurimorum [in dicta scientia medicine] ibidem asistentium testimonium deliberatione prehabita pro sufficienti et ydoneo extiterit approbatus, nos ipsum ad examinationem[5] publicam admisimus; quo etiam in publico examine eorundem magistrorum testimonio sufficienti reperto, volentes eundem prout rationi congruit de suo labore honorem debitum reportare, eidem domino Arnaldo de Riaria legendi ordinarie disputandi repetendi et omnes alios actus magistrales exercendi qui ad cuiuslibet magistri in medicina officium expectare noscuntur in dicto generali studio Ilerdense et etiam ubique terrarum auctoritate qua[6] fungimur plenariam potestatem et licentiam ducimus concedendam,[7] ipsum dominum Arnaldum ad honorem magisterii[8] in medicina nichilominus assumentes.[9] (fo. 136v) Et quoniam ad consumationem cuiuslibet negotii apetendus est finis laudabilis per quem saltem apareat principium et medium precessisse, ideo dominus Arnaldus de Riaria prelibatus a predicto domino Jhoanne Maseti in magistrali cathedra existente cathedram magistralem in signum excellentie, librum in signum sapientie, birretam in signum glorie, osculum in signum dilectionis amicitie, et benedictionem in signum benedictionis eterne, sibi non presumendo set seipsum anima et corpore humiliando, petiit iuxta morem sollempniter exhiberi; qui quidem dominus Jhoannes Maseti[10] ipsi domino Arnaldo de Riaria tanquam benemerito predicta insignia per eum petita ibidem sollempniter ministravit.

In quorum testimonium sibi presentes[11] [litteras] sigilli officii cancellarie apensione fecimus comuniri. Datum in cathedrali ecclesia Ilerdense .iii. idus februarii anno a nativitate domini M°CCC°[XL]IIII°, presentibus et ibidem asistentibus reverendo in Christo patre domino Jacobo dei gratia episcopo Ilerdense pluribusque venerabilibus dominis doctoribus magistris bacallariis in jure canonico et civili medicina et artibus canonicisque militibus civibus peritis religiosis ac universitate dicti studii Ilerdensis qui ibidem convenerant ad sollempnitatem omnium predictorum.

1. *del.* vice
2. *corr. ex* ubi
3. *del.* decem
4. *del.* medicina
5. *corr. ex* executionem
6. quam *MS*
7. *corr. ex* concedendus
8. *corr. ex* ministerii
9. *del.* et de predictis omnibus ad eternam rerum memoriam
10. *del.* in medicina magister
11. *del.* publicum instrumentum concessimus

3.

(fo. 138v)

dominus A. de Riaria bacallarius in medicina diversa literarum studia
[decoravit studendo et laudabiliter conversando] et specialiter in generali
studio Montispesullani[1] tam audiendo quam omnes cursos suos [perfecte]
legendo prout nobis de predictis per quoddam publicum instrumentum ibi
confectum x^a die mensis marcii anno domini M° CCC.XX.VIII° extitit facta
fides [insuper etiam][2] in illis partibus publice practicando[3] prout fidedignorum relatibus nobis constat eundem bacallarium nobis presentatum per
venerabilem

1. *del.* ubi
2. *del.* decoravit laudabiliter conversando ac fruentem medicinalis scientie
   per quam tam legendo in dicto Montispesullani studio quam
3. *del.* etiam seminavit

The Art of Teaching and Learning Law: A Late Medieval Tract

Thomas E. Morrissey

I. Introduction

Around the year 1400 the name of Franciscus de Zabarellis, or Zabarella for short, was very well known in legal circles. He had been born in 1360 near Padua and had spent his early years of education in Padua. In 1378 he had gone to Bologna where he spent five years studying law with Johannes de Legnano. When Legnano died in 1383 Zabarella transferred to Florence where he received the degree of doctorate in both laws in 1385 and began to lecture in law at the *Studium Generale* there. Five years later in 1390 he accepted an invitation to transfer back to his home city of Padua where he taught for almost two decades until summoned once again to Florence as bishop-elect in 1409. Then only a few months later he was called to the papal curia as a cardinal, the position which he held until his death at the Council of Constance in September, 1417.[1]

In his career then Zabarella spent twenty-five years teaching law to students from all over Italy and Europe. But he was more than just a successful university professor. He was also known as a legal counsellor and spokesman and so at various times he found himself employed as an ambassador to the king of France, an envoy to the pope in Rome, and advisor to the Carrara government in Padua and later to the Venetian government.[2] In addition his legal opinion was asked on such questions as the deposition of the emperor, the unfortunate King Wenceslaus in 1400.[3] He was a familiar and friend of some of the famous men of his day. These included the heirs of Petrarch and such notable humanists as Coluccio Salutati, Poggio, Vergerio, Barzizza, Emmanuel Chrysoloras and others.[4] His opinion was sought by the king of Cyprus and by the bishop of Magdeburg, and we even find that the Council of Pisa in 1409 cited his opinion in defence of that council's actions against two papal claimants.[5] On other occasions the Venetian government used his talents to settle disputes over territory in Dalmatia, the emperor-elect Sigismund appointed him to the commission that was to attempt to resolve the quarrel of the Teutonic Knights against the Kingdom of Poland. Among his other burdens at the Council of Constance was the debate over the theory of tyrannicide and of course the foremost concerns of unity and reform.[6]

There was never any question about Zabarella's skill and knowledge. If we ask how successful was he as a teacher, we can only answer by pointing to certain signs. We do know that he was a popular teacher. On numerous occasions he was asked by students to give the customary address upon the awarding of the doctorate to one of the graduates at Padua.[7] Students moreover came from all over Italy and many other lands of Europe to study with him.[8] Cardinal Cesarini, Nicholas of Cusa, Nicholas de Tudeschis, Paulus Vladimiri of the University of Cracow and many others looked up to him as either their teacher or one whose teachings greatly influenced their own thoughts.[9] After his death the humanist Poggio delivered the formal eulogy in the name of the Council of Constance and there survived another anonymous eulogy which spoke of the care he had for the poor, especially poor students.[10] We can verify this claim for in at least one case a student transferring from Bologna came to his house with no money. Zabarella not only took him in and supported him for the course of his studies but also introduced him into the leading humanist circles of the day and from these encounters Arnold of Rotterdam was able to bring back to the Netherlands the knowledge of Petrarch.[11] Furthermore in 1405 after he had been absent from Florence for some fifteen years efforts were made to bring him back to the university in Florence. Another story reported that when in early 1408 Venice planned to send him as part of an embassy to the Duke of Savoy, the students proclaimed that they wanted him to stay home to teach them and protested so violently that his appointment was cancelled.[12] Finally we know from many letters of his friends, fellow humanists, protégés and students of the warm and lasting bonds that all felt with Zabarella.[13] It is with some interest then that we can turn to the tract which he composed for teachers and students on the art of teaching and learning law.[14]

When Zabarella composed this tract is unknown, nor is there any indication where it was composed. There are indications in the text itself that he wrote the tract later in his career since he referred to his opinion 'after much experience'. The recent discovery of a substantial revision and expansion of Zabarella's legal commentaries including this tract, as described by Stephan Kuttner,[15] makes the dating of the final version more likely to be in the period after 1400 toward the very end of Zabarella's life and career.

Zabarella begins by explaining that he does not intend to offer any new or startling ideas but rather to put together in compact form some suggestions that immediately appear to be sensible and which are based on his many years of experience with students.[16] His work, therefore, provides a student and teacher handbook for the Faculty of Law at the University of Padua around 1400 as well as some tips on how to succeed if one really tried hard.[17] His comments were directed to the teacher, to the student and to both considered together. Many of the remarks may appear to be platitudes to a modern audience; perhaps they were to Zabarella's audience.

The tract praised certain standard virtues which from time immemorial were supposed to be the hallmark of the devoted legal student and scholar: hatred of crime, a love of knowledge and wisdom, perseverance and diligence in investigation.[18] The student was to be diligent and attentive to all the details and circumstances of a question; the professor was to be a model both in his life and in his actual manner of teaching.[19] To give concrete application to this last demand Zabarella stressed that just as it is not enough to tell the soldier to shoot the arrow or to draw his sword and fight, so too the law professor must give instructions not just by words but by actual practice.[20]

II. The Teacher

Since in his scheme the teacher was to play such an important role for the young student, Zabarella went into some detail on what he should be like and how he should act. At the outset he demanded that there be some order in his life; he should not take on too much lest his health be harmed (and consequently his students suffer) nor should he on the other hand take too much time off.[21] When the teacher was there in front of his class, Zabarella was very blunt in what he expected of him and on what the teacher should avoid. The fact that Zabarella mentioned certain items indicates that at least in some cases teachers had these failings. Thus the professor was supposed to have spent the time in class preparation so that he knew what he was talking about; he should not uselessly return to what he had already said, nor should he be so disorganized that he had to backtrack and say: 'I should have told you that . . .'[22] If the teacher himself did not know what he was saying, was hesitant and uncertain where his line of argument was leading, how was the poor student to be able to follow it to the end?[23] When he was speaking, let the teacher speak with a clear and fluent delivery, not shouting at the class nor in a monotonous singsong, but with moderation, liveliness, and consistency. After all the major point was that he be fully and completely intelligible to his audience. Hence he should not speak too quickly nor abruptly, nor should he on the contrary go too slowly as though he were exhausted.[24] He should pause at the proper place to give emphasis and unity to what he had to say and to allow his audience a breather. In this way they would be able to grasp what he had to say and he could catch his breath. He should avoid excess verbiage, incorrect usage, unnecessary interpolations, and too often using certain pet phrases. If not, as Zabarella warned, the class would lose track of his argument and concentrate on counting how many times he used whatever words had become his trademark.[25]

Specifically Zabarella urged the use of correct and precise terminology, the avoidance of barbarisms, and similar failings. He asked: how was the teacher to instruct the class in advanced studies if he appeared to his students as basically uneducated, as ignorant and ridiculous because he did not know what was expected of little boys in the lowest classes who had been exposed to the rudiments of grammar?[26] He advised the teacher: no matter how learned you might be in law, if you could not express yourself clearly and correctly, they were just going to laugh at you, and so it was worth the time and effort to acquire these skills. On this line of reasoning he suggested that a person with an outlandish accent do something about it if he expected his students to follow his argument. Zabarella also added that no matter how many years of experience one had as a teacher a little periodic brushing up on these basics would do a lot of good. If you wanted to know what you sounded like, then ask some of your more faithful auditors; especially at the beginning of one's career this would be useful and from these admonitions one could improve, correcting the weak points and increasing one's stronger qualities.[27]

Dealing with more specific instances, Zabarella went on to consider the bond between the speaker and the spoken word. If the audience were turned off by the speaker, then they would obviously not accept the message either.[28] Medieval rhetoric had always spoken of the need to make the hearer benevolent, attentive, and receptive.[29] Zabarella knew well that rejection of either part (the medium or the message) often meant the rejection of both.[30] Therefore adapt yourself to the audience. Nothing was more useless than the vain attempt to appear more learned which resulted from the use of improper and obscure words. Pedantry only produced ridicule. Every discipline or field of study had its own vocabulary and method of procedure, and to mix two of them as for example philosophy and law, only resulted in a dual confusion.[31] The teacher did not really explain what he was supposed to teach and the hearers who did not know the alien phraseology did not grasp what it was that they were being taught. So too attempts to appear more erudite and literary only resulted in mixed metaphors. What was more imprudent than for a teacher to render himself either unintelligible or only barely understood? On the contrary, Zabarella said, we always praised teachers when we said that they were clear and could be understood.[32] In this area nothing was worse than the teacher who went off on a tangent at some point and got involved in a very complicated problem or disputed point of little relevance to the main part of his topic. Often such teachers spent an entire class on these chases and so after years of lectures they had covered only a part of what was supposed to be taught in one year. This was the reason, Zabarella added, that something of a locked-step programme had been devised in the past so that each part of law would be covered in a set space of time and those appointed to teach were instructed as to what they were expected to deal with in that semester.[33] In this way in the course of a certain number of years the whole text of the law would be treated. Such a mandate might be very restrictive and one could find arguments for and against the locked-step programme, but it was understandable why it had come into being.[34] Did this mean that the teacher was never to go into details on any point? Far from it! Rather the teacher was to avoid useless detail and unnecessary repetition.[35] Furthermore he should teach the students how to find out things for themselves rather than bringing out everything on every topic. In a word the teacher was to treat the student as one did with a thirsty person, that is, show him the way to the fountain of knowledge. Beyond that all repetition became pointless. Let the students learn how to discover, to argue, and to investigate on their own; it would be better, far better, for them than any attempt at spoonfeeding.[36] Zabarella admitted that this advice was not new even for his own day, that he was merely echoing the sage words of a great canonist and teacher, Pope Innocent IV, in the latter's legal commentaries from the thirteenth century.[37]

How should a teacher handle his material? Traditionally in medieval times there were two main schools of thought: topically and schematically. In law the first method would cover the legal corpus under certain headings, choosing materials from a variety of sources and places as they pertained to a particular topic. The latter method would cover the legal corpus in the order in which it was compiled, book by book, title by title, and chapter by chapter.[38] In either method when something of major importance came up it was imperative that the teacher delayed on this, repeating it even two or more times until the students had it as though from memory.[39] Zabarella observed that many students put marks in the margins of their books at such points.[40] Even more to the point Zabarella insisted that the teacher consider his audience carefully. He urged that one bring in elements of relaxation to the lectures, an anecdote or a bit of humour.[41] Were the students beginners, moderately advanced, or fully trained students? Obviously for each audience the techniques of teaching were different. He suggested as a model instruction of St. Paul on the explanation of the faith to new converts (I Corinthians 3:1–2) that one should not give meat to babes but milk. With little ones food was prepared in small bites; so too for those beginning legal studies the text of the law should be broken down into sections that were easily grasped.[42] The instructor should warn the class that this point was important, and that one was of lesser import, and so on. He should summarize periodically so that the students could see how things fitted together. If it was necessary or useful he should just treat the text of the law and leave out the glosses and commentaries until the students were more capable of handling these. In fact at this early stage of their careers these glosses might be of more a hindrance or distraction than a help for the students.[43]

With the moderately progressed students obviously more difficult material could be introduced. Still the major points should be stressed and the finer points of law could be left to the advanced classes.[44] Zabarella admitted that sometimes the impossible situation arose when the teacher faced a class composed from all three levels. All he could recommend in this case was that you should use your prudence and hope for the best. His chief concern was that on any level the instructor should not either belabour the obvious or omit a major point of controversy because it was difficult.[45] Difficult topics took longer and so the teacher should spend the time on them. An item that was obvious to the class might provide the teacher with an opportunity to present a parade of erudition, but it would be merely that, ostentation and useless show. Such a procedure was vulgar and counter-productive; a good teacher knew when to speak out and when to be silent.[46] Zabarella added that many other points could be raised on the teacher but that this about summed up his advice and it was time to address himself now to the student of law.

III. The Student

What about students? How should they approach their task? What was expected of them? Zabarella started off with a piece of advice basic to all ages and times. Before the student went on to advanced studies, he had to make sure of the basic skills. For Zabarella this meant: know your grammar and how to write. For if the student did not have these, how was he ever going to understand the legal texts?[47] It went without saying but he said it anyway, that he presupposed that this problem had long before been taken care of in the teacher.[48] After basic language skills the next in priority was training in logic and rhetoric so that the student could see how an argument was constructed and follow its course.[49] He observed that in his day some felt that these skills were superfluous. If the ancients had felt that way we would not even have the science of law was his considered judgement in response. Moreover if you wanted to be read, then you had to write legibly, clearly and well.[50] The legal scholars whom the people read possessed these qualities. It was also good to know something about philosophy, especially the principles of natural philosophy, and of course moral philosophy. The latter was especially important since in a sense, Zabarella explained, all law was intended to be a particular embodiment of a general moral law.[51]

Zabarella admitted that these prerequisites meant that the student had to spend some time before beginning legal studies, and so he would be a bit older, but the delay was worth the time, provided of course that the student did not spend so long and become so enamoured of these other studies that he lost the taste for law, its discipline and methods.[52] In a personal note Zabarella added that after grammatical studies he himself spent two full years and part of a third in logic and philosophy before he devoted himself full-time to law, and once he began in law he did not turn back. Once the students had completed their legal studies then it was time for and advisable to keep in contact with literature and other disciplines. For you could not really be adept in your own field if you were totally ignorant of others.[53]

However, while still a student of law it was advisable to remove all other books that might serve as a distraction from your studies.[54] Concentrate on what was at hand if you really desired to progress. Go to the sources, the laws themselves and the glosses and the commentaries on the laws; do not always remain two or three removes from the texts. Know the laws themselves, especially what were the principal texts and which were related ones.[55] If you were just beginning your studies, you should find a colleague who was more advanced and who could therefore aid you in difficulties. Let him be like a father and friend to you. Know your sources, your texts, and their meanings. This admonition could not be repeated too strongly. When you had difficulties with these, go to your more advanced friend for help, or to some other source and in this way you would not lose the time uselessly. Your friend would help you overcome the difficulties that arose from inexperience. Later as you became more experienced you could do the same for others.[56]

Zabarella then interjected a criticism that seemed to bother him. He did not want to seem to say that all law was a matter merely of memory as some critics claimed, but the fact was that it was much easier if certain basic information was on the tip of your tongue at all times.[57] If this were taken care of, then there would be plenty of time for the truly complicated and subtle problems that arose in legal argument. Besides, all the subtlety in the world would not help the person who could not remember the basic legal maxims and traditions, and the same was true of any field of learning.[58] There were of course all sets of mnemonic tricks that had been devised for that purpose,[59] and Zabarella added that each person should seek out and use the one that worked best for him. He considered it absurd and offensive to resort to black magic or some more perverse techniques to attempt to gain this skill.[60] On the contrary, Zabarella admonished the student: do not lose sight of your goal in this development of your memory and end up as a kind of showman and not really understanding what you are spouting.[61]

It was good, he advised, to discuss and debate with your *confrères* regularly. This would prevent you from falling into the fatal error of relying too much on your own judgement and ability. In this regard it was necessary to remember that the purpose of these sessions was mutual help, and not self-glorification. To seek this latter path was to diverge from the way to true knowledge and growth. The results were usually less than desirable: a person who was garrulous, quarrelsome, or in general unpleasant.[62]

As to the student's personal habits and way of life, Zabarella was well aware of what student life has always been like. His first admonition was for students to use their time wisely.[63] Do not study so long that you were worn out and as a result learned nothing from such efforts. On the other hand there were students not refreshed by sleep so that the class room was their dormitory, and when they did sit down to study they could not keep their eyes open and so again nothing was achieved.[64] Others were so irregular in their eating habits and schedule that when they did come to table they were famished, they over-ate and again as a result they were rendered useless for many hours later. Even worse many suffered from stomach disorders for years afterwards, or from other diseases. Some even suffered from brain damage or insanity.[65] Therefore in planning your schedule of study, rest for both mind and body should be arranged.[66] Allow enough time for study to get your work done; do not strain or violate your natural constitution as you would only lose this way. A weakened body was no support for a tired mind. Eat carefully and do not rush your meals.[67] In regard to wine, Zabarella advised that students should go as lightly as possible in their consumption, especially if the wines were more powerful. Do not let your stomach nor your brain succumb to the clouds. At any rate give yourself some time before you start studying again.[68]

As to when students should eat their main meal, Zabarella wisely added that this was a matter of natural disposition. But some time for physical exercise was a must. Zabarella's personal choice was for a light meal and then study, and later the heavier meal according to one's physical needs with perhaps a short siesta in the early afternoon.[69] The hours of sleep were also geared to a person's physical constitution but in general seven or eight hours were the norm.[70] If you tried to cut corners on this at night, nature very often would steal in during the day to make up her loss.[71] So too the best hour for study—morning or afternoon—was a matter of choice.[72] But if you carefully attended to these matters in accord with your nature, you could get your work done. Usually in any event you arose at dawn for school and until the third hour, that is, until mid-morning, you were in class. Then there was a break for something to eat, and then perhaps a short rest before you returned to your studies. This depended somewhat on the season of the year and the amount of daylight available. No matter what, a proper schedule should be drawn up and diligently followed as has been stressed so often.[73]

Since he was addressing himself to students in the law schools of the late middle ages, Zabarella naturally dealt with two other parts of student life peculiar to that era. First he expected that the students would become skilled, if not doctors, in both laws, civil and canon law, and so he asked with which branch of law the student should begin his legal studies. His answer was that the student should begin with the field in which he intended to concentrate, so that from the outset he would be imbued (his imagery is based on a citation from the Roman poet Horace) with certain habits of mind and ways of thinking, and become quick and familiar with the terminology peculiar to one's specialty. He admitted that not all agreed with this advice but from experience it appeared to him as the most useful way.[74] Secondly, as his final admonition, writing for a medieval audience, Zabarella urged them to be men of faith and prayer.[75] In this way, he said, you would attain as a student and as a teacher your goal in this life: having a good name now and eternal happiness hereafter.[76]

This tract which we have discussed was the work of a medieval canonist and lawyer who was also an early humanist of the Renaissance as well as a leader in the movement striving for unity and reform in the Church at the time of the Great Western Schism.[77] The tract has survived unpublished for close to six hundred years, but in its practicality and reasonableness, one can ask if the course of years has robbed it of its value or has time weakened its admonitions. In his own life, from all that I have been able to reconstruct, Zabarella lived according to these norms that he urged.[78]

History Department
State University of New York
College at Fredonia
Fredonia, New York 14063

REFERENCES

1. For details on Zabarella's life and his importance for his era, see: Giuseppe Vedova, *Memorie intorno all vita ed all opere del cardinale Francesco Zabarella Padovano* (Padua, 1829); Antonio Zardo, 'Francesco Zabarella a Firenze (il Cardinale Florentino)', *Archivio Storico Italiano* Series 5, 22 (1898) 1–22; August Kneer, *Kardinal Zabarella (Franciscus de Zabarellis, Cardinalis Florentinus) 1360–1417* (Dissertation, Münster, 1891); Pietro Pinton, *Appunti biografici intorno al grande giurista et umanista card. Zabarella* (Protenza, 1895); Gasparo Zonta, *Francesco Zabarella (1360–1417)* (Padua, 1915); Walter Ullmann, *The Origins of the Great Schism* (London, 1948), Appendix: 'Cardinal Zabarella and His Position in the Conciliar Movement', pp. 191–231; Brian Tierney, *Foundations of the Conciliar Theory* (Cambridge, 1955), Pt III, chap. 4: 'Franciscus Zabarella', pp. 220–37; Gregorio Piaia, 'La Fondazione filosofica della teoria conciliare in Francesco Zabarella', in *Scienza e Filosofia all'Universita di Padova nel Quattrocento* [Contributi all storia dell' Universita di Padova, 15] (Trieste-Padova, 1983), 431–61; Thomas E. Morrissey, 'Franciscus de Zabarellis (1360–1417) and the Conciliarist Traditions', Unpublished Ph.D. Dissertation; Cornell University, Ithaca, New York 1973. In the tract on which this paper is based Zabarella referred to Johannes de Legnano as 'my famous teacher'; see Munich, Bayerische Staatsbibliothek, Codex Latinus Monachensis [Clm] 14134, fo. 150^r: 'clare fame preceptor meus dominus Johannes de Legnano'. In Vienna, Oesterreichische Nationalbibliothek, Cod. Lat. 5513, fos. 200^v–201^r, has a number of dates from Zabarella's life, e.g., that he received his licentiate in canon law at the University of Bologna under Johannes de Legnano and that he began to teach as a doctor in both laws at the end of his twenty-fifth and start of his twenty-sixth year; he then began his teaching at Florence, see Francesco Novati, 'Sul riordinamento del studio fiorentino nel 1385', *Rassegna bibliografica della letteratura italiana* anno iv (1896) 322. Zabarella died on September 26, 1417 and on the next day in the name of the assembled council the famous humanist, Poggio, delivered a eulogy on Zabarella

before the assembly, see Hermann von der Hardt (ed.), *Magnum oecumenicum Constantiense concilium* (7 vols.; 1696–1742), I:IX:537–546.

2. From Zabarella's embassy to the court of the King of France in the winter of 1404–5 two of the addresses he gave there have survived and have been published: see Zardo, *Francesco Zabarella*, pp. 144–6, 147–9; the address he delivered to Pope Boniface IX in 1398 while on a mission to him from the government of Padua has also survived, see: Terenzio Sartore, 'Un discorso inedito di Francesco Zabarella a Bonifacio IX sull' autorita del Papa', *Rivista di Storia della Chiesa in Italia* 20 (1966), 375–88; for Zabarella's service for the government in Venice, see : *I Libri Commemoriali della Repubblica di Venezia. Regesti* Tomo III [Monumenti Storici pubblicati della R. Deputazione Veneta di Storia Patria, vol. IV, Serie Prima, Documenti vol. VII] (Venezia, 1883), 340–1; later Venice also wrote to Zabarella to ask his help at the Council of Constance, see: Heinrich Finke *et al. (eds.), Acta concilii Constantiensis* (4 vols.; Münster, 1896–1928), iii. 213.

3. *Consilia* (Milan, 1515), #154, fo. 78[v a–b].

4. Some of the letters that Salutati and Zabarella exchanged have been published, see : Francesco Novati (ed.), *Epistolario di Coluccio Salutati* [Fonti per la Storia d' Italia pubblicate dall'Istituto Storico Italiano, 4 vols., 15,16,17, 18:I–II] (Rome, 1891–1905) vol. 18, pt. II, pp. 347–9, 350–61; vol. 17, 422, 379. Zabarella served as legal advisor to the heirs of Petrarch, see his *Consilia* (Milan, 1515), #79/II [two *consilia* were numbered as #79 in this edition] fo. 36[vb]–37[ra]. Of the others mentioned Vergerio was his longest and closest friend and the two collaborated on a number of works during the friendship lasted from 1390 to 1417. Many letters of Barzizza and Zabarella survive and it is clear how often Zabarella provided him financial support as well as friendship; on these contacts see: Thomas E. Morrissey, 'Franciscus de Zabarellis (1360–1417) and the Conciliarist traditions', pp. 1–21.

5. For the citation of Zabarella's writings in support of the Council of Pisa, see Johannes Vincke, *Schriftstücke zum Pisaner Konzil. Ein Kampf um die öffentliche Meinung* (Bonn, 1942), pp. 136, 140. His responses to the others who sought his advice are found in his *Consilia* (Milan, 1515), #137 (to the King of Cyprus), #70 (to the bishop of Magdeburg); R. Creytens, 'Un "consilium" de François de Zabarella et de Jacques de Piemont rélatif aux observances dominicaines', *Archivum Fratrum Predicatorum* 22 (1952), 346–80.

6. For Zabarella's ideas and his work at the Council of Constance, see: Thomas E. Morrissey, 'Cardinal Zabarella on Papal and Episcopal Authority', *Proceedings of the Patristic, Medieval and Renaissance Conference* [Villanova University] 1 (1976) 39–52; 'The Decree "Haec Sancta" and Cardinal Zabarella. His Role in its Formulation and Interpretation', *Annuarium Historiae Conciliorum* 10 (1978), 145–76;

'After Six Hundred Years: The Great Western Schism, Conciliarism and Constance', *Theological Studies* 40 (1979), 495–509; 'Franciscus Zabarella (1360–1417): Papacy, Community and the Limitations upon Authority', in Guy F. Lytle (ed.), *Reform and Authority in the Medieval and Reformation Church* (Washington, D.C., 1981), 37–54; 'The Sun and Moon Image: A Late Medieval Critic', *The Jurist* 42 (1982), 170–9; 'Emperor-Elect Sigismund, Cardinal Zabarella and the Council of Constance', *Catholic Historical Review* 69 (1983), 353–70; 'The Call for Unity at the Council of Constance: Sermons and Addresses of Cardinal Zabarella (1415–17)', *Church History* 53 (1984), 307–18; 'Cardinal Franciscus Zabarella (1360–1417) as a Canonist and the Crisis of His Age: Schism and the Council of Constance', *Zeitschrift für Kirchengeschichte* 96 (1985), 196–208, 'Cardinal Zabarella and Nicholas of Cusa: From Community Authority to Consent of the Community', *Mitteilungen und Forschungsbeiträge der Cusanus Gesellschaft* 17 (1986), 156–76; 'The Crisis of Authority at the end of the Fourteenth Century: A Canonist's Response', *Mediaevalia* 9 ([1986 for] 1983), 251–67; ' "More Easily and More Securely": Legal Procedure and Due Process at the Council of Constance', forthcoming in Sweeney and Chodorow (eds.), *Popes, Teachers, and Canon Law in the Middle Ages*; and Friedrich Merzbacher, 'Die ekklesiologische Konzeption des Kardinals Francesco Zabarella (1360–1417)', in *Festschrift Karl Pivec* [Innsbrucker Beiträge zur Kulturwissenschaft, Bd. 12] eds. Anton Haidachers and Hans Eberhard Mayer (Innsbruck, 1966) 279–87. His involvement with and work for Venice is illustrated in *I Libri Commemoriali della Repubblica di Venezia. Regesti.* iii. 340–1, and in *Monumenta spectantia historiam slavorum meridionalium* vol. 9 (Zagreb, 1878), 215–24, 267–9; vol. 12 (Zagreb, 1882), 137–8, 139–46, etc. Sigismund's appointment of Zabarella to the commission at the Council of Constance trying to arbitrate and resolve the dispute between the Kingdom of Poland and the Teutonic Knights is noted in Finke, *Acta concilii Constantiensis*, ii. 241, and dated to May, 1415.

7. Many of these addresses are contained in the manuscript from Vienna mentioned above in note 1, Cod. Lat. 5513, along with another manuscript from Austria, Stift Sankt Paul in Lavantthal [a manuscript formerly at the Hospital ad Pyrhum], Codex pap. 31 [27.1.7].

8. Walter Brandmüller noted that among those who took official part in the proceedings at the Council of Constance ninety-nine of Zabarella's students were listed, 'Simon de Lellis de Teramo: Ein Konsistorialadvokat auf dem Konzilien von Konstanz und Basel', *Annuarium Historiae Conciliorum* 12 (1980), 230, while the lists provided by Andrea Gloria (ed.), *Monumenti della Universita di Padova 1318–1405* I–II (Padua, 1888) and by Gasparo Zonta and Johanne Brotto (eds.), *Acta Graduum Academicorum Gymnasii Patavini ab anno MCCCCVI ad annum MCCCCL* (Padua, 1922), show the students who studied with

Zabarella and were promoted by him came from Germany, Hungary, Poland, Austria, Bohemia, perhaps also from Croatia, Spain and France, as well as from most cities of any size in Italy.

9. Cardinal Nicholas of Cusa from Germany, Paulus Vladimiri from Cracow, Cardinal Giulano Cesarini, Nicholas de Tudeschis (later Archbishop of Palermo) were just a few of the more famous people influenced by Zabarella. For Nicholas de Tudeschis, see Knut Wolfgang Nörr, *Kirche und Konzil bei Nicholas de Tudeschis (Panormitanus)* [Forschungen zur kirchlichen Rechtsgeschichte und zum Kirchenrecht, Band 4] (Cologne, 1964) and Charles Lefebvre, 'L' Enseignement de Nicolas de Tudeschis et l'autorité pontificale', *Ephemerides Iuris Canonici* 14 (1958), 312–39; for Cesarini, see Gerald Christianson, *Cesarini: The Conciliar Cardinal. The Basel Years, 1431–1438* [Kirchengeschichtliche Quellen und Studien 10] (St. Ottilien, 1979) and 'Cardinal Cesarini and Cusa's "Concordantia" ', *Church History* 54 (1985), 7–19; on Cusa, see : Thomas E. Morrissey, 'Cardinal Zabarella and Nicholas of Cusa', with the literature cited there especially the studies by P. Sigmund, M. Watanabe, J. Biechler *et al.*; for Paulus Vladimiri, see Stanislaus F. Belch, *Paulus Vladimiri and His Doctrine Concerning International Law and Politics* (2 vols.; The Hague, 1965).

10. Von der Hardt, I:IX:549.

11. Mark Dykmans, 'Les premières rapports de Petrarque avec les Pays-Bas', *Bulletin de l'Institute historique belge de Rome* 20 (1939), 109–21.

12. Alessandro Gherardi, *Statuti della Universita e studio Fiorentino dell' anno 1387* [Documenti di Storia Italiana pubblicati a cura della R. Deputazione sugli Studi di Storia Patria per le provincie di Toscana, dell' Umbria e delle Marche, Tomo VII] (Firenze, 1881), p. 386; Jacobus Philippus Tomasini, *Gymnasium Patavinum* (Udine, 1654), p. 21.

13. One could mention that Zabarella must have been known to the composer Johannes Ciconia who dedicated two motets in his honour and to the poet, Antonius Baratella, who among other works wrote a lament on Zabarella's death. In addition the many letters from his friends reveal the relationships he had and finally even those who disagreed with him often sought his advice and respected his opinion.

14. The manuscripts of this tract *De modo docendi et discendi ius canonicum et civile* with which I have worked are four codices: Munich, Bavarian State Library, Clm 14134, fos. 147^v–152^r; Vatican City, Biblioteca Apostolica, Vat. Lat. 2258, fos. 364^v–369^v; Tübingen, University Library, Mc 58, fos. 111^r–121^r; and Stift Sankt Paul in Lavantthal (Austria) Codex S. Pauli in Carinthia 79/4 [28.4.9], fos. 34^r–39^r. Dr. Dieter Girgensohn of the Maz-Planck-Institut für Geschichte at Göttingen has written to me since this article was completed of a whole group of other codices which he has uncovered in his extensive research. Dr. Girgensohn has been preparing for some time a study of Zabarella which will include a critical edition of Zabarella's tract based on all the

manuscripts available. Hence what I have as an appendix to this article is in the way of a working edition rather than a final and critical edition since it is based only on the four codices known to me and not the others now being transcribed and collated by Dr. Girgensohn. In the notes that follow the citations to the text will be to this working edition and to the line numbers therein as found in the appendix. The text is based on the Munich codex correlated and compiled with corrections and additions from the other three.

15. Zabarella several times in the tract prefaced his recommendation as 'post multas experiencias' [line 97], 'cum enim ut experiencia ostendit' [line 94], 'post tamen multas probaciones' [line 603] and at another point in his discussion talked of a certain method and stated that he could not speak on it as it was not in use when he left school 'in meo tempore' [lines 10–11]. Both of these would indicate that he composed the tract at least in its final form some years after he had completed his studies at Bologna and then Florence in 1385, and that after a good deal of trial and error as a teacher he was giving his opinion after a long time. Both would therefore point to a date in the later part of his teaching career which had stretched from 1385 to 1410. I have concluded that the tract dates from some time after 1400, and that Zabarella composed it in Padua where he taught in those years between 1390 and 1410. The references to his career and experiences are reinforced by the evidence put forward by Professor Stephan Kuttner and his observations that the Vatican manuscripts of Zabarella's legal commentaries including a version of this tract were a result of late work and revision; see Stephan Kuttner, 'Francesco Zabarella's Commentary on the decretals: A Note on the editions and the Vatican manuscripts', *Bulletin of Medieval Canon Law* New Series 16 (1986), 97–101, esp. 100–1.

16. In the notes that follow the citations to the text of Zabarella's tract will be to the text as found in the appendix, here lines 4–6: 'non est meum propositum de hac re doctrinam novam cudere sed ea sola que ab experto cognovi prout menti se offerent'.

17. There were precedents for this type of tract and other writers later than Zabarella who delivered their advice in a variety of forms such as guides for correct writing and conversation and even for letters home; see: Eva M. Sanford, *'De disciplina scholarium*. A Medieval Handbook on the Care and Training of Scholars', *Classical Journal* 27 (1932), 82–95; Lillian G. Berry, 'A Fifteenth-Century Guide to Latin Conversation for University Students', *Classical Journal* 23 (1928), 520–30; L. Frati, 'L' Epistola "De regimine et modo studendi" di Martino de Fano', *Studi e memorie per la storia dell' Universita di Bologna* 6 (1921), 19–29; Bernardo Alfonso Rodriguez (ed.), *Juan Alfonso de Benavente, Ars et doctrina studendi et docendi* [Bibliotheca Salamanticensis II, Textus I] (Salamanca, 1972).

18. Lines 11–13: 'Communia utrique sunt timor dei [dei missing in Clm],

odium criminum, amor ad scienciam et sapienciam, studii perseverancia, diligencia investigacionis.' In the anonymous eulogy mentioned earlier and printed in Von der Hardt, I:IX:549, the writer cited the key virtues according to Isidore of Seville and noted them in Zabarella. Since this citation begins with the words 'timor odiumque delectio atque census' it is possible that Zabarella in his text was also echoing Isidore.

19. Lines 17–20, 24–5.
20. Lines 26–31.
21. Lines 38–9.
22. Lines 39–42. It is worth noting that here as so often in this treatise Zabarella interjected the personal reference 'ut nonnullos vidi'.
23. Lines 42–3.
24. Lines 43–51. Zabarella again referred to concrete examples: 'ut aliqui . . . ut alii', and noted that many teachers dropped their voices especially at the end of a statement: 'maxime in fine oracionis'.
25. Lines 53–5, 51, 57–9. Once again Zabarella referred back to his personal experience: 'quendam vidi'.
26. Lines 65–9.
27. Lines 71–7. The text here shows that Zabarella was referring to his own action of brushing up on the basic skills.
28. St. Augustine had stressed the importance of 'making instruction pleasant and appealing in order to hold attention'; cited by Charles Sears Baldwin, *Medieval Rhetoric and Poetic (to 1400)* ([New York, 1928]; Gloucester, Mass., 1959), p. 65, from St. Augustine's *De doctrina Christiana*.
29. Donald C. Lemen has shown that the aim of making the audience well disposed (*benevolum*), attentive (*attentum*) and willing to receive information (*docilem*) goes back to the classical Roman tradition of rhetoric of Cicero and Quintilian, *Rhetoric in Greco-Roman Education* (New York, 1957), pp. 112–13. But this tradition in turn looked back to the Greek philosophical, rhetorical and oratorical tradition, especially Aristotle's *Rhetorica*, 'For it makes a great deal of difference to persuasion . . . how the speaker strikes the audience—both how the hearers think he regards them, and in addition how they are disposed toward him.' See Baldwin, *Ancient Rhetoric*, pp. 17–18. For a good part of the medieval world this tradition was filtered down to them through St. Augustine's *De doctrina Christiana* and later borrowers from this work, e.g., Rabanus Maurus, who cited that triad from Augustine (*benevolus, attentus* and *docilis*); see Harry Caplan, 'Classical Rhetoric and the Medieval Theory of Preaching', in Raymond F. Howes (ed.), *Historical Studies of Rhetoric and Rhetoricians* (Ithaca, N.Y., 1961), p. 77.
30. 'The consideration of the hearer is in a degree necessary in all teaching', was a maxim from Aristotle quoted by Baldwin, p. 23. Zabarella suggested that the teacher find the mode of instruction that was best

accommodated to all ('modum ... qui commodis omnibus gratior') [lines 83–4] and he should aim for a goal that not only the subject taught (the message) but also the way it was taught (the medium) would be approved ('ut non tantum ipsas res sed eciam ipsum dicendi modum comprobent') [lines 89–90]. The saying of St. Gregory the Great, 'whose life is despised so is his preaching', was often quoted in the medieval world (see Caplan, 'Classical Rhetoric', p. 85) and so Zabarella's insistence on the moral qualities of the teacher would fit in here as well. Both how the teacher taught and what he was seen as made up the medium. Marshall McLuhan would have fully agreed.

31. Lines 90–1, 92–3. Again the practical reference by Zabarella 'as I have seen some teachers do'. A medieval Franciscan handbook, *Ars concionandi* contained similar advice as Caplan noted, 'use ordinary words, do not coin words or you will be ridiculous' (p. 79). St. Augustine had put it very simply, 'He who teaches will rather avoid all words that do not teach. If he can find correct words that are understood, he will choose these.' Baldwin, *Medieval Rhetoric*, p. 65.

32. Lines 94–102. Once more Zabarella refers to abuse in practice 'as some do'.

33. Zabarella urged that the instructor only bring in what was necessary for the class to understand the point at issue and went on to describe the opposite of this, the teachers who go in the other direction (lines 102–7). He then brought in the legislation that was enacted to constrain these types to cover the material as stipulated; lines 107–9. Arthur A. Norton, *Readings in the History of Education. Medieval Universities* (Cambridge, Mass., 1909), cited the decree which was passed at the University of Bologna precisely because of the problem with some professors in this regard, pp. 112–14.

34. Lines 111–12.

35. Lines 120–2.

36. Lines 117–20, 115–17.

37. Innocent IV's famous *Commentaria in V libros Decretalium* (Frankfort 1570) which he composed while he was only Sinibaldo Fieschi (*c.* 1200–54) but issued as the commentary of a prominent canonist by him while he was pope (1243–54).

38. Lines 128–33. These methods had become well established in the law schools as can be seen by the description attributed to a famous commentator on Roman law, Odofredus, of the way he had learned from his master to teach law at Bologna in the thirteenth century: 'Concerning the method of teaching the following order was kept by ancient and modern doctors and especially by my own master, which method I shall observe: First, I shall give you summaries of each title before I proceed to the text; second, I shall give you as clear and explicit a statement as I can of the purport of each law [included in the title]; third, I shall read the text with a view to correcting it; fourth, I shall

briefly repeat the contents of the law; fifth, I shall solve apparent
contradictions, adding any general principles of law [to be extracted
from the passage] . . . and any distinctions or subtle and useful problems
(*quaestiones*) arising out of the law', Charles Homer Haskins, *The Rise
of the Universities* (Ithaca, New York, 1923, 1965), p. 42. The famed
canonist and contemporary of Innocent IV, Hostiensis (Henricus de
Segusio) described a similar procedure in his commentary which he
completed in 1253, see Hans-Jürgen Becker, 'Simone da Borsano, ein
Kanonist am Vorabend des Grossen Schismas', in *Rechtsgeschichte als
Kulturgeschichte. Festschrift für Adalbert Erler zum 70. Geburtstag* unter
Mitwirkung von Adolf Fink, ed. Hans-Jürgen Becker *et al.* (Aalen,
1976), 193–4.

39. Lines 150–4. Odofredus had expressed the same plan in his description:
'And if any law shall seem deserving, by reason of its celebrity or
difficulty, of a repetition, I shall reserve it for an evening repetition',
Haskins, p. 43.

40. Lines 154–5.

41. Lines 159–61.

42. Lines 162–83.

43. Lines 191–4, 201–5. As Haskins noted, Odofredus claimed to be
bringing in an innovation: 'And I shall read all the glosses, which was
not the practice before my time', *The Rise of the Universities*, p. 43.

44. Lines 211–15.

45. Lines 218–20. Here Zabarella also pointed out that with more advanced
students one can take the time to show what the standard commentary
on the text was (the *glosa ordinaria* as it was called), what different
commentators had said on this text, the arguments in favour of the view
in the standard interpretation or the reasons for his own disagreement
with this. His only provision was that the instructor carefully distinguish between the importance and level of difficulty of the material.

46. Lines 234–45.

47. Lines 249–53.

48. Lines 257–8.

49. Lines 265–7.

50. Lines 270–5.

51. Lines 276–84. For a discussion of this medieval view, see Paul E.
Sigmund, *Natural Law in Political Thought* (Cambridge, Mass., 1971).

52. Lines 287–91.

53. Zabarella spoke of the two or three years ('duobus primis annis ad plus
tribus premissis doctrinis immoretur') [lines 292–3] spent in these
related studies of logic and philosophy before going on to the study of
law but added that then he came to this study as a trained inquirer
which could not be said of those who began to study law with no
preliminary training [lines 293–5]. Zabarella would have been in his mid
teens for these studies for he started his legal programme at Bologna at

the age of eighteen in 1378. His studies in logic and philosophy would presumably then have been from *c*.1375–8 ('ego . . . duos annos et partem tercii apposui studiis logice atque philosophie') [300–3] in Padua which was a very lively and active time in those days for the tradition of Petrarch who had died there in 1374 was still very much alive. His studies in grammar and rhetoric would have been going on while Petrarch was still alive in Padua and he himself was at the start of his teens. Zabarella added that it was good and not at all dangerous for those finished with their studies to continue contact and interest in these other disciplines [lines 309–16].

54. Zabarella's advice during legal studies was to give full attention to these and not to go back to the other studies and reading (lines 304–5); he considered this very important and so repeated the admonition not to leave these other books around so as to avoid distractions (lines 307–9).

55. In the tract Zabarella points out the inanity of those who never get to the text because they spend all their time on the secondary sources (lines 318–33). He urged that the student go through the texts very carefully and methodically, going back over them as much as and as often as was necessary until he had grasped them, even getting down to the individual paragraphs and phrases, if not syllables (lines 337–42).

56. Again Zabarella indicated the importance of this piece of advice by beginning with the words 'I can not say it (insist on it) too often' [lines 334–49]. He added that the student should seek help at a proper hour ('ydoneo tempore'), that he should not make a pest of himself ('et illi non ingrato eum visitet') and be polite in his requests ('atque humiliter interroget'). Finally he expected that as the student became more advanced he would return the favour and be devoted and humane in helping those who came after him (351–2).

57. Lines 365–7. Zabarella said of these critical logicians that they were talking about matters which they did not know, and nothing was stupider than to do this, 'illi vero logici locuntur de his que non sapiunt quo nil est inanius' (lines 370–1). He freely admitted the necessity of some degree of memory (lines 373–5).

58. Lines 376–8, 353–4, 359–60.

59. Lines 380–81, and then Zabarella added that some people (quidam enim . . .'), while others ('alii'), and then certain people ('nonnulli') all had their own ways of dealing with this problem.

60. Lines 388–90.

61. Lines 469–71.

62. Lines 481–8. Haskins, pp. 44–5 pointed out that the three mainstays of the medieval academic world were lectures, reviews, and repetitions. Zabarella observed that even in these private sessions the proper attitude had to be kept and a self-centred approach would only result in disaster [lines 488–510, 535–6).

63. Lines 567–8.

64. Lines 568–72. Haskins again presented the picture given by a medieval writer of university life which showed a similar view: 'Many eat cakes when they ought to be at study, or go to sleep in the classrooms' (p. 64).
65. Lines 572–77.
66. Lines 577–9
67. Lines 579–85. The two images that Zabarella presented here, the first of the futility of trying to pour more water into an already filled vase as analogous to putting more demands on an exhausted body or mind, and the second the traditional instructions of parents of all ages to their children that they should chew their food carefully, must have been immediately acknowledged by his audience.
68. Lines 585–9. Zabarella advised here that he did not need to elaborate on his counsel since these things could be known from common sense ('ipsa naturali prudencia') [line 588]. He then added that in all of this to prevent an addled mind from too many demands put upon it, it was important to allow breaks ('interpelacione aliqua') [lines 590–1] so that the mind would be refreshed and able to continue to study and be more retentive ('recreata mens ad continuendum stadium fit retencior') [line 592]. He did advise that practice famous at many academic institutions and which Jacob Bronowski described so well in *The Ascent of Man*, the walk or stroll for which professors were known at Göttingen and other places, 'sive deambulas in camera vel per civitatem vel extra' (lines 624–5), but all of this was geared to make you more apt for studying (line 626).
69. Lines 596–7. After presenting the two schools of thought ('censent aliqui . . . ; alii e contra'), Zabarella once more called upon his many years of experience to suggest what appeared to him to be advisable as more useful [lines 597–9].
70. Lines 601–5; again appealing to his long years of experience, Zabarella advised seven or eight hours of sleep (line 605).
71. Lines 605–7.
72. Lines 610–15.
73. Lines 615–23.
74. Lines 550–9. The citation from Horace is drawn from Book I of his *Epistles*, Epistle 2, line 69.
75. Zabarella urged that if his audience would heed the advice he had just given in the body of the tract and were men of faith and prayer, they would succeed, lines 627–36.
76. Lines 636–8.
77. In his eulogy for Zabarella (printed in Von der Hardt), the humanist Poggio elaborated on Zabarella's reputation as a jurist (I:IX:541–542), stressed the fact that Zabarella deserved chief credit for pressuring Pope John XXIII to come to Constance (I:IX:540), had laboured in the most turbulent days of the council with a willingness to speak out on critical issues and disputed points (I:IX:544), and that his reputation was such

that if he had lived he might very likely have been the new pope elected at Constance (I:IX:541).

78. Von der Hardt published also the anonymous sermon on the death of Zabarella which spoke of his care for the poor while he was at Padua, while in the Roman curia and at Constance, called him the father of the poor ('velut pater pauperum') (I:IX:549), repeated the judgement that he was considered by all worthy of the papacy ('ut omnium iudicio summo sacerdotio dignus esset') but that he died in the struggle for reform and unity ('pro conservatione Ecclesiae et pro reparatione Ecclesiae') (I:IX:551).

Appendix: Text of Tract with Critical Apparatus

M = Munich codex, Clm 14134

T = Tübingen, Mc 58

V = Vatican City, Vat. Lat. 2258

S = Stift Sankt Paul in Lavantthal, codex 79/4

A Tract of Franciscus de Zabarellis (1360–1417)

In nomine sancte et individue trinitatis Amen. Incipit tractatus de modo docendi et discendi ius canonicum et civile reverendissimi in Christo patris domini francisci de Zabarellis cardinalis florentini.

Circa quod advertendum est quod non est meum propositum de hac
5 re doctrinam novam cudere sed ea sola que ab experto cognovi prout menti se offerent literis mandare vel in hoc venturus post me preiudicans si quid viderint vel certius vel ordinacius vel eleganciori stilo de quo hoc nichil fui curatus me posse tradere sed pocius eis viam aperiens in quo etiam opere si qua superflua vel diminuta vel inordinata tradita
10 legerint debent esse faciles ad indulgendum si insuetum iter ingressus aliquando erraverim tanquam homo non vacuus errore et hoc premisso ut de proposito dicere incipiamus. Considerandum est quod quedam tam in docente quam in discente communiter requiruntur; quedam sunt utrique precipua et singularia ita uni quam non alteri conveniunt.
15 Communia utrique sunt timor dei, odium criminum, amor ad scientiam et sapientiam, studii preseverancia, diligencia investigacionis et alia huiusmodi inter que illud videtur potissimum ut curet videre fundamentum eorum que per alios dicta sunt ut non facile adhereat nisi

motiva et rationes ei videantur urgere ad quod percipiendum sit
20 diligens in videndo iura et rationes quibus moventur; sepe enim ex
eisdem movebitur ad oppositum vel intelliget illa non urgere ac sibi
aliter dicendum videbitur quod tamen non facile affirmet sed studeat
iuribus et racionibus munire et hec ipsa notare ut si a memoria labantur
habeatur ubi perquiri possunt, precipue in docente ut excellat moribus
25 et facundia. In discente sunt ea que dico alibi sed hec quamquam vera
sint non tamen satisfaciunt ad omnino plene intelligendum, nam sicuti
in artificiis manualibus ad instruendum alium non sufficit ei dicere sic
esse sagittandum vel sic in pugna ducendum gladium nisi apprehensa
sagitta ipse instruens eam baliste vel arcui applicatam emittat vel ipsum
30 gladium manu tractans educat ostendens pocius quam sermone depro-
mens qualiter agendum sit. nostra est intencio ante oculos ponere quid
docentis sit et quid discentis officium quod dic ut in sequentibus.
   Quero que docenti documenta maxime tradenda sunt ut in promptu
habeat que fugiat et que sequatur; dic premittendo quod licet in hac
35 questione dicatur de preceptore et in sequenti de auditore non nulla
tamen que uni applicantur etiam alteri conveniunt. Et hoc premisso dic
quod ad docentem qui vult in docendi exercicio perseverare precipue
pertinet ut vitam ordinet studio ita tempora distinguens ut non vexetur
natura super quam possit nec vacet ocio ultra quam expediat. leccio-
40 nem eciam quam vult tradere ita curet intelligere ut cum erit in cathedra
non vacillet nec ad dicendum redeat dicens, ut nonnullos vidi, volui sic
dicere; qua autem constancia poterit auditor proficere si doctor ipse
tanquam dubitans nescit opinionem suam et sermonem firmare; non
etiam tepide vel flendo ut aliqui nec clamorose ut alii neque tanquam
45 inarticulatam cantus melodiam pronunciet sed vivaci et constanti voce
medium quoddam inter altum et depressum tenens et illud solum
advertens ut bene et complete ab auditoribus intelligatur ad quod
potissime suffragabitur si dicciones non truncate quod plerique maxime
in fine oracionis faciunt sed perfecte explicabit et se non tanquam
50 currens accelerabit nec rursus tanquam fatigatus ultra quam oporteat
retardabit nec interpellacionem faciat ubi sensus oracionis non est
perfectus sed pausata et continua oracione prosequatur distinguens
diccionem a diccione atque ubi perfecta est oratio morulam quandam
faciens ita et ut sibi respirandi et auditoribus percipiendi tempus
55 tribuat. Evitet eciam omnino verborum superfluitatem ne ut quidam ex
non recto loquendi usu verba interponat ad rem explicandam non
necessaria veluti quemdam vidi qui tociens verbum scilicet aut videlicet
interponebat ut auditores omissa lecionis attencione persisterent in
numerando quot vicibus illis in lecione usus fuisset. Alium eciam alias
60 valde peritum qui tociens verbum dico repetebat ut esset non modica
pars lecionis; alii frequenter verba intelligitis vos et similia inpertinen-
cia que cum in omnibus eciam in communi sermone vitanda sint nisi
cum oportet, tamen maxime in preceptore precavenda qui enim alios
instruit. hunc expedit in omnibus precipue in sermone et specialiter
65 cum doctrinam aliis tradit esse irreprehensibilem. diligens enim sit ut
congrua utatur oracione nec barbarismos faciat quale enim est eum qui

superiores sciencias docet huius inferioris que non tam scienciam quam
sciendi modus et condimentum est esse ignarum atque ex hoc ludibrio
haberi apud pueros in gramatica mediocriter doctos; ob hoc si evenit ut
70 is qui alias in sapiencia iuris clarus est doctor gramatice non sit
quantum satis est peritus consultius est eciam in etate grandiore
aliquam operam illi arti impendere quam semper per omnem vitam
patere derisui quamobrem et si non essem prorsus eius artis ignarus
tamen ne in accentu et huiusmodi errarem ei postquam aliquot annis
75 canones docueram tempus aliquod apposui maxime in videndo Prisciani opus ut vim vocabulorum et alia illam artem concernentia non
ignorarem. ad hec autem percipienda de se ipso an scilicet verbis
superfluis vel incongruis utatur velut doctor per sibi fidos auditores ab
eo eciam super hoc rogatos admoneri maxime in primis annis quibus
80 incipit docere. Sic enim facile potuerit se corrigere cum de suis erroribus
fuerit admonitus sciscitetur eciam sepe ab eisdem fidis qualiter modus
suus legendi sit auditoribus acceptus; quid eciam in eo laudent sed
magis quid dampnent ut ad hoc redditus attentus illum modum
exequetur qui communis omnibus gratior fuerit sicut enim rebus in
85 omnibus medius plurimum valet, sic potissimum in lecione in qua
diversis auditoribus tradenda, illa est forma recipienda quam ipsi
saltem pars maior probaverit; parum enim prosit quis cum audit
aliquid referri modo sibi non grato et e contra multum qui audit ita
tradi [aliquid referri] ut non tantum ipsas res sed eciam ipsum dicendi
90 modum comprobet. Super omnia vero caveat ne verbis utatur impro-
priis et obscuris ut non nullos vidi qui ut subtiles et doctiores habeantur
docentes in iure nituntur verbis philosophicis uti quo nichil potest esse
ineptius; verbis enim propriis gaudet queque sciencia que cum ad aliam
transferre volueris duo mala secuntur quia nec docens plene rerum quas
95 docere vult naturam explicat nec auditores illorum vocabulorum ignari
clare percipiunt que docentur. Sunt et alii qui ut peritiores credantur
vocabulis ambiguis et obscuris sermone transponendo eciam interdum
verba loqui curant. Quid autem imprudencius quam cum qui professus
est se alios instructurum studiose ita loqui ut intelligi vel nullo modo vel
100 saltem non sine multa difficultate possit. Cum e contra soleamus in
laudem preceptorum eos appellare claros qui scilicet et clare intelligant
et clare doceant. Sit insuper attentissimus ut illa sola doceat que ad
intellectum legis vel canonis et glossarum sufficiant quod contra plures
faciunt qui per latissimas et plurimas disputaciones eciam quandoque
105 non nimium pertinentes ita se delatant ut parum in textum per totum
annum possint procedere unde evenit ut in multis annis auditoribus
tradere non possint id quod anno uno tradendum fuerat, cui transgres-
sioni volentes antiqui obviare per certas partes annum distinxerant
inter quas de publico stipendiati tenebantur expedivisse volumina.
110 Illum autem morem quo ad ipsius distincionis formam quia in meo
tempore non fuit in usu non possum probare vel dampnare sed certe
propositum et intencio distinguencium plurimum commendanda ut
occasio prestaretur docentibus non retinendi occupatos auditores per
longa temporum dispendia quod precavens legislator per certos paucos

115 annos omnium librorum iuris civilis leccionem coartavit.
Doctor ergo solis illis tradendis operam det que non possint auditores per se ipsos facile percipere quem ad modum enim sicienti satis est ostendisse fontem absque eo quod id quod natura instruerit edoceat que forma potandi sit; ita sufficit auditoribus illa declarare per que possint reliqua
120 ad illam rem pertinencia intelligere per se ipsos. Nichil ergo inutilius quam post apertam exposicionem legis vel canonis per infinita vagari quesita nisi forte sit aliqua questio vel ex post facto pendens vel alias ita difficilis ut eius explicacio videatur opportuna pro intellectu materie que traditur et facile erit ipsi preceptori cognoscere; qua consideracione
125 ductus Innocentius Quartus in prologo suo Commentarii super hanc compilacionem scribit quod tam doctor quam auditor dum in scolis legunt multa de suis glosis potuerunt omittere et studio camere pro discussionibus et diffinicionibus causarum pro tempore reservare. Formam autem recitandi duplicem esse constat. Una est quam in commen-
130 tariis secutus sum in qua non attento glosarum ordine proceditur per notabilia, contraria et questiones; altera est secundum glosarum ordinem procedatur prima scribentibus vel legem seu canonem repetentibus accomodatur, reliqua docentibus. Et quoniam non nulli ex preceptoribus optarent hanc formam per me et scribendo servatam fuisse;
135 cogitent id quod verbum est quia si primum unum notabile, consequenter una questio, postea contrarium aliquod, scribendo explicaretur et sic rursus pro materie prolixitate pluries fieret, huiusmodi inordinata permixtio nulla esset operis forma ut dici posset cum de uno loco ad alium revertimur quod tali contrario puta primo vel secundo et sic
140 ulterius. Id quod queritur possit reperiri, docendo autem hoc cessat inconveniens. Sed quam facile sit hunc scribendi ordinem adaptare ad docendi modum patebit in exemplo quod subicio infra questione quinta. Non est eciam pretermittendum quod ad preceptorem non parum pertinet exhibere se gratum auditoribus. Nam ut Quintilianus
145 ait ut notatur *de magistris* capitulum 'pluraliter' sciencia valescere nequit nisi sanata fuerit tradentis accipientisque concordia et huic consonum est ut in cathedra sit letus et vigil ut ex primo auditores ad amatores sibi conciliet; exaltare eosdem excitet ad attente audiendum, ad quod eciam specialiter eos parumper exaltando vocem admoneat
150 cum aliquid difficile vult explicare vel singulare aliquid aut notabile per eos diligenter intelligi et memorie commendari quo eciam tempore non numquam utile est vel bis vel eciam pluries replicare ita ut perfecte possit quod ambiguum est intelligi et quod singulare seu notabile menti firmiter inherere. Ad quod eciam consequendum admonendus erit
155 auditor ut in margine signum aliquod scriptorio stilo imprimat quo facilius possit illud alias cum queretur inveniri atque uti; assolet non longo itinere fatigare parvas sessiones respirandi causa interponere. sic in preceptore optime convenit ut post expeditam lecionis partem precipue si gravior aliquis articulus iam explicatus animos laxaverit
160 auditorum aliquid iocosum et festivum et ad risum provocans intromittere studeat ut ex illo recreati auditorum animi ad percipienda reliqua

et prompciores fiant et retenciores sed et precipua cura consideret qui
illi sint quos habet instruere. Aliter enim cum rudioribus et novis, aliter
cum mediocriter instructis, aliter cum profectis auditoribus est agen-
165 dum. Nam quem ad modum in ponderibus humeris robustioribus
applicamus pondera graviora tenerioribus leviora, non secus in leccione facienda. Unde Apostolus primo ad Corinthios tertio scribens,
lac inquit, potum vobis dedi non escam, nondum enim poteratis sed
eciam nunc quid potestis ad huc enim carnales escis [*de penitentiis et*
170 *remissionibus*, capitulum 'deus qui'] quod imitatus canonis lator admo-
net eos qui missi fuerant ad instruendos noviter conversos ad fidem ut
eos paulatim instruant in fide confessionis formam, oracionem domini-
cam, et symbolum que sunt fidei principia eos sollicite edocentes; ita
ergo iuris preceptor si contingerit ut hii quos habet instruere sint
175 novicii, curet eos instruere circa principia ut eciam iuris vocabula eis
exponat et textum aperiat ponendo casum brevem quem dicimus
summarium quod summatim et verbis paucis legis vel canonis explicat
effectum, principalem deinde legem vel canonem dividat in particulas
[ff de doli exceptione 'literaliter']. res enim divisione sit lucidior ut enim
180 volentibus cibo refici opus est non uno bolo quod nec natura patitur
totum panem transglutire sed per singulas buccellas. Sic eciam in
auditoribus oportet longiores partes in breviores scindere particulas
quo faciliores sint ad percipiendum; non nulli tamen prius dividunt
quam sumarium ponunt quibus non resisto. Priorem tamen ordinem
185 imitatus sum quia videtur ad reddendum auditores attentos valde
accomodum sumatim premittere quid est id quod est explicandum.
Tercio loco casum ponat longiorem seu in terminis et facta contingen-
cia quod est quasi ante oculos ponere rem ipsam, quem ad modum
acciderit postea literam distincte et punctatim legat eciam indicando
190 ubi punctus faciendus et qualis an planus qui orationem perfectam esse
indicet an suspensivus qui eam ad huc pendere significet. Et si quid
notabile in litera fuerit ammoneat ut notent et calamo extrinsecus
signent. non omittat etiam ostendere ubi principaliter colligitur summarium; quinto loco notabilia colligat et ita commode hoc et quod
195 supra dixi et summario et divisione referat ut volentibus hec scribere
pateat comoditas et hec iunioribus sufficiunt; nam sicuti pictores
antequam figuram pingendam incipiunt parietem cemento fulciunt ut
habilis fiat ad colores suscipiendos et ymaginem retinendam sic et in
istis qui erudiuntur expedit ut animi pocius inbuti sint doctrine
200 primordiis quatenus ydonei fiant ad intelligenda que in doctrina illa sint
difficiliora et ob hanc causam non nulli iuris preceptores volentes suos
caros bene ad doctrinam disponere consueverunt eisdem tradere in
primis annis volumina iuris absque glosis ne occasionem captent
vagandi per glosas, sed in textu tanquam firmo fundamento figant
205 memoriam; alia tamen consideracione utilius videtur eciam ab ipso
inicio eisdem libros tradere glosatos; quamquam enim non videantur
ydonei ad ipsas glosas intelligendas, tamen ut incipiant discere eas
legere consultum videtur ut attendant cum preceptor exponit vel legit

easdem in quibus eciam quandoque sunt aliqua notabilia vel versus
210 quos debent iuniores menti perdiscere.

Sin autem evenerit ut auditores sint mediocriter instructi preceptor
hos instruat in glosis et materiis difficilioribus, plus tamen cum eis
insistat quam cum provectis quibus tamquam facile percipientibus
quequam difficilia, non oportet exhibere eandem curam sed istis de
215 punctis fortioribus facienda erit admonicio ut advertant diligenter; ad
quos eciam plenius excitandos studeat aliquid novi ex ingenio suo
proferre, verum quia in generali studio premissa auditorum divisio
rarissime reperitur. Sunt enim in eodem auditorio novicii mediocriter
instructi et provecti; expedit ut preceptor simul prout oportunum est
220 satisfaciat ut ergo novicii suam porcionem accipiant, quandoque
premissum summarium scilicet divisionem et reliqua prius expediat,
deinde satisfaciendo mediocribus et provectis ad apparatum glossarum
accedat et eas notando opponendo vel querendo expediat prout melius
esse putaverit; si quid etiam alii scribentes aliter dicunt vel eciam ipse
225 aliter vult dicere quam glossa illud non obmittat et studeat quantum
fieri poterit sustinere glosam vel si non poterit explicet rationem que
videatur urgere, quod si per glosas non habeatur intellectus legis vel
canonis ad plenum illa eciam adiciat que vel alii vel que ipse circa hoc
senciat et ex hoc explicite non oportebit ut insistat in explicandis
230 questionibus extra glossam nisi ex ea causa quam supra, eadem
questione documento nono premisimus. Illud pretera negligendum
non est quod aliter cum leccio facilis, aliter cum difficilis, est agendum.
imprudentis enim est et rerum distinctionem non agnoscentis parem
curam tam levibus quam arduis agendis apponere. cicius itaque leviores
235 lecciones et paucioribus explicet verbis; in gravibus morosius et
ampliore oracione persistat donec existimet ab auditoribus perfectam
acceptam esse doctrinam. Est et illud advertendum non esse in preceptore laudabile id quod nonnulli ostentacionis causa faciunt quid ut
appareant in iure copiosi plurimum in iurium multorum allegacione ad
240 idem propositum insistunt que quandoque parum quandoque nil et
pocius contrafaciunt et vulgaria sunt in quibus immorari diucius non
est auditoribus expediens nec apud doctiores commendabile. Sufficit
ergo illa inducere que quod intenditur probant vel saltem bene faciant
ut ita sit in sermone diligens quod nec dicenda taceat nec proferat
245 reticenda; plura forte alia documenta preceptoribus tradenda forent
sed hec ad presens mihi non occurrunt.

Iam tempus exigere videtur ut explicentur illa que oportuna sunt in
auditoribus ut percipiant facile et celeriter proficiant. Quero de huiusmodi circa quod admonendus est auditor ut eius prima cura sit
250 antequam ad scienciam iuris properet ut in grammatica sit quantum
expedit instructus nec scribendi sit prorsus ignarus. plurimum enim
valet si que a preceptore traduntur possit reportare item ut cum incipit
intelligere possit ymaginaciones suas mandare literis. evenit enim ut
quandoque scolaris diligenter intendens studio non nulla cogitet que
255 postea doctor probavit et que forte sibi postea non redibunt in mentem
quod in me sum expertus, cum que opiniones et motiva cum audiebam

occurrerentur quas postea doctor percomprobavi; longe autem maior
necessitas est in preceptore ut scribere non ignoret quatenus possit que
in cathedra recitare voluerit in forma redigere consilia que ab ipso in
260 iure petita fuerint, repeticciones et disputaciones notare aut si contigerit
ut oportet ut possit commentarios scribere; non sit semper opus habere
coadiutorem in scribendo nam eciam ut expertus sum cum imminet
materia difficilis et perplexa videtur pene impossibile alteri eam dictare
uti multociens experimentum feci et tandem fuit opus ut ipse conscri-
265 berem. Post instructionem gramatice non parum est utile intelligere
principia logice propter noticiam argumentorum quorum in iure non
parvus est usus sed et in rhetorica valde proderit saltem mediocriter
instructum esse. Est enim pars civilis sapiencie adinventa que maxime
fuit ad causas ordinandas et inde oratores quibus habundavit vetustas.
270 nos autem propter inopiam illius pericie hoc genere non sine nostrorum
temporum confusione caremus, quam indigenciam si priora tempora
passa forent non habuissemus iuris consultos qui civiles leges tam
accincta et gravi oraccione dictarunt ut sine iniuria possint eorum
volumina quo ad textuum pulcritudinem et elegenciam ceteris aliarum
275 facultatum voluminibus anteferri. sunt preterea in ipsa oratoria facultate documenta que multum prodesse possunt advocatis et omnibus
causidicis, quamquam autem philosophia naturalis non videatur ad
sapienciam iuris maxime pertinere quia tamen in iure de omnibus que
humanam vitam respiciunt tradi oportet maxime competit ut idem
280 futurus iuris auditor saltem naturalia principia non ignoret; nam si
respicis iuris consultos invenies eos non ignorasse philosophiam ac et si
de naturali non curas ipsam saltem moralem non negligas. Hec enim
non est aliud a iure nisi quia in ipsa de moribus agitur in genere, in iure
autem distincte et ad casus particulares fit applicacio. fortassis autem
285 dices nimium temporis exigi volentibus proficere in omnibus premissis
sed non arbitrare me consulere ut vacetur premissis facultatibus ea
mente ut ibi proficearis; hoc enim vidi non tam prodesse quam obesse,
cum scilicet hii qui diucius in artibus logica et philosophia fuerunt
immorati ad iuris sapienciam se contulerunt iam enim in alio sciencie
290 genere habituati non facile disponuntur ad habitum percipiende iuris
prudencie. hec igitur mens est ut qui post gramaticam ad iuris sapienciam est accessurus duobus prius annis ad plus tribus premissis
doctrinis immoretur quibus si diligenter institerit non in formis sed
quasi formatus statim incipiet scienciam iuris intelligere quod non sic
295 evenit his qui horum rudes ad iura transmittuntur. hii enim non parvo
tempore indigent ut incipere possint solide intelligere; longa eciam
differentia est in ordine subtiliter intelligendi inter imbutum predictis
facultatibus seu saltem earum principiis et alium eorum prorsus
ignarum. hinc videmus maximam partem eorum qui commentarios in
300 iure scripserunt inscios non fuisse premissarum facultatum. Ego in me
perpendi quod illi qui de gramatica simul mecum egressi ad iura se
contulerunt non prius expediti sunt quam ego qui duos annos et partem
tercii apposui studiis logice et philosophie. cui tamen hoc contigerit
memor sit quod cum primum in sciencia iuris audire incipit numquam

305 alterius voluminibus immoretur sed a se penitus amoveat. simile nihil
enim magis accelerat proficiendi utilitatem quam in ea sola sciencia
versari quam proficis, unde talibus consultum est dum in scholis
audiunt eciam cum ex iuris studio lassati sunt, pocius ab omni leccione
abstinere quam poeticos auctores quod non nulli faciunt lectitare. non
310 idem est in doctoribus qui iam fundati sunt in iuris sapientia; sine
periculo ergo sepe multo cum fructu possunt captatis temporibus ocii
sui partem accomodare ad intelligendas et si non perfecte saltem
quantisper alias facultates. ex hoc namque fiunt eciam in iuris sapiencia
doctores; habent enim omnes facultates communem quandam coniunc-
315 tionem ita ut non possit quis facile in una esse perfectus si ceterarum sit
omnino ignarus. et ob hanc causam ut auditor non distrahatur ad
aliquid aliud cogitandum summe necesse est quod alios in camera
libros non habeat quam eos quibus percipiendis intendit. quod contra
faciunt aliqui qui credentes proficere cicius lecturas seu commentarios
320 ab inicio student habere in quibus eciam legunt et obmittunt textum et
glosarum studium. Hoc autem nichil aliud est quam textum supponere
ubi nullum precessit fundamentum ut quendam vidi qui omissis
textibus et glossis lecturis operam dederat. cum autem promocionis sue
tempus instaret inventus est ita textuum et glosarum indoctus ut vix
325 appareret scire in eis legere. sunt et alii qui cum curant habere
repertoria et in his omisso leccionis studio divagantur. hec autem sicuti
preceptoribus sunt valde accomoda ut cum eis possint adinvenire
glossas vel alia dicta quibus in allegacionibus, consiliis et leccione
habent uti; ita sunt auditoribus valde nociva tamquam per que studium
330 leccionis intermittitur quo nil potest eis esse dampnosius. hoc igitur
auditor evitet et in primis annis maxime vacet ut textum intelligat et
memorie commendet legum et capitulorum principia et ad quid principaliter allegantur, et quia forte non plene sibi sufficit doctrina precep-
toris qui cum habeat eciam provectoribus intendere, non potest diutius
335 insistere circa rudiores, adhereat auditor novus alteri peritiori quem
cum dubitat interroget et hunc veluti patrem colat et frequentet. sic
enim faciens sepe plus per illum proficiet quam in scolis. ipse vero cum
studere voluerit primo totam literam legis vel canonis seu paragraphi
aut versiculi quam intelligere vult perlegat et iterum repetens comode
340 per singulas dictiones immoretur ut pene sillibas ipsas infigat memorie
nec ab hoc desistat donec volvendo et revolvendo et literam per
singulas oraciones construendo sibi videatur intelligere; quod si dubitet
redeat ad eum quem prediximus provectorem si habet secum in domo
socium ut hii sunt quibus super est, unde possint tales suis alere
345 sumptibus. si vero facultatibus ad hoc non habundat sollicitus sit
associare se provectoribus ad communes sumptus subeundos ut in
generalibus studiis consuevit et si contigerit ut in domo secum tales non
sint extra domum querat aliquem et ydoneo tempore et illi non ingrato
eum visitet atque humiliter interroget. nam sic agendo brevi tempore
350 consequetur ut tantum per se intelligat quod aliis rudioribus poterit ad
eorumdem quibus dubitaverint declaracionem suffragari reddendo in
hoc pietatis et humanitatis vicem quam ipse ab alio fuerit consecutus. in

ipso vero studii ordine hoc eciam observet ut quanto amplius potest
elaboret menti mandare que didicit et quia non possunt singula retineri
355 saltem meliores leges vel capitula studeat recordare ad quod non parum
proderit si in aliquo parvo folio principia legum vel capitulorum et que
meliora notabilia conscripserit et hoc quocumque iverit secum habeat
et eciam inspiciat cum datur comoditas; sicut enim ut in scolis dicere
solebam non obliviscitur quis eorum quod habet in promptu ut suarum
360 manuum vel oculorum ita sit et in doctrina ut memoria ea sola perdit
que sepe non aspicit quamvis autem in quacumque facultate ad
intelligenda eius documenta sit opus memoria tamen maxime in iure in
quo qui dicuntur probare oportet auctoritate aliqua textus vel glosarum vel racione in ipso iure fundata, neque tamen ob hoc verum est
365 quod nonnulli logici garziunt affirmantes scienciam iuris non consistere
in disserendi subtilitate sed in eorum que in iure statuta sunt memoria
commendare. Sunt enim in iure innumerabiles difficultates ad quas
explicandas opus est ingenio pene divino ut facile constat his qui sunt in
iure saltem mediocriter periti qui quanto periciores tanto sunt huius rei
370 certiores. illi vero logici locuntur de his que non sapiunt quo nil est
inanius. Licet ergo sint hortandi auditores ut memorie que discunt
reponere studeant non ex hoc eis dicitur ut de subtiliter intelligendo
non sint solliciti; ac admoneantur de memoria, quoniam ipsa de iure
deficiente frustra tenetur quis subtilia cogitare si ei promptu non sit ea
375 versibus et rationibus munire. Nam sine lege non est de iure loquendum, *C. de collacionibus*, 1. *illa*, sed neque in alia ulla facultate
quisquam poterit esse bene doctus nisi traditiones illius habeat im-
promptu. hoc advertentes studiosi legum civilium vel canonicarum
solent multa remedia experiri ut fiat eis solidior memoria. Quidam enim
380 leccione capitis cum herbis calidis utuntur existimantes expedire
memorie capud siccum esse; alii aliis unccionibus. nonnulli eciam
dicuntur solliciti de faciendo artem notoriam ut brevi tempore et
absque multo labore omnia ut existimant sciendi genera proficiant qua
in re clare fame preceptor meus dominus Iohannes de Lignano quem-
385 dam probo delusit. nam cum ille diceret communiter dici quod ipse
preceptor per artem ipsam notoriam didicerat, verum, inquit, isti ferunt
sed nosci qua racione usque ad sanguinem et certe ille quidem. neque
enim aliquem unquam vidi qui illius artis suffragio profecisset. Dicitur
eciam nomina ignota que ibi scripta sunt non angelorum esse sed
390 demonorum unde viro catholico prorsus spernenda et cavenda est.
Sunt et alii anxii per discendi memoriam quam dicunt artificialem et isti
penitus videntur ignorare ad quod illa profuit. non enim valet ut diu
retineas sed ut prompte percipias et brevi conserves et si expedit recites
quod sepe sum expertus. Et quia pauci solent intelligere precepta
395 Ciceronis eam tradentis facile poteris huius habere periciam, si cogitaveris hanc a naturali quam excitat habere dependenciam, videmus enim
eciam indoctos qui cum volunt alicuius meminisse signum aliquod
faciunt puta nodum in corrigia quo viso recordantur eius quod facere
disposuerant; sic et apud eos qui volunt plurium meminisse multa signa
400 seu ymagines erunt necessarie in quo non nulli decipiuntur qui pro

habendis locis pluribus ubi locare possint ymagines fingunt ymaginarium palacium cum multis aulis, cameris et columpnis et ad retinendam
huiusmodi palacii memoriam in tantum laborant quod cum ibi collo-
cant ymagines earum non facile recordantur. ad quem evitandum
405 errorem consultum est ut cum huius artis opus habueris vel in resump-
cione argumentorum vel ambasciate vel huiusmodi recurras ad locum
qui cum suis omnibus partibus ita tibi sit memorie ut nil in hoc oporteat
laborare; sicut exempli causa domus quam diu habitasti cum ergo fit
argumentum attende medium concludendi et de allegatis iuribus,
410 considera legem vel canonem qui maxime faciet huius similitudinem in
loco aliquo domus, picta hoscio primo colloca ut si allegatur *de causa
possessionis et proprietatis*, 'cum ecclesia' ibi parvam ecclesiolam ymaginariam collocabis et hoc sufficiet cum locum aspicies ut illud capitulum continuo menti occurrat et per consequens suffraganti naturali
415 memoria ex hoc medio excitata totum argumentum. Si ulterius arguet
allegando *de restitutione spoliatorum*, 'cum ad sedem,' finge nudum in
cathedra sedentem, in secundo loco puta muro qui est prope hostium et
sic ultra ut dum ille verbis insistit fundando argumentum, tu recurre per
420 ymagines quas locasti; sic non erit magna difficultas in memorando de
multis argumentis quod si ille per rationem arguit ut quod beneficium
non potest sine canonica institutione obtineri vel quod non debet quis
cum aliena ditare, iactura pro recordacione, primi constitues episco-
pum et clericum ad eius pedes cuius digito anulum inmittit; pro
secundo aliquem honestum et tibi notum hominem qui rem alterius
425 inventam ei restituit vel similes ymagines prout tibi commodiores
occurrent; quamquam enim non contineant totam facti seriem tamen
cum suffragio memorie naturalis ut prediximus parva ymago eciam non
omnino propria sufficiet sicuti iam dictum est de nodo in corrigia facto
quo inspecto res reminiscimur factorum etiam illi nodo inpertinencium
430 quanto ergo magis ymago in aliquo similitudinem representans sufficiet; quas eciam ymagines pot
eris si tempus aderit efficere conpleciores ut cum domi vis aliquam
repeticionem vel sermonem menti commendare, tunc divisione facta in
particulas singulis particulis ymagines ut fieri poterit conformiores
435 acomodabis ut locis singulis collocabis nec labores singulis verbis
ymagines coaptare, id enim nimis dispendiosum sed solis partibus
principalibus ut una recitata reliqua sine difficultate se offerant reci-
tanda tenorem autem repeticionis, sermonis seu oracionis qui maxime
in sermone seu oracione contextualiter discendus est breviter et absque
440 difficultate per memoriam naturalem proficies si comodissime et morose processeris exempli causa vis menti exponere textum ewangelii
Iohannis "In principio erat verbum et verbum erat apud deum" et
reliqua que secuntur si centies milies totum simul perlegeres parum plus
menti haberes quam quando nodum inchoaveras; fac ergo secuti super
445 de cibo per particulas sumendo diximus ut paulatim discas primo illa
verba "In principio erat verbum" que sepius tecum dicendo repetas,
postea consequenter illa "et verbum erat apud deum" deinde utramque
particulam coniunctim sepius tecum dicendo repetas donec menti

tenaciter sunt infixa deinde procede similiter ad reliqua et cum didiceris
450 unam partem, puta decimam vel aliam iuxta prolixitatem eius quod
proficere vis, subsiste et illam partem quam didicisti milies si expedit
repete quousque tam firmiter infixa sit quod de facili non elabatur;
subinde similiter procede in eo quod restat, sic tamen quod cum
senseris attediari animum interpollacionem facias debitam. Si sic egeris
455 expertus pluries hoc affirmo cito eciam longum textum menti proficies;
quantum autem ad superiorem artificialem memoriam ego quantum ad
loca pertinet sepe nodis digitorum pro locis usus sum collocando in
singulis singulas ymagines et ita hoc modo vel superiori pro locis
accipiendo domus quam tunc habitabam partes mihi notas multas
460 rationes in communi ratiocinio vel cum allegantur in iure per advocatos
argumenta plurima per eos facta audiendo ambasciatam partes diver-
sas sine difficultate resumpsi; ergo quod vix credebam semel audiens
quemdam sermonem ad populum quem predicacionem dicunt apposita
cura locando particulas in suis locis totum eciam cum allegationum
465 quotenus domum reversus his qui eundem audierant retuli multo eciam
maiora de aliis qui huic arti vacant per amplius audivi; sed ut
prediximus hec ars quamquam utilis ad ea que dicta sunt ex tempore
referenda non tamen valet ad illam memoriam de tradiccionibus iuris
menti habendis ad quam proxime studiosos exhortati sumus. utuntur
470 preterea non nulli hac ipsa artificiali memoria ut admiratori sint apud
alios quod cum sine periculo inanis iactancie non committatur; ab hoc
abstineas ut utere cum exigit necessitas; est et alia cura per eum
auditorem habenda qui iam adeo profecit ut possit in glossa et in aliis
commentatorum scriptis studii diligenciam apponere ut non cursim
475 multa simul legat sed omnino comode ita ut sententialiter memorie
commendet et de motivis et iuribus quibus illi moventur secum
meditetur an sue menti sint consona; ne torpor eum apprehendat ut
acquiescat eis nisi quantum vero sibi suadet et ut intelligat radicitus
sedulo volvendo membranas inspiciat an allegata iura id ad quod
480 indicuntur probent; de re cum eciam supra questione secunda diximus
non expedit ampliare sermonem. valet eciam plurimum frequens cum
aliis sociis pericioribus collacio disputacio nam et accuciores reddit et
que profecerant tenacius imprimit mentibus; ostendit eciam plerumque
falsum esse quod verum ei existimaverant et ita liberantur ab errore
485 quo nullus potest esse periculosior; quam facile incidunt hii qui de suo
presumentes ingenio illud tantummodo verum arbitrantur quod iudicio
suo probant nichil aut parum existimantes aliorum iudicium et hoc
errore nullus potest esse maior. qui enim se non posse unquam errare
confidit is primo graviter in deum et sacram doctrinam committit cum
490 hoc solius dei sit; deinde ineptum se reddit ad ulterius proficiendum;
quam ob rem ab hoc maxime cavendum nec suo tantum fidendum
ingenio quin et aliorum iudicio saltem probatorum et plurium velimus
nos conformare cognoscentes uti catholicos decet nos facile posse
tamquam homines decipi nec gloriantes de nostro subtiliori ingenio sed
495 gratie dei attribuentes quidquic in nobis est laude dignum, quod vero
redarguacione nostris culpis et humane infirmitati ut ergo fructus

amplissimos qui ex disputacione percipiuntur assequi possimus, ad eam
rem quantum in nobis fuerit studeamus esse non inhabiles. hoc autem
assequimur si cum fraterna caritate proficiendi quod zelo cum aliorum
500 cogitationibus nostras mansuete conferimus non clamorose ut plerique
nec pertinaciter ut alii nec subvertere alios intendentes ad quod aliqui
nimium solliciti sunt victi suo perverso inanis ostentacionis proposito
que omnia inter bonos omnino fugienda sunt sed illud solum optantes
ut qui simul disputant nobiscum et versa vice cum eisdem et ipsi nos
505 proficiamus nec illud insuper obmittendum puto in quo vidi quam
plures errare qui ut multum periti existimarentur accurati sunt se fore
in qualibet repeticione vel disputacione in arguendo ostentare unde
consquens est ut omisso studio leccionis ordinarie vagetur in perquerendis argumentis quod non est aliud quam dum quis itinerat intermit-
510 tere iter et per diverticula divigari quo fit ut qui eos longe itinerando
sequebantur eosdem interea post terga linquant et hii sicuti precedunt
illos sciencia ita eciam ex consequenti et fama itaque illi priores qui
perversa via contenderunt ad famam ubi putaverant alios preire
postponuntur sed et aliud malum non minus proximo eisdem accidit
515 nam cum sciencia suos habeat ordines quos interrumpunt cum ulterius
in sequentibus leccionibus fit mencio de prioribus quas studere omiser-
ant non perfecte possunt eas intelligere; hinc evenit ut tarde vel
numquam ad perfeccionem sciencie perveniant ut ex hoc ludibrio fiunt
precipue cum videntur alii qui solebant esse posteriores in existima-
520 cione sciencie multum eos antecedere. sic ergo dum credunt ante
tempus assequi gloriam id agunt ut quo tempore fuerint assecuti
sciencam et veram famam; primo sciencam non acquirunt cuius
ordinem intermiserunt et famam perdunt si quam videbantur sibi
comparasse ideoque nulla quacumque ratione qui proficere cupit
525 lecciones intermittat ut sit in aliquo de gloria sollicitus; tantum studeat
bene proficere et numquam deerunt laudatores. nolo autem ut ex hoc
penitus credatur me dampnare illos qui arguunt sed tunc tantum cum
propter vacare argumentis intermittunt lecciones quo nichil profi-
ciendo celeriter studio magis obvium est. si qui tamen lecciones
530 quandoque volunt arguere hoc maxime convenit cum incipiunt esse
provecti quo tempore post bene visam leccionem potuerunt aliquid
temporis in hoc apponere et hii sint admoniti ut post data responsa et
factas replicaciones et covenienter solutas non sint pertinaces quasi
hostiliter volentes eos evertere qui cathedram tenent hoc enim non fit
535 sine iniuria et ubi credunt videri periciores existimantur quandoque vel
garruli vel contumeliosi vel alias viciosi, si quod est aliud vicium hiis
assine et quoniam de provectis dicere cepimus hiis videtur consulendum
ut postquam ydonei esse incipiunt ad egrediendum de scolastico studio
non precipitantes maturent. visum enim est quod si tunc persistunt per
540 aliquod tempus confirmant in memoria tenaciter que didicerant et tunc
quia possunt sicut consonum est rationi in colloquibus scolasticis et in
repeticionibus et disputacionibus quas vel ipsi faciunt vel in quibus cum
fuerint per alios ipsi arguunt vel eciam in leccionibus quas ceteris
diebus legunt ostendere suam periciam et ex hoc facile consequuntur

545 tantam existimacionem ut eciam postquam doctores facti sunt cito
habeantur in numero doctorum de quibis sit existimacio, ad quem
locum non facile aut saltem non cito hii proveniunt qui properant ad
doctoratum antequam fundatam habeant scolasticam scienciam et in
ipsa reputacionem et ita ubi crediderunt alios prevenire festinando
550 preveniuntur ab eis; quia vero permixtum de auditoribus hactenus
locuti sumus qui vel legibus vel canonibus student incitat dubitacio
quam sepe vidi agitare. si quis est qui velit in utraque sciencia proficere
a qua sit melius inchoare? qua in re diversos audivimus diversa sentire
sed illud per experienciam cognovimus inchoandum esse ab illa in qua
555 quis vult se maxime exercere. qui igitur in canonibus versari cupit ab his
incipiat ut cum recens est memoria imbuatur institucionibus canonicis
que postea tenaciter inherent, iuxta illud Horacii, quo semel est imbuta
recens servabit odorem testa diu; quod contra evenit si a legibus fecerit
exordium; vidi enim paucissimos eorum qui post legalem ad canonicam
560 accesserint scienciam fuisse umquam in ea perfectos; iam enim imbuti
legalibus institucionibus quasi cibo saturati non transmittunt canonicam doctrinam ad penetralia nec tenacem videntur habere posse
memoriam in canonibus. unde fit ut raro possint ad habendam
perfectam et promptam in eis periciam precipue quo ad materias
565 canonicas pervenire. si quis vero vult finaliter legibus intendere ab eis
exordiatur; postea det operam canonibus quantum cognoverit expedire. Super omnia sit attentus auditor ut cum debita moderacione
tempora dispenset; quidem enim tantum persistunt in studio ut mens
affecta tedio nichil solide percipiat. Alii non recreantur sompno quan-
570 tum opus est et hinc sunt quasi dormitantes dum audiendo leccionem
vacandum est, et cum volunt domi studere non sufferentibus oculis pro
sompno nihil acute possunt intelligere; alii a cibo nimis diu abstinent
unde fit ut cum mense accumbunt voraciter cibum et ultra mensuram
sue nature ingurgitent quo impediti multis horis minus ydonei sunt ad
575 studium et haec minima sunt. accidunt enim sepe istis egretudines longe
stomaci distemperaciones et alii morbi varii, ita eciam ut quod aliquando visum est cerebrum taliter distemperetur ut insaniant; ita ergo
vacandum est studiis ut non omittantur que refectioni mentis vel
corporis sunt necessaria. Satis enim temporis ad studium conceditur; si
580 frustra non consumpseris nec violando naturam cicius proficis, ymo
deficis quia deficientibus nature viribus et mente ultra quam opus est
lassata quidquam legere contingerit effluit tamquam pleno vase si quid
infunderis; cum itaque refeccionem corpus interpellat non subtra-
has sed ita ut cum debita mora cibum mastices et quasi semidigestum
585 transmittas ad stomachum. A vino autem quantum fieri potest abstineas, precipue si, ut sunt vina potenciora, fumosum sit sed utere
mediocri quod nec acerbitate sua stomachum nec fumositate cerebrum
offendat in quibus rebus quia ipsa naturali prudencia leviter dinoscun-
tur, opus non est pluribus insistere. si tamen illud admonueriumus
590 quod cum studendo aliquam diu mentem attentam tenueris interpelacione aliqua opus est tantum ut que legeris mente consolides tantum ut
recreata mens ad continuendum studium fit retencior; sed de cibo

disputant aliqui quo ad horam que ydonea sit studenti ut reficiatur.
cum enim ut experiencia ostendit non bene sufferat natura ut ociosi
595 puta vacantes studio leccionis qui corporeos labores non habent bis in
die fiant saturi; censent aliqui studenti competere ut prandium sumat et
abstineat a cena; alii e contra. mihi post multas experiencias visum est
utilius esse sibi prandio levi uti taliter ut statim possint intendere studio
et in cena refici quantum oportet et post parvum lectum petere; nam
600 licet aliqui post cenam studeant minus tamen gravat matutinum
studium et plus affert commodi ad subtiliter intelligendum. quot vero
horis opus sit lecto decumbere quia varie sunt nature non potest certa
tradi doctrina; post tamen multas probaciones perpendi quod per
totam diem naturalem xxiiii horarum desiderat natura pro sompno
605 saltem vii et forte octo et si contingat quod in nocte tantum quinque
dormias aut sex, inter diem sompnus te invadit et suppletur quod
deperditum est et si violare naturam volueris non propterea plus studes
et si plus incumbis libris minus proficis quam si nature debitum suum
tradidisses. hora vero surgendi mane est post expletam digestionem;
610 aliquando stomachus eructuat et studium tuum reddit inquietum. Quid
vero sit studio tempus comodius sepe queritur; nonnullis matutinum,
aliis serotinum studium preferentibus qua in re natura cuiuslibet
diligenter attendenda est. Si enim comodius vigilias serotinas quam
ante lucanas sufferas, tibi serotinam cum ante cenam; alteri cui gratius
615 est oppositum ante lucem vigilandum est; communiter autem receptum
est in generalibus studiis ut usque ad horam terciam noctis studio
vacent postea reficiantur eciam facta parva mora donec cibus fundum
stomachi petierit lecto decumbant et surgant post quinque sex vel
septem horas ut proxime diximus et hoc hieme; cum vero dies sit
620 longior tunc secundum temporis varietatem horas oportet immutare
quod cuique clarum est; sed licet hora mutetur distinctio tamen
temporis in hora refeccionis et ordine et in tempore sompni sicut
premissum est non variatur. Postremo illud in omnibus ante oculos
habeant ut quidquam agis sive cibo reficiaris aut sompno sive deambu-
625 las in camera vel per civitatem vel extra, causa respiracionis et spacii
totum ordinetur ad studium ut in hiis quantum satis est immoreris
semper cum proposito confestim ad studium redeundi. hec que premisimus si custodieris et in deo fiduciam habueris dicendo singulis diebus
oraciones tibi notas et maxime quod valde religiosum est et honestum si
630 officium gloriosissime Virginis Marie devote legeris vel si es clericus ad
hoc obligatus totum officium ecclesiasticum et missam quanto pluries
potueris saltem diebus festivis libenter visitaveris, cito sicuti ab experto
videor affirmare posse in causam et terminum felicem studii tui
scolastici consequeris si fueris auditor et si preceptor effectum tui
635 propositi in cito docendo et auditores tuos ad optatum studiorum
suorum finem rationabiliter perducendo facilius continges et utrique sic
agenti deus in hoc seculo vitam letam et clari nominis famam prestabit
et in futuro cum electis gloriam sempiternam. Amen.

[Explicit tractatus de modo docendi ius canonicum de francisci de caba
640 cardinalis florentini amen.] [only in T]

[T: Item incipit unus tractatus de modo docendi et discendi ius
canonicum compositum per dominum franciscum de zabarellis cardi-
nalem.]
[Title: Zabarellis: Zarabellis M;]

645 [M, f 147ᵛ (150ᵛ); T, f 111ʳ col. A; V, f 365ʳ col. A; S, f 34ʳ]

(4) advertendum est: est not in T,V; (5) sola: solum T; experto: experte T;
cognovi:cognovit T; (6) vel: nichil S; venturus:venturis V, venturum T;
certius vel: cercius T; (7) eleganciori: eliganciori T; de quo hoc:[de] not in T,
de quo hic M,S; nichil: vel T; (8) fui T,V,S: fuit M; curatus: accuratus V; me:
se V; viam: mea M,T,S; eciam: et eciam T; (9) inordinata: ordinate V;
debent: debebunt V; (10) indulgendum: intelligendum T; insuetum: (insitum
crossed out, insuetum M) in stretum T; erraverim: enarraverim M; (11)
vacuus: fatuus T; errore: errare T; (12) quod quedam: quod que M; in
discente: discente V; (14) utrique: que T; singularia: summaria M; (14)
quam: que T; timor dei: timor M,T, S; (15) criminum: et criminum T; (16)
diligencia investigacionis: diligencia que vestigationis T; (17) huiusmodi:
huius M; illud:ita T; (19) motiva:per motiva S, motivam M, motivacio T;
ei:et T; urgere:regere T [regere in superscript in S]; ad quod: ad quid T; (20)
in videndo: in vendendo T; moventur: movetur T; (21) ad oppositum: ad
propositum T; illa non urgere: illa vero regere T; ac sibi: et T,V, sic sibi V, si
sibi T; (22) videbitur: videor V; quod tamen:quod et T; sed:et T; (23) munire:
in iure T; hec ipsa: hoc ipsam V, per hec ipsam T; a memoria: e memoria
M,V, ex memoria T; habeatur: hanc V; (24) possunt: possint V; (25) in
discente: indistincte T; (25) sed hec:debet hec T; quamquam: que quam V;
sint:sit T; (26) ad omnino:ad non T; intelligendum:interdum T; artificiis:
iuristificibus T; (27) alium:aliud T; sagittandum:vatigandum T, sagit tandem M; (28) in pugna: impugnare T; ducendum; dicendum (corrected in
superscript to ducendum) T; (29) eam: eum T; arcui: alicui T; applicatam: ad
placitum T; emittat: emitet T; (31–2) quid docentis sit et quid discentis
officium quod dic ut in sequentibus: not in T; quod docentis sit et quod
discentis officium quod dic ut in sequentibus S, quid docentis sit et quid
docentis sit discentis officium (repetition underlined to be omitted in M);
(33) Quero:Tertio quero V; docenti: docendi T; tradenda: tradenta V; sunt:
not in V (34) sequatur: sequetur T; (35) non nulla: non nullam T; (36)
applicantur: appellantur T; etiam: et T; (37) exercicio: exercere T; (38)
distinguens: distigrues T; (39) nec vacet: nec vacat M; ocio not in T; (40) erit:
erat T; cathedra: chadedra T; (43) opinionem: opi T; vel flendo: quasi
fluendo T, quasi flendo V,S; ut aliqui: ut alius vi T; (44–5) nec: aut T;
clamorose : clamose T,V,S,M; tanquam inarticulatam: ut inarticulatam T;

inarticulatam cantus melodiam: inarticulativa cantus melodia V; (45) pronunciet: pronunciavit T; (47) ut bene: ut plene T; ad quod: ad quid T; si not in T; (48) non truncate: intricate T, (intricate written also in superscript in S); plerique: plerisque que T; (49) et se:et si T,V; currens: curres T; (50–1) fatigatus: vatigatus T, (quam fatigatus ultra repeated in M); interpellacionem: interpollacionem M,S,V; faciet: facit T, faciet S,V, faciant M; (52) pausata et continua: pausate et continuate T, pausate et continua V, pausata (changed to pausate in superscript in S) et continuata; (52–3) prosequatur: prosequeretur M, presequeta T, prosequitur V, prosequetur S; distinguens: distigruens T; diccionem a diccione: distinctionem a diccione T, diccions a diccione V; (54) ita et ut: ita ut V, ita ut et T,S; respirandi: repirandi T; (55) tribuat: tribuet T; eciam:et T; ut quidam: ut quid M; (57) veluti quemdam: veluti quedam V; (59) quot: quam T; usus: visus T; (60) verbum: hoc verbum T; (61) intelligitis vos: intelligitis vos, auditis T,V; (62) [precipue in sermone et specialiter cum doctrinam aliis tradit] not in T,V,S, marked in M to be omitted; sunt: sint M,V,S; (63) tamen: tame T; (65) tradit: tradidit T; sit: sic T; (66–7) faciat: facit T; superiores sciencias: superiore sciencia V, superiorem scienciam T,S; (68) sciendi modus: sciendi modos; et: est et T; (68–9) condimentum: M,T,S,V [for fundamentum?]; haberi: habere T; apud: aliquos T; (69–70) ob hoc: ab hoc T, [M?]; ut is: ut his T; (70–1) clarus est: est not in T; quantum satis est: quantum sit M, tantum est T, quantum satis S; (71) grandiore: gradiore T, grandiori V; (74) huiusmodi: huius M; (74–5) aliquot annis: aliquos annos T, aliquod annis S; docueram: domeram T; aliquod: aliquot S; (75–77) Prisciani opus [*Institutiones grammaticae libri XVI*]; ut: et T,V, (et in superscript added in S); (77) ad hec: ad hoc M; percipienda: percipiende T; an: non T; verbis: verbum M; (78–9) incongruis: ymo congruis T; velut: velit V,S; fidos: fides T; ab eo eciam: ab eciam T; (79) rogatos: egrotas M; quibus: in quibus T; (80–1) sic: si T; potuerit: possit V, poterit T, potuit (corrected in margin to alias potuerit) S; de erroribus: (erratoribus crossed out T), de suis erratibus M,T,S, de suis erratus V; fuerit: fuit V; (81) sciscitetur: sciscitet T; sepe:sequitur T; fidis: fides T; (82) quid eciam: quidam eciam T; (83) quid dampnent: dampnent T; (83–4) ut ad hoc: ut ex hoc V, S, ut ex hac T; redditus: [changed in superscript to reddatur S]; attentus: accentus T; exequetur: exequatur V,T, exequitur S; (84–5) gratior: grator T; fuit: fuerit T, V,S; medius: modus T,V, (changed to modus in superscript in S); [*de restitutione spoliatorum*, c. fi.[nale] inserted in T] [a reference to the Gregorian Decretals, II.13.19, de restitutione spoliatorum, the last chapter entitled "Pisanis ac Lucanis," see Aemilius Friedberg, ed. *Corpus Iuris Canonici* 2 vols. (Leipzig, 1879), II:290–291]; (86) auditoribus: autoribus T; (87) saltem: saltim T; probaverit: approbaverit T,V; prosit: proficit T,V,S; (88) referri: referre T; e contra: contra V; (89) non tantum: (non added in superscript in M); sed eciam ipsum: sed ipsum eciam T,V,S; (91) doctiores: doctores T; (93) enim: ergo V; queque: quequam V; ad aliam:

ad alia M; (96) que: quod T,V; et alii: etiam alii T; peritiores: peritores T,S; (97) obscuris: obscuro M,V; eciam: not in V; (98–9) quam cum: quam eum V,S; instructurum: instruiturum M; (101–2) claros: cleros T; qui: quod T; clare: clase T; qui scilicet et clare intelligant et clare doceant: qui scilicet et clare intelligant et clare not in V; sit: sicut S; (103) sufficiant: not in T; (104) latissimas et plurimas: latissimas M, latissimas [et plurimas added in marginal note in S]; eciam: et T; (105) delatant: delatavit M, dilatant V, sedi latant T; in textum: per textum T, in textu V; (107–8) tradendum fuerat: repeated and then cancelled in T; antiqui: aniqui T; obviare: obvirare T; (108) per certas partes: per certas per certas partes V; (110) Illum autem: autem illum autem (with first autem crossed out in T); morem: mor*oe* T; (110–11) in meo tempore: meo tempore T,V; (112) intencio: intercio T; distinguencium: distingruencium T; commendanda: commendanda est V,S; (113–14) occupatos; occuperatos T; per longa temporum:per longa tempora T; (115) omnium: omnem T,V,S; (116) possint: possunt T; (117–18) sicienti: sciente .t; absque eo: ab se eo T; (118–19) instruerit: instruit T,V,S; edoceat; edoceas T,V; qua forma:quot forma V, quatenus scilicet forma T; potandi: potandum T,V; (119–20) possint: possunt T; intelligere: intellige T; (121) quam: quod T; (121–2) vagari: fagari M; nisi forte sit: nisi sit forte T; questio: questi T; (122) ex post facto: que ex facto V, in facto T; (122) alias: alia T; (124) facile: hoc facile T,V; (125) Innocentius Quartus in prologo suo [sui: T] Commentarii [commenti V, continenti T] = Innocentii IV Apparatus super decretalium libris quinque, München, Bayerische Staatsbibliothek, Clm 6350, 2⁰ xiv c., fol. 1ʳ col. A; (127) potuerunt: possunt S (corrected in margin to potuerunt), poterunt V; (128) causarum: casuum V; pro tempore: in tempore T; (128–9) formam autem recitandi duplicem: formam recitandi duplicem added in margin in S, formam autem c. recitandi duplicem V; constat: not in V; quam: quod T; (129–30) in commentariis: commentariis M; (130) secutus sum: imitatus sum T,V,S; in qua: mihi qua T; in qua non attento repeated in S; (131) altera est: altera est ut V,S; (132) prima: primo T; vel legem: vel legentibus M,S; (133–4) quoniam: qui V; ex: not in V; preceptoribus: acceptoribus V; (134) optarent: aptarent V; scribendo: scribendi T; (135–6) primum: primo T,V,S; si primum unum notabile, consequenter una questio: si primo unum, consequenter non questio T,S; (138) permixtio: permisto T, permiscio V; (139) revertimur: remittimur V, remittuntur T,S; (140) queritur: communiter (but corrected in superscript to queritur) S; reperiri: reperire T; (141–2) ordinem: modum T, ordinem correct to modum in superscript in S; subicio: subito S; (143) pretermittendum: premittendum T; (144) parum: modicum (corrected in margin to parum) S; (144–6) exhibere se gratum auditoribus nam ut Quintilianus ait ut notatur *de magistris* capitulum penultimum M, exhibere se gratum auditoribus non ut Quintilianus ait scio coalescere nequid nisi selata fui tradentis accipientisque concordia T, exhibere se gratum ut notatur *de magistris*

capitulum pluraliter auditoribus nam ut Quintilianus tus V; the reference is
to the chapter in the Gregorian Decretals, V.5.4, [ed.
Friedberg, (Leipzig,
1879) which is the next to last chapter entitled not "Pluraliter" but "Quia
nonnullis," where Pope Innocent had ordered provision to pay teachers so
that they could teach poor students; the reference to Quintilian is not an
exact quotation since Quintilian had written "eloquentia coalescere nequit,
nisi sociata tradentis accipientisque concordia," *Marcus Fabius Quintilianus
institutio oratorie*, edited by M. Winterbottom [Oxford Classical Texts] 2
vols. (Oxford: Clarendon Press, 1970), 2.9.3, vol. I, p. 95; as can be seen the
text here is: "scientia valescere nequit nisi sanata fuerit." scientia: scio T;
valescere: coalescere T,V, (valescere corrected to convalescere in superscript
in S); nequit: nequid T; (146–7) sanata: sonata V,S, selata T; fuerit: fui T;
huic: habuit T; est ut in: ut T; (147–8) in cathedra: cathedra T; ex primo: ex
prime T; ad amatores: ad amores M, ad amorem T,V,S; (148–9) conciliet:
conscilient T; exaltare: ex altero V; eosdem: easdem S; excitet: exercitet T; ad
attente: attende V, attendentem T; audiendum: audient debent T; ad quod:
ad quid T; (149) parumper exaltando vocem: parum per exaltandum voce T;
admoneat: admoneant T; (150) aliquid: aliquod V,S; (152) utile est: utile M;
(152) vel bis vel eciam: bis vel eciam T,S,V; perfecte: perfecta T; (154) ad
quod eciam consequendum: ad quid et consequendum T; (155) auditor:
(adiutor then crossed out) auditor V; aliquod: aliquid T; (155–6) imprimat:
imprima T; facilius: facius V; (156) cum queretur inveniri: cum querentur M,
cum queritur V, queretur illud inveniri S, queretur illud invenire T; (156–7)
assolet: assolent T,V,S; non longo: longo T,V; fatigare: fatigati V, fatigari S;
parvas: personas [partly crossed out] parvas T; sessiones: possessiones T;
(157–9) sic in preceptore optime convenit ut post expeditam lecionis partem
precipue: not in T, sic in preceptore optime convenit ut post expeditam
lecionis partem precipue V,S (illegible note in superscript S); (159) iam:
iamiam T; explicatus: explicios T, explicitus V; (159) laxaverit:laxaverit in S
(changed to lassaverit in superscript), lassaverit T.V; (160–1) auditorum
aliquid iocosum et festivum et ad risum provocans intromittere studeat ut ex
illo recreati: not in V [has only auditorum animi]; aliquid: aliquod T,S;
festivum: festinum T,S,M; intromittere:intermittere T; percipienda: percipiendum T,V,S; (162) et retenciores: retenciores M; sed et: sedet T; (164)
profectis: pervectis T, perfectis V, provectis S; (165–6) in ponderibus
humeris robustioribus applicamus pondera graviora tenioribus leviora: in
ponderibus [humeris not in T] leviora [rest of text missing] T, in ponderibus
est agendum [underlined to be omitted] humeris rustioribus applicamus
pondera graviora tenerioribus leviora V; (167) facienda: faciendum V,S, non
faciendum T; (167–8) Unde: un T; Apostolus primo ad Corinthios tertio
scribens: applus ad continet his scribes T, apostolus primo [prime V, primus
M] ad Corinthios iii⁰ Corinthis scribens V, reference is to I Corinthians 3:2;
lac inquit potum vobis dedi: lac inquit vobis potum dedi potum T, lac inquit

vobis dedi potum V, lac inquit vobis potum dedi S; (168–70) nondum: nudum T,V; poteratis: potantis T; sed eciam nunc: sed ned nunc, T,V,S; quid potestis: quidem potestis T,V.S; ad huc enim carnales : ad huc carnales T; notatur: in S; reference to the Gregorian Decretals, V. 38. 8, *de penitentiis et remissionibus*, the chapter entitled "Deus qui," see: E. Friedberg, *Corpus Iuris Canonici* 2 vols. (Leipzig, 1879), II: 886; S gives the most exact reference to this text, V gave no reference but one was later added in the margin in lighter ink; quod: quid T; (171) eos: eo T; qui missi: nisi T; (172) paulatim: palatim T; (172) contingerit: contigerit V; quos: quo T; sint:sit T; (176) ponendo: pontes T; quam: quem V,S; (177) summarium: sive maximum T; summatim: sumatym V; (178) particulas: particulos T; (179) [ff de doli exceptione 'literaliter'] T has no citation reference, ff de doli except 1. i. V,S, ff de doli exceptione "literaliter" in M; the reference is to the Code of Roman Law, the Digest, 44.4.1: "Paulua libro septuagesimo primo ad edictum quo lucidius intelligi possit haec exceptio prius de causa videamus quae proposita sit deinde quem ad modum dolo fiat per quae intelligimus quando obstet exceptio deinde ...", see *Justiniani Augusti digestorum seu pandectorum codex Florentinus olim Pisanus phototypice expressus*, Vol. II, facsicolo viii, (Roma:Danesi Editore, 1909), fol. 318, col. a; the exact reference is to *Digestum*, de doli mali et metus exceptione, "Literaliter." (181) transglutire: de glu transglutire T; (181–3) sic eciam: sic et V; eciam: eciam est: in S but then the st was lightly crossed out; longiores partes in breviores: longiores partes in brevioribus oportet longiores partes in breviores: longiores partes in brevioribus oportet longiores partes in breviores T; scindere: deinde T; quo faciliores: ut faciliores T; (183–4) percipiendum: percuciendum M; quam: quod T; ponunt: ponant T,V,S; imitatus: invitatus T; (186) sumatim: statim V; quid est id quod est explicandum: quid est id est quod est explicandum T; (187) casum:causam T; ponat: not in V, ponit T; facta: facti T,S,V; (189) acciderit: accederit T; (189–90) indicando: iudicando T; faciendus: faciendum T; (191) indicet: iudicat T, indicat V; eam: eciam T,V; significet: significat T; Et si quid: si quid T,V,S, Et si quod M; (192) notabile: eciam notabile V,S, est notabile notabile T [sic]; (192–3) notent:notant T; signent: signet T; (193) non omittat: non amittent T; (193–4) colligitur: intelligi V; quinto loco: quarto loco S; (194–5) commode: commune T; hoc: de hoc T, hec V,S; et divisione: et de divisione T; (195–6) referat: referas T; hoc: hec V,S; pateat: patet T; (197) antequam figuram: antequam picta figuram T; (197) incipiunt: incipient T, incipiant V,S; (197) parietem: parientem V; cemento: cimento T; (199) istis:hiis T,V; (200) quatenus: quantis M; (200–1) in doctrina illa: in doctrina T; sint: sunt M,T; ob hanc causam: ob hac causa T; (201–2) suos caros: suas cauros T; bene: beati T; ad doctrinam: ad iuris doctrinam T,V,S; consueverunt: consurever-unt T; (202–3) eisdem: eidem T; in primis annis: in primis antiis T; occasionem: accomi M; (203–4) captent: caperet T; vagandi:negandi di T; (205–6) videtur eciam: videtur et T; ab ipso inicio: ab isto inicius T; (206)

tradere:trade T; videantur: valeantur T; (207) intelligendas: intelligendos T; ut incipiant: incipient T; eas: eos T; (208–9) ut attendant: et attendunt T; exponit vel legit: legit vel exponit V; easdem: eosdem T; (209) quandoque sunt aliqua notabilia: quandoque aliqua sunt notabilia V; (211) evenerit: enoverit V; (212) difficilioribus: difficilibus T; (213–14) insistat: insistet T,V; provectis: provectioribus V, provencioribus T; tamquam: tam T; quequam: quoque T; (214) difficilia: difficilima T; (215–16) facienda: fanenda T; diligenter: diligencius T; eciam: ecius T; (217) in generali studio: in generalibus studiis T,S,V; (218–19) auditorio: adiutorio T; mediocriter instructi et provecti; mediocriter [singuli crossed out] singuli T; expedit ut preceptor: not in T; simul: not in T, singulis V,S; (220) porcionem accipiant; porcionem [s. then crossed out] accipiant V; (222) et provectis: provectis V; (223) eas:eos T; opponendo: apponendo T; (224) putaverit: putavit T; si quid etiam: si quidem T; (224) vel eciam: vel ut T; (226) explicet: explices M; rationem: rationi T; (227) urgere: rigor T; quod si per: quia si per[V?], quod super T; (228) illa eciam: eciam illa V; addiciat: addicias T; que vel: vel que T,V,S; ipse: ipsa T; (229) et ex hoc: et hoc T, et hec per V; explicite: explicito V; (230) questionibus: questi T; extra glosam: ex glosa T; ex ea causa: ex causa ea T; (230–1) eadem questione documento nono: not in T, documento quarto V; (231–2) illud: id quod V; negligendum non est: not negligendum est V; (232) quod aliter cum leccio facilis, aliter cum difficilis: quod aliter cum leccio difficilis, aliter cum facilis T,V,S; (233) enim: enim enim [repeated] M; (233) et rerum: ut rerum T, [S et rerum with ut in superscript]; (234–5) cicius: illegible word written above in S; et paucioribus: paucioribus T; (235–6) explicet: explicit T; oracione: sermone V; (236–7) perfectam acceptam: perfectam ipsarum acceptam T,V,S, perfectam exceptam M; (237–8) preceptore: preceptione T; laudabile: esse laudabile S; id quod: illud quoted M,T,V; nonnulli: non ulli T; (239) plurimum in iurium multorum: plurimum eciam iurium multorum V; (240) insistunt: insistant V; nil: nichil V,S; (241) et vulgaria: vel vulgaria T,V,S; (242) doctiores: doctores T,V (243) quod: quid T; probant:probent T,V,S; bene faciunt: benefaciant M,V,S; (245) reticenda: retinenda T; (245–6) forent: foret T; hec: not in V; (246) non occurrunt: occurrunt T,V; [etc.: only in M]; (247) videtur ut explicentur: videtur M, videtur (ut explicentur illa added in superscript) S, ut explicentur illa T,V; illa que: que M; (248–9) Quero: Quarto itaque quero T,V; circa: ita T; (249) prima cura sit: primo cura sit T; (250–1) in gramatica: gramatica V; sit quantum expedit instructus: sit quantum expedit sit instructus V; (251–2) sit prorsus: prorsus sit V; valet:neque T; si que: si scilicet que T; (252–3) possit: ut possit V; cum incipit intelligere: incipit is missing in M; (253) suas: suis T; evenit: si enit T; (254–5) non nulla: non nullam T; probavit: probabit T,V,S; et: not in T; (255–6) forte sibi: forte T; non: nisi T; redibunt: redirent V,S; reddent T; in mentem: in mente T; quod in me sum: quod immensum T; cum: cui T,V; (256–7) que: quedam T,V,S;

occurrerentur: occurrerunt V, occurrunt T, occurrerent S; quas: quos M; (257–8) percomprobavi: comprobavi T,S, comprobavit V; longe autem: longe aut M; preceptore: preceptione T; (258–9) possit: posset T; voluerit: noluerit V; in forma: in formam T,V,S; (260) repeticciones: receptiones T; (260–1) contigerit: contingerit T, [but second n underlined to be omitted] S; ut oportet: ut optet S; ut possit: et possit V,S; commentarios: commentaciones T; (261–2) semper: per T; coadiutorem: coadiutorium T; (263) materia: tuam[?] T; (263–4) dictare: dicare M; uti: ut T; multociens: multis M, S [corrected to multociens in superscript]; (264–5) ipse: ipso T; ipse in S [but ipsam in superscript]; parum est: parum est parum est [repeated] M; (265–6) est utile: utile est T,V; quorum in iure: quorum eciam in iure T,V: (266–7) non parvus est: non est parvus T; sed et in: sed in T; rhetorica: rethorica T; valde: not in T; saltem: saltim T; (268) Est enim: Est enim V; sapiencie: sapienca S; (268) maxime: maxime[*que*] (crossed out in V,S); (270) inopiam: inopia T; (271) temporum: tempore M, temporis S,V; caremus: carens M; (272–3) passa: fassa T; accincta: accencta T; (273) gravi: graviorem T; oraccione: not in T; (275) voluminibus: voluminis E (corrected in margin to voluminibus); (275–6) preterea: autem T, [illegible word crossed out in S]; documenta: documente T; (277–80) videatur ad sapienciam iuris maxime pertinere quia tamen in iure de omnibus que humanam vitam respiciunt tradi oportet maxime competit ut idem futurus iuris auditor saltem: videatur ad sapienciam iuris auditor saltem M, videatur sapienciam iuris maxime competit ut idem futurus numerus saltim T; (281–2) ac: ad T, at M,S; ipsam saltem moralem: ipsum saltim morale T; (282–3) hec: hoc M; aliud a iure: aliud [illegible word crossed out] a iure V; (284) distincte: distincto T; casus: causus T; (285) dices: dicis V; (285) proficere: not in V, illegible marginal note in T; (285–6) in omnibus premissis sed non arbitrare me consulere ut vacetur premissis facultatibus: in omnibus premissis facultatibus M, premissis sed non arbitraris me consulere ut faceret premissis facultatibus T, sed non arbitrimus(?) me consulere ut vacet premissis . . . S; (286–7) ea mente ut: ea mentent T; (287) obesse: abesse T; (288) in artibus logica et philosophia fuerunt: logica et fuerunt philosophia fuerunt T; (288–9) fuerunt: fuerant V; immorati: immorate T; iam enim: nam enim T; (290) disponuntur: disponunt T, disponitur V; (294–5) formatus: formato T; incipiet: incipiat T; sic evenit: evenit sic V; (295) rudes: rudos T; (296) ut: et T; possint: possit V; (297) intelligendi: intelligendum T; (298) saltem: saltim T; eorum: earum V; et: atque T; (300) premissarum: premissorum V; (301) egressi: ingressi T; (302) ego: ergo T; (303) et philosophie: atque philosophie T,V; (304) memor: tueor T; (305) alterius: alterius sciencie V; immoretur: immorescet T; (305) sed a se: a se T; (305) amoveat: amoneat T; simile nihil: nichil T,V, nichil simile S (nichil in superscript); (307) talibus: talis T; (308) eciam: et T; (309) poeticos auctores: pocius arictores T; (310) sunt: super V; (310–11) in: not in V; ergo: ymmo

T,V; multo: multa M; (312) intelligendas : intelligendos T; (312–3) saltem: saltim T; fiunt eciam: eciam M, namque fuerint T, fiunt eciam S (fiunt in superscript); (313–4) iuris: una S; habent enim: enim habent T; (315–6) ceterarum: certarum T; sit omnio: omnino sit T,V,S; (316–8) ad aliquid aliud: ad aliud aliud M, ad ad aliud S; alios in camera libros: alios libros in camera V; (318) non habeat: not in V; (319–20) aliqui qui: aliqui V; proficere: perficere T; lecturas: lecturis S (corrected in superscript); ab inicio: ab ipso inicio T,S,V; (320) textum: tectum M,S,V; (321–22) supponere: super proposito (? illegible) V; ubi nullum: ubi M; (322–3) precessit: processit V, processerit T,S (changed in margin to processit); quendam: quedam M; textibus: testibus T; (323) lecturis: in lecturis T,V,S; (324–5) indoctus: indoctos M; appareret; apparet V,T; scire: not in V; in eis: in ipsis T,V; (325–6) qui cum curant: qui curant T,S; repertoria: reportoria T,V; omisso: obmisse T; (326) leccionis: leccio T; (329–30) tamquam: tamque T; potest: potuit T; (330–31) dampnosius: dampnasius T; hoc: hec V, nec T; et in: ut in T, ut et in S (ut in superscript); (331–2) textum: textus V,S; commendet: commendat T; legum et: legum seu T,V; (333) et quia: quia T; (334) cum habeat: tamen habeat M, S (cum in superscript in S); provectoribus: provatori T; intendere: hoc intendere T; (335–6) periciori: peritori M; dubitat: dubitet T; (336) frequentet: frequenter T,V; sic: et T; (338) totam: tam T; (339) quam: quem V,S, quod T; (340–2) dictiones: not in V; (4) dictiones immoretur ut pene sillibas ipsas infigat memorie nec ab hoc desistat donec volvendo et revolvendo et literam per singulas: repeated in superscript in S; (340) sillibas: silbas T, sillabas V; (341) nec: de nec V; (342) quod si: quod sibi T; (343) provectorem: provectiorem V; (344) possint: possent T; alere: allegare T: (345) ad hoc: ad hec M; habundat: habundant T; (346–7) provectoribus: pervectoribus T; subeundos: subeundo T; ut in generalibus studiis: et in generalibus studii T; (347) in domo secum: in domo M, (secum marginal addition in S); (348) et ydoneo: ydoneo T; (350) consequetur: consequitur T,S; ut: et V; (350) quod: quia T; (351) eorumdem: eorum T,V,[?]; quibus: de quibus T,V; (351) dubitaverint: dubitaverunt M,T; suffragari: suffragarii T; (352–3) quam: quam ut V; ipse: ille ipse V; fuerit: fuera T, [fuerat in superscript in S]; studii: studio V; (354) mandare: mendare T; (355) saltem: singula saltim T; (355–6) recordare: recordari T,V,S; non parum proderit: non parum non proderit V; (356) et que: et quedam V,S et quidam T; (357–8) conscripserit: conscripsit T; et: not in S; eciam: not in V; cum: not in V; (359) quod habet: qui habet T,V, que habet S; in promptu: imprompta T; (360) perdit: perdat V; (361–3) ad intelligenda: ad intelligendo M; eius: cuius T; qui: que V,S; (363–4) textus: texto M; glosarum: glosa M; (365) non nulli: non T; garziunt: gazriunt V, garriunt T,S; iuris: numquam T; (366) subtilitate: subtilitatem T; (367) commendare: not in T,V; innumerabiles: innumerabilia T; difficultates: facultates T; (368–9) explicandas: applicandas T; ut facile: et facile V; sunt: sciunt T; saltem:

saltim T; (370) que: qui M,T; (372) ex hoc eis; ex eis hoc T; (373) Ac: ad M, sed T; admoneantur: admonentur V, amoventur T; tenetur; tenentur T; de iure: in iure T; (374–5) ea versibus: mens T, ea iuribus V,S; (375) munire: invenire T, illegible-ere M; (375–6) Nam sine lege non est de iure loquendum: Nam sine lege C. de colla. illa non est de iure loquendum V, loquendum: loquendi; [C. de collacionibus, 1. illa: C. de colla 1. illa in M,V,S; T gives no citation] the text is: Nam sine lege non est de iure loquendum; and the reference is to de collationibus, 1. illa(m) which is in *Corpus Iuris Civilis. Codex Iustinianus* ed. Paulus Krueger (Berlin: Weidmann, 1875), p. 250, fasc. 7; (= VI.20.19) in this the Codex speaks of a situation it is trying to resolve where a person has died intestate and where there has arisen a dispute over the rights of the different heirs: "De collatione vero dotis vel ante nuptias donationis . . . multi dubitatio orta est, superstitibus quidem . . . contendentibus eo; quod nulla constitutio super huiuscemodi collatione posita est, nepotibus vero mortuae personae non tantum huic resistentibus. . . . Talem igitur subtilem dubitationem amputantes praecipimus." (377) quisquam: quisquis T; (378) hoc: hec V; advertentes: advertens T; (378) studiosi: studiose T, studioso V; (379–80) eis: in eis T,V; solidior: solidor T; leccione: *locon* M, locoe S; calidis: caudis T; (381) capud: aliud T, caput S; alii aliis: alii T; (381) nonnulli: non ulli T; (382–3) artem notoriam ut brevi tempore et absque: not in T; multo: multa T; (383) existimant: existiment T; (383–4) proficiant: proficient T; qua in re: qua iure T,V; clare fame: clara fame M; (384–5) quemdam: quamdam M,T; probo: probe M,V,S; quod ipse: quod idem T,V,S; (386) didicerat: deciderit T; verum: unum S; (387) qua racione: qua racione studendo T,S,V; usque ad sanguinem: usque ad saguinem T; (389) eciam: enim T; (389) ibi: sibi V; esse sed: esse T; (391) alii anxii: anxii V, alii ausi T; (392) penitus videntur: videntur penitus V; (392) ad quod: ad quid T,V; illa: not in T; profuit: prosit T,V,S; ut: dum ut V; (393–4) brevi: orevi V; quod sepe sum: quod spe sum V, quod sepe sum (sum written in superscript) S, quod sepe [sum not in M] M; (395–6) habere periciam: periciam habere V; periciam: periciem M; si cogitaveris: si consideraveris T,V,S; (396–7) dependenciam: condependenciam T; cum: not in V; (398) nodum: nondum V, ne dum T; in corrigia: in cot rigia T; (398–9) quo viso: quo visu T; facere: de facere T; disposuerant: disposuerunt T, disposuerint V; volunt: voluerint V,S, voluerunt T; (399–400) plurium: plurimum S; meminisse: meminissi T; necessaria: necessarie V; (400–1) pro habendis: pro bandis M; locare possint: possint locare V; (401–2) ymaginarium: ymaginariam T; (404) earum: eorum T; (405) huius: huiusmodi V; habueris: humeris T; (406) vel huiusmodi: vel huius M, huiusmodi; (407) cum: eum T; ita tibi sit: ita sit T; in hoc oporteat: in hoc te oporteat T, V; (408) fit: sit T; (409) attende: addende T; (410) faciet: facit T,V; huius: et hoc T, et huius V,S; similitudinem: silitudinem V; (411) colloca: collata T,S; (411–12) si allegatur *de causa possessionis et proprietatis* 'cum ecclesia' = reference to the Gregorian Decretals, II. 12. 3 (Friedberg, II:276); 'cum ecclesia': cum eciam T; (412–3) ecclesiolam: eclesiam T; collocabis: collorabis ＼T; (413) ut illud: et illud T; (414–5) suffraganti: suffragati V, suffragante T,S; ex hoc medio: ex hoc modico T,V; (415) excitata: excita T; ulterius: alterius T; (416) allegando *de restitutione spoliatorum*, 'cum ad sedem' = reference to the Gregorian Decretals, II.13.15 (Friedberg, II:288); (418) ut dum: et dum V,S, et tamen T; verbis: in verbis T,V; (418–19) fundando: fundendo T; quas: qua V; memorando: memoriando T; (419–20) de multis: de multis et multis V; (420–1) beneficium: beneficium ecclesiasticum T,V, (ecclesiasticum added in superscript) S; canonica: cam sa T; obtineri: [haberi: underlined to be deleted in S]; (422) ditare: dittare T, ditari V,S; (422) primi: primo T; (423–4) et: vel T; anulum: in annulum T; aliquem: aliquem [hostum crossed out in V]; (425) ei: et T; (426) occurrent: occurrunt V; contineant: contineat T; totam: totum M; (427) eciam: et T; (428) sufficiet: sufficiat T; (429) quo inspecto: que inspecte M,S (both corrected [in superscript in S] to quo inspecto); (429) res: not in T,V,S; reminiscimur: reminiscuntur T; illi nodo: illo nodo S; (430) in aliquo similitudinem: in aliqua similitudine V; sufficiet: sufficiat T; (432) aderit: adherit V; (432–3) aliquam: aliqua M; commendare: commendari T; tunc: dic T; (434) particulis: partibus T; (434) singulis: simul M; ymagines ut fieri poterit: ymagines non poterit fieri T, fieri: fiere V; (435) vel: et T,V; (436) id enim: idem enim T; (437) principalibus: principibus M; offerant: offerat T,V: (438) tenorem: ecorem M; sermonis seu oracionis: vel sermonis vel oracionis T, vel sermonis seu oracionis V,S; (438–9) qui maxime in sermone seu oracione: not in T; (440–1) proficies: perficies T; si: not in T; commodissime: comodosissime T; morose: moroso M; (441) exempli: et exempli V; exponere: reponere T,V; ewangelii: evangelii T,V, evengelii S; [reference is to John I:1] (442) apud deum: apud deum et deus erat verbum T; (443) centies milies: centies T; perlegeres: relegeres T; parum: parum parum T; (444) quam quando nodum: quando non dum T,S, quam quando non dum V; (444–5) fac ergo: facitur ergo T, ffac V; ergo: igitur V,S; secuti: sicuti T,V; super de cibo: de cibo T; (445) paulatim: palatim T; discas: dicas T; primo: prima S; illa verba: illa M; (446) sepius: scriptis T; (448) coniunctim: coniunctam T; (449) sunt: sint T,V; infixa: infixe T; (449) didiceris: dixeris T; (451) subsiste: subsisti T; milies: miles V; (452) quod de facili non elabatur: [quod not in T] de facili modo elabatur T; (453) similiter procede: procede M; sic: sit V; (454) animum: animi M; facias debitam: debitam facias T, debitum facias V; (455) hoc: hec V; (457) nodis: nodos M,T; (459) accipiendo: accipientes T; (459–60) habitabam: habitam V; mihi notas: innotas T, mihi not in S; rationes in communi ratiocinio: communes in communium raticinio T, rationes in communi ratiocino V; (460) allegantur: allegatur V, allegaturis T; (461–2) audiendo: audiendam T, vel audiendo V; ergo: ymo V; (462–3) credebam: credebam possibile V; ad populam: a populum M, ad populu V; quem: que V; (463–4) apposita: apposito T; locando: locanda T; totum: totam T; (464–5) allegationum: allegationem T; quotenus: quotenus (?)V, quotis (?)M; qui eundem audierant: qui eundem audierunt T, qui eum de audierant V; retuli: rotuli M; multo eciam: multa eciam V; (466) vacant per amplius: per amplius vacant T,V; (467) quamquam: quam V; (468) illam: illa V; (469) habendis: [habendi crossed out] habendis V; (470) hac: ac V; admiratori: admiracionem T; (471–2) periculo: pacto T; inanis iactancie: inanis iactacio T; ab hoc: ad hoc T,S, ad hec M; abstineas: abs mens T; ut: et T,V; utere: utetur S; (472) exigit: erigit V; alia: alii M,S (473–4) profecit: proficit T; aliis: aliorum V; commentatorum: comintatorum T; (474–5) cursim: currisim T; legat: legature T; commode: comede T; (475–6) sententionaliter: finaliter V; commendet: commendat T; illi: illa V; (477) sue menti: sua menti T; ne torpor eum: nec torpor eum V, ne eum T; (478) vero: racio V; (479) sedulo: sedule T; (479–80) id: illud T; ad quod: ad quid T; indicuntur: inducuntur T,V,S; probent: probant T; de re cum: de qua re cum S,V, de qua re (cum not in T); supra questione secunda: secunda questione supra V, supra questione quinta T, supra questione secunda [changed in superscript to quarta] S; (480–1) diximus: dixerimus T,V; ampliare: amplius M, ampliore V; valet: nam T; (482) disputacio: et disputacio V; (483) profecerant: proferant T; eciam plerumque: plerumque eciam V; (484) falsum esse: id falsum est T, ad falsum esse V, id falsum esse S; (484–5) quod verum ei: quod T, quod verum V,S; liberantur: liberamur V; quam: quem V; (485–7) qui de suo presumentes ingenio illud tantummodo verum arbitrantur quod suo iudicio probant: qui de suo [presumentes not in M], qui de suo presumantes ingenio V, qui de suo presumens ingenio T, [ingenio illud tantum modo verum arbitrantur quod suo iudicio probant: not in M but in T,V,S]; (487) existimantes: existimans M; (488) qui enim se non posse: qui enim non posse M; unquam: numquam T,V; (490–1) ulterius: ulterum T; ab hoc: ob hoc T; (491–2) fidendum: fiendum M; quin: quid quin T; iudicio: iudico S; (492–3) plurium: plurimum V; uti catholicos decet: ut catholica decet T; (494) nostro: nostra M, nostro V; (494–5) sed: si T; quidquic: quicquid V, quodquic T; quod vero: quod non V, quod pro T; (496) infirmitati: infirmitatis T; (497) amplissimos: amplissimas T; qui: que T; percipiuntur: incipiuntur T; assequi: sequi T; (498) fuerit: fuit T; hoc: hec V; (499) cum: eum T; (500–1) nostras: nostras S (changed in superscript to nostris); conferimus: conferemus M,T,S; clamorose: clamose T,V,S; pertinaciter: pertineciter T; (501–2) nec: neque V; ad quod: ad quid T; solliciti: solici T; (502) proposito: proposite M; (503) que omnia inter bonos omnino: que omnia inter bonos omnia M, que omnia inter bonos oracio T; (504) et versa vice: vel vice versa T; eisdem: eosdem V, eiusdem T; nos: non T; (506) periti: peritim T; (506) existimarentur: existimentur V,S, existimant T; sunt: sint T; fore: forem T; (507) repeticione vel disputacione: disputacione vel repeticione T; (507–8) arguendo: argumentando T; consequens est: sequens est T, consequens [est not in V]; (508) ordinarie: ordinare M; vagetur: vaget T; (508–9) perquerendis: quirendis T, perquirendis V; aliud: ad M; (510) quo fit: que fit T,S; (510–11) ut qui: (qui inserted in margin in M); longe itinerando: itinerando longe T,V; terga: tergam T; (511–12) hii: not in T; illos sciencia: illas sciencias T; (512) itaque: nam V; (513–14) putaverant: putabant V; preire: perire S; postponuntur: ponuntur T; sed et aliud malum: sed et ad illud malum M, sed et ad aliud malum T; (515) cum sciencia: sine sciencia T; suos: suas S; interrumpunt: interrumpit M,S; (517) hinc: huic T; ut tarde: vel tarde T; (518) sciencie: sentencie T; perveniant ut ex hoc ludibrio fiunt: not in T, perveniat et ex hoc ludibrio fiunt V, perveniant et ex hac ludibrio fiunt S; (519–20) videntur: vident T; existimacione: estimacione V; (521) id: (hic in M but then crossed out and id written over it); (521–2) fuerint: fuerant T,V,S; assecuti: assecuturi V; veram famam; vanum famam S; primo: et primo T; (524) nulla: non ulla T; quacumque: not in V; (525) ut sit: nec sit V,S, nec si T; (525) tantum: tamen T; (527) dampnare: dampnere T; (527–8) cum: non T; intermittunt: intermittenti T; (529) magis: in legis V; obvium: obviam V; lecciones: underlined in S to be omitted; (530–1) volunt: voluerint T, voluerunt V,S; provecti: perfecti T; (531) potuerunt: poterint S; (532) apponere: opponere M; sint: sunt T; responsa: reversa S; (533) sint: sit T; quasi: quam T; (534–5) evertere: vertere V; qui: not in T tenent: tenet T; enim: tamen T; fit: sit T; iniuria: in via M; ubi: id M; credunt: credam T; (535–6) vel garruli: garruli V; viciosi: incensi T; (536–7) si quod: quod T; de provectis: provectis T; (537–8) cepimus: cempimus T; hiis: hic M; ut [que] postquam: [que cancelled out in M], not in T,V,S; (538) egrediendum: ingrediendum T; studio: studi T; (540–1) didicerant: dedicrat T; sicut: sic T; (541–2) colloquibus: collacionibus V, coloribus T; quas: quasi T; (543) fuerint; fuint T; (543–4) leccionibus: electionibus V; ceteris: certis V; periciam: periciem M,S; (544) et ex hoc facile: ex hoc facile V; (545–6) facti sunt cito habeantur: factio habeant T; (546) sit: fit T; (547) facile aut: facileaut T; proveniunt: perveniunt T; (548–9) antequam fundatam habeant scolasticam scienciam: habent scolasticam antequam fundatum habent scolasticam scienciam T; et in ipsa: et ipsam T, et in ipsam S; (550) permixtum: permixtim M,T,S; de auditoribus hactenus: hactenus de auditoribus T,V; (551–2) incitat: incipit T, incidit V,S; agitare: agitari V; (552–3) proficere: proferri proficere T; a qua sit: a qua sit a qua sit [repeated] T; (553–4) qua in re: quo iure T, qua iure V; illud: not in V; (554–5) cognovimus: agnovimus T; quis: quo M; (556) institutionibus canonicis: institutionibus canonicis S; (557–8) iuxta illud Horacii quo semel est imbuta recens servabit odorem test diu: reference is to the Roman poet Horace, Epl. 1, 2, 69 (= Book I, Epistola 2, line 69), *Q. Horacii Flacci Sermones et Epistulas*, ed. Rudolf Helm (Zurich and Stuttgart: Artemis Verlag, 1962), p. 222; imbuta: imbute T; testa: scesta T; (558–9) quod contra evenit si a legibus facerit exordium vidi enim paucissimos eorum: T,V,S, not in M; (558) evenit: venit

T, evenerit S; fecerit: facerit M, fecit V; (559–60) canonicam: canonicum T; accesserint: accresserint V; umquam: numquam M,S,V, namque T; (560–1) perfectos: perfectus T; iam enim: amem T; quasi: quam T; saturati: statuati T; (561–2) transmittunt: transmittam T; canonicam doctrinam: canonicam scienciam S (corrected in margin to doctrinam); (563) memoriam: memoria T; (564) periciam: periciem M,S, perinciam T; (565) pervenire: provenire T; si quis vero vult: si quis vero M,T; (566) exordiatur: exordiat T; det: debet T; (567–8) attentus: attenta T; dispenset: dispensat T; (568–9) quidem: quid M, qui enim T, quidam V,S; nihil solide: solide T; (569) Alii non: Alii vero M, Alii vero non S; recreantur: recreant T; (570–1) et hinc sunt quasi dormitantes dum audiendo leccionem. vacandum est: not in V, et huic sunt [quia crossed out, quis written above] dormitantes dum audiendo leccionem. vacandum est T; (572–3) nimis diu: mᵒtnis diu T; fit: sit T; mense: mensse V; voraciter: veraciter T,V; (574) impediti: prepediti M,V, propediti S; minus: numeris T; (574–5) ad studium: ad studendum V,S, ad statuendum T; et haec minima sunt: et haec immora sunt M,S, et haec minora V; istis: iste T; (575–6) egretudines: egritudines T,V; varii: variis T; (576–7) ut quod: etiam quod T; quod aliquando: aliquando quod V; (578) refectioni: refectam M; (579) enim: omni T; temporis: tempori T; (580) ymo: ergo M,S; (581) et mente ultra quam: ultra quam et mente M; (582–3) quidquam: quicquid V; contingerit: conterit M, centingit T,V, contigit S; infunderis: infuderis M,V; (585–6) autem: not in V; precipue: precipuo V,S; si ut sunt: ut sunt V, si ut [si ut repeated] sunt T; (587) cerebum: celebris T, cerebru V; (588) leviter: not in T; (589–90) illud: id V; admonuerimus: ammoverimus T; quod cum: quantum T, quod tamen S; aliquam: aliqua T, aliquandum S; (590–1) tenueris: te civeris T; interpelacione: interpollacione S; tantum: tamen T, tum ut V,S; mente: mentem M,T; (591–2) consolides: consolidos M; tantum ut: et T, tum ut V,S; recreata: creata T; mens: metis T; continuendum: continuandum M,V,S; (593) sit: not in T; (594) non bene: no bene T; sufferat: sufficerent V; (595) qui: que T; corporeos: corpore eos T; (596) fiant: fiunt T; saturi: faturi M, statim T; prandium: predium T; (597) e contra: contra T; (598) sibi: not in T; taliter: utiliter V; possint: possit T,V; (599) et post parvum lectum petere: et parvum lectum petere M, et post parum lectum competere T, et post parum [tempus in superscript] lectum petere S, et post parum lectum petere V; (599–601) nam licet aliqui post cenam studeant minus tamen gravat matutinum studium: nam licet post cenam cum gravat matutinum studium M; (601) et plus affert: et affert M, et plus auffert T; (601) commodl: commode M; quot: quod T; (602) lecto: lectio T; potest: post T; (603–4) post tamen: potest tamen [with potest corrected to post in superscript] S; multas (doctrinas) probaciones: [doctrinas underlined to be omitted] in S; per totam diem: totam diem T; (605) saltem: saltim T; (605–6) contingat: contingit V; in nocte: nocte M [in crossed out], V; dormias: dormas M; (606–7) suppletur: supplet T,S; quod deperditum est: deperditum est S, deperditum T,V (quod, est not in T,V); (607–8) plus studes: plus M, plus studeas V,S; incumbis: incumbes T; minus: immo T; (608) debitum suum: debitam suam T; (610) aliquando: alioquando M,V; (610–11) quid: quod T,S; commodius: modius T; nonnullis: nonnullus T,V; (612) studium: studiis T; qua in re: quo T; cuiuslibet: cuiusque T,V; (613) attendanda est: not in V; Si enim: nam si T,V,S; commodius: commodiut T; vigilias serotinas: vigilias M; (614–5) sufferas: sufferos T; tibi sero cum ante cenam: tibi sero tamen ante cenam V,S, tibi sero tamen ante eciam T; alteri cui gratius est: alteri cui gratus T; (615) oppositum: appositum T; vigilandum: violandum V; (616) ad horam noctis terciam: ad horis terciam noctis M, ad horam noctis sterciam T, ad horam tercia noctis V; (618) lecto: lectio T; decumbant: decumbat T; (619) cum vero dies: cum dies non T; (620) varietatem: val etatem T; immutare: mutare T; (621–2) mutetur: invitetur T; temporis: tempore T; ordine: [hordine: with 'h' then crossed out] V, [in ordine with 'in' then crossed out] T; (623) variatur: variantur T; (623) in omnibus ante oculos: ante omnia pre oculis V; (624) quidquam: quicquid V, quidquid S, quitquam M; aut: a V; (624–5) deambulas in camera vel per civitatem vel extra: deambules scilicet in camera vel per civitatem vel extra V, deambules in camera vel extra M, deambules in camera vel per civitatem vel extra T; causa: tam T; (626–7) ad studium ut in hiis quantum satis est immoreris semper cum proposito confestim ad studium redeundi: ad studium redeundi M, ut in hiis quantum satis est immoreris et in deo fiduciam habueris cum proposito cum confestim ad studium reddendi T, ad studium ut in hiis quantum satis est immoreris semper cum proposito confestim ad studium redeundi S; (627–8) premisimus: premisi T; (628) et: not in V; (629) religiosum est: religiosum es T; et honestum: et honestum est V; (630) gloriosissime: glorissime T; devote: devoto V; (631) obligatus: obligatas V; ecclesiasticum: ecclesiasticum [ecclesiasticum repeated] V; quanto: quanta V; (632) ab experto: ab expertor T; (633) affirmare: confirmare T; in causam et terminum: in etam et terminum V, in metam et terminum S; mecum et camicium T; (634) si fueris auditor et si preceptor: not in T; effectum: tum T; propositi: proposito T; (636) suorum: tuorum V; (636) perducendo: producendo V; facilius: facilem T, facillime V; continges: contingentes T; sic: sit V; (637) famam: famem T; (638) Amen: not in V; (639–40) [Explicit tractatus de modo docendi ius canonicum de francisci de caba (sic!) cardinalis florentini amen]: only in T.

[V has additional paragraph at end linking the present tract with a *repetitio* of Zabarella entitled 'Cum omnes' that follows.]

University, Administration, Taxation and Society in Italy in the Sixteenth Century: The Case of Fiscal Exemptions for the University of Pavia

Mario Rizzo

Among the privileges most frequently granted to universities in the Middle Ages, great importance was attached to fiscal immunities, which exempted members of universities from certain fiscal burdens payable by the rest of the population.[1] Together with jurisdictional privileges, fiscal exemptions gave university members a status that marked them off from ordinary citizens. So advantageous were these fiscal privileges, that the universities did everything in their power to prevent any attempt to rescind or restrict them, as occurred in the University of Pavia in the course of the sixteenth century. Faced with the difficult overall position in Lombardy and the pressures exerted by hostile social forces, students and professors alike fought fierce fiscal battles over a long period. The central Milanese authorities and the Pavia community were involved in a complex series of disputes, alliances, and attempts at mediation. This is evidence of the clearcut and profound link between the university and the society of the time.

1. The origins and organization of the University of Pavia

The *Studium papiense* began in 1361, when Galeazzo II Visconti, lord of Milan, obtained the privilege needed to found the *Studium* from the Emperor Charles IV.[2] The University of Pavia falls into that category of *studia* that Jacques Verger has defined 'foundation universities' (arising, that is, through the initiative of an authority and strictly tied to its interests), as opposed to 'spontaneous universities', which developed autonomously on the basis of pre-existing scholastic and cultural nuclei.[3] This rather rigid classification has been partially revised by Jacques Le Goff and Stephen C. Ferruolo, who argue that 'spontaneous universities', too, were to a certain extent linked to extra-university authorities, whether lay or ecclesiastical.[4] While avoiding over-schematic simplifications, it is still useful to distinguish between universities which developed essentially *ex consuetudine*, such as Bologna, Paris, Oxford, and Montpellier,[5] and universities founded *ex privilegio*. Some medieval universities such as Toulouse, Rome, and Naples were set up by popes or emperors.[6] Towards the end of the Middle Ages and during the Renaissance, with the changing political circumstances, other local or national authorities in their turn promoted new *studia*. Already in the course of the fourteenth century (somewhat earlier than other European countries) the kings of Castile, León, and Aragon founded various universities, the most eminent of which were Salamanca and Valladolid.[7] It was, however, mainly in the following two centuries that universities multiplied in Europe. New foundations arose in Spain (Perpignan, Huesca, Barcelona, Saragoza, Palma, Sigüenza, Alcalá de Henares, Valencia) and in France (Grenoble, Orange, Aix-en-Provence, Dole, Poitiers, Caen, Nantes, Bordeaux, Valence, Bourges).[8] Many universities emerged in the German area, through the efforts of emperors, local princes, bishops, or cities (Vienna, Heidelberg, Cologne, Erfurt, Würzburg, Leipzig, Rostock, Greifswald, Freiburg, Bâle), while other *studia* were created in the age of reform (Marburg, Königsberg, Jena).[9] Through the efforts of certain princes, several universities were set up in Bohemia, Poland and Hungary, including Prague, Cracow and Pécs.[10] The fifteenth century saw university centres being set up in Scandinavia (Upsala and Copenhagen), in Flanders (Louvain) and Scotland (St Andrews, Glasgow, and Aberdeen).[11] In the Italian case, the political divisions of the peninsula and the rivalries between the various states stimulated the foundation of numerous universities between the fourteenth and sixteenth centuries.[12] Alongside Pavia, we may recall Turin, Florence, Pisa, Siena, Ferrara, Urbino, Macerata and Messina, to name but a few.

Quite apart from political and cultural prestige, Galeazzo was encouraged to found a university because of the need to provide for common legislation which would strengthen the unity of the recently formed duchy and the need to train highly qualified personnel for the state administration.[13] The choice of Pavia as the site of the

Lombard *Studium* was encouraged by the desire to win over the city (which had only reluctantly yielded to Galeazzo's rule), its favourable geographical position, and above all its cultural tradition. The University of Pavia consisted of two faculties, law and arts, the latter including philosophy, grammar, theology, medicine, and mathematics. The faculty of law was undoubtedly the most important, which is explained not only by the interests and the requirements of Galeazzo's state, but also by Pavia's old legal tradition. The dukes of Milan constantly exerted strict control over the university,[14] which subsequently, during the Spanish domination, passed under the protection of the Lombard Senate, as is apparent from the New Constitutions promulgated by Charles V in 1541.[15] In defending the prerogatives of the *Studium*, and, in particular, its monopoly in the field of higher education, the senate proved to be less motivated and effective than the dukes. The times had undoubtedly changed and the attitude of the senate towards the university also suffered from the influence exerted by religious and patrician forces who ran or financed educational structures competing with the *Studium*.[16]

Together with the documents of foundation and various provisions specifically promulgated by the Milanese authorities, the statutes of the *universitates scholarium* and the two teaching bodies were the main source of law guiding the life of the University of Pavia and were a major reference point for the academic world.[17] Under Spanish rule the professors were appointed by the senate, which also fixed the salaries; the professors were paid by the state, not by the students, even though they received certain emoluments from students during the degree examinations.[18] The senate had certain powers of discretion as regards setting the level of salaries, though this had to be compatible with the state's financial situation. Moreover, the importance of the subject taught and the prestige of the teacher was usually also taken into account, with the result that a system of payments characterized by great inequalities developed.[19] This was certainly not peculiar to the University of Pavia in the sixteenth century, since great differences in salary are to be found in Pavia even at the end of the fifteenth century and in other Italian and European *studia* at various stages in their history.[20] When used correctly, discretion was a useful instrument for the recruitment of professors but at times it gave the senate the chance to bestow inappropriate favours.[21] It should, however, be said that from the second half of the sixteenth century and in particular in the seventeenth century the senate, to a certain extent, submitted to (but, probably, also encouraged) the growing 'municipalization' of the teaching staff. For various social and financial reasons, the professors were mainly recruited from among the citizens of Pavia.[22] This was a common occurrence in Italian universities in the sixteenth and seventeeth centuries (a similar tendency can be noted at Bologna, Perugia, and Pisa after 1570).[23] In Pavia, together with the lack of finance, it contributed to restricting the concrete exercise of the senate's powers of discretion.

Split between the two *universitates* (*iuristarum* and *artistarum*), the students of the University of Pavia were organized into nations, on the basis of a geopolitical criterion.[24] Every nation elected its advisor, who represented it and looked after its interests. Every year the advisors met in the cathedral to elect the rector of their faculty. The two students elected as rectors had a series of important functions: they represented the university in official ceremonies, protected the rights of their fellow students in the faculty, collaborated with the advisors in the control of the restless student world, and exercised their jurisdictional powers over students in disputes that did not require the intervention of extra-university authorities.

2. The administrative hierarchy and the fiscal system in the state of Milan in the sixteenth century

After a long struggle with France, Charles V finally acquired the state of Milan in 1535, linking it to his own empire by means of a personal union, but ensuring that it had ample administrative autonomy.[25] The fear that excessive centralization would bring about centrifugal trends led both Charles and his successors to be prudent. Moreover, the geographical distance certainly did not facilitate direct control of the dominions, and political decisions inevitably suffered from the slowness in communications.[26] The Spanish bureaucracy itself would have been unable to bear the weight of a totally centralized administration. Indeed, no European country in the sixteenth century had a really modern bureaucracy. However, the very fact that Lombardy was no longer independent necessarily required a minimum of centralization, partially limiting local powers. Inevitably Charles's Milanese policy was part of the more general policies pursued in the wider context of the empire.

The ex-duchy was an essential element for hegemony in Europe, giving Spain control over the Italian peninsula and hence the Mediterranean chessboard, ensuring links between the emperor's central-northern and southern dominions.[27]

The representative of the king of Spain in Lombardy was the Governor, who had the power to issue laws (called *gride*),[28] oversee the administration, assess the pleas of his subjects, grant grace and commute sentences. The collaboration with the Milanese authorities was not always smooth, and disputes arose in particular with the Senate.[29] Quite apart from being the Supreme Court of the state of Milan, the Senate had many administrative functions, one of which was the management of the University of Pavia. Also very important were the financial authorities, i.e. the *Magistrato Straordinario* and the *Magistrato Ordinario*. The latter, in particular, took on increasing importance, since it handled most of the income, as well as military finances. Besides their strictly administrative tasks, the financial authorities also had the powers of courts on fiscal matters. The main link between the centre and the periphery in the state of Milan were the *Podestà* and the *Referendari*. The *Podestà* represented the central Milanese government in the provincial capitals. Appointed by the Governor, they too had administrative and court functions, as was the custom of time, in the absence of a clearcut separation of state powers. The *Referendari* were the local representatives of the *Magistrato Ordinario*. Resident in the provincial capitals and with jurisdiction over their respective provinces, these civil servants oversaw all local fiscal matters and acted as a link between local issues and the *Magistrato*. Like all sixteenth century Lombard cities, the municipal administration in Pavia was run by an *élite*.[30] The most important Pavia families were represented on the *Consiglio Generale* (the general town council) by a hundred-odd *Decurioni*,[31] who dealt with the major issues but delegated most of the city's administration to a much smaller executive council. The *Consiglio Generale* also appointed many municipal officials, including the *dazieri* (excisemen).

For a long time historians argued that Spanish rule suffocated Lombardy's flourishing economy with extreme fiscalism. In recent years scholars have revised this adverse opinion, reappraising the consequences of Spanish fiscalism and contesting the traditional image of the ruinous decline suffered by the Lombard economy.[32] Although less oppressive and deleterious than previously thought, the fiscal pressure brought to bear by the Spanish on the state of Milan was nevertheless very heavy, higher overall than in the ducal period. In addition to conserving various ordinary taxes (i.e. those which were collected periodically) which went back to the ducal period, such as the horse tax and the salt tax,[33] the Habsburgs introduced new taxes. Pressed by impelling military needs, in 1536 Charles V instituted the new *mensuale* tax for the state of Milan, consisting of a monthly tax of 20,000 *scudi*. Reduced in 1537 to 12,000 *scudi* a month, it was temporarily suppressed between January 1546 and August 1547 only to be definitively reintroduced from September 1st 1547, at the rate of 25,000 *scudi* a month. Conceived of as a temporary tax and therefore defined as an occasional levy, the *mensuale* in actual fact became the most important ordinary tax and was the backbone of Spanish finances in the state of Milan, even though formally it remained an occasional levy throughout the period of Habsburg domination. The *mensuale* was levied in a complex and inequitable way. The first stage was that the *Magistrato Ordinario* shared the tax between the various provinces of the state, essentially using the antiquated schemes of distribution of the horse tax and the salt tax; in the second stage, every provincial *camera* assigned a certain tax quota to the individual communities in the province, and finally the local authorities made a further division among the individual taxpayers in the community. Within each community the quotas not paid by those who enjoyed exemption ended up by further penalizing those who were obliged to pay, for the latter in effect had to pay for themselves and also for those who enjoyed fiscal immunities. In the course of the sixteenth century the procedure for distributing tax was partly modified, eliminating some of the most serious disparities and reducing the exemptions, as we shall see below.

The *mensuale* quotas assigned to the cities were mainly levied indirectly, by means of many duties on goods and foodstuffs, whose collection was usually contracted out. The *camera* gave the contractors full powers and rights to levy taxes from the taxpayers, in return for a fixed annual sum established with the Milan financial authorities, who thus did not have to worry about the costs and uncertainties involved in levying taxes. While direct taxes were applied only rarely in the cities, the surrounding countryside areas usually paid the *mensuale* by means of direct taxation on individuals, property, or crops (these taxes went under various names such as the *perticato, testatico, focatico,* and *imbottato*).[34] Levied in this way, the *mensuale* should have provided for the financial needs of the state and, in particular, the huge military expenses. Unfortunately for the Lombard subjects of the king of Spain the *mensuale* was not sufficient and the Spanish repeatedly imposed a series of occasional levies, which did not, however, become payable on a regular basis. Last but not least, there was the problem of housing and feeding the numerous troops stationed in the state of Milan.[35] Contact with the soldiers was particularly feared by the population, above all because the soldiers were frequently guilty of misdemeanours and rarely complied with the billeting regulations laid down by the government, causing much expense and considerable damage to those who had to put them up. The burden of billeting affected the rural community in particular, since, despite frequent disputes and breaches, the cities and city landowners were generally exempt throughout the sixteenth century.

3. University fiscal legislation in Pavia from the foundation of the university to the beginning of Spanish rule (1361–1541)

Legislation on university fiscal exemptions was not completely unified, sometimes granting very extensive immunities, but on other occasions explicitly providing for more limited privileges. Modelled on the privileges of various famous contemporary universities, such as Paris, Bologna, Oxford, Orléans, and Montpellier, the imperial diploma of 1361 and the papal bull of 1389 granted all university members exemption from taxes. The imperial diploma in fact ordered:

Quod quidem Studium eiusque studentes nec non rectores, doctores, bacalarios, officiales atque ministros, famulos et familias eorum et cuiuslibet eorundem, quocumque nomine censerentur, qui fuerint per tempora, cuiuscumque etiam dignitatis, status, ordinis seu conditionis, predicti et singuli eorum extiterint, omni eo privilegio, libertate, immunitate, indulto et gratia quibus Parisiensis, Bononiensis, Oxoniensis, Aurilianensis et Montis Pexulani Studia, seu alia quecumque Studia generalia privilegiata noscuntur, huius nostre concessionis gratia, perfrui semper volumus et gaudere per omnia, ac si privilegium, libertas, immunitas, indulta et gratia huiusmodi presentibus de verbo ad verbum essent inserta.[36]

However, the statutes of the *universitas iuristarum*, dating back to 1395, referred explicitly only to town duties, stating that students should not pay more than the citizens of Pavia.[37] This was an apparently restrictive interpretation, which would seem to preclude any particular fiscal privileges, with the exception of the free introduction of lawbooks in the city. When Lombardy fell under Spanish rule, even the New Constitutions of 1541 dealt only with duties, declaring professors and students exempt:

Possunt omnes Doctores, et Scholares quarumcumque nationum, modo non sint banniti, nec rebelles nostri, libere, et omni impedimento cessante Papiam ire, in ea habitare, stare, et conversari, ab eaque recedere cum sua familia, vestibus, libris, utensilibus, pannis, laneis, lineis, sericeis, et alia suppellectili necessaria, et opportuna pro usu eorum sine solutione alicuius pontis, portus, gabellae, aut cuiusvis datii, cujuscunque civitatis, aut loci huius Dominii.[38]

Although with some differences, both the New Constitutions and the statutes apparently indicated more restrictive forms of fiscal immunity, especially when compared with the privileges of some of the most famous universities. *De facto*, however, in the fifteenth century the legislation of the dukes usually guaranteed the University of Pavia widespread and reassuring exemptions, basically inspired by the original ducal and papal concessions, and based on common law, although there were some changes in the legislation.[39] Significant in this sense, for example, was the order issued by Duke Ludovico Maria Sforza on January 14 1496, stating among other things that:

Tenore igitur praesentium, ex certa scientia, motu proprio, et de nostrae plenitudine potestatis praedictos Doctores, omnes, et singulos utriusque Collegii Papiensis seu alterius eorum, Jurisconsultorum scilicet et Artistarum, Philosophorum, et Medicorum, qui sunt, et per tempora erunt in infinitum cum omnibus ejusdem familiae, seu de eorum familia simul in communione habitantibus, ad unum panem et vinum pro eo tempore quo simul cohabitabunt, et donec tales Doctores erunt in humanis, ac Cancellariis Collegiorum, et eorum Bidellis generalibus, et specialibus exemptos, et immunes facimus, a quibuscumque collectis, talleis, taxis, praestitis, mutuis, subsidiis, contributionibus, functionibus, Andatis, plaustris, superindictis, Navigiis, Angariis, et Perangariis, Hospitationibus, et aliis quibuscumque oneribus, et positionibus qualiacumque sint, et quibusvis nominibus onera ipsa nuncupentur realibus, etiam pro bonis alibi sitis, et ubivis jacere contingant in futurum, realibus, personalibus, et mixtis, tam impositis, quam de caetero imponendis, quomodolibet, et qualis ex causa, tam cogitata, quam incogitata, tam per nos, et Cameram nostram Ducalem, et Commitalem, aut ejus Offitiales, quam per Communitatem Papiae, et aliam quamvis Communitatem, vel universitatem, vel personam etiam tempore Guerrae, aut Pestis, reservatis semper Datiis ordinariis, onere salis, et quibuscumque aliis ordinariis oneribus, ad quorum solutionem, et contributionem teneri volumus.[40]

Fiscal privileges were a great financial advantage for the members of the University of Pavia, students and teachers alike. The property they possessed was mostly exempt from taxes. Duty privileges, totally or partially, exempted university members from taxation applied to basic consumer goods, such as corn, wine and meat, the main foodstuffs of the times.[41] Generally, these privileges were implemented in a two-stage process: the privileged normally paid at the gates of the city and were subsequently reimbursed by the excisemen. In the case of students, the reimbursement was paid to the advisors of the student nations on the basis of a list presented to the excisemen; subsequently, the advisors distributed the money among the members of their nation, according to the amount owed to each member.[42] Usually the university members could be exempted from charges payable for billeting soldiers, guard duty in the defence of the city and other similarly unwelcome tasks.[43] As in many other Italian and European universities, in Pavia the students could benefit from reduced-rate rents for rented accommodation.[44]

Apart from certain changes in legislation and a few occasional restrictions, fiscal immunities remained in force until the beginning of the sixteenth century and were extended to the entire university population, 'tanto per ragione commune, quanto per li privilegi concessi per li passati Prencipi di questo stato'[45] ('both under common law and by virtue of the privileges granted in the past by the Lords of this State'). The sixteenth century, however, saw a great change marked by intense conflict between the university world, the rest of the Pavia community and the Milanese authorities, over the relative burden of taxation.

4. The disappearance of student fiscal exemptions

In the course of the sixteenth century the students of the University of Pavia lost those fiscal exemptions that had previously been attached to their status. It is likely that there was a gradual erosion of student fiscal privileges rather than a drastic abolition due to a single order issued by the central Milanese authorities. It may be that before disappearing completely these exemptions were sometimes temporarily suppressed or limited, as a consequence of the needs of the central Lombard treasury and the difficulties that had periodically troubled the life of the *Studium* in the sixteenth century. Archive records make it possible to reconstruct at least partially the chronological development of events. We know that in the mid-sixteenth century, students and professors fought together—and with a certain degree of success—to maintain their fiscal exemptions.[46] After the reintroduction of the *mensuale* (which increased its fiscal burden) in 1547 Pavia decided to increase the duties on corn, wine and meat, and double all other duties.[47] This was so as to be able to offset the increase in tax Pavia had to pay. Having been duly authorized by the *Magistrato Ordinario*, the city contracted out the collection of the increase in duties, without any further special conditions apart from the stipulation that the governor should be paid 200 *scudi* to repair the town's fortifications. The generalized collection of the new duties immediately caused serious problems. The members of the university appealed directly to Governor Ferrante Gonzaga, pointing out their traditional exemption from any occasional levy, such as the *mensuale*, and begging him to order the town authorities to respect this inalienable right. The governor agreed, and in January 1548 ordered that students, professors, and university officials be 'preservati secondo il solito' ('exempted as usual').

The dispute was far from being resolved and dragged on for a further year, involving the members of the university, the tax farmers, and the Pavia and Milanese authorities. Despite Gonzaga's order, the situation remained extremely tense and at the beginning of February, the rectors of the two faculties sent a new petition to the governor, repeating their protests once more on behalf of teachers and students. On February 11 Gonzaga confirmed the previous order and extended it explicitly—as the members of the university had requested—to their servants and the professors resident in Pavia, to whom the exemption had not apparently always been granted; at the same time, however, don Ferrante stressed the need to avoid defrauding the central treasury. When the order had been received, the *Magistrato Ordinario* transmitted it to the *Refer-*

endario of Pavia, instructing him to oversee its implementation personally. Not convinced, the *Referendario* asked for further instructions, openly revealing his support for the townspeople, who expressed their deep concern over the abuses committed by the members of the university who defrauded the central treasury.[48] Finally, on February 27 the *Magistrato* once more instructed the *Referendario* that the exemption was to be complied with, though care should be exercised to avoid fraud. Even the *Magistrato*, however, pressed by a difficult financial situation, did not approve of the university's exemptions and was thus sensitive to the complaints of the Pavia community, sharing their fears. Thus it was that at the beginning of March, the *Magistrato*, effectively departing from Gonzaga's orders (and its own previous instructions), ordered the *Referendario* to take steps to get the members of the university to agree to a payment of the 200 *scudi* previously earmarked for fortification works in return for their exemption from the duty on meat. It was a brave attempt to prevent the total exemption of members of the university from the additional duty burden, but the vehement reaction of professors and students soon made itself felt with the Milanese and Pavia authorities.[49] After ten days of frenetic exchanges of supplications, orders, and various letters, the *Magistrato* gave way, instructing the *Referendario* that the members of the university (whose tax exemptions had just been extended to servants who lived in with them) should be allowed to keep their immunities 'omnino, et senza piu altra difficulta ne dilatione' ('totally, and without further hindrance or delay'). Once the legal dispute about the legitimacy, appropriateness, and extent of the immunities had been established, further complications linked to their concrete application arose. In April it was once more the meat duty that caused the greatest friction between the town and the students. The *Referendario* wrote to the *Magistrato*:

Se la citta li volle far dar li denari delle exemptioni della predetta carne a caduno per caduno, acio non segua grande fraude, essi scolari non voleno, ma voleno esser satisfati secondo le liste qualle dano li lori consiglieri, et la citta non volle, per che se iustifica che sopra le predette liste li dano infinita de boche de piu de quelle che sono, et a voler giarir queste liste con essi consiglieri, si vene ogni giorno a litte e contentione con essi, se anchora la citta volle deputar beccaria che gli dia la carne exenta non voleno, et dicano voler li denari, se la citta anchora gli volle dar una suma de denari fazendo acordo con loro per una volta tanto, fra essi scolari non poteno acordar.[50]

(If the city, in an attempt to avoid serious fraud, tries to pay each student the money due for the exemption from duty on meat, the students refuse, demanding to be reimbursed under the list of names presented by the advisors of the student nations; the city, however, does not accept this, since the lists mention many more students than exist in reality; and if we try to discuss the list with the advisors, we end up by quarrelling. If the city wishes to instruct a butcher to supply students with duty-free meat, the students refuse and say they want the money. If the city, once in a while, decides to pay the students a certain sum of money, they will not manage to agree among themselves as regards the division.)

In May further problems arose between the tax farmers, the *Referendario* and the students regarding the payment of exemptions.[51] Between June and July there were fierce disputes regarding the decision of the *Magistrato* to defer the payment of the sum due in restitution to those enjoying immunity; following loud protests from the university, the *Magistrato* once again had to change his mind and proceed to pay the sum. In February 1549 the students turned to the *Magistrato* in defence of their fiscal privileges, which had once again been violated. Although reaffirming the exemption from the duty increases, the *Magistrato* took the opportunity to exclude the servants of the students explicitly, and also the students from Pavia itself: a step backwards vis-à-vis the student gains of the previous year.

As this affair shows, half way through the sixteenth century the students of the University of Pavia certainly still retained a number of fiscal privileges, even though we do not know exactly to what extent. Sources speak explicitly only of exemption from occasional levies and from increases on duties, without specifying whether the students had to pay part of these duties or not (almost certainly they were not entirely exempt).[52] Moreover, some provisions such as those relating to servants, seem to be subject to major variations. Whatever the case may be, it is still a fact that students maintained, at least partially, their fiscal prerogatives and were still able to defend their rights, although the bitter struggle between 1547 and 1549 indicates that these prerogatives, which probably for some time had been periodically disputed and which had perhaps even been subject to occasional limitations, were now in grave danger.

The situation was very different some twenty years later in 1572, when the university asked the governor to restore student immunities, together with other measures designed to increase the flow of students to Pavia.[53] Obviously, in these years the students' position regarding the fiscal problems had worsened considerably. The confirmation of the complete .suppression of student exemptions came from a vast administrative and financial survey, called *Visita general del Estado de Milan* (general inspection of the state of Milan). Ordered by Philip II, it was led in the 1580s by one of his faithful lieutenants, the *Visitador* don Luis de Castilla. The general inspections periodically involved the entire Milanese state structure and affected most of Lombard society. Inspired by the Habsburg sovereigns' policy of cautious centralization, these inspections were an attempt to control local administration, harmonizing it with the needs of Spanish imperial policy and correcting various excesses perpetrated by the Milanese authorities and civil servants.[54] In charge of the visits were the *Visitadores*, special magistrates appointed personally by the King and reporting directly to him. The *Visitadores* carefully checked the behaviour of civil servants and magistrates, from the lowest levels to the highest ranks, to identify abuses, corruption, and inefficient administration. Moreover, by means of these visits, the central powers wanted to get a clear picture of the resources available and the forces at work in the Milanese dominion.

Given the vast scope of the inspection, every visit lasted for years and was divided into numerous 'trials', each of which included various interrogations of the witnesses. One of the most important visits was undertaken between 1581 and 1591 by don Luis de Castilla. In the section dedicated to the senate, de Castilla dealt with the University of Pavia, questioning professors, administrators, and notaries, and finally presenting a series of queries to the senate, which defended itself with as many *responsiones*. The interrogations are most interesting, because the direct evidence of some protagonists enables us to see the life of the members of the university from inside, revealing various aspects of the mentality and customs of the times, as well as certain rivalries existing both among the members of the university and between the latter and the rest of society.[55] The precious evidence contained in the *responsiones* gives us a chance to assess the senate as the institution supervising the management of the *Studium*.

In one of its replies, denying any responsibility in the matter, the senate admitted that the student exemptions had effectively disappeared and explained that the new situation had been the result of the long period of war in which Lombardy had been involved in the first half of the sixteenth century; having once re-established peace securely, student immunities had not been restored, both because the state coffers really were empty and because of the fiscal authorities' excessive severity.[56] This explanation seems plausible, since it indicates two major causes in the decline of student exemptions: the economic uneasiness caused by the wars and, in particular, the needs of the central treasury. During the interrogations, some witnesses even stressed that the tormented affairs of the mid-sixteenth century had profoundly shaken the immunities of university members in general.[57]

Anxious to exculpate itself the senate also stressed its attempts to restore student exemptions. Had such moves been successful, the Senate declared, it would have encouraged the recovery of the *Studium*, while the increased flow of students, financially speaking, would in its turn have fully compensated for the concession of fiscal immunities.[58] This argument appears on several occasions, in the course of the visit as in previous documents,[59] and does not seem to be without grounds. We cannot prove, however, with any certainty that the number of students in Pavia declined in the course of the sixteenth century, since we do not have the matriculation records, which have made it possible to establish patterns of student attendance in other European universities.[60] Moreover, even if the records had come down to us, in all probability they would not have been of much use, since sixteenth-century sources all stress their poor state and unreliability.[61] Not even the graduation records help us determine student attendance, both because of the obvious limitations of this kind of source, and because the Pavia lists are incomplete. Since no accurate quantitative analysis is possible we must base our conclusion exclusively on the evidence of contemporary accounts. Although heterogeneous and the fruit of subjective impressions, these generally suggest a certain decline in student enrolments.[62]

The fact that the university community existed must have been financially beneficial to the town, increasing the consumption of various products (foodstuffs, clothing, books), encouraging the rise of new shops and taverns, and stimulating the property market because of the student demand for rented accommodation.[63] The presumed link between restored immunities and a flourishing university was often quoted by witnesses giving evidence to the *visita.* Although dictated in particular by personal interests, these remarks should not be underestimated. Admittedly, the fame and prosperity of a university centre did not depend on the mere existence of fiscal exemptions. At least as important were other factors, such as the quality and the renown of the teachers, the order and tranquillity of university life, and the competition of other nearby universities which could 'steal' students and professors.[64] It should not be overlooked that in the course of the sixteenth century in Lombardy the educational monopoly previously exercised by Pavia's public *Studium* weakened, since it was threatened and partly supplanted by alternative centres of higher education which developed through the initiative of religious orders and the town's guilds, the expression of an emerging town *élite*.[65] During the early modern period, the development of other educational institutions weakened numerous Italian, Spanish and French universities. The greatest threat to universities was generally posed by colleges run by religious orders, and in particular by the Jesuits, who organized a *de facto* European network of colleges. The *Studia* sometimes had to protect themselves from other competitors as well, such as town grammar schools, the colleges of the nobility, academies, and private teachers.[66] The loss of the educational monopoly undoubtedly removed many students from the universities, since the young who were eager to learn, gain professional qualifications, and raise themselves socially through higher education studies could resort to other alternative educational institutions, frequently more attractive and easier to attend than traditional universities. On the other hand, as far as the University of Pavia is concerned, its traditional immunities must really have been an attraction for anyone intending to become a university student. The fact therefore that the *Studium* was deprived of its privileges might easily have led students to prefer other universities or other educational institutions. Moreover, the sudden restoration of student immunities might have facilitated the restoration of the rectorate, which fell into disuse in Pavia in the second half of the sixteenth century.[67]

5. Conflict over the fiscal exemptions of the professors

The frequent references to exemptions contained in the *Visitador*'s records show just how sensitive the university was to this problem.

Interestingly enough, witnesses—all university professors, officials, and notaries—placed the members of the university on the same plane, whether they were students, teachers, or members of the non-teaching staff, as if all these categories had been equally deprived of their traditional fiscal immunities. In actual fact, during the six-teenth century great fiscal differences emerged within the university world. Until the mid-sixteenth century the position of the professors and the students was substantially the same but subsequently their respective fiscal positions changed markedly, even though occasion-ally the two groups did fight together for common causes. The professors did not totally wash their hands of students' exemptions, partly because a high number of enrolments meant an increase in what the professors received from the students when they graduated. However, the professors were paid a fixed salary by the state, regardless of payments made by the students. This may perhaps help to explain why the professors were in actual fact much more concerned with the defence of their own fiscal privileges than with student privileges. Just how it came about that only the students lost their exemptions, while the professors (and the university officers) kept theirs, albeit with great difficulty remains to be clarified. The documentation in our possession makes it possible for the time being only to advance a few hypotheses as to why this happened. The professors presumably had greater political influence, partly because they often belonged to socially high-ranking groups. Despite quite often sharp differences and disagreements regarding certain basic problems, the professors were generally more united and effective than the students, both because of their professional expertise, and because the students were a much more heterogeneous group. For these reasons, although unable to prevent their privileges from being frequently attacked, the professors probably were able to bring greater pressure to bear on certain decisions taken in Milan, and were thus able to defend their interests more effectively. In addition, there were fewer professors than there were students, so that we can assume that the maintenance of the professors' exemptions cost the Lombard fiscal authorities less than it did to keep students' immuni-ties.

Although entirely plausible, these considerations do not fully explain why professors kept their privileges whereas the students lost theirs. In this respect the explanation recently put forward by Maria Carla Zorzoli should be borne in mind, whereby the decline in student exemptions may be explained by the great decrease in foreign students in Pavia and the development of the university colleges, which gave a whole range of financial and legal privileges to their members.[68] Our belief is that while these developments are extremely interesting, they are of secondary significance. It is true that at the end of the sixteenth century and in particular during the seventeenth century the number of foreign students in Pavia decreased while the number of students in the colleges increased, even though both these phenomena need to be explored more fully. Nevertheless these late sixteenth-century developments alone cannot account for the disappearance of student exemptions. More probably they contributed to the maintenance of the new *status quo*, and had the effect that any suggestion of reintroducing the abolished exemptions did not appear to be a particularly urgent or significant problem in the eyes of most of the authorities. As we have seen, student exemptions were fiercely contested already in the course of the first half of the sixteenth century, and around 1570 were completely abolished. The crisis in the exemptions began long before the end of the sixteenth century and to understand this we need to refer to a series of economic, administrative, social, and university factors. The fact that the fiscal disputes also involved the professors shows that an interpretation limited only to the student world is inadequate. Clearly in the sixteenth century, university fiscal privileges (all of them and not just student privileges) gave rise to frequent complaints: the dispute on the subject was already very much in the open.

In 1537 the professors asked for and obtained the reconfirmation of their exemption from putting up billeted soldiers, after several violations had occurred and some professors had been forced to put the soldiers up in their own homes.[69] There were numerous disputes regarding the *mensuale*, from 1536 onwards.[70] Although the exemptions of the professors were promptly upheld by the Milanese authorities, the Pavia administration repeatedly tried to change the *status quo*. In the 1540s the professors turned to the governor on several occasions to safeguard their exemption from the *focatico* tax, and both Del Vasto in 1542 and Gonzaga in 1547 upheld their cause.[71] Again in 1547 Gonzaga reconfirmed the professors' immunity from the salt tax.[72] Between 1555 and 1557 new disputes arose over the question of exemptions regarding the billeting of soldiers. In the course of the dispute the professors threatened a sort of strike, complaining about the chronic delays with which they were paid. In a memorandum presented to the governor the professors stated that:

Essi lettori se si vedranno privati de loro Privilegi, et ugualati a ogni persona plebea, oltre che non son pagati de suoi salarij, restando egli anchora creditori di uno anno e mezo, per non havere sin adesso il Refferendario essequito la commessione di Vostra Signoria Illustrissima, hano deliberato resolutamente lasciare la professione di leggere. Il che non si pensa che Vostra Signoria Illustrissima debbi permettere che occorra come quella che e' ferventissima protettrice de studi et dilligentissima conservatrice degli ordeni di Sua Maesta.[73]

(Because they are deprived of their privileges, and placed on a par with any plebeian person, quite apart from the fact they have not been regularly paid and are still owed a year and a half of pay, since the *Referendario* has still not executed the Governor's orders, they have decided to give up teaching. They also point out that the Governor should not allow matters to deteriorate to this stage since he is, after all, a fervent protector of studies and a very diligent executor of his Majesty's orders.)

In this particular instance the professors did not obtain all they wanted, for the question at issue (viz. immunity from billeting) remained unresolved. In the meantime the professors' fears were heightened since violations of all kinds were becoming increasingly frequent. The professors now turned directly to Philip II, hoping that he would intervene in their favour. On July 23 1555 Philip solemnly confirmed the privileges of the professors and the university officials, the exemption being expressly extended even to times of war.[74] In the following years, thanks perhaps to the royal document and in particular to the restoration of peace in Lombardy, the conflict probably became less acute, though it was not resolved definitively. In 1578 the *Deputati alla Provvisione* of Pavia officially attested the professors' immunity from ordinary taxes and occasional levies, after disputes arose on this matter.[75] In 1582 the professors had to present a new plea to the governor in defence of their fiscal privileges.[76] Sometimes the individual professors found themselves involved in fiscal diatribes, complaining about the Pavia authorities' behaviour.[77] Overall, the fiscal disputes continued into the first half of the seventeenth century, with sometimes very violent clashes, while the Milanese authorities became increasingly vigilant in this respect, sometimes temporarily suspending the exemptions until certain situations had been investigated. Although repeatedly confirmed, professors' fiscal privileges came increasingly under fire.[78]

This brief review gives some idea of the innumerable difficulties that the professors had to face, already in the course of the sixteenth century, to protect their fiscal privileges. The senate, the governor, and even the king intervened to safeguard these privileges, but this was not always sufficient to guarantee that local authorities observed them. After every official confirmation of immunity, there was a whole series of violations, complaints and disputes of various kinds between the professors and the city authorities when the orders of the central power came to be implemented. A sort of fiscal guerrilla warfare broke out, characterized by an interminable series of wearying skirmishes fought without ever reaching a definite solution. Indeed, the passage from legislation to its enactment was often difficult, and the orders of the central authorities were sometimes ignored at a local level. The issue was further complicated by the complex bureaucratic channels that both parties' petitions and the orders of the authorities had to go through. The Governor's order (sometimes following a royal letter) often had to obtain the approval of the senate, which sent the approval to the *Magistrato Ordinario*, which in its turn referred the matter to the *Referendario* of Pavia, whose job it was to see that the decisions of the higher authorities were implemented locally in collaboration with the excisemen and the *avvocati fiscali* in Pavia. It is hardly surprising, therefore, that a whole series of bottlenecks and inefficiencies arose and that some of the authorities involved in the bureaucratic *iter* could conjure up obstacles or interpret the orders transmitted by the superiors with excessive freedom.

The nature and significance of fiscal conflicts can be appreciated through the greater quantity of petitions presented by the parties to the senate, the *Magistrato*, the governor and even the sovereign. The professors often saw their privileges being threatened and, in asking for them to be observed, emphasized their age-old existence, stressing the importance of immunities for the life of the *Studium* and minimizing the financial damage that the community might suffer. For its part the city denounced the unfairness of a situation which by favouring several people disproportionately, further increased the city's fiscal burden. The local administration often referred to those sections of legislation and to case law which gave (or, at least seemed to give) a restrictive interpretation of these immunities, in exactly the same way as the members of the university referred to those aspects of legislation and common law that were most favourable to them. The community denounced the abuses committed by members of the university, who sometimes exploited their privileges to defraud the central treasury, extending them to goods and people with no right to benefit from them.[79] Among the students these illicit practices were facilitated by the poor state of the enrolment records.[80] The excesses of certain university members were even feared by the Milanese authorities, who, though invariably reconfirming the exemptions, urged the local authorities time and again to be on their guard for any attempt at fraud.

6. The causes of the disputes over university tax liability

During the sixteenth century the question of fiscal immunity was undoubtedly of great importance in the history of Pavia's academic life, involving all those who belonged to the university world at different times and with different outcomes. The theme of exemptions seems to be very significant, partly because in this area of university life the correlation between the affairs of the *Studium* and the political, financial, and social conditions of the state of Milan was manifest. While to a large extent maintaining the pre-existing administrative structure, Spanish rule in Lombardy caused some inevitable changes. Because of the frequent transfers of responsibility and the recurrent consultations between the various levels of power, the red tape increased often slowing down and complicating the solution of various university problems. From time to time the various authorities gave orders or refused to obey the orders of others; they would ask for opinions and consultations, and would complain of interference in their sphere of influence. All were, however, heavily conditioned by the chronic lack of funds afflicting the university budget. The lack of finance often forced the Lombard administration to a severely restrictive university policy that prevented officials from going beyond simple day-to-day administration. In this sense, the general financial situation of the state of Milan was of decisive influence. The huge military demands of the crown and the consequent financial squeeze imposed on other sectors inevitably affected the university too, making it difficult to

raise funds or obtain various favours and benefits which it had
obtained without great difficulty in previous ages.

As often happens, economic hardship sharpened social conflict
and, in particular, sharpened fiscal disputes, accentuating the contrast between those who enjoyed great privileges and those who did
not, or who were in some way damaged by these privileges. Thus it is
not surprising that the prolonged wars and the consequent deterior-
ation in the economic and financial situation made it increasingly
burdensome, and, in particular, unpleasant for the city to respect the
university exemptions. For these same reasons, on the other hand,
the university members strove to remain exempt from fiscal burdens,
which became steadily heavier on the population. While the many
military commitments of the Spanish required growing finance and
the central Treasury's chests were increasingly empty, even the
Milanese financial authorities often came to share the positions of
the Pavia community. It is no accident that the documentation of
the fiscal battles is particularly rich in the 1540s and 1550s, a very
difficult period for the state of Milan, which experienced the final
acts in the long war between France and Spain for domination in
Italy, and which subsequently had great difficulty in restoring its
economy. It is equally significant that the senate justified the
disappearance of student immunities by reference to the financial
crisis that followed the sixteenth century wars, thus directly linking
the problems of state finance with university life. In this respect, the
question of the city's increase in taxes seems to be central. The
reintroduction of the *mensuale* caused a further increase in the fiscal
burden and led the city to increase the duties and operate a
generalized collection. In this way, however, Pavia clashed with the
privileged group of university members, whose determined opposition was inevitable. There was substantially a chain reaction
in which the effects of the fiscal needs of the state had repercussions
on the local situation in Pavia and the interests of the university
world.

If this link between state finance and the university needs to be
stressed, consideration must also be given to the influence exerted on
university problems by the changes in the Lombard fiscal system,
which in the course of the sixteenth century underwent a major
change thanks to the introduction of the general rating system,
called the *estimo*, which began under Charles V and was completed
under Philip II.[81] The general *estimo* was for Lombardy a first,

though very imperfect affirmation of the principle of generality and impersonality vis-à-vis taxes on which modern finance is based. The historical importance of the *estimo* favoured by the Habsburgs resides above all in the greater fiscal equity that it introduced and in the fact that this long and tormented fiscal matter favoured significant developments within Lombard society, even beyond the initial intentions of the promoting authorities. On the legal plane these developments in part eliminated the discrepancies which were associated with the different status of taxpayers, so that the nobles lost various privileges, the merchants had to give up the total exemption of trade from ordinary taxes, and the rural areas surrounding the cities saw their fiscal dependence vis-à-vis the city decline. It was certainly not easy to obtain these results, since the disputes between the various social groups and the various state bodies were numerous and harsh, given the complex network of conflicting interests. Much remained still to be done to achieve a satisfactory organization of the fiscal system, but the sixteenth-century *estimo* was a first, major step in this direction, rationalizing the fiscal structure and to a certain extent reducing discriminations between taxpayers. Although not directly linked to the *estimo*, the university's fiscal position was, however, part ot this social and economic context. The abolition of student exemptions and the pressure exerted by the city against the professors' privileges are plainly analogous with two essential aspects of the history of the *estimo*, namely the restriction of certain fiscal privileges and the struggle undertaken by several underprivileged groups against the privileged.

The University of Pavia certainly felt the effect of these influences brought to bear by Lombard society. Besides these causes which we may define as external, we must also consider other factors more specifically related to the *Studium*'s internal history. The attack on the university's fiscal privileges cannot be divorced from the decline in several traditional institutions which had typified the late-medieval *Studium*, and constituted a major reference point for the entire Pavia university world. There was a decline in the rector's power and influence and in the final decades of the sixteenth century the position of rector was almost invariably vacant, probably weakening students' jurisdictional privileges. The written texts of the university statutes were lost and were not adequately replaced, despite some vain attempts to revive them. This decline affected the structure of the university, university life as a whole suffered (although it is not possible to state that it remained without appropriate provision), and probably even the fiscal privileges to some extent suffered from the difficulties experienced by the *Studium*. Moreover, the crisis in the rectorate contributed to making the position of the students even more precarious vis-à-vis the fiscal authorities, often depriving them of their traditional spokesman, the rectors.

In the second half of the sixteenth century the University of Pavia went through an age of transition, during which old and new coexisted. At that time the *Studium* was very different from the flourishing university of the late Middle Ages, bogged down as it was by a series of major structural problems and threatened by the decisive competition exerted by religious orders and the town's guilds. It would, however, be quite wrong to dismiss that period of its history as totally negative, since the university kept a certain cultural and institutional vitality, and had not yet been finally relegated to a secondary role within the Lombard educational system. Moreover, although it is true that the University of Pavia suffered considerable decline, numerous transformations arose, which were sometimes painful but at least in part inevitable, as occurred with the fiscal exemptions. The university world suffered the consequences of the profound changes which were gradually emerging within Lombard society.

The relationship between the university, the central Milanese powers, and the city community is one of the most interesting aspects of university life in Pavia in the sixteenth century. Even those characteristics, which in theory would seem to isolate the *Studium* from the social context should instead be considered in relation to it: this is precisely the case of fiscal immunities, which, while legally sanctioning the peculiarities of the university world, in actual fact constituted one of the main reasons for contact with the reality outside the university. In the sixteenth century the relationships between the university and the most powerful elements in the state were sometimes characterized by fierce conflicts, and on other occasions by relative collaboration. As we know, the Senate was the main protector of the *Studium*, but sometimes it showed no authentic interest nor an effective will in safeguarding university interests. Although unable to resolve all the problems under which the university laboured, adequate funding would certainly have contributed, apart from anything else, to alleviating the difficulties,

restoring order to academic life, and reviving the prestige of the
Studium. However, nothing really effective was done and what *was*
done more often than not did not go beyond what was immediately
necessary for the university's survival. As regards the running of the
university, it was precisely this frequent lack of interest, sometimes
verging on negligence, which is the worst fault that can be imputed
to the senate, far more detrimental to the institution than its
connivance at certain abuses and its favouritisms, which though
rather unpleasant were typical of the age. Quite apart from its
dealings with the senate, the university often had dealings with the
financial authorities and the governor, the king's representative in
the state of Milan. On some occasions, the university also had direct
contacts with the central powers of the Empire, in Madrid, and with
the king of Spain himself.

Even the complex relationships between the *Studium* and the
Pavia community were affected by the general condition of the state.
These relationships were characterized by a series of increasingly
frequent clashes, followed by periods of collaboration, then irrecon-
cilable rivalries, followed by converging interests, and finally followed by sharp invective, offset by exaggerated praise.[82] When seen
from the community's point of view, this apparent schizophrenia
reveals a certain consistency, marked by the city's interests. For a
city like Pavia, the university was a source of prestige, as well as
headaches. Not being exceptionally important as an economic,
political, religious, or military centre, Pavia was known and
esteemed in particular for its cultural vitality, thanks to the *Studium*.
At the same time the presence of the university members brought
significant economic benefits to the city, stimulating commercial
activities and enlivening the property market. For these reasons the
community not only tolerated the existence of the university, but
even tried to defend it and where possible to increase its prosperity,
insofar as this coincided with the interests of the city. Other aspects
of university life were, however, disadvantageous or, at least, not
accepted by the community, which hence radically changed its
attitude towards the university. This helps to explain the attempts to
reduce university exemptions, the city's resentment at the disorder
caused by the students, and the insistent requests for harsher
measures in dealing with them.[83] In a nutshell, the city was trying to
keep the economic advantages and good image that the *Studium*

gave it, while eliminating the aspects that were harmful to it such as the fiscal inequalities and the disruption of public order.[84]

7. Conclusion

Having analysed the fiscal position of the University of Pavia, it is only natural to see whether it was a unique case in the Italian and European university environment, or whether, on the contrary, other universities had similar experiences. The reply is far from simple for various reasons. Perhaps the greatest difficulty for a thorough comparative survey lies in the limitations of the extant secondary material which is often generic and too condensed, and which basically regards medieval universities only in their cultural and institutional aspects.[85] The references to fiscal privileges are not lacking, but refer in particular to the provisions laid down in the statutes, and not their actual implementation or their evolution over a period of time. Moreover, though widely distributed among European universities, fiscal privileges were not (and could not be) identical everywhere, since the conditions of the *studia* were different just as the fiscal systems of the various countries were different. Finally, to avoid excessive oversimplification it is appropriate to distinguish between those fiscal disputes which were the result of fiscal discrepancies and sometimes the cause of open hostility towards certain university members,[86] and more intense, harsh, and persistent conflicts characterized by systematic attacks against university fiscal privileges *per se*, which were carried on with determination until some exemptions were rescinded. Every fiscal battle is part of its own local context and has several original characteristics, which can be reduced to a single cause only with great difficulty. Despite this it is possible to make a few comparisons, which to a certain extent help us to understand the Pavia fiscal position more fully.

As regards the early modern period, cases of heated fiscal disputes are documented as are suspensions of university fiscal privileges for varying periods sometimes long, sometimes short. During the course of the fifteenth and the beginning of the sixteenth century the fiscal exemptions of the University of Louvain were repeatedly at the centre of clashes between the members of the university and the community. In 1473 Duke Charles the Bold, fighting against the king of France, ordered his subjects to pay an occasional levy, that the members of the university had to pay, too.[87] Although forced to make some temporary concessions, the University of Louvain kept its fiscal exemptions substantially unscathed, at least until the last twenty-five years of the sixteenth century, when the city (which was extremely loyal to Philip II) suffered the ravages of the war between the Spanish and the Dutch rebels. It was not only fiscal privileges but also the life of the university overall that was upset by the events of those years. On the other hand, the fortunes of the University of Louvain began to improve in the last decade of the sixteenth century, and even its fiscal exemptions regained importance and respect.[88]

In the last years of the fourteenth century and throughout the fifteenth century, the University of Toulouse saw its fiscal privileges threatened but the French kings intervened in their defence.[89] Disputes and violations also affected the fiscal rights of the University of Paris, one of the most prestigious and important in Europe. Already at the end of the fourteenth century various episodes of intolerance against the university's exemptions occurred, but its privileges were confirmed without hesitation by the Pope or the King of France. It was in particular during the Hundred Years War that fiscal strife heightened and the violations by the Parisian authorities and by other powerful authorities in France became much more serious and recurrent. Several restrictions to the enjoyment of university fiscal exemptions were introduced, excluding for example the students who did not actually attend lessons and certain university officials. Even vigilance regarding abuses committed by the members of the university became more severe. However, although the pressure exerted on the exemptions had increased considerably, the French monarchy never failed to stress the right of the members of the university to enjoy fiscal immunities. If the concrete application of these royal orders was often inadequate, it must be stressed that even at times of great crisis for the country, university exemptions were systematically reconfirmed albeit with some limitations. At the end of the war the situation in the University of Paris became relatively more tranquil and, although losing most of their rights and autonomy from state power, the university members regained a certain fiscal security. Their fiscal privileges substantially survived for the entire duration of the *ancien régime*, even though there were further violations, as on the occasion of the payment of the extraordinary taxes imposed by Louis XIV towards the end of the seventeenth century.[90]

The Universities of Paris, Toulouse and Louvain faced disputes and sometimes considerable fiscal restrictions, demonstrating the fact that fiscal conflicts were certainly not negligible problems nor, presumably, limited to a few *studia*. However, these three universities managed to maintain their fiscal privileges for all of their members (and not just the professors or the students), partly thanks to the support given by the state authorities they fell under. But this did not happen in Lombardy, where the students entirely lost their privileged fiscal status and the Milanese authorities did not always defend the privileges of the *Studium* with the necessary determination, partly because they were subject to competing pressures in favour of other educational institutions. On the other hand, besides this basic difference, we also find a very significant similarity between the events in Pavia and the other three universities. As in Pavia, in Paris, Toulouse, and Louvain the most heated fiscal disputes generally occurred in periods characterized by the tensions of war, social conflict or public calamities.[91] All this undoubtedly confirms the important influence of extra-university forces on academic life, and in particular on fiscal matters.

Several observations can be made regarding the fiscal position of several important Italian universities in the sixteenth century. The professors and the students of the University of Bologna retained very wide fiscal privileges throughout the sixteenth century, and very probably in the seventeenth century too.[92] In Naples the members of the *Studium* continued to enjoy their fiscal privileges throughout the seventeenth century.[93] The reform undertaken between 1614 and 1616 by the Viceroy Count of Lemos partially modified the organization of the university, but did not affect its fiscal exemptions.[94] The fiscal position of the University of Naples was clearly different from that of Pavia, even though the kingdom of Naples and the state of Milan were both under Spanish rule and thus shared several features, despite many profound differences. Among these differences which influenced university fiscal conditions, and which it will be appropriate to examine in the future, it is important to recall that the fiscal reform in Lombardy was not paralleled by a similar reform in the kingdom of Naples, even though in Southern Italy the fiscal burden and backwardness of the fiscal system were even greater than those in the state of Milan.

Even the University of Padua could count on conspicuous fiscal exemptions in the sixteenth century.[95] The Padua *Studium*, which together with the Bologna *Studium*, was the richest in traditions, received numerous foreign students and professors in the course of the sixteenth century. To this extent it was unlike the other universities in the peninsula, which gradually lost their international prestige. It was in fact an Englishman by the name of Fynes Moryson, who gave us the unequivocal confirmation that at the end of the sixteenth century the students of the Padua *Studium* enjoyed considerable fiscal privileges. A Fellow of Peterhouse College, Cambridge, in 1590 Moryson undertook a long journey through Europe, in the course of which he meticulously wrote down a vast quantity of details and personal reflections in his diary.[96] Moryson spent three months at the University of Padua at the end of 1593 and the beginning of 1594, and a further three months at the end of 1594 and the beginning of the following year, acquiring as a result a certain insight into the life of the University. Regarding fiscal privileges, Moryson wrote: 'The Vniversity hath great priuileges as in perticular, all Students haue Immunity from tributes during life through the State of Venice.'[97] Moryson himself directly benefited from some of these reductions: 'My selfe retorning from Padoa towardes England, and hauing the testimony of the Vniversity (vulgarly called Matricola) that i was Student thereof was thereby freed from many small payments in that State, as six Soldi demaunded at the Gate of Padoa, and eight Soldi at the gate of Verona, and some Quatrines for the passing of bridges, and the like.'[98] A careful observer of university matters, Moryson also recorded the fiscal exemptions granted to certain members of various German and Dutch universities.[99]

Seen against this background of other Italian and European universities, the sixteenth-century fiscal affairs of the University of Pavia are, though not unique, certainly rather singular, in particular as they are characterized by almost uninterrupted conflict, and by the definitive and total suppression of student exemptions. This drastic and unfavourable outcome differs notably from the cases mentioned above, in which the restrictions of the fiscal rights of university members were only partial or temporary. It is to be hoped that in the near future the development of new research will make it possible to delineate an overview of the real fiscal conditions of European universities during the early modern period, providing sufficient data for a comparative analysis on a larger scale. The theme of university fiscal exemptions certainly deserves greater attention than has been given so far. We believe that a deeper understanding could not only enrich the history of universities, but could also usefully contribute to the study of fiscal matters, which is an important aspect of socio-economic history.

Università di Pavia
Dipartimento Storico Geografico
Sezione di Storia
Strada Nuova 65
27100 Pavia
Italy

REFERENCES

List of abbreviations
AGS = Archivo General de Simancas
ASM = Archivio di Stato di Milano
ASPU = Archivio di Stato di Pavia, Università
BUP = Biblioteca Universitaria di Pavia

1. Cf. Jacques Verger, *Le università del Medioevo* (Bologna, 1982), p. 90; Sven Stelling-Michaud, 'La storia delle università nel medioevo e nel Rinascimento: stato degli studi e prospettive di ricerca', in Girolamo Arnaldi (ed.), *Le origini dell' Università* (Bologna, 1974), p. 188; Pearl Kibre, *Scholarly Privileges in the Middle Ages. The Rights, Privileges, and Immunities of Scholars and Universities at Bologna, Padua, Paris, and Oxford* (London, 1961), p. 325; Jacques Le Goff, 'Les Universités et les pouvoirs publics au Moyen Age et à la Renaissance', in Jacques Le Goff, *Pour un autre Moyen Age. Temps, travail et culture en Occident: 18 essais* (Paris, 1977), p. 207.
2. For the origins of the University of Pavia, see Pietro Vaccari, *Storia dell' Università di Pavia* (Pavia, 1957), pp. 1–35; Beniamino Pagnin, 'L' istituzione dello "Studium generale" di Pavia', in *Discipline e maestri dell' Ateneo pavese* (Pavia, 1961), pp. 17–35; Hastings Rashdall, *The Universities of Europe in the Middle Ages* (2 vols.; Oxford, 1895), i. 106, ii. 53–4.
3. Verger, pp. 75–81, 189–98. See also Stephan d' Irsay, *Histoire des*

universités françaises et etrangères des origines à nos jours (2 vols.; Paris, 1933), ii. 129–33; Rashdall, i, 'table of universities', 10–15, 19–21, ii. 102; Stelling-Michaud, pp. 157–8; Herbert Grundmann, 'La genesi dell' Università nel Medioevo', in Arnaldi, pp. 87–8.

4. Cf. Le Goff, 'Les Universités et les pouvoirs publics', pp. 200–1; Stephan C. Ferruolo, 'The Paris Statutes of 1215 Reconsidered', *History of Universities*, v (1985), 1–14, especially p. 1. See also *Id.*, *The Origins of the University: the Schools of Paris and Their Critics 1100–1215* (Stanford, 1985).

5. Cf. Stelling-Michaud, pp. 177–80; Rashdall, i. 89–177, 271–344, ii. 113–36, 319–61; Alan B. Cobban, *The Medieval Universities. Their Development and Organization* (London, 1975), pp. 48–109; Charles Homer Haskins, 'L'origine delle università', in Arnaldi, pp. 36–9; Verger, *Le università del Medioevo*, pp. 57–77. For Bologna, see also Giorgio Cencetti, 'Studium fuit Bononie', in Arnaldi, pp. 101–51.

6. Cf. Grundmann, pp. 88–9; Rashdall, ii. 22–30, 157–70; Cobban, pp. 25–6, 175; Verger, p. 79. For Naples, see also Francesco Torraca, 'Le origini – L'età sveva', in *Storia dell' Università di Napoli* (Naples, 1924), pp. 1–16; Gennaro Maria Monti, *Per la storia dell' Università di Napoli. Ricerche e documenti* (Naples, 1924), pp. 8–9.

7. Cf. Rashdall, ii. 65–85; Cobban pp. 24–5, 183–4; Richard L. Kagan, *Universidad y sociedad en la España moderna* (Madrid, 1981), pp. 105–6. For Salamanca, see also Vicente Beltrán de Heredia, 'Los orígenes de la Universidad de Salamanca', *La Ciencia Tomista*, 81 (1954), pp. 69–116.

8. For Spain, see Rashdall, ii. 86–107; Cobban, pp. 118, 184–5; Kagan, *Universidad y sociedad*, pp. 105–9. For France, see Rashdall, ii. 179–208; Cobban, pp. 118–19; Jacques Le Goff, 'La conception française de l' université à l' époque de la Renaissance', in *Les Universités Européennes du XIVe au XVIIIe Siècle. Aspects et Problèmes. Actes du Colloque International à l' Occasion du VIe Centénaire de l' Université Jagellonne de Cracovie – 1964* (Geneva, 1967), pt. ii, *La conception des universités au moyen âge et à la Renaissance*, p. 95.

9. Cf. Rashdall, ii. 232–80; Cobban, pp. 118–19, 191–2; Stelling-Michaud, pp. 180–1; Max Steinmetz, 'Die Konzeption der deutschen Universitäten im Zeitalter von Humanismus und Reformation', in *Les Universités Européennes*, pt. ii, pp. 114–27. For Vienna, see also Franz Gall, 'Gründung und Anfänge der Wiener Universität', in *Les Universités Européennes*, pt. i, *Les premières universités de l' Europe centrale au moyen âge*, pp. 48–55. Towards the end of the sixteenth century a young English student who was visiting the Continent noted in his diary that: 'Germany hath very many vniversityes, for after the decay of the Imperiall and Papull power, besydes those of olde founded vpon priuiledges graunted by them, each absolute Prince, and some free Cittyes (which are very many in Germany) haue founded an vniversity in some cheefe Citty of theire Provinces.': Fynes Moryson, *Shakes-*

*peare's Europe. A Survey of the Condition of Europe at the End of the 16*th *Century. Being Unpublished Chapters of Fynes Moryson's Itinerary (1617)* (New York, 1967), p. 306.

10. Cf. Rashdall, ii. 211–32, 283–90. See also the articles about Cracow, Prague, and Pécs in *Les Universités Européennes*, pt. i, pp. 13–47.

11. Cf. Rashdall, ii. 259–63, 290–315; Cobban, pp. 76, 118–20, 192–3. For Louvain, see also Jacques Paquet, 'Bourgeois et universitaires à la fin du Moyen Age. A propos du cas de Louvain', *Le Moyen Age*, lxvii, 3 (1961), pp. 325–40.

12. Cf. Richard L. Kagan, 'Le università in Italia, 1500–1700', *Società e Storia*, 28 (1985), pp. 277–80; Eugenio Garin, 'La concezione dell' Università in Italia nell' età del Rinascimento', in *Les Universités Européennes*, pt. ii, pp. 84–6; Rashdall, ii. 4–5, 31–61.

13. Cf. Dante Zanetti, 'L' Università di Pavia. Note brevi di una storia millenaria', *Pavia economica*, September–December (1977), 15–16. See also Le Goff, 'Les Universités et les pouvoirs publics', pp. 204–5, 213–4; Cobban, pp. 218–34, especially pp. 219–20; Sven Stelling-Michaud, 'Quelques remarques sur l'histoire des universites à l' époque de la Renaissance', in *Les Universités Européennes*, pt. ii, pp. 78–9.

14. Cf. Dante Zanetti, 'Università e classi sociali nella Lombardia spagnola', in *I ceti dirigenti in Italia in età moderna e contemporanea. Atti del convegno di Cividale del Friuli – 1983* (Udine, 1984), pp. 29–30; Vaccari, p. 33; Anna Giulia Cavagna, *Libri e tipografi a Pavia nel Cinquecento* (Milan, 1981), p. 28.

15. 'Senatus (. . .) universitatis quoque papiensis curam habebit, lectores deputabit, et amovebit, salaria constituet, et denique alia faciet, veluti facere consueverat.': 'Constitutiones Dominii Mediolanensis, liber I, constitutio III, De Senatoribus', in *Statuti e ordinamenti dell' Università di Pavia dal 1361 al 1859* (Pavia, 1925), p. 155.

16. Cf. Giacomo Parodi, *Elenchus privilegiorum et actuum publici Ticinensis Studii a seculo nono ad nostra tempora* (Pavia, 1753). See also Maria Carla Zorzoli, *Università, dottori, giureconsulti – L' organizzazione della "facoltà legale" di Pavia nell' età spagnola* (Padua, 1986).

17. Cf. Verger, pp. 67–8; Vaccari, pp. 36–8. Three statutes have come down to us, respectively relating to the law students, the law professors and the professors of arts and medicine. These statutes are published in *Statuti e ordinamenti dell' Università di Pavia.*

18. For the organization of the University of Pavia in the Spanish age, see Zorzoli; Mario Rizzo, 'L' Università di Pavia tra potere centrale e comunità locale nella seconda metà del Cinquecento', *Bollettino della Società Pavese di Storia Patria*, xxxix (1987). On the question of emoluments and salaries in late Mediaeval and Renaissance universities, see Le Goff, 'Les Universités et les pouvoirs publics', p. 204; Cobban, pp. 175–6.

19. Cf. Rizzo, 'L' Università di Pavia tra potere centrale e comunità locale'.

20. For fifteenth-century Pavia, see Dante Zanetti, 'À l' Université de Pavie au XVᵉ siècle: les salaires des professeurs', *Annales E.S.C*, xvii (1962), pp. 421–33. For Florence, see Armando F. Verde, *Lo Studio fiorentino 1473–1503. Ricerche e documenti* (3 vols.; Florence, 1973; Pistoia, 1977), i. 282, 290. For Naples, see Ercole Cannavale, *Lo Studio di Napoli nel Rinascimento. 2700 documenti inediti* (Naples, 1895), pp. 43–81. For Bologna, see Guido Zaccagnini, *Storia dello Studio di Bologna durante il Rinascimento* (Geneva, 1930), pp. 65–6, 84 ff., 196 ff. For Rome, Pavia, Naples, and other Italian universities, see Marina Roggero, 'Professori e studenti nelle università tra crisi e riforme', in Ruggiero Romano and Corrado Vivanti (eds.), *Storia d' Italia – Einaudi* (Turin, 1981), Annali 4, *Intellettuali e potere*, p. 1042. For the German universities, see Cobban, p. 203. For Louvain, see Jacques Paquet, 'Salaires et pré-bendes des professeurs de l' Université de Louvain au XVe siècle', in *Studia Universitatis Lovanium, Faculté de Philosophie et Lettres*, 2 (Leopoldville, 1958).
21. Cf. Rizzo, 'L' Università di Pavia tra potere centrale e comunità locale'.
22. Cf. Zorzoli, pp. 27–9, 46–7, 51, 137–211; Elena Brambilla, 'Il "sistema letterario" di Milano: professioni nobili e professioni borghesi dall' età spagnola alle riforme teresiane', in Aldo De Maddalena, Ettore Rotelli and Gennaro Barbarisi (eds.), *Economia, istituzioni, cultura in Lombardia nell' età di Maria Teresa* (3 vols.; Bologna, 1982), iii. 79–160; Rizzo, 'L'Università di Pavia tra potere centrale e comunità locale'.
23. Cf. Roggero, 'Professori e studenti', p. 1045. For fifteenth-century Padua, see Jacques Le Goff, 'Dépenses universitaires à Padoue au XVe siècle', in *Pour un autre Moyen Age*, pp. 153–4 ('nationalisation, c' est-à-dire tendance a sè limiter, au moins en ce qui concerne les maîtres, à un recrutement local.').
24. For the student nations in general, see Pearl Kibre, *The Nations in the Medieval Universities* (Cambridge, Mass., 1948); Cobban, pp. 151, 183, 191, 213.
25. For the administrative system of the state of Milan, see Domenico Sella, 'Sotto il dominio della Spagna', in Giuseppe Galasso (ed.), *Storia d' Italia – UTET* (Turin, 1984), xi. 21–59; Alessandro Visconti, *La pubblica amministrazione nello Stato milanese durante il predominio straniero (1541–1796)* (Rome, 1913); Salvatore Pugliese, *Condizioni economiche e finanziarie della Lombardia nella prima metà del secolo XVIII* (Turin, 1924), pp. 105–41; Ugo Petronio, *Il Senato di Milano: Istituzioni giuridiche ed esercizio del potere nel Ducato di Milano da Carlo V a Giuseppe II* (Milan, 1972).
26. Cf. Fernand Braudel, *Civiltà e imperi del Mediterraneo nell' etá di Filippo II* (Turin, 1976), 2nd edn., pp. 379–421. For the Spanish Empire and its administration, see John H. Elliott, *La Spagna imperiale 1496–1716* (Bologna, 1982), pp. 182–203, 285–302.
27. Cf. Geoffrey Parker, *The Army of Flanders and the Spanish Road, 1567–*

1659. The Logistics of Spanish Victory and Defeat in the Low Countries' War (London, 1972); Federico Chabod, *Storia di Milano nell' epoca di Carlo V* (Turin, 1971), pp. 5–149; Mario Rizzo, 'Militari e civili nello Stato di Milano durante la secondà metà del Cinquecento. In tema di alloggiamenti militari', *Clio* xxiii, 4 (1987), pp. 563–96, with the bibliography quoted there.

28. Sometimes the *gride* were no more than public notification of private letters sent expressly by the Sovereign to his representative in Milan. On other occasions, they were the result of independent initiatives by the Governor.

29. All this was often worsened by the ambitious, authoritarian and in any case conceited personalities of many Governors. Sons of the most prestigious Castilian families, these men resented the competition of the local authorities. The latter, in their turn, were extremely jealous of their privileges and were certainly not afraid of the Governors. Thus cultural and psychological factors exaggerated the primarily institutional conflict between the Spanish and Lombard parts of the administration.

30. Cf. Enrichetta Lucconi, 'Economia società amministrazione a Pavia "spagnola" 1562–70', degree thesis (Pavia, 1979–80); Maria Clementina Costa, 'Economia società amministrazione a Pavia a mezzo il secolo XVI', degree thesis (Pavia, 1976–7).

31. This was the name given to the heads of local administrations in some Italian states in the early modern period. The term goes back to Roman times.

32. Cf. Domenico Sella, *Crisis and Continuity: the Economy of Spanish Lombardy in Seventeenth Century* (Cambridge, Mass., 1979), *passim*; *Id.*, 'Sotto il dominio della Spagna', pp. 48–59, 119–23; Giovanni Vigo, *Fisco e società nella Lombardia del Cinquecento* (Bologna, 1979), *passim*; Luigi Bulferetti, 'Il problema della "decadenza" italiana', in *Nuove questioni di storia moderna*, (2 vols. Milan, 1981), ii. 803–45; Pugliese, pp. 145–313.

33. These two taxes, introduced in the fifteenth century, were the nub of the Dukes' finances. The horse tax was introduced in 1442 to cover the stabling expenses of the Duke's cavalry. The assignment of the cavalry to the communities was based on haphazard criteria and was sometimes almost casual, not taking into due account the territorial extension of the individual communities, their wealth or their population density. In 1493, this changed when the requirement to provide stabling facilities was replaced by a monetary tax but it was still based on an anachronistic and basically iniquitous division. The origin of the salt tax goes back to the obligation all Lombard communities had to acquire a certain number of bushels of salt. In 1534 Francesco II Sforza, Duke of Milan, converted the compulsory purchase into a monetary tax, ordering all rural communities (but not cities, who thus remained exempt from the

new tax) to pay the *camera* two *soldi* for each bushel which they had
been liable to purchase previously.

34. The *perticato* (from *pertica*, which means 'perch') was a tax on land
measured in perches applied proportionately to the quality of the land.
The *testatico* (from *testa* meaning 'head') was a poll tax, while the
focatico (from *fuoco*, a 'hearth') was a direct tax collected from families.
Finally the *imbottato* (from the verb *imbottare*, meaning 'putting in
barrels') was a tax on the production of wine, grain and other farm
produce.

35. Cf. Rizzo, 'Militari e civili nello Stato di Milano'.

36. 'Diploma dell' Imperatore Carlo IV, 13 aprile 1361', in *Statuti e
ordinamenti*, pp. 3–4. 'Statuimus et etiam ordinamus (. . .) quod
docentes, legentes et studentes ibidem omnibus privilegiis, libertatibus,
immunitatibus et indulgentiis, concessi doctoribus, legentibus, magistris
et scolaribus et presertim in eadem Sacra Pagina in Bononiensi et
Parisiensi Studiis commorantibus, gaudeant et utantur.': 'Bolla di
Bonifacio IX, 16 novembre 1389', in *Statuti e ordinamenti*, pp. 6–7.

37. 'Volentes scolaribus qui amore science facti sunt exules, favores impendere sicut decet, statuimus et ordinamus, quod scolares quoad ipsorum
commoda pro civibus reputentur et quod in veniendo ad civitatem
Papie et redeundo pro ponte et pro bulletis, item pro introitu et exitu
rerum quas deferunt usus sui causa, et non causa mercimonii, solvere
debeant eo modo et prout solvunt cives Papie et non ultra. Insuper
volentes Studium ampliari et ut librorum copia reperiatur, statuimus et
ordinamus, quod omnes, etiam non existentes alicuius facultatis, possint undecumque apportare libros iuris canonici vel civilis ad civitatem
Papie, etiam causa vendendi, sine aliqua solucione gabelle.': 'Statuti
dell' Università dei Giuristi, LXVI, De privilegiis scolarium', in *Statuti e
ordinamenti*, p. 57.

38. 'Constitutiones Dominii Mediolanensis, liber IV, constitutio XVI, De
Gymnasio Ticinensi, et in eo studentium immunitate', in *Statuti e
ordinamenti*, p. 156.

39. Cf. Zorzoli, pp. 36–7, 85–8.

40. 'Lodovico Maria Sforza Duca di Milano, Conte di Pavia etc. concede
larghe esenzioni ed immunità ai Collegi dei Giureconsulti, degli Artisti,
dei Filosofi e dei Medici della città di Pavia, ai loro ufficiali e rispettive
famiglie, 14 gennaio 1496', in *Memorie e documenti per la storia dell'
università di Pavia e degli uomini più illustri che vi insegnarono* (2 vols.,
Pavia, 1877–8), ii. 13–15.

41. AGS, Visitas, 292, fo. 1480v. See also ASM, Studi p. a., 390, c, 20, fo.
5r. A detailed treatment of the feeding habits and related problems of
the time can be found in Dante Zanetti, *Problemi alimentari di una
società preindustriale* (Turin, 1964).

42. AGS, Visitas, 292, fo. 1440r.

43. Cf. Zorzoli, p. 87. See also Le Goff, 'Les Universités et les pouvoirs
publics', p. 203.

44. Cf. Le Goff, 'Les Universités et les pouvoirs publics', p. 207; Kibre, *Scholarly Privileges in the Middle Ages*, pp. 57, 270–1; Haskins, p. 41; Stelling-Michaud, 'La storia delle università nel medioevo e nel Rinascimento', p. 189; Kagan, *Universidad y sociedad*, pp. 234–6; Moryson, *Shakespeare's Europe*, p. 429; Verger, p. 109.

45. ASM, Studi p. a., 390, c, 20, fo. 7r. See also BUP, Miscellanea Ticinensia, iii. 20.

46. This reconstruction of events is based on archive data found in ASM, Studi p. a., 390, c, 1–3, 6–9, 11–17, 20; e 406, a.

47. A petition by the rectors refers to 'il novo carigho dela masina imposta sopra le farine, qual importa circa soldi 16 denari 9 per sacho, et il carigho del dattio del vino, qual importa soldi 4 per brenta, et il carigho deli altri datij novamente dupplicati.': ASM, Studi p. a., 390, c, 1. In a letter to the Governor we find the following: 'Hora essendo per la communità di Pavia, per la nuova imposta delli scudi trecento milla, fatta una additione sopra il datio della Macina, e specialmente soldi quindeci imperiali per caduno sacco di formento oltre l' ordinario; et così anco dupplicati li datij dell' intrata, et poste certe additioni sopra il datio della carne': ASM, Studi p. a., 390, c, 20, fo. 7v.

48. 'Però chi dovesse tener esenti li sudetti dal detto datio, cadauno scolare domandaria la esentione per brente sei di vino et sachi tre formento per loro et suoi servitori, de manera che le puono considerar de quanta importanza saria questa cosa, per che credo non siano manco di boche 800, et non dimancho la vigesima parte di loro, non credo faccia intrar grano ne vino per che la magior parte stano a dozina, o comprano il grano et vino in la città, se parà a qualchuno che faccia casa gli occorerà il predetto grano et vino, de manera che Vostra Signoria puono considerar la confusione che in questo nasceria, et danno alla cesarea camera, o vero a questa città, al uno de quali l' havesse da patir.': ASM, Studi p. a., 390, c, 6.

49. 'Restringendosi alla detta summa de scudi 200, sarebbe cossa di confusione tra essi privilegiati, et non se gli pagarebbe il loro interesse; et non si vede per qual raggione si debba pagar una parte et non l' altra (...) Et perchè si è vociferato come le Signorie Vostre fano dificulta che i scholari quali acomprano vituaglie in Pavia o vero stano a donzena non habbino a sentir commodo alchuno del privilegio del datio del intrata cossa qual si pensa non esser raggionevole. Per tanto pregano essi scholari che le Signorie Vostre voglino levar tal difficultà et committer che loro privilegi sijno integralmente servati come sperano.': ASM, Studi p. a., 390, c, 13.

50. ASM, Studi p. a., 390, c, 15.

51. On May 5 1548 the *Magistrato* wrote to the *Referendario*: 'E' venuto da noi il Magnifico Rettore degli Artisti di quello studio a nome de tutti li Magnifici Lettori Rettori, et Scolari di quello studio, facendone intendere le molte difficultà, che se interponeno nel darli la loro essentione per privarli d' essa: il che ci pare molto inconveniente, et contra la mente

de Sua Eccellentia. Però risolutamente se vi dice et strettamente se vi commette, che debbiate farli rendere el denaro de l' importanza de tale sua essentione et della carne, de tre in tre mesi dandoli o facendoli dare di presente il denaro de l' importanza de tal' essentione delli primi tre mesi dell' anno presente, et a Calende di Luglio prossimo per altri tre mesi, et così de tre in tre mesi in l' avvenire: facendo fare tale pagamento in mano delli suoi consiglieri, cioè delli consiglieri delli Iuristi per li Scolari suoi, et delli consiglieri delli Artisti per li suoi Scolari, et per quello numero d' essi Scolari che essi consiglieri daranno in nota, che sia sottoscritta dalli suoi Rettori debite referendo, che facciano fede sopra el carico della conscientia sua, che effettualmente li Scolari, et suoi servitori, che seranno nominati sopra la nota, che sottoscriveranno ut supra, sono presenti nella Città, et nello studio, et li suoi servitori sono veri servitori, et non furtivi, et così servareti et farete omnino servare, non ostante altre nostre in contrario scritte, et per modo alcuno non gli lasciarete causa di ritornare da noi a dolersi, che non se gli serva questo ordine.': ASM, Studi p. a., 390, c, 20, fo. 10r. Information on the dispute between the *Referendario* and the contractor are found in ASM, Studi p. a., 390, c, 16–17.

52. In February 1580, at the Governor's request, the Senate pronounced itself in favour of University immunities (ASM, Studi p.a., 406, a). Recalling the provisions on which its opinion was based, the Senate affirmed: 'Ipsos vero scholares (. . .) non solum a pedagijs sed etiam a vectigalibus quibuscumque pro rebus ad victum, et vestitum pertinentibus immunes et exempti esse debere, ut eo secure ire, et redire inde possint absque alicuius oneris solutione.' The Senate then recalled the orders of Gonzaga in 1548, 'quibus mandat eam immunitatem tam scholaribus quam doctoribus omnino servari debere.'. The expression 'eam immunitatem' would appear to refer to the total exemption from duties quoted above, and hence it could be argued that the immunity extended both to ordinary duties as well as special surcharges. This is only a probability, not a certainty, however.

53. ASM, Studi p. a., 372, 7.

54. The question of the *visitas* still remains almost totally unexplored even today. In the historiography relating to the state of Milan there are few hints about these general inspections, and those that do exist are essentially brief passages or general descriptions, which do not derive from any direct knowledge of the documentary material. Here however are the main titles: Chabod, *Storia di Milano*, pp. 324, 411, 420–2; Sella, 'Sotto il dominio della Spagna', pp. 22, 39–41; Petronio, *Il Senato di Milano*, pp. 98–101, 175–80; Aldo De Maddalena, 'Malcostume e disordine amministrativo nello Stato di Milano alla fine del Cinquecento', *Archivio Storico Lombardo*, iii (1963), pp. 261–72; Federico Chabod, 'Usi e abusi nell' amministrazione dello Stato di Milano a mezzo il Cinquecento', in *Studi storici in onore di Gioacchino Volpe* (2

vols.; Florence, 1958), i. 94–194. The latter is the only true study really investigating the records of a *visita*. Given the slightness of the secondary literature, I would like to quote the title of my degree thesis: Mario Rizzo, 'Senato, comunità locali, corporazioni, Ateneo pavese nella "visita general" di don Luis de Castilla (1581–87)', degree thesis (Pavia, 1984–5), *passim* and especially pp. 23–30.

55. See Rizzo, 'L' Università di Pavia tra potere centrale e comunità locale'.

56. In the eleventh *responsio* the Senate wrote: 'Quod neglectis, et fere abrogatis privilegis ad nihilum reciderit, hec eadem Academia Ticinensis, affirmari vix posse creditur, cum, et magnus ad eam confluat, ac confluxerit semper studiosorum numerus, et quae illi concessa sunt privilegia, ut pote in corpore iuris conscripta, non tam abrogata, quam coangustata dici possint, quaestorum aerariorum istius status ita cogente ob publicas necessitates imperio. Quod si quid propterea pristinae amplitudinis amisit, id omne ad notissima bellorum incommoda referendum est, quibus Gallia haec Cisalpina tamdiu exarsit, ea namque adhuc perdurare certum est, tametsi bellum Dei optimi maximi benignitate finem acceperit, postquam exhaustis Fisci loculis, nec adempte immunitates scholasticis restitui, nec sat digna professoribus honoraria persolvi potuere.': AGS, Visitas, 294 bis, pp. 16–17; see also p. 19.

57. According to one witness, the critical phase went back to the governorships of Del Vasto and Gonzaga, i.e. between 1538 and 1555 (see AGS, Visitas, 292, fo. 1442v). Don Alfonso d'Avalos d'Aquino, Marquis of Vasto, came to Milan as a Governor in February 1538 and died in his post in March 1546. After a six-month interim governorship by the Milan military commander, Charles V sent Ferrante Gonzaga to Milan in October 1546, who remained there until March 1555, when he was removed from the post by order of the King: cf. Giuseppe Gargantini, *Cronologia di Milano dalla sua fondazione fino ai nostri giorni* (Milan, 1874).

58. In the fourteenth *responsio* the Senate wrote: 'Si ademptae Rectoribus, et toti scholasticorum Universitati bellicis perturbationibus immunitates, restitutae pacatis rebus non fuerunt, id Senatui vitio verti non potuit, qui ita fieri debere, et postulavit, et etiam flagitavit, sed illis quidem, qui Quaestoris offitio praefecti, publicorum proventuum studiosi usque adeo fuerunt, ut quicquam his comminui nefas semper esse crediderint, absque speciali Regiae Maiestatis assensu, quamvis non comminutos, sed etiam longe auctum iri Senatus censeret, quod tantum vectigalibus incrementum accessisset, ex maiori Scholarium numero, qui ad eam ex externis quibusque regionibus, confluxissent, ut fructus, immunitatis huius damnum exuperaret.': AGS, Visitas, 294 bis, p. 19. The external documentation to the *visita* confirms that the Senate effectively had backed the restoration of student immunities on at least one occasion in 1580 (see ASM, Studi p. a., 406, a).

59. On the *visita* see AGS, Visitas, 292, fos. 1409r, 1440r. Previously, in the memorandum quoted above dated November 11 1572, Graziano wrote: 'Quando sopra gl' altri fiorì lo studio di Pavia e di Bologna, fu per i privilegi concessi a scolari forestieri, et il ritornare li privilegi porta gran bene et utile a la Città et al paese di Pavia, nè può tornar in danno del Principe o de la sua Camera, essendo ch' è 1 numero de Scolari aumentato, lascia maggior copia de denari al Paese, che non fanno pochi scolari col pagare et perdere le loro immunità.': ASM, Studi p. a., 372, 7.

60. See Lawrence Stone, 'The Size and Composition of the Oxford Student Body 1580–1910', in *Id.*, *The University in Society* (2 vols.; Princeton, 1974), i; James K. McConica, 'Scholars and Commoners in Renaissance Oxford', in *The University in Society*, i; Kagan, *Universidad y sociedad*, pp. 240–74; Mark H. Curtis, 'The Alienated Intellectuals of Early Stuart England', *Past and Present*, 23 (1962), pp. 25–43; Joan Simon, 'The Social Origins of Cambridge Students, 1603–1640', *Past and Present*, 26 (1963), pp. 58–67; Lawrence Stone, 'The Educational Revolution in England 1560–1640', *Past and Present*, 28 (1964), pp. 41–80; Walter M. Mathew, 'The Origins and Occupations of Glasgow Students, 1740–1839', *Past and Present*, 33 (1966), pp. 74–94; David Cressy, 'The Social Composition of Caius College, Cambridge 1580–1640', *Past and Present*, 47 (1970), pp. 113–15; Richard L. Kagan, 'Universities in Castile 1500–1700', *Past and Present*, 49 (1970), pp. 44–71; *Id.*, 'Law Students and Legal Careers in Eighteenth-Century France', *Past and Present*, 68 (1975), pp. 38–72. For criticism of these studies, see Fritz K. Ringer, 'Problems in the History of Higher Education: A Review Article', *Comparative Studies in Society and History*, 19 (1977), pp. 239–55; Lawrence Stone, 'Comment', ibid., pp. 256–7; Fritz K. Ringer, 'Counter-Comment', ibid., p. 258; Roger Chartier and Jacques Revel, 'Université et société dans l' Europe moderne: position des problèmes', *Revue d' Histoire Moderne et Contemporaine*, xxv (July–September 1978), pp. 353–74; Laurence W. B. Brockliss, 'Patterns of Attendance at the University of Paris, 1400–1800', *The Historical Journal*, 21, 3 (1978), pp. 503–44.

61. Cf. Rizzo, 'L' Università di Pavia tra potere centrale e comunità locale'.

62. Cf. AGS, Visitas, 292, fos. 1412r–v and 294 bis, p. 19; ASM, Studi p. a., 372, 7 and 390, c, 6 and 456. See also Moryson, *Shakespeare's Europe*, p. 431; Zanetti, 'L' Università di Pavia', pp. 17–18.

63. Cf. AGS, Visitas, 292, fo. 1440r. See also Chabod, *Storia di Milano*, pp. 275–6; Le Goff, 'Les Universités et les pouvoirs publics', pp. 206–7; Paquet, 'Bourgeois et universitaires', pp. 326, 338.

64. 'La qualità et eccellenza dei lettori credo sia quella che fa in più reputatione il studio, e crescere il numero de i scholari', observed a professor questioned by the *Visitador* (see AGS, Visitas, 292, fo. 1412r). He then added: 'Dopoi li studij de Turino, et Piacenza impediscono

assai che non vengano tanti scholari. Et anchora mi pare che si dottorano a Milano.': Il che tutto cede in danno et diminutione di questo studio, et si doveria advertire che li Gesuiti che ciò fanno non lo facessero.': AGS, *Visitas*, 292, fos. 1412r–v. See also Kagan, 'Le università in Italia', p. 278.

65. Cf. Maria Carla Zorzoli, 'La formazione dei giuristi lombardi nell' età di Maria Teresa: il ruolo dell' università', in De Maddalena, Rotelli and Barbarisi (eds.), *Economia, istituzioni, cultura in Lombardia*, pp. 743–69; *Id.*, *Università, dottori, giureconsulti*, pp. 213–322, 377–8; Brambilla, 'Il "sistema letterario" di Milano', pp. 79–160.

66. Cf. Nino Cortese, 'L' età spagnola' in *Storia dell' Università di Napoli*, pp. 227–32; Zaccagnini, *Storia dello Studio di Bologna*, pp. 162–4, 303–4; Roggero, 'Professori e studenti', pp. 1056–9; Kagan, 'Le università in Italia', pp. 307–10; *Id.*, *Universidad y sociedad*, pp. 84–100, 203–4; Brockliss, 'Patterns of Attendance at the University of Paris', pp. 516–18, 541, 543.

67. AGS, Visitas, 292, fos. 1408r–1409r, 1429r, 1440v.

68. Cf. Zorzoli, *Università, dottori, giureconsulti*, pp. 88–9.

69. ASM, Studi p. a., 390, c, 20, fo. 3r.

70. ASM, Studi p. a., 390, c, 20, fos. 6r, 11r–v.

71. ASM, Studi p. a., 406, a and 390, c, 20, fos. 6r–7v.

72. ASM, Studi p. a., 390, c, 20, fo. 7v.

73. ASM, Studi p. a., 406, a.

74. Here is the text of the order sent to the *Magistrato Ordinario*: 'Magnifici spectabiles, fideles dilecti, Conquesti sunt apud nos Professores Ticinensis Gymnasij, quod et si eis competat iure ipso Communi immunitas ab omnibus oneribus extraordinarijs, etiam patrimonialibus, eaque comprobata ab olim Principibus istius nostri Status Mediolani presertim a Duce Francisco Secundo Sfortia de anno Domini Millesimo quingentesimo trigessimo tertio fuerit observata perpetuo, tenore etiam temporibus bellicis, vos tamen motos quorumdam ordinum iussionibus, et precipue vuormatiensium per Serenissimum, et Invictissimum Romanorum Imperatorem Carolum Quintum patrem nostrum colendissimum factorum de anno Domini millesimo quingentesimo quadragessimo quinto, quae nuperrime, ut in isto Statu Mediolani observarentur, eadem Maiestas Caesarea mandavit, ea ratione adductos, quod pro arcendo bello in sub alpinis Regionibus vigente, fuerit indicta onera extraordinaria subditis Mediolanensis Dominij, et ob id vos velle eos cogere ad huiusmodi onerum solutionem, nulla habita ratione suorum privilegiorum, ac antiquae suae possessionis; Nobis propterea humillime supplicando, ut predictam eorum immunitatem, ac Bidellorum generalium ipsius Ticinensis Gymnasij conservare, ac tueri, nostra Regia, et Ducali benignitate dignaremur, Nos vero eorum petitione benigne admissa, considerantes, quod agitur de ijs, quae publicam utilitatem concernunt, ut etiam, et ipsi professores ardentiores fiant ad

propaganda litterarum artiumque omnium liberalium studia eis
annuere omnino decrevimus. Tenore igitur presentium vobis commit-
tendum esse duximus serio iniungentes, ut eorum professorum ac
Bidellorum generalium immunitatem, ac exemptionem iuxta seriem
eorum privilegiorum, ac seu antiquum eorum morem, et possessionem
omnino observetis, et ab omnibus ad quos spectet, et in futurum
spectabit quomodolibet inviolabiliter observari faciatis, omni penitus
impedimento molestia, ac contraditione cessante, non obstante etiam
tempore belli, nec obstantibus aliquibus legibus, si quae forsan contrario disponere videretur, aut alijs ordinibus, quibuscumque precipue
vuormatientibus, ac denique alijs omnibus in contrarium facientibus,
etiam si talia essent, de quibus specialis, et individua mentio hic
facienda esset. Quibus omnibus, et singulis eorum tenores hic pro
sufficienter expressis, et insertis de verbo ad verbum habentes, quo ad
hunc effectum, tantum, ex certa nostra scientia, motu proprio et
potestatis plenitudine derogamus, et derogatum esse volumus, et iube-
mus expresse, quia sic est enixe mentis nostrae, Decernentes has nostras
vim habere secundae, tertiae, et peremptoriae iussionis, quam vos
tanquam ex enixa nostra voluntate procedentem executioni mandabi-
tis.': ASM, Studi p. a., 406, a. As we said, the royal order is dated July
23 1555; transmitted to the Governor on January 9 1556 it was sent to
the Senate for the customary approval which was given on January 15
of the same year.
75. ASPU, Acta Studii Ticinensis, 34/1578.
76. ASM, Studi p. a., 406, a.
77. ASPU, Acta Studii Ticinensis, 34/1586; ASM, Studi p. a., 391.
78. ASM, Studi p. a., 406, a. See also Zorzoli, *Università, dottori, giureconsulti*, pp. 27, 38–43.
79. Cf. Zorzoli, *Università, dottori, giureconsulti*, pp. 41, 47; Zanetti,
Università e classi sociali, p. 234.
80. AGS, Visitas, 292, fo. 1409r.
81. Cf. Vigo, *Fisco e società*.
82. Cf. Zorzoli, *Università, dottori, giureconsulti*, p. 329; Le Goff, 'Les
Universités et les pouvoirs publics', pp. 202, 206–10; Paquet, 'Bourgeois
et universitaires', p. 336.
83. Cf. Rizzo, 'L' Università di Pavia tra potere centrale e comunità locale'.
84. Cf. Paquet, 'Bourgeois et universitaires', p. 325.
85. Cf. Chartier and Revel, 'Université et société dans l' Europe moderne',
p. 353.
86. Cf. Le Goff, 'Les Universités et les pouvoirs publics', p. 207; Kibre,
Scholarly Privileges in the Middle Ages, p. 326.
87. Cf. Paquet, 'Bourgeois et universitaires', pp. 332–8; Léon Van Der
Essen, 'Un conflit entre le duc Charles le Téméraire et l' Université de
Louvain à propos du paiement des impôts en 1473', *Bulletin de la
Commission Royal d' Histoire. Académie Royale de Belgique*, xc (1926),
pp. 242–57.

88. Cf. Léon Van Der Essen,'Les tribulations de l' Université de Louvain pendant le dernier quart du XVIe siècle', *Bulletin de l' Institut Historique Belge de Rome*, 2 (1922), pp. 61–86; R. Van Uytven, *Stadfinanciën en stadsekonomie te Leuven van de 12e tot het einde der 16e eeuw* (Brussels, 1961), pp. 83–92, 648, 656, 660, 713.

89. Cf. Juliette Puget, 'L' Université de Toulouse au XIVe et au XVe siècles', *Annales du Midi*, xlii (1930), pp. 351–4.

90. Cf. Kibre, *Scholarly Privileges in the Middle Ages*, pp. 99–101, 129–32, 135–7, 148–9, 158–63, 168, 173–4, 179–226, 326–30; Jacques Verger, 'The University of Paris at the End of the Hundred Years' War', in John W. Baldwin and Richard A. Goldthwaite (eds.), *Universities in Politics. Case Studies from the Late Middle Ages and Early Modern Period* (Baltimore and London, 1972), pp. 56–9, 60–4; *Id.*, *Le università del Medioevo*, p. 223; Cobban, p. 95; Laurence W. B. Brockliss, 'The University of Paris in the Sixteenth and Seventeenth Centuries', doctoral diss. University of Cambridge, 1976, pp. 38–45.

91. Cf. Kibre, *Scholarly Privileges in the Middle Ages*, pp. 326–7; Paquet, 'Bourgeois et universitaires', p. 332; Van Der Essen, 'Un conflit entre le duc Charles le Téméraire et l' Université de Louvain', pp. 242–4; Puget, pp. 351–2.

92. Cf. Kibre, *Scholarly Privileges in the Middle Ages*, pp. 21, 40, 52; Zaccagnini, *Lo Studio di Bologna nel Rinascimento*, p. 151.

93. Cf. Cannavale, *Lo Studio di Napoli nel Rinascimento*, pp. v, xii; Gennaro Maria Monti, 'L' età angioina', in *Storia dell' Università di Napoli*, pp. 21, 73, 103–4; Riccardo Filangieri di Candida, 'L' età aragonese', in *Storia dell' Università di Napoli*, pp. 151–9, 172–4; Nino Cortese, 'L' età spagnola', in *Storia dell' Università di Napoli*, pp. 236, 249, 362.

94. An eminent politician, patron of such celebrated writers as Cervantes, Lope de Vega and Gongora, and a man of letters himself, *don* Pedro Fernandez de Castro, seventh Count of Lemos, held the prestigious post of Viceroy in Naples from 1610 to 1616. He had studied in the University of Salamanca, and was inspired by it when promoting the reform of the Naples *Studium*. Cf. *Diccionario de Historia de España* (2 vols.; Madrid, 1968), 2nd edition, ii. 682; Cortese, 'L' età spagnola', pp. 255–64.

95. Cf. Kibre, *Scholarly Privileges in the Middle Ages*, pp. 56–8, 65, 75, 83–4.

96. Cf. the introduction by Charles Hughes to Moryson, *Shakespeare's Europe*, pp. i–xlvi; Dante Zanetti, 'Dalle note di viaggio di Fynes Moryson: le attività accademiche e la vita materiale all' Università di Padova alla fine del Cinquecento', in *Studi in onore di Gino Barbieri* (3 vols.; Pisa, 1983), iii. 1651–75.

97. Moryson, *Shakespeare's Europe*, p. 432.

98. Moryson, *Shakespeare's Europe*, p. 129. See also *Id.*, *An Itinerary Containing His Ten Yeeres Travell through the Twelve Dominions of*

Germany, Bohmerland, Sweitzerland, Netherland, Denmarke, Poland, Italy, Turky, France, England, Scotland & Ireland (3 vols.; Glasgow, 1907), i. 380.
99. For the University of Leiden, see Moryson, *Shakespeare's Europe*, pp. 375–6 ('Each Student hath yearely 80. Stoupes of wyne allowed free from assise or tax, and six vessels of Beare at two shillings sixpence starling the vessel lesse then the ordinary price the Cittizens pay, and they with whome they dyett, take this allowance in theire names and right, besydes that the Professors and Students are free from all other taxes and tributes.'). For the German universities, see Moryson, *An Itinerary*, i. 11 ('From Luneburg I returned to Hamburg, whither I and my company might have had a Coach for 4 Dollors but we misliking the price hired a waggon for three Lubeck shillings each person to Wentzon, three miles distant from Luneburg. Here the Duke of Lunebergs territory ends, to whom each man paid a Lubeck shilling for tribute, my selfe only excepted, who had that priviledge because I went to study in the Universities.'); and p. 119 ('From Breme we passed foure miles through wild fields, yeelding some little corne, and thicke woods, and in sixe houres space came to a poore house; where each man paid for dinner five lubecke shillings. Here those which carried any merchandise paid tole: and one man having a packe which a man might carry on his shoulder, paid foure lubecke shillings for the same: but all that goe to study in Universities, or be no Merchants, are free from this imposition.').

Experimental Science in Early Nineteenth-Century Oxford

G. L' E. Turner

I

The use of demonstration apparatus to teach experimental philosophy on Baconian principles was practised by individual lecturers at Oxford and Cambridge universities at the end of the seventeenth century. This method of teaching, generally called the lecture-demonstration, brought about the widespread popularization of science during the eighteenth century, a phenomenon recognized in 1789 by James Keir, when he wrote:

The diffusion of a general knowledge, and of a taste for science, over all classes of men, in every nation of Europe, or of European origin, seems to be the characteristic feature of the present age.[1]

Such wide dissemination resulted in a demand for scientific instructions that gradually became institutionalized. The University of Oxford, because of its examination structure, was comparatively slow to include the experimental sciences formally in its curriculum. There is, however, plenty of evidence that science lectures outside the classical curriculum were enthusiastically attended by a considerable proportion of undergraduates during the eighteenth, and the first half of the nineteenth centuries.[2]

The beginnings of the lecture-demonstration may be seen in the early years of the Royal Society, at the meetings for which Robert Hooke was required to produce 'three or four considerable experiments' on each occasion. William Whiston, Newton's successor in the Lucasian chair at Cambridge, taught the Baconian programme using much apparatus, and his published and illustrated lectures set a pattern for over a century. Because of his supposed heretical views,

Whiston left Cambridge for London in 1710 and continued his lecture courses at a coffee-house in conjunction with an instrument maker.[3] The man who began the study of experimental philosophy at Oxford was the Scot, David Gregory, who became Savilian professor of astronomy in 1691. Three years later he was followed from Edinburgh by John Keill, who started in 1700 a lecture course using apparatus, some of his own devising. John Desaguliers, another highly successful lecturer in London, had spent three years lecturing at Hart Hall, Oxford, before his move to the capital in 1713.[4]

The tradition established by Newton remained strong at Cambridge, and the importance of natural philosophy was confirmed in 1782 by the establishment of the Jacksonian professorship of natural and experimental philosophy. The will of the founder actually required an abundance of 'fact' to be demonstrated. The first holder of the chair was Isaac Milner, who, with his successor, Francis Wollaston, concentrated his teaching largely on chemistry. Wollaston began by lecturing alternately on experimental philosophy and chemistry, performing, it is said, no fewer than 300 experiments annually.[5] He handed over his apparatus to Samuel Vince, who was elected in 1796 to the Plumian professorship of astronomy. Vince advertised a course of lectures in 1793 which placed a strong emphasis on mathematics and astronomy, but which relied heavily on practical demonstrations.[6]

Extremely large cabinets of apparatus were acquired by all the lecture-demonstrators, whether at the universities in Britain, Holland, France, and the United States, or by the travelling lecturers such as Stephen Demainbray or Benjamin Martin, and many others.[7] A third class of cabinet 'maker' came from the nobility and wealthy landowners. John Stuart, third earl of Bute (1713–92), was a patron of science as well as of literature and art. He had a very extensive collection of minerals, a library of books on natural history and botany, and a cabinet. This was sold at auction in 1793 in 255 lots, the number of individual items being around 500.[8] The chemical laboratory was sold separately. When the future King George III was born in 1738, Lord Bute was twenty-five, and from the evidence of his correspondence was at that time interested in scientific apparatus. It seems clear that in science as well as in matters of state, Lord Bute had a profound influence on the king. At Kew, the king kept a cabinet of experimental apparatus that numbered well over a thousand items, and much of it remains today in the London Science Museum.[9] Stephen Demainbray was employed as the lecture-demonstrator to the royal household during the 1750s, and he it was who expanded the collection. Eventually, when it was decided to discontinue the maintenance of the Kew Observatory, where the instruments were kept, the mechanical and physical apparatus was sent in 1841 to King's College in the Strand, for use in 'a general course of Experimental Philosophy'. A permanent base for lecture demonstrations was provided in London by the foundation in 1799 of the Royal Institution by the American, Benjamin Thompson, known as Count Rumford. The prospectus by Rumford, published in 1799, bore the title: *Proposals for forming by subscription in the Metropolis of the British Empire, a Public Institution for diffusing the knowledge and facilitating the general introduction of Useful Mechanical Inventions and Improvements, and for teaching, by Courses of Philosophical Lectures and Experiments, the application of Science to the Common Purposes of Life.*[10] This foundation is world famous for its lecture-demonstrations that continue to the present, and for the fundamental and far-reaching research of Humphry Davy and Michael Faraday, to mention but two. After the departure of Rumford in 1802, Davy came to the Royal Institution from Thomas Beddoes' Pneumatic Institution at Bristol, and his lecture-demonstrations were an immediate success, so much so that the dry and far more theoretical lectures of Thomas Young had to be terminated.[11]

The model was soon followed by the London Institution, founded in the City of London in 1805, which became the largest and best endowed of the new style of scientific establishments of the early nineteenth century.[12] Its purpose was to 'promote the diffusion of Science, Literature, and the Arts'. Large premises were built, which were opened in 1819. In the first year there were five different series of lectures, the subject of one being 'Elements of chemistry and its connection with arts and manufactures', while another was entitled 'Experimental philosophy; or the useful application of natural philosophy to society by hydrostatics, mechanics, optics, and the use of the steam-engine and other machines'. This was just the sort of syllabus taught at Oxford by Charles Daubeny from 1822 (chemistry), and by Stephen Rigaud from 1810 (experimental philosophy), although the location in the Ashmolean building was minute and ill-equipped compared with London.

The skills required by technical advances during the early nineteenth century made it necessary for the workers to understand the principles that underlay the tasks required of them. Craft training had in earlier times been undertaken by the apprentice system of the guilds, but the new era demanded a new approach. A most important movement was that of the Mechanics' Institutes, which became so popular that it has been estimated that 610 existed in England and Wales by 1850.[13] What is regarded as the inspiration for these institutes is the Andersonian Institution at Glasgow, where George Birkbeck, professor of natural philosophy, gave lectures for artisans in around 1800.[14] The first that was formally founded was the Edinburgh School of Arts in 1821, which is now the Heriot-Watt University. Here courses on chemistry, natural philosophy, applied chemistry and applied mechanics were given. The London Mechanics' Institute was founded in 1823 and continues today as Birkbeck College, in the University of London. The syllabus comprised chemistry, mathematics, hydrostatics, applied chemistry, astronomy and electricity.

In North America, the first lecture-demonstrations were performed at Harvard College from 1727.[15] At the end of the century, from 1790, Transylvania College at Lexington, Kentucky, acquired apparatus, a considerable purchase being made in Paris in 1821.[16] Similar purchases, worth $1446, were made by the college of Charleston, South Carolina, at much the same period.[17] In the 1830s, the Seminary at Quebec bought a consignment of apparatus in London, and later sent staff on buying trips to Paris.[18] These few examples will serve to indicate that a pattern similar to that in Europe was being repeated elsewhere.

II

The world in which the University of Oxford found itself by the beginning of the nineteenth century was, then, full of enthusiasm for science and technology, from the king down to the artisan. In 1800, the university introduced examinations in classics and mathematics, but not in the physical sciences at that time. The latter were included in the examination system in 1849 with the formation of the honour school of Natural Science.[19] It was this that brought about the building of the new University Museum in Parks Road, the Gothic pile erected between 1855 and 1860.[20] Here were housed the science professors (with the exception of those at the Botanic Garden), with their departments of chemistry, experimental philosophy, mineralogy, geology, medicine, and anatomy, plus an observatory for the Savilian professor. Thus the Ashmolean Museum building in Broad Street was finally replaced as the scientific institution of the university.

The Ashmolean Museum, opened in 1683, contained the chemical laboratory and the lecture room for natural history, as it was named.[21] It was in this room that the lecture-demonstrations were performed from 1714 by John Whiteside (1714–29), James Bradley (1730–60), Nathaniel Bliss (1760–2), Thomas Hornsby (1763–1810), and Stephen Rigaud (1810–32).[22] Occasionally an anatomy was performed and teaching of mineralogy and geology was done from time to time. Pressures for the expansion of teaching in science, and for space to hold the growing collection of the museum, forced a series of departures from the old building. The University Press which occupied the Clarendon Building, paid for out of the profits of Lord Clarendon's *History of the Rebellion*, moved to a new site in 1830, leaving space that was taken by the geological collections and by the cabinet of physical apparatus. The initiative was taken by Rigaud, whose title was reader in experimental philosophy, and William Buckland, reader in mineralogy from 1813, and also reader in geology from 1818.

The critical years for Oxford were around 1790, when Thomas Beddoes was lecturing on chemistry. He published a devastating criticism of the Bodleian Library in 1787, pointing out a neglect to keep up with scientific journals and scientific books, comparing it unfavourably with some small-town subscription libraries.[23] From his extensive travels, Beddoes thought the Bodleian to be one of the worst conducted public libraries in Europe, unfit for an institution instructing the youth of a great commercial state. Beddoes himself lectured diligently on chemistry, his income being the students' fees from those who voluntarily attended the lectures. Beddoes was a friend of Dean Jackson of Christ Church, one of the instigators of the new examination system of 1800. Beddoes left Oxford in some disgust in 1792 for Bristol, where he set up the Pneumatic Institute, employing there the young Humphry Davy.

The last of the old style chemical readers was Robert Bourne, who succeeded Beddoes in 1794. His approach to the teaching of chemistry was schoolmasterly and practical: to provide students who were to become MPs, landed gentry, manufacturers, and physicians, with a basic knowledge of the properties of matter. But a change had been initiated by the criticisms of Beddoes, and three new professorships were established under the will of George Aldrich. They were filled in 1803 as follows: professor of the practice of medicine, Robert Bourne; professor of anatomy, Christopher Pegge; professor of chemistry, John Kidd. It is interesting to note that the stipend of the chemical professor was augmented by a grant from the Crown in 1817, as had been the stipends of the readers in experimental philosophy and mineralogy in 1813.

A leading reformer and chemist of the first half of the nineteenth century was Charles Daubeny, who, after taking his BA at Oxford, graduated in medicine in Edinburgh in 1818. Elected to the Aldrichian chair of chemistry in 1822, he immediately asked for and received a large grant to buy chemical apparatus and he tried to undertake research.[24] He added to himself the Sherardian chair of botany in 1834, and in 1840 the chair in rural economy, so had both the means and incentive to move out of the basement of the Ashmolean Museum to a large new building erected at his own expense adjacent to the Botanic Garden. This move occurred in 1848. Daubeny was a campaigner and pamphleteer endeavouring to counter the 'neglect' of science in Oxford, and to promote the educational value of chemistry, apart from its economic value. He was in at the foundation of the British Association for the Advancement of Science, and was responsible for inviting it to meet at Oxford in 1832.[25]

Turning now to what is today called physics, we find Thomas Hornsby, an eighteenth-century pluralist, who collected successively the positions of Savilian professor of astronomy 1763, Radcliffe Observer 1772, Sedleian professor of natural philosophy 1782, and Radcliffe Librarian 1783. He also conducted the lecture-demonstrations on experimental philosophy in the Ashmolean, having a collection of apparatus that was valued in 1790 at £375.[26] The course continued in the tradition of the beginning of the eighteenth century, the subject headings being mechanics, optics, hydrostatics, and pneumatics. Hornsby had reacted quickly to new discoveries, and in 1785 he delivered a course specifically on 'The different Kinds of Air', based on the discoveries of Priestly. It included the theory of balloons, and one should give the Ashmolean extra credit here, because the assistant in the chemical laboratory, James Sadler, had the previous year been the first Englishman to go up in a balloon.[27] On the death of Hornsby in 1810, Rigaud took over the teaching of experimental philosophy. He had, in fact, been groomed to take over, and had deputized when Hornsby was ill. It is also not surprising that he had experimental skills, since he was the grandson of Stephen Demainbray, the King's astronomer at Kew and the man responsible for keeping the cabinet of physical apparatus there. Rigaud held the Readership till his death in 1839 concurrently with the Savilian chairs first of geometry and then of astronomy, to which he moved in 1827. However, when Robert Walker succeeded Rigaud in 1839 he did so as reader in experimental philosophy in its own right, not now annexed to a Savilian professorship. The full independence and importance of the subject was finally shown by the conversion to a professorship in 1860, the date of the opening of the new University Museum. In effect, Walker was the first professor of physics at Oxford. A quantity of apparatus still exists from his era, and may be seen in the Museum of the History of Science.

III

The account given above has brought in the names of those who lectured in the physical sciences during the first half of the nineteenth century, and has outlined the movements from building to building as pressures increased. What remains to be done is to consider just what was taught, and how far new developments in science were reflected. Also, how did the audience of young men react to the teaching? Here a great deal of work needs to be undertaken. Because experimental sciences were not part of the examination structure, either before or after 1800, there are no statutes to look to for guidance. But there were syllabuses printed for the use of those who attended the lectures, and some of these may be found. They indicate a very traditional scheme of experimental demonstration, one which changes hardly at all until the 1790s, after which some of the new discoveries are inserted. A mathematical approach is apparently deliberately avoided, because few students had sufficient knowledge of mathematics. But there are some lecturers who add some geometrical or analytical workings in smaller type or as an appendix. Rigaud, obviously a very careful and systematic man, who had an informed interest in the history of science, collected syllabuses, and his collection, including some of his own, is now kept (thanks to a donation by the Radcliffe Trustees in the 1930s) in the Oxford Museum of the History of Science. Examples of Rigaud's printed syllabuses for 1812, 1813, 1821 and 1824 exist, increasing in extent from 20 to 48 pages. The main headings are: introduction, matter and motion, mechanics, hydrostatics, pneumatics and hydraulics, meteorology, optics, electricity, magnetism. Intercomparison shows that novelties and new experiments from the world outside were constantly added in. To pick out a few, one may name the polarization of light, Fraunhofer's spectra, the Italian Professor Amici's reflecting microscope, wave theory, Captain Kater's pendulum experiments and the new standards of length, and the friction of carriages on rail-roads. It is clear that this was the period when natural and experimental philosophy was turning into the physics and applied physics of the end of the nineteenth century. While the teaching of the classics that led to the examinations for the BA was in the hands of the colleges, the university provided unexamined courses in the sciences that attempted to satisfy the intellectual curiosity aroused by the 'taste for science' held to be the 'characteristic feature of the present age'.

The trouble was not the capabilities of most of the science professors, but the attitudes to science of those college men who governed the teaching and the examining for the BA in Literae Humaniores. And the Rudiments of Religion allowed no discretionary power to the examiners; failure here meant no degree at all. As adherence to the Thirty-Nine Articles was required, the university was attacked for religious exclusiveness. Criticizing Oxford, *The Athenaeum* wrote, in 1834, 'The universal spread of extra-academical knowledge, and the tone of utilitarianism ... render it impossible that the course of education, which was the admiration of our forefathers, can be tolerated by their descendants'.[28] The editor pointed out that science was intimately mixed up with the prosperity and well-being of society, and should be included in every course of liberal education. He went on to complain that Oxford neither encouraged science among its students nor paid its professors as much as 'a pittance sufficient to meet even the most moderate views in life'.

Indeed, critics were all around, even inside the university, and the reason for this was that fundamental changes were taking place. As Arthur Engel puts it, in his even-handed essay, crucial to the intellectual conflicts and institutional changes at Oxford in the first half of the nineteenth century was the question of whether the university was to provide careers for academic men, and, if so, what sorts of careers these were to be in terms of functions, status, and income.[29]

It must be remembered that, at the beginning of the century, the Oxford don was by profession a clergyman, not a teacher, for holy orders and celibacy were conditions for holding a fellowship. The pattern was that after ten years or so the fellowship was relinquished for a living generally in the gift of the college, and probably for marriage. But by the end of the nineteenth century, most college fellows were career teachers, spending all their lives in the profession. While this crucial change was in process of taking place, the increasing strictness introduced into the examination statutes led to a growing number of private coaches.[30] This may provide a reason for the complaint that professorial lectures were ill-attended. Professor Daubeny wrote a letter to Convocation on 24 February, 1839, to explain that he had cancelled his chemical course because of low numbers.[31] His high point had been in 1828 with 45 auditors; in 1840, after his cancelled year, he could muster a total of only 10 auditors: 4 graduates, 3 undergraduates, and 3 who were not members of the university. Daubeny thought that professorial lectures ought to be compulsory, and that they should be examined and an attendance certificate issued. Yet another cause for the turning away from science was the onset of the Tractarian movement from 1830 onwards: in the eyes of the Oxford establishment science was just not relevant.

The attitudes within the University of Oxford cannot be completely fathomed by a reading of the statutes, the minutes of the hebdomadal board, or the position papers of those pressing for reform. What is necessary is an investigation into those who did choose to pay up their fee and attend the lectures of the various professors. Attendance registers do, luckily, exist. The late J. M. Edmonds, curator of the geological collections, had amassed a great deal of information on course attendance, and he had also identified most of the names on the registers. His papers have been deposited at the Museum of the History of Science, where they are being edited for publication by the librarian, Mr A. V. Simcock. The brief analysis below is derived from the MSS Edmonds 10–28, but must be taken as preliminary and as an indication only, since the full analysis of the courses is complicated through some being split into parts either in terms of level or in terms of topic. In Tables 1 and 2 the attendance registers of Daubeny's course in chemistry, Rigaud's course in experimental philosophy, Buckland's courses in mineralogy and geology are compared in various ways: total numbers, average per course, the percentage of doctors, MAs, BAs, and undergraduates at each course, and the numbers of non-university auditors. The information is also presented in the form of histograms in Tables A to D.

Of the members of the university who attended the courses, undergraduates accounted for between one-third and two-thirds in all four subjects. The geology course attracted the largest audience, the chemistry the smallest. On the other hand chemistry always attracted the largest number of non-university auditors (albeit a handful). Geology lost its appeal dramatically after 1840, collecting in that year only 11, to be compared with the 87 of 1824, a peak. Mineralogy doubtless had less of a theological interest, hence lower numbers. It went down from 1834, with only 9 auditors compared with a peak of 57 in 1817. Chemistry hit a low point from 1839 to 1844, when there began a slight rise. But experimental philosophy maintained a very steady interest through all its varied topics and for the whole of the period considered, 1811 to 1831 (i.e., to the end of the Ashmolean period before the move to the Clarendon Building).

Table 1 Attendance at Oxford Science Lectures, 1818–48

Subject	Chemistry	Exp. Philos.	Mineralogy	Geology
Years of Lectures	1822–49	1818–39	1814–49	1814–49
Number of Courses	29	40	33	33
Total Attended	439	725	818	1055
*Average Attendance per Course	15	18	25	32
Average Attendance of Non-University Auditors per course	2.7	1.2	1	1

*Rounded figures

Table 2 Average Attendance at Oxford Science Lectures, 1818–48

Subject	Chemistry		Exp. Philos.		Mineralogy		Geology	
Years of Lectures	1822–49		1818–39		1814–49		1814–49	
	N	%	N	%	N	%	N	%
Doctors	0.2	1	0	0	0.5	2	1	3
MA	5.3	35	1.9	10	7.7	31	7.8	25
BA	4	26	4.7	26	7.6	31	7.9	25
Under-graduates	5.6	37	11.6	64	9	36	15.2	47
*Total	15	100	18	100	25	100	32	100

*Rounded figures

The peak attendance was 40 in 1818, Lent term, and the lowest 4 in 1827, Easter term, but this is a freak figure. The large numbers of MAs attending is noticeable in all courses, except experimental philosophy (which attracted not a single Doctor).

These figures may be compared with those taken from the register of James Bradley's lectures on experimental philosophy from 1746 to 1760. The average attendance was 37 at a course, and the charge was three guineas, giving an average income of £116. As two or three courses were given each year, the income was appreciable. During the fifteen-year period, 1221 men attended Bradley's lecture-demonstrations.[32] This is a remarkable number considering the size of the university, for around 1750 the average yearly matriculation was just 200, so in fifteen years some 3000 would have entered, thus showing that about one third of the university came to hear and view Bradley's performance.

Little is known about the disposition of the lecture rooms in the Ashmolean Building. A visitor from Denmark made a simple drawing of the horseshoe seating in three tiers during his 1777 visit, but that is all.[33] A lithograph of 1823 is probably the only representation of a lecture given during the first half of the nineteenth century. It shows William Buckland demonstrating fossils to a gathering of 52 in a room on the western side of the upper ground floor of the Ashmolean. An analysis of the auditors has been

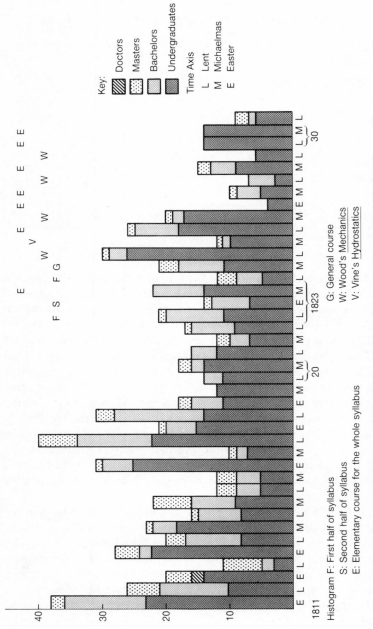

Figure A: *Courses in Experimental Philosophy, S. P. Rigaud 1811–31.*

Histogram F: First half of syllabus   G: General course
          S: Second half of syllabus   W: Wood's Mechanics
          E: Elementary course for the whole syllabus   V: Vine's Hydrostatics

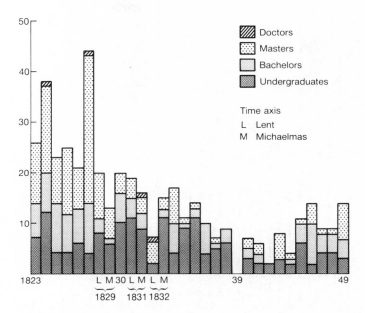

Figure B: *Courses in Chemistry*, C. G. B. Daubeny, 1823–49.

published in 1976 by the late J. M. Edmonds and the late J. A. Douglas. They showed that the 52 in the audience was composed of 3 heads of colleges, 19 Fellows, 8 BAs not Fellows, 19 undergraduates, and 3 who were not members of the university.[34] The disposition of the facilities for science teaching on the first floor of the Clarendon Building in rooms vacated by the Press is known from a drawing, dated May 1831, done by the architect Sir Robert Smirke.[35] The space given over to Rigaud is labelled: 'Room for Lectures on Natural and Experimental Philosophy'. There is a U-shaped 'Reader's Table', four cases on the walls for apparatus, a book press, and a special table marked: 'Model of Steam Engine'.[36] The lecturer behind his bench faced nine rows of benches, the back five being raked, and Smirke has labelled this part: 'Seats for about 70 Students'. Clearly, there were expectations for the future, for Rigaud had only reached a total of 40 auditors in 1818, and for his elementary course in 1830 had an audience of not more than 14. In the opposite corner of the building was a space marked by Smirke as a 'Room for Lectures on Geology and Mineralogy', which had

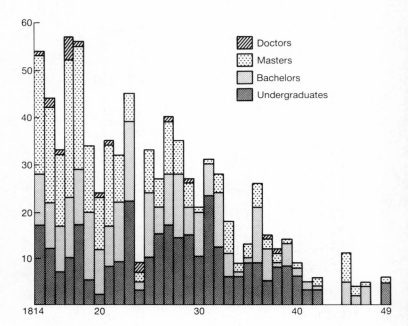

Figure C: *Lectures in Mineralogy*, W. Buckland, 1814–49.

benches to seat around 65. This space was needed in 1834, but audiences soon fell away (Table D).

It has been shown that during the first half of the nineteenth century there was a very considerable demand for scientific knowledge at all levels throughout the Western world. Should Oxford, as one of the premier universities, have welcomed the teaching of science more wholeheartedly than it did? Or was Oxford right to hold it at arm's length, as had been done with the older professions of medicine and law, by sending students who had completed their course in the *litterae humaniores* to the London hospitals and the Inns of Court? Oxford saw itself as a guardian of knowledge and not a creator of it: science would be better done elsewhere. Reforms in teaching methods, incentives to make students work, the proper design of examinations, these were necessary and were carried out. But if a university is there to train the mind of the young is it also necessarily obliged to fill it with practical facts? If today many universities do just that, is it right to assume that all should do so,

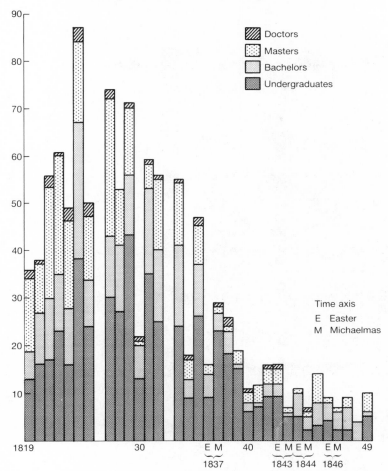

Figure D: *Lectures in Geology and Palaeontology*, W. Buckland, 1819–49.

and that this is a fair criterion by which to judge the University of Oxford 150 years ago?

History of Science and Technology Group
Imperial College of Science
Sherfield Building
London SW7 2AZ

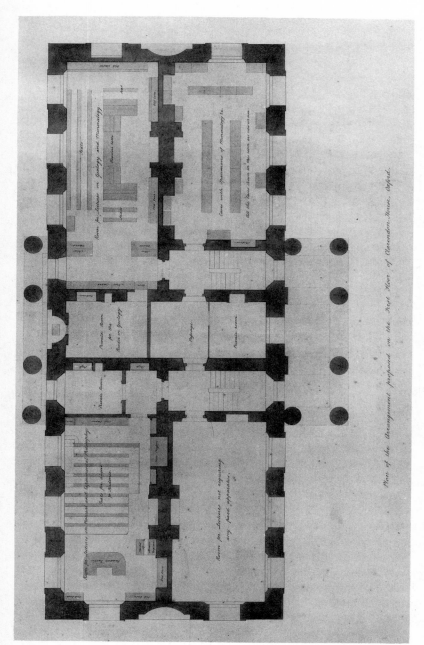

Figure 1: Plan of the Arrangement proposed on the first floor of the Clarendon House, Oxford, 1831.

REFERENCES

1. J. K. [James Keir], *The First Part of a Dictionary of Chemistry &c* (Birmingham, 1789), p. iii.
2. G. L'E. Turner, 'The Physical Sciences', in L. S. Sutherland and L. G. Mitchell (eds.), *The History of the University of Oxford* v. The Eighteenth Century (Oxford, 1986), 659–81.
3. W. Whiston, *Memoirs of the Life and Writings of Mr William Whiston, containing memoirs of several of his friends also* (London, 1749), 135ff, 235ff.
4. See the Preface to J. T. Desaguliers, *A Course of Experimental Philosophy* (2 vols.; London, 1734–44). Nicholas Hans, 'The Rosicrucians of the Seventeenth Century and John Theophilus Desaguliers, the Pioneer of Adult Education', *Adult Education*, 7 (1935), 229–40.
5. R. T. Gunther, *Early Science in Cambridge* (Oxford, 1937), 81.
6. Ibid., 82f.
7. A. E. Musson and E. Robinson, *Science and Technology in the Industrial Revolution* (Manchester, 1969), especially chapter 1; Jean Torlais, 'La Physique expérimentale', in René Taton (ed.), *Enseignement et diffusion des sciences en France au XVIIIᵉ siècle* (Paris, 1964), 619–36; J. R. Millburn, *Benjamin Martin: Author, Instrument-maker and 'Country Showman'* (Leyden, 1976); Geert Vanpaemel, 'Experimental Physics and the Natural Science Curriculum in Eighteenth Century Louvain', *History of Universities* vii (1988) 175–96.
8. G. L'E. Turner, 'The Auction Sale of the Earl of Bute's Instruments, 1793', *Annals of Science*, 23 (1967), 213–42.
9. J. A. Chaldecott, *Handbook of the King George III Collection of Scientific Instruments* (London, 1951).
10. Reprinted in *Proceedings of the Royal Institution*, 6 (1872).
11. References to Beddoes are in Dorothy A. Stansfield, *Thomas Beddoes M.D. 1760–1808: Chemist, Physician, Democrat* (Dordrecht, 1984); Turner, 'Physical Sciences', 666–8; A. V. Simcock, *The Ashmolean Museum and Oxford Science 1683–1983* (Oxford, 1984), 35, n. 91; and D. A. Stansfield and R. G. Stansfield, 'Dr Thomas Beddoes and James Watt: Preparatory Work 1794–96 for the Bristol Pneumatic Institute', *Medical History*, 30 (1986), 276–302. On Young, see G. N. Cantor, 'Thomas Young's Lectures at the Royal Institution', *Notes and Records of the Royal Society*, 25 (1970), 87–112.
12. J. N. Hays, 'Science in the City: The London Institution, 1819–40', *British Journal for the History of Science*, 7 (1974), 146–62.
13. Musson and Robinson, *Science and Technology*, 181f.
14. T. Kelly, *George Birkbeck* (London, 1957).
15. I. Bernard Cohen, *Some Early Tools of American Science: An Account of the Early Scientific Instruments ... in Harvard University* (Cambridge, Mass., 1950).

16. Leland A. Brown, *Early Philosophical Apparatus at Transylvania College* (Lexington, Kentucky, 1959).

17. Barbara Hughes, *Catalog of the Scientific Apparatus at the College of Charlston: 1800–1940* (Charlston, South Carolina 1980).

18. Paul Carle, 'Le cabinet de physique et l'enseignement des sciences au Séminaire de Québec', *Cap au Diamant* (revue de la Société historique de Québec), autumn 1985.

19. F. Sherwood Taylor, 'The Teaching of Science at Oxford in the Nineteenth Century', *Annals of Science*, 8 (1952), 82–112. On the development of the examination system at early nineteenth-century Oxford generally, see M. Curthoys, 'The Early Years of the Oxford Examination System, 1800–1830' (unpublished conference paper).

20. A. V. Simcock, *The Ashmolean Museum and Oxford Science 1683–1983* (Oxford, 1984).

21. R. F. Ovenell, *The Ashmolean Museum 1683–1894* (Oxford, 1986).

22. Turner, 'Physical Sciences'; Simcock, *Ashmolean Museum*.

23. E. Robinson, 'Thomas Beddoes, M.D., and the Reform of Science Teaching in Oxford', *Annals of Science*, 11 (1955), 137–41; Thomas Beddoes, *A Memorial Concerning the State of the Bodleian Library* (Oxford, 1787).

24. For many references, see Simcock, *Ashmolean Museum*, 36, n. 93. For the chemistry laboratory and equipment, much of which remains, see C. R. Hill, *Museum of the History of Science: Catalogue 1 Chemical Apparatus* (Oxford, 1971); the Appendix has the 1823 inventory of apparatus bought with a vote of £200.

25. Jack Morrell and Arnold Thackray, *Gentlemen of Science: Early Years of the British Association for the Advancement of Science* (Oxford, 1981).

26. Bodleian Library, MS Top. Oxon. c.236, ff. 3–13; R. T. Gunther, *Early Science in Oxford*, xi (Oxford, 1937), p. 195.

27. J. E. Hodgson, 'James Sadler of Oxford, Aeronaut, Chemist, Engineer and Inventor', *Transactions of the Newcomen Society*, 8 (1927–8).

28. *The Athenaeum*, No. 344, 31 May 1834, in a review of Daubeny's Inaugural Lecture on the Study of Botany.

29. Arthur Engel, 'The Emerging Concept of the Academic Profession at Oxford 1800–1854', in L. Stone (ed.) *The University in Society* (2 vols.; Princeton, N.J., 1975) i. 309.

30. Ibid., p. 313.

31. Charles G. B. Daubeny, 'To the Members of Convocation', 24 February 1839 (Papers relating to the Proceedings of the University, 1839 Bodleian Library, Oxford).

32. Turner, 'Physical Sciences', 673. Bradley's attendance list in the Bodleian Library, MS Bradley 3, is printed in R. T. Gunther, *Early Science in Oxford*, xi, 359–98.

33. Kongelige Bibliotek, Copenhagen, MS Ny kgl. Saml. 377 e, f.67r (The Travel Diary of Thomas Bugge, 1777). The plan, redrawn, is reproduced in Simcock, *Ashmolean Museum*, opposite p. 12.

34. J. M. Edmonds and J. A. Douglas, 'William Buckland, F.R.S. (1784–1856) and an Oxford Geological Lecture 1823', *Notes and Records of the Royal Society*, 30 (1976), 141–67.

35. Oxford University Archives, UD/11/1/2 & 3.

36. Most likely the working model of a James Watt beam engine by Watkins & Hill of London, now on display in the Museum of the History of Science. It is illustrated in colour on Plate VIII in G. L'E. Turner, *Nineteenth-Century Scientific Instruments* (London, 1983).

The Threat to Authority in the Revolution of Chemistry

Hans-Georg Schneider

The authority of any teaching rests on the certainty of the knowledge which it conveys. If the knowledge expounded by recognized scholars to their students should prove to be of dubious reliability, then their authority is open to question. Thus, scientific progress and changing theories are natural enemies of authoritarian tradition.

This is especially so when knowledge develops at a faster rate than usual, for instance during scientific revolutions.[1] In such cases, the traditional authorities cannot cope with the upheavals taking place, but at the same time are unable to prevent them from happening. Attempts to stop them lead to a break with tradition. Then begins a phase when social ties are loosened and the 'scientific community' is transformed and formed anew. When authority is re-instated, it is on a new basis. A path is laid for a new way of thinking which unfolds itself within the community espousing it, so that a new tradition emerges. Its continuing success dictates further research and teaching, and as its credibility increases, so does the authority of those who represent the new tradition.

The political and the chemical revolutions of 1789

It was already clear to those living at the time of the French revolution of 1789 that parallel to the political upheavals which they were experiencing, far-reaching changes were taking place in the field of knowledge and learning.[2] These changes were not confined to political, moral, and religious spheres, but affected several areas of the natural sciences as well. Above all, in 1789, with the publication of A. L. Lavoisier's (1743–94) *Traité Elémentaire de Chimie*,[3] chemistry experienced the decisive revolutionary change which has since become known as the 'revolution of chemistry'.[4] The spectacular change in chemical knowledge which took place at that time led to the overthrow of alchemy and to the foundation of chemistry as a modern science. It is significant that the process did not take place in the quiet academics' studies and chemical laboratories, but with full publicity. It was accompanied by a level of public interest which is seldom accorded to science. John Playfair (1748–1819) wrote as early as 1782 in England: 'Chemistry is the rage in London at present'.[5] In 1786, in Paris, Antoine François de Fourcroy (1755–1809) stated that 'Everyone nowadays is studying chemistry'.[6] Three years later, he added: 'Never has a scientific subject aroused so much general interest, and never has it been more widely studied than chemistry in the past twelve years.'[7] Another French chemist of the time, Christophe Opoix (1745–1840) went as far as to note that: '. . . even the ladies have been keen frequenters of the lecture-halls, without feeling out of place.'[8]

The originator of this surge in public interest in chemistry was first of all, as already mentioned, the Frenchman Antoine Laurent Lavoisier. In his presentations at the Paris Academy, in his numerous publications, and not least through strident propaganda, he heralded a fundamental disruption in chemical knowledge.[9] He predicted that the chemistry of the future would have a radically altered shape. Lavoisier claimed that the then dominant 'Phlogiston Theory' of the German Georg Ernst Stahl (1659–1734) was a mere fanciful notion, which had to be overthrown. In his view, it was based on an illusion, since the 'phlogiston' introduced into chemistry by Stahl did not exist in reality. It was nothing more than a prejudice. As such, it had fuddled the thinking of chemists and prevented progress. If, however, chemists were prepared to give up the notion of 'phlogiston' and to rely only on facts, then it was possible to found a true science of chemistry.

This message of Lavoisier's fell on fertile soil. It awoke a new hope, to which old promises attached themselves, promises of the kind which had previously been associated with alchemy. The recognized authorities in the field were startled by the inflammatory tone of Lavoisier's announcements. Was everything that they had previously taught nonsense? The phlogiston theory was the first theory ever to gain universal recognition in chemistry. Its influence on eighteenth century thinking was virtually unchallenged for decades. What did this theory purport? Where were its strengths and what were its weaknesses?

Phlogistic and Antiphlogistic Chemistry

The chemistry of the second half of the eighteenth century was characterized by a convergence and separation of currents and developments, which were in part a realization of centuries-old traditions, and in part pointers to future discoveries. As is the case with most nodal points in historical processes, it contained a variety of incomparable parts, all striving for a new order—characterized by the simultaneity of aspects which were in part left-overs from the past, and in part heralds of a new future. Alchemy's influence on chemistry had not yet been overcome. Even into the eighth decade of the eighteenth century, the Aristotelian elements, earth, water, air, and fire were a widely recognized concept. At the same time, Newton's theories of cosmology and gravitation were spreading from Great Britain to the European continent. The latter's decisive influence on chemistry lay in its linking of the proof of chemical substances to their weight. Any chemical substance, in so far as it really exists, has mass, and because it has mass it must also have weight. The ascertainment of weight was thus raised to the status of a criterion for the existence or non-existence of chemical substances. The application of this criterion led to the improvement of measurement techniques and in particular to the development of more accurate scales and balances in the late eighteenth century. Another consequence of the weight criterion for the existence of chemical substances was the exclusion of a number of obscure influences which had been said to have an effect on chemical reactions. Improved quantification through measurements, weighing and calculations led to the banishment of the 'spirits', 'beings', and 'principles' whose evocation had been characteristic of alchemy.

Eighteenth century chemistry was also significantly influenced by 'pneumatic' chemistry, which was concerned with the investigation of the chemical nature of the various 'airs'. Instigated primarily by Joseph Black (1728–99) in Edinburgh, these investigations eventually led to the discovery of the gases carbon dioxide, hydrogen, oxygen, and nitrogen. This was accompanied by the recognition that gases take an active role in chemical reactions and can also change from a gaseous state to a solid one, and vice versa.

The one concept which intellectually held together all these different currents of alchemy, Newtonian physics, improved quantification in chemical research and particularly in pneumatic

chemistry, was the Phlogiston Theory with its prime influence on
chemical thinking throughout the eighteenth century. It claimed that
all combustible materials contained a particular substance, phlogiston, which conferred their combustible quality on them. The process
of combustion was explained by the phlogiston leaving the burning
substance; combustion ended when no phlogiston remained in the
burning material. According to this concept, a burning candle over
which a jar is placed will go out after a short while because the air in
the jar will be so enriched with phlogiston, i.e. so 'phlogistonised',
that no more phlogiston can leave the candle. Therefore the candle
goes out, unless the jar is opened and fresh air let in to absorb more
phlogiston.

After the discovery of oxygen by Joseph Priestley (1733–1804) in
1774, Lavoisier proposed that instead of phlogiston leaving a
burning substance, the burning substance absorbed oxygen which
reacted with it chemically. Lavoisier was thus able to explain the
weight gained by burning metals, a phenomenon inexplicable using
the phlogiston theory. Lavoisier even succeeded in proving experimentally that the weight of the oxygen used up was equal to the
weight gained by the metal. Lavoisier's oxygen theory of combustion was quickly accepted by many, and even taken up by some
chemists who in other respects remained true to the concept of
phlogiston.

The accuracy and success of Lavoisier's oxygen theory of combustion was matched by its inaccuracy and misdirection with regard to
his theory of heat. Lavoisier claimed that heat was a chemical
substance, which he classed as an element. He named it 'Calorique'
and put it at the top of his list of chemical elements. This erroneous
concept of the nature of heat contaminated all the rest of his
chemical theory, since energy transformations are present in all
chemical reactions. Lavoisier also believed that oxygen was the basis
of all acids, a kind of acidifying principle ('principe acidifiant')
present in all acids and giving them their acidic qualities. This bold
speculation was wrong too. There are acids which do not contain
oxygen, for example, hydrochloride acid.

Owing to these aggravating errors in Lavoisier's theory, as well as
to other contradictions and difficulties which cannot be elaborated
on here, the new chemistry, known as 'antiphlogistic' chemistry as
from 1785, met with strong opposition. When Lavoisier claimed in
1785 that phlogiston was a mere illusion, not necessary for the

explanation of chemical processes, and could be dispensed with, the fight between phlogistians and antiphlogistians broke out in earnest. Its climax came in the years 1789/90, and it faded out in the mid-nineties. By 1795 the battle of opinions had been decided in favour of the new chemistry. The chronological parallels between the chemical revolution and the French revolution are thus obvious. The immediate prehistory of the French revolution also began in 1785 with the so-called 'necklace-trial', which exposed the French court to public ridicule. In 1789 came the outbreak of revolutionary violence. By 1795, the revolution in the narrow sense of the word was finished. The institution of the directorate began a phase of relative stability on a republican basis. In the case of both revolutions, in politics as well as in science, the decisive breakthroughs thus took place parallel to each other, on a wave of emotional and violent public outburst.

Public Attention and Public Embarrassment

Lavoisier's success in putting over his new views was aided by the fact that, at that time, there was considerable public interest in chemistry primarily directed at the theory of combustion. This and the question of whether or not phlogiston existed were at the centre of public attention. Thus the French chemist Jean Claude Delamétherie (1743–1817) reported in 1789: 'The nature of combustion is nowadays one of the most important questions in chemistry, and one could even say that the solution to all other problems that concern us depend on the solution to this one.[10] In Germany, the well-known chemist Friedrich Albrecht Carl Gren (1760–98) admitted in 1790: 'Among all the newer systems, . . . no other has aroused so much attention as that of Herr Lavoisier in Paris'.[11] His compatriot, Lorenz Crell (1744–1816) mentioned the 'great attention' being paid to 'this important matter'.[12] Sigismund Friedrich Hermbstädt (1760–1833), Lavoisier's most important supporter in Germany, spoke in 1792 of the 'sensation caused by Herr Lavoisier's system among German chemical opinion'.[13]

In the face of these developments, the phlogistian authorities, who still held to the old theory, were put to a hard test. What had previously been universally acknowledged and accepted was now forced into retreat, and suddenly needed defending. Those who were not only involved in research, but who also taught chemistry and needed to instruct their students and answer questions, were put into a difficult position. The public nature of the 'battle of the two sects'[14] was often painfully embarrassing to them, undermining their authority as teachers and making it impossible to inspire confidence in their text-books. For example, Georg Friedrich Hildebrandt (1764–1816), professor of chemistry at Erlangen, complained that the argument was having a negative effect on reputations: 'As long as it remains undecided whether we should believe in a combustible element or an oxygen element, unbiased chemists, excellent authors and teachers are unable to explain anything without coming up against uncertainties; the more often one attempts to give a lecture on chemistry in general, and keeps coming upon sentences where one can hardly speak without favouring one system or the other, the more unpleasant it becomes.'[15] He added: 'It is therefore desirable that the matter should be decided'.[16] Johann Bartholomäus Trommsdorff (1770–1837) found himself in a similar situation. He was a professor at the University of Erfurt, but also ran a private training institute for apothecaries, and so felt the problems of teaching particularly acutely. In 1793, he wrote: 'The battle between the two opposing systems is now being fought too fiercely for it to last very long, and I hope that some verdict will soon be arrived at'.[17] In 1794, Trommsdorff was still declaring that he would acquaint his audience with both systems: 'I am neither a phlogistian nor an antiphlogistian; I know and respect both systems, and make them both known to my audiences'.[18] Two years later, however, when the public battle had been decided in favour of the antiphlogistic side, he too admitted 'that it does more harm than good to attempt to portray two or more systems side by side in one textbook'.[19] Instead, he made the new theory the basis of his teaching. Heinrich Friedrich Link (1767–1851) also spoke of the necessity of having 'at least one well-founded theory, for the sake of both teacher and pupils'.[20] Likewise, Wilhelm August Lampadius (1772–1842) agreed that 'I must make use of one system in my lectures'.[21] Eventually, 'after a difficult struggle within myself, and by overcoming constant doubts',[22] he persuaded himself to accept the antiphlogistic system.

One widely recognized phlogistian authority in German chemistry at the time was Johann Christian Wiegleb (1732–1800). He too called for the battle to end, in order to avoid lasting damage to chemistry. Wiegleb explained: 'Two parallel but totally opposed theories can only damage science if they continue to compete with one another. One of them must be overcome once and for all, and repudiated in future'.[23]

Uncertainty about the issue led not only to a proliferation of minor theories, but to an immense diversity of chemical terms. These increased confusion rather than helping to facilitate the understanding of chemical facts. One chemist wrote to Trommsdorff's *Journal der Pharmacie*, groaning: 'Heavens, how many languages will German chemists start to speak next? we already need dictionaries to understand each other. What an immense amount of work is needed for any beginner to find his way through this tangled mass of words'.[24]

Faced with this background of confusion, linguistic chaos, and the feeling that a secure foothold and certitude were nowhere to be found, many chemists instinctively sought for guidance and simplicity; there was an increasing longing for order and a new certitude. This longing gradually strengthened their preparedness to come to a mutual agreement, despite continuing doubts and reservations. Professor Hildebrandt of Erlangen, for example, expressed his 'heartfelt longing for a final decision'.[25] Friedrich August Westrumb (1751–1819) admitted to the readers of the *Chemische Annalen* that he hoped 'that the bright day will soon dawn' when the fight would be over. 'I will be full of warm thanks and true admiration', said Westrumb,' for the men who can show us the pure light of truth and lead us out of the maze of hypothesis . . . and back onto the level . . . path of nature'.[26] The Dutch apothecary Petrus Johannes Kasteleyn (1746–94) expressed his longing for certainty and consistency in words which convey a vivid feeling of a desire bordering on despair for a return to certitude: 'For my own part, I will grab at any kind hand able to lead me just one step nearer to certainty and truth; without worrying whether it was leading me towards the path of Stahl or Lavoisier'.[27]

What could show more clearly how the proliferation of scientific theories and the lack of common ground between the basic conceptions were felt as a deficiency? The dissolution of the unity which had existed under the phlogiston theory had left a social and intellectual vacuum which did not even allow the different parties to speak the same language when discussing the same subject. The lack of common ground on which to corroborate conflicting arguments, the consequent instability, and the lack of an established climate of opinion made the scholars involved feel so unsure of themselves that this state of affairs could not endure for long. Any indication of a pending agreement or of a rapprochement of views was acclaimed optimistically. In 1796 Wilhelm August Lampadius at last saw 'the forthcoming return of that happy time when the most assiduous scientific work can once more be undertaken by all nations in peace and undisturbed.'[28] The new *Chemische Annalen*, he wrote to Lorenz Crell, 'are already showing us the dawn of such a time'. This must, he said, 'be welcome to all scientists'.[29] Hermbstädt too observed 'a gradual rapprochement of scientific principles'.[30] This made a 'very pleasing impression' on him, since he believed that such a reconciliation 'will greatly contribute to scientific progress'.[31]

The same was happening on an international level; here too the realization that opinions were once again becoming reconciled was welcomed. For instance, Fourcroy declared in 1796: 'Between Herr Gren and the French chemists, at least, harmony now reigns with regard to the acceptance of all new facts, which is a very happy omen for progress in chemistry. Their example seems set to be followed by a large proportion of the German chemists.'[32]

Conformity and the Establishment of a New Authority

The longing for certitude, harmony, and mutual acknowledgement led the chemists involved in the conflict developing new ways of relating to each other, based not on intolerance and conflict, but rather on agreement and mutual respect. It became usual to refer to colleagues to consolidate antiphlogistic teachings. In France, for example, Armand Seguin (1765–1835) called on 'such worthy chemists as Dr. Black, Messieurs Lavoisier, de la Place, Pictet, Landriani etc. etc.'[33] to declare that the new chemistry could not possibly be wrong. Likewise, Fourcroy stated: 'Many famous professors have already adopted the teaching presented in this book. Messieurs de Morveau, van Marum and Chaptal have shown themselves to be convinced by its truth and simplicity'.[34]

Madame Lavoisier had been the first to use this means. As early as 1788, when she published her French version of Kirwan's *Essay on Phlogiston* (London 1787), she made clever use of the almost instinctive persuasive power of the approval of a large number of people for a particular point of view. In the preface of her translation, she wrote: 'The majority of French scholars have followed the example of this ardent defender of the new teaching. Monsieur de la Place, Monsieur Monge and Monsieur Meusnier, in numerous memoranda; Monsieur de Fourcroy, in his lectures in Paris; Monsieur Chaptal in Montpellier; Monsieur le Febvre de Guineau, who holds the new Chair of Physics founded by the King at the Collège-Royal. They have all banished phlogiston from their writings and lectures: and the success of their works and the size of their audiences both prove that public opinion is in no way hostile to them.'[35]

Even Lavoisier himself was strengthened in his scientific views in this way. In 1791 he wrote to Chaptal in Montpellier: 'I am receiving letters from everywhere with news of new converts.'[36] The practice of mutual endorsement became so widespread that Fourcroy could soon speak of a 'reunion of the French chemists'.[37] Of course, the antiphlogistians most often referred to their leader, Lavoisier. The fact that his fame had spread throughout Europe not only added to the persuasive power of his arguments, but also strengthened the credibility of his followers. Again and again the statement that this or that idea came from the famous Lavoisier unmistakably implied that this alone was a powerful indicator of truth. It was then only a short step from wide acceptance of Lavoisier's theories, to the claim that they encapsulated absolute truth. It was a step which the young Seguin, for example, had no hesitation in taking. Seguin, who in 1790 called Lavoisier the 'creator of modern chemistry',[38] wrote the following on the link between acclamation and truth: 'Now that these truths have received the endorsement of time, and are strengthened by the support of practically all the chemists and physicists of Europe, we can say with the greatest confidence that there is no certitude in chemistry which is based on clearer evidence.'[39]

A similar process was taking place in Germany. In Berlin, Hermbstädt, who translated Lavoisier's *Traité Elémentaire* into German, based his defence of the antiphlogistic system mainly on the authority of Martin Heinrich Klaproth (1743–1817). In order to demonstrate that the step he had taken was in no way foolhardy, he named in addition a whole list of other well-known chemists: 'But if my opponents are really inclined to make this criticism, then at least I can pass a part of it onto the shoulders of these worthy men, whose fame is so much greater than mine . . . I refer to Kirwan, Klaproth,

Black, Girtanner, de Morveau, Mayer, Hindenburg, Klügel etc. Nothing is of more importance for the new system than the conversion of someone like Kirwan or Klaproth.'[40]

Altogether, it is clear that the change in attitudes that was taking place was due in no small way to the fact that each author quoted the authority of the other. Since there was no absolutely definite proof either for or against phlogiston, the new ideas were eventually elevated to truths by mutual affirmations and were consolidated into their more permanent form at least to some extent by mutual approval. Occasionally there were also collective references as, for example, when Kirwan, in his *Essay on Phlogiston*, designated German chemists in general as the decisive authority in chemical matters: 'Germany is the place that all newer nations must visit if they wish to perfect their mineralogy and metallurgy, just as the ancients visited Greece in order to improve their rhetorical skills. The Germans and the Swedes have gradually improved and refined the old teaching; and their devotion to it is still immovable.'[41]

These feelings were reciprocated. In 1801, Michael Hube (1737–1807) commented that one significant reason why the new French chemistry had met such opposition in Germany was that anything English had been regarded particularly highly: 'The notorious battle of the antiphlogistians would not have been fought with so much venom in Germany if the well-known figures who set the tone at that time had not been so prejudiced as to admire only that which came from England.'[42] The predisposition which the English and North German chemists felt towards each other was grotesquely linked to the fact that the House of Hanover was then on the throne in England.

In Sweden, an integral part of good scientific manners consisted of extolling the opinions of one's colleagues and eulogizing and praising one another as highly as possible. Johann Gottlieb Georgi (1729–1802), who translated the *History of Iron* by Sven Rinman (1729–1802) into German (Berlin 1785), mentioned this 'custom of the Swedish chemists' in his preface: 'If they are not declared enemies, they exalt each other to the best of their abilities and circumstances.'[43]

The Transition from Personal to Factual Authority

If one takes a broader view of the great changes in knowledge which took place during the chemical revolution in the late eighteenth century, it becomes apparent that the temporary abrogation of authority was due mainly to three factors. Firstly, in the wake of the Enlightenment, the eighteenth century experienced a general questioning of tradition and authority. This happened not only in France, but was the case all over Europe. It simultaneously affected all areas of society. Secondly, another by-product of the eighteenth century Enlightenment was the tendency to raise experience and logic to the status of new authorities. According to the new beliefs, secure knowledge cannot be gleaned from tradition, but must be based on experience and logic. The weakening of the authority of individuals went hand-in-hand with the strengthening of the authority of facts and logical or mathematical proofs. Thirdly, as this implies, expectations of truth and perception were altering. People were ceasing to believe in personal authority, because this was no longer expected to be a source of truth and certainty. People were beginning to believe in experience and logic because these were the new sources from which truth and certainty were expected to flow.

The upheavals in the expectations of truth which took place at the height of the Enlightenment, the transition from authority based on individuals to that based on facts, was by far the most momentous change that western humanity has experienced in its intellectual history. It was accomplished in the wake of the victory of science. In the shock-waves which shook Europe after the French Revolution two hundred years ago, the credibility of personal authority was finally shattered and rejected. It was replaced by the kind of modern factual knowledge which sees its validity as rooted in the structures of reality itself, seemingly detached from all human activities.

However, this upheaval simultaneously created a problem which has since undermined and disrupted western intellectual life like a smouldering fire—a problem which is characteristic of everything modern, and which at the end of the twentieth century has gained an ominous relevance. It lies in the fact that belief in the validity of factual knowledge is once again taking on the form of the credibility of individuals and groups. The rise and fall of empirical and rational science is mirrored by the rise and fall of scholars and experts who represent that science. The authority of scientific and technical facts has recently been proven to be just as uncertain as the authority of individuals. They are interdependent—but the modern world has not yet succeeded in reconciling the two forms of authority. The solving of this problem is one of the enduring spiritual and human challenges of our time.

St. Cross College
Oxford, OX1 3LZ

REFERENCES

1. For more about scientific revolutions see particularly: A. C. Crombie (ed.), *Scientific Change* (London and New York, 1963); Thomas S. Kuhn, *The Structure of Scientific Revolutions* (Chicago, 1962; 2nd edition, revised, Chicago, 1970); I. Lakatos and A. Musgrave (eds.), *Criticism and the Growth of Knowledge* (Cambridge, 1970); I. B. Cohen, *Revolution in Science* (Cambridge/Mass. and London, 1985).
2. More about this parallelism in: Hans-Georg Schneider, 'Die Parallelität der Revolutionen in Chemie und Politik um 1790', *Mitteilungen der Fachgruppe Geschichte der Chemie in der Gesellschaft Deutscher Chemiker* (Frankfurt), 1 (1988), 26–40; I. B. Cohen, 'The Eighteenth-Century Origins of the Concept of Scientific Revolution', *Journal of the History of Ideas*, 37 (1976), 257–88; A Levin, 'Venel, Lavoisier, Fourcroy, Cabanis and the Idea of Scientific Revolution: The French Political Context and the General Patterns of Conceptualization of Scientific Change', *History of Science*, 22 (1984), 303–20.
3. A. L. Lavoisier, *Traité Elémentaire de Chimie* (Paris, 1789).
4. Bernadette Bensaud-Vincent, 'A Founder Myth in the History of Sciences? The Lavoisier Case', in, Loren Graham, Wolf Lepenies, Peter Weingart (eds.), *Functions and Uses of Disciplinary Histories*, Vol. VII (Dordrecht, 1983), pp. 53–78; C. E. Perrin, 'Revolution or Reform: The Chemical Revolution and Eighteenth Century Concepts of Scientific Change', *History of Science*, 25 (1987), 395–423; C. E. Perrin, 'The Chemical Revolution: Shifts in Guiding Assumptions', in, A. Donovan, L. and R. Laudan (eds.), *Scrutinizing Science, Empirical Studies of Scientific Change* (Dordrecht 1988), pp. 105–24.
5. John Playfair, *The Works of John Playfair Esq., Late Professor of Natural Philosophy in the University of Edinburgh* (4 vols.; Edinburgh, 1822) vol. 1, p. lxxxv.
6. Antoine François de Fourcroy, *Elémens d'Histoire Naturelle et de Chimie*, 3rd edn. (5 vols.; Paris, 1789), vol. 1, *Avertissement*.
7. A. F. Fourcroy (1789), as note 6.

8. 'Lettre de M. Opoix, Maître en Pharmacie à Provins, & Membre de plusieurs Académies: à M. De la Métherie, Sur la Nouvelle Théorie, *Observations Sur la Physique* (Paris), 34 (1789), 76–8.
9. For Lavoisier's works see : *Œuvres de Lavoisier* (6 vols.; Paris, 1864–93); bibliography in, J. R. Partington, *A History of Chemistry* (London, 1962, 1970), iii. 368–74.
10. Jean Claude Delamétherie, 'Discours Préliminaire', *Observations Sur la Physique (Paris)*, 34 (1789), 29.
11. Friedrich Albrecht Carl Gren, 'Prüfung der neuern Theorien über Feuer, Wärme, Brennstoff und Luft, II, Lavoisier's System, *Journal der Physik*, ed. F. A. C. Gren, Professor zu Halle, 1, 2 (Halle und Leipzig, 1790), 295–325.
12. Lorenz Crell, *Chemische Annalen* (1791), ii. introduction.
13. S. F. Hermbstädt, 'Ueber Oxygen und Phlogiston; vom Hrn. Professor D. Hermbstädt', *Chemische Annalen* (1792), ii. 209–22.
14. G. F. Hildebrandt, 'Vergleichende Uebersicht des phlogistischen und des antiphlogistischen Systems', *Chemische Annalen* (1793), i. 536–60.
15. G. F. Hildebrandt (as note 14).
16. G. F. Hildebrandt (as note 14).
17. Vom Hrn. Trommsdorff in Erfurt, *Chemische Annalen* (1793), i. 257–8.
18. Johann Bartholomäus Trommsdorff, 'Meine lezte Erklärung in Betreff der phlogistischen und antiphlogistischen Streitigkeiten', *Journal der Pharmacie* (1794), i, pt. 2, pp. 103–8.
19. J. B. Trommsdorff, 'Lehrbuch der pharmaceutischen Experimental-chemie für practische Apotheker und Aerzte' (review of his own book by himself), *Journal der Pharmacie* (1796), iv, pb. i, pp. 341–6.
20. H. F. Link, *Herrn Lavoisier physikalisch-chemische Schriften* (Greifs-wald, 1792), iv, p. V.
21. W. A. Lampadius, *Sammlung practisch-chemischer Abhandlungen und vermischter Bemerkungen* (Dresden, 1795), i. 138 f.
22. C. Schiffner, 'Wilhelm August Lampadius', *Beiträge zur Geschichte der Technik und Industrie*, 12 (1922), 40–50.
23. Johann Christian Wiegleb, 'Beweißgründe des geläuterten Stahlischen Lehrbegrifs vom Phlogiston und der Grundlosigkeit des neuen chemischen Systems der Franzosen', *Chemische Annalen* (1791), ii. 388.
24. Anonymous, Von Herrn S + + + in M., *Journal der Pharmacie* (1796), iii, pt. i, pp. 312–15.
25. G. F. Hildebrandt (as note 14).
26. 'Einige Bemerkungen, verschiedene Gegenstände der neuen Chemie betreffend, vom Hrn. Berg = Commissair Westrumb', *Chemische Annalen* (1792), ii. 33–36.
27. 'Bemerkungen über ein Schreiben des Hrn. Prof. Grens zu Halle an Hrn. Apotheker van Mons zu Brüssel, Vom Hrn. Apotheker P. J. Kasteleyn in Amsterdam', *Chemische Annalen* (1794), i. 28–38.
28. Vom Hrn. Prof. Lampadius in Freyberg, *Chemische Annalen* (1796), i. 258–62.

29. Lampadius (1796), as note 28.
30. 'Einige Versuche und Bemerkungen, die antiphlogistische Chemie betreffend, In einem Briefe vom Hrn. Prof. Hermbstädt an den BR von Crell', *Chemische Annalen* (1793), ii. 479–86.
31. Hermbstädt (1793), as note 30.
32. A. F. Fourcroy, article 'Chymie', *Encyclopédie Methodique* (Paris, 1796), iii. 573.
33. A. Seguin, 'Abrégé des Principaux Phénomènes qui Dépendent de l'Action du Calorique', in, *La Médecine Eclairée par les Sciences Physiques* (Paris, 1791), i. 135.
34. A. F. Fourcroy (1789), as note 6.
35. Madame Lavoisier, 'Préface du Traducteur', in, R. Kirwan, *Essai sur le Phlogistique et sur la Constitution des Acides* (Paris, 1788).
36. Edouard Grimaux, *Lavoisier, 1743–1794* (Paris, 1896), p. 126.
37. A. F. Fourcroy, *Système des Connaissances Chimiques* (Paris, 1801), i. 47.
38. A. Seguin, 'Observations Générales sur la Respiration et sur la Chaleur Animale; lues à la Société Royale de Médecine, le 22 Mai 1790', *Observations Sur la Physique* (Paris), 37 (1790), 467–72.
39. Seguin and Lavoisier, 'Premier Mémoire sur la Respiration des Animaux', *Mémoires de l'Académie des Sciences, Année 1789* (Paris, 1793), pp. 566–84.
40. 'Ueber Oxygen und Phlogiston; vom Hrn. Professor D. Hermbstädt', *Chemische Annalen* (1792), ii. 209–22.
41. Richard Kirwan, *Essay on Phlogiston and on the Constitution of Acids* (London, 1787), Introduction, p. 8.
42. Michael Hube, *Vollständiger und faßlicher Unterricht in der Natur-lehre* (4 vols.; Leipzig, 1801), i. Vorrede.
43. Sven Rinman, *Geschichte des Eisens* (Berlin, 1785), translator's preface, p. viii.

The Modern World, Sciences, Medicine, and Universities

Notker Hammerstein

In the immediate aftermath of World War II, German and Austrian historiography witnessed the emergence of a new assessment of the old 'German Empire', the Holy Roman Empire of the German nation. Not only did the experience of Nazi domination, with its perverted, hypertrophied, and exaggerated nationalism, give rise to a quest for a new inner security, a new and better historical self-understanding, and a different sort of model of political existence: it also introduced an initially rather tentative reassessment of the settled and seemingly assured results of the great German history writing of the nineteenth and early-twentieth centuries. The brilliant judgements of Heinrich von Treitschke, which had for so long defined concepts of the early-modern German Empire, now seemed possessed of an exaggerated clarity; doubt was also cast on the conclusions of many of his more recent followers, such as Max Lenz, Georg von Below, Hermann Oncken, Friedrich Meinecke, Erich Brandenburg, and Karl Brandi. These names are just an arbitrary selection, of course, and others like Carl Alexander von Müller and Heinrich Ritter von Srbik might also be added. There ceased to be an uncritical acceptance of their vision of German history as engaged in a laborious, long-drawn-out evolution up to the modern 'moral' national state. Even though each new scholar in his history writing only ever introduced modifications of detail or polemical distinctions,[1] the cumulative effect of the new analysis was to bring about a fundamentally different assessment of early-modern and modern German history.

From now on in fact the need was felt to rethink and revise the whole so-called 'borussian' mode of history-writing. Interest ceased to be focused in the first place on the achievements of the Branden-burg–Prussian territories, and their supposed or actual contribution to German unity and greatness. There was an abandonment of the hitherto prevailing assumption that the North German territories under the leadership of Prussia had saved the decaying political fabric of Germany, prevented further German decline, and brought an end to the 'unfortunate multiplicity of stages' in the Empire. Above all, there was a retreat from the idea that this older mode of living together of the Germans was somehow foolish, or as Samuel von Pufendorf had put it, 'monstrous'. Changes in the contemporary situation of the Germans transformed the whole historical question, and made it possible to take a more detached view of older established judgements.

According to these older conceptions it could not have been expected of the Emperor and the Empire that they would promote the restoration of a German State in the period after 1648. Since the irruption of Protestantism, the ancient and long-dilapidated constitution of the Empire had degenerated into a 'hateful lie', as Treitschke had put it in his famous *History of Germany in the nineteenth century*. It was not merely the borussian historians but also many of the Protestant ones that Treitschke was following when he started out from the assumption that 'the imperial dominion was rooted in a lost past, and therefore found its natural opponents in the secular princes, whose energies were on the increase, while its adherents were drawn from the rotten and degenerate portions of the Empire'.[2] This latter part had originally been 'Ecclesiastically endowed' Germany.

It 'constituted the kernel of the Austrian party—that luxuriantly flourishing spiritual province of German life which, having been restored to the Roman Church through the victories of the Counter-Reformation, henceforth led an easy life under the lax rule of the crosier, rejoicing in nepotism and sensuality. . . . The powerful Catholic nobility likewise adhered to the Emperor, exercising control through its prince-bishoprics over three of the electorates and a number of the princely thrones of the Empire, and finding in the service of the Archducal House of Austria comfortable sinecures for its sons. . . . In the sloth of a national life of this character the well-grounded sense of proportion, characteristic of the national genius, had begun to disappear. An epoch of intolerable troubles had broken the courage of the burghers and had accustomed the common man to prostrate himself before the powerful. Our free-spirited tongue learned to decline into a slavish obedience, and adopted that cringing phraseology which has not to this day been entirely discarded. The unprincipled *raison d'état* of the age exercised its pernicious influence even on civic life. . . .'

This corruption and decay, said Treitschke, could be traced at least as far back as the emergence of Martin Luther, but it was first found in its most truly oppressive form in the period that followed the Treaty of Westphalia, between 1648 and 1806. For about 150 years the history of this non-state of the German Empire slumbered on, with Germany the epitome of spineless inactivity, moral subservience, and a hollow culture of tasteless pastiche. Only in a few of the larger North German Protestant territories was there any hint of backbone at this period, and it was here that the first hints appeared of the resurgence that blossomed and came to full maturity in the nineteenth century. Treitschke's remark that 'over this decayed life of the community there was spread the glamour of a history dating back from a thousand years' seemed to be about all that could be said in mitigation.[3]

Of course, such judgements were rather more extreme than the generally prevailing conception of the Holy Roman Empire. Nonetheless for a long time the opinion persisted that in this 'Gothic' regime it was the Protestant North that stood for progress, freedom, political reason, and the future of the Germans. The same view was taken of the Empire as it was of Europe in general at this time: it was the non-Catholic countries that were really setting the trends.

But here the experience of the Third Reich was instructive, for it suggested that this judgement was too much conditioned by the national state and the *Kulturkampf* standpoint of the nineteenth century. It was also felt that it made no historical sense to regard one or several centuries as periods of 'underdevelopment' or as amounting to missing stages in the development of a people, a country, or a region. Thus twenty or thirty years of neutral investigation of this supposed state of affairs has shown up the extent to which it was in truth an assessment conditioned by its time, and cannot accurately be called historical as such. The result of this recent research has been to rediscover and restore to general awareness wholly positive elements even in these years of German history.[4]

But this process is not really what I shall be discussing here: it is merely meant as an example to demonstrate how much historical conceptions can be limited by their time, and equally immensely influential in their time. This history of the conception of the Holy Roman Empire of the German Nation is however loosely connected to my subject: I want to reflect very generally on once-cherished

nineteenth-century ideas and views about the progress, development, and cultivation of modern science and its institutions. In my
opinion these old views still have a far-reaching influence on our
picture of what was really crucial, positive, and future-orientated in
this area in the Early Modern Era. I am talking about questions that
relate to the whole arena of debate about the so-called 'scientific
revolution'.[5]

The central issue in my discussion will not so much be this so-
called 'revolution' itself, but more fundamentally the effect and
meaning of it for the history of the universities in the early modern
era. Although I will focus on the German connection as the one I
know best, it needs to be borne in mind that as I shall occasionally
indicate, similar phenomena are also observable in other countries. I
hope that the result will be a more discriminating view of the
development of European universities in the early modern era from
the one that has all too often prevailed before. Questions about
'progress', about development to a better and more modern world,
and about outstanding advances made in the non-Catholic territories etc. . . . , are as much germane to Germany today as they were
to the Holy Roman Empire and its history.

There are three classic approaches to this topic: there is the one
adopted by certain Marxist historians, whose premise is that the
emergence of the Natural Sciences in the seventeenth century
represented a decisive stage in the transition from a Feudal to a
Bourgeois order: then there is the view of many historians of the
Natural Sciences and of Medicine, that this phenomenon is to be
seen as the beginning of the modern world; and thirdly, there is the
less dogmatic view that although the sudden world-transforming development of these sciences is really a nineteenth- and twentieth-
century phenomenon, it is nonetheless solidly grounded in the
seventeenth century. Whatever approach we adopt, the whole
process must clearly be regarded as one of the most important,
decisive, and definitive for our modern world. What a book published recently called 'the birth of modernity'[6] is intimately connected with the 'countableness', measurableness, and arithmetical
analysis of the world and of interpersonal relations. The modern
atomistic individual, like the modern economy, the this-worldly view
of things, the 'disenchantment of the world', as Max Weber called it,
were all crucially formed and defined in tandem with this 'scientific
revolution'. Modernity is accordingly a function above all of a

peculiar aptitude for research into nature, of a transformation in the quality of the natural sciences and medicine, and also of a highly-developed technology. Not that this is generally presented as a process having only one cause. All kinds of different factors are put forward as equally capable of explaining the sudden rush into modernity since the seventeenth century. Yet there remains an overwhelming impression that it was chiefly the triumphal march of the 'sciences' that defined the remorseless progress into our world.[7]

I am not going to tackle this whole complex of issues, but I do want to point to one circumstance that needs elucidation in relation to it. My argument concerns the elevated conception which the second half of the nineteenth century had of technical and natural-scientific progress as the sign of modernity in the sphere of knowledge, and I want to point to the insignificant role assigned to the universities in this view of things. In 1966 Sir E. Ashby wrote: 'The history of this scientific revolution lies almost completely outside the universities'.[8] But this would mean that the universities completely rejected anything to do with the emergence of the modern world. For it is widely accepted that the nineteenth century was correct in supposing that the Natural Sciences are, as Emile du Bois-Reymond put it in 1878,[9] the 'absolute organ of culture', and that the history of the Natural Sciences is the 'real history of mankind.' In 1985 James E. McClellan III wrote in similar vein:

In the seventeenth century organized science turned away from the traditional setting of the medieval universities and established itself in extra-university circles of several sorts. . . . The emergence of these institutions makes clear that the organizational revolution accompanying the cognitive and methodological redefinitions making up the Scientific Revolution as a whole marks the end of one era in the institutional history of science, that of the medieval university, and the beginning of another, the age of the learned scientific societies.[10]

It would be easy to find more examples of these and similar judgements on the emerging European Academies and their scientific community. It is a view that seems to correspond in certain ways to the conclusions that emerge from a consideration of the two English universities, many French ones, most of the Spanish, a host of Italian, and also many German universities. And yet the strange fact is that it was in these very institutions that the triumphal march of the disciplines in question took place in the nineteenth century; or, to be more precise, the advances occurred in those institutions that had organized themselves according to the pattern of the German university reforms of the beginning of the nineteenth century, as inspired by Humboldt. The interesting thing in fact about these German universities, frequently taken as models and patterns for the rest of Europe, is that in their Humboldtian manifestation they consciously clung to forms and modes of existence that went back to the early-modern era and indeed to the high or late medieval period. Even while seeking curricula and ideals that were more in tune with their own times, they remained much as they had been for generations. To that extent judgements like the following must be misleading:

> Thus most seventeenth- and eighteenth-century European universities showed marked signs of decay, which gave ample grounds for demands for the dissolution of whole institutions. At the same time, scientific research had emigrated completely outside the universities. The English Royal Society, which came to maturity in the seventeenth century, was followed in the eighteenth by the Académie française, which for a long time stood as the leading centre of scholarship in Europe. Thus there grew up alongside the universities a new scholarly profession, following a practice which clearly contradicted that of the traditional learned class committed to the transmission of inherited knowledge: this new class pioneered the advance of learning and in particular pushed on with the development of natural-scientific knowledge. ... For the most part, European universities in the seventeenth and eighteenth centuries saw an increasing tendency towards decline such as had been perceptible since the end of the Middle Ages and the beginning of the territorial states.[11]

To cite one further such view, albeit one that is less categorical and clearly more discriminating, we may go to Crosland: 'Anyone who has studied science in the eighteenth century in England or France may consider universities as peripheral to the development of science and it is useful to have the temporary weakness of some universities placed in a broader context'.[12] This is a widely-held view long enshrined in history of science and history of medicine textbooks.[13] I believe it is as false as it is widespread.

It is a way of looking at things that takes a great deal for granted. First of all, there is its most obvious and in fact most important presupposition: that the path to modernity passes through Natural-

Scientific and Medical knowledge and that a fundamental break with the traditional concept of philosophy was made by Descartes. Even someone as well informed as Charles B. Schmitt makes the assumption that the teaching and development of the Natural-Scientific-Medical disciplines are *the*, or at least always *one*, decisive touchstone for 'modernity', and for the future-orientatedness of learning in a university. Admittedly, Charles Schmitt does correct a general impression that the Italian universities of the Renaissance (which are the ones he is interested in), contributed nothing at all to the development of these disciplines and that Aristotelianism was pretty much a hindrance to them. In fact his research has success-fully exploded this as a prejudice. The real issue for him nonetheless remains the place assigned to these disciplines within the canon of the learned sciences, a place whose importance allowed them, in his view, to lead the way to the modern world.[14] In following another route and seeking answers to a rather different question, J. Ben-David came to a similar conclusion when he was working on *The Scientist's Role in Society*[15] in the early 1970s. In this very shrewd book, based on sociological arguments, he emphasizes that the natural sciences as 'a central element in the emerging conceptions of progress' must be acknowledged to have made the decisive contribu-tion to the inauguration of the modern world. Like Schmitt and others he notes the erroneousness of the view commonly held in the late-nineteenth and early-twentieth centuries, according to which it was technical or purely internalist factors that brought about the enormous explosion of these sciences from the seventeenth century on. According to him, the triumphal march of the new way of thinking and style of research is to be attributed to social and historico-political factors in conjunction with the mental outlook of the men of the time, first of all in England and then in France. In his opinion universities, their professors and their scholars contributed very little. In general the process of development passed the universities by completely, because their main role was to serve as places to train theologians, jurists, and medical men. The universities were so wedded to their role as training centres for practical and socially-useful professions that they did not develop into 'research institutions'.

Ben-David argues that the preoccupation with revolutionizing the natural sciences that emerged first of all in England and was eventually focused paradigmatically in the Royal Society had impli-cations beyond the natural-scientific realm. The methods, approaches, and types of research orientation involved could be carried over to the study of society as well. There were hints of this at the time, but it very quickly led to a self-limitation by the 'scientists', for in a society as open as the English such discussions would have led to unrest and the questioning of the established social order. Limiting themselves as it were by their own choice to the purely scientific dimension of their researches into nature, they managed to retain enough freedom of manoeuvre to be able to establish a 'scientific community' that transcended national borders and spread out over Europe. The indisputable success of this scientific movement made even absolute sovereigns feel it was desirable to make use of its results for their own states and to encourage the advancement of science free from government control. In the eighteenth century England quickly sank into a state of mediocre amateurism, and the torch of the new scientific knowledge and enlightenment forward passed to France. The freedom that the absolute state allowed to the French *savants* to publish their results produced a great deal of improvement in the quality of their work.

Brockliss has recently given a very penetrating picture of conditions in the French universities which shows how uneven was the development of the different branches of knowledge there in the eighteenth century.[16] This too in its way fits in with the conclusions I have been discussing. While in theology and jurisprudence and in all the disciplines of practical philosophy the picture is one of definite stagnation, on the fringes of the arts disciplines, in the natural sciences, and sometimes also in medicine there was still plenty of room for manoeuvre. Not only did this permit the assimilation of scientific advances, but it also allowed the gradual development of methodologies that at the same time suggested new concepts of social order and encouraged the formations of different theories about the common life of men in the state. Brockliss has quite rightly shown the extent to which the significance of these curricular changes for the French Revolution has hitherto been seriously underestimated. He is not actually concerned with the question which I have been discussing of the role of the sciences in the emergence of the modern world, but his conclusions add further to the picture built up by other authors. Thus they could encourage the opinion that this picture is a true and accurate one.

This association of the 'scientific revolution' with the development of modernity is also crucial for another contentious issue, although it is one I shall not be discussing at any length here: I will restrict myself to a brief reference to this question and its implications. I am alluding to the way this theory excludes any possibility that the formation of the early modern states grew out of the Renaissance or Humanism, or that the door to modernity was opened by the Reformation. For the assumption here is that it was not *humaniora* that surrounded the cradle of modernity but *realia*, which were ultimately conceptualized in the triumphal march of the sciences in the nineteenth and twentieth centuries. The key role in all this is credited to England and France, with the Netherlands also having a significant part. And according to this argument, the decline of the universities, indeed the irrelevance of the universities between the late sixteenth and nineteenth centuries is a product of the same phenomenon. Their role as training institutions for Church and State made them capable of contributing little to the real development of the most significant disciplines. Although the process was manifested in a slightly different form in the Netherlands, this was only because of its pragmatic-Calvinistic character and the nature of its civic order.[17]

I shall not be concerned here with the broader issues raised by these theories. What I do want to do is propose a few correctives to the overall picture on the basis of observations particularly on the role of the universities in Central, East-Central, and Northern Europe. These will, I hope, encourage a much greater appreciation of hitherto neglected examples and developments in a sphere beyond that of the West European and Mediterranean universities. If this inquiry suggests that there are significant differences between the two spheres, the suspicion would be that, as Crosland rightly noted in another connection, 'national culture' and 'national systems' have made their own contributions to our 'common cultural heritage'.

I have always personally been convinced that it was in fact the Renaissance and Humanism that crucially paved the way for the development of early modern Europe, for the inauguration of modernity, and for the modern understanding of Economics. However, the Renaissance and Humanism were not initially of any very great importance for the universities. For Humanism did not in fact create a novel system of knowledge *per se*, but rather promoted a distinctive understanding of certain specific disciplines. The disciplines concerned were treated according to a kind of philological-early historical methodology. The preference was for morally uplifting subjects, the method was characterized by an appeal *ad fontes*, and Antiquity was the norm and measure of truth. Antiquity was seen as something belonging to the past that should nonetheless be brought to life again as a norm and framework within which universal criteria of value were to be sought.[18] All these ideas fitted in very well with the general shape of the universities, and the form in which they had been developing, both from the institutional point of view and from the point of view of their ordering of the sciences into faculties. Inevitably it was chiefly the *Humaniora* and the *Artes* that were stimulated and renewed, especially the disciplines of the Trivium, but also those of the Quadrivium.[19]

The truth is, however, that this methodology affected not only the Arts Faculties; it affected the Higher Faculties too, even if the effect was apparently only superficial. The mere fact that improved texts and purified editions of normative texts became available led to changes of emphasis and new approaches in certain disciplines. This might initially mean a polishing-up of appearances rather than any profound changes. But from the point of view both of methodology and of content it led in time to a much more earthbound and this-worldly conception and understanding of the sciences. The new strongly practical-moral orientation combined with radical aesthetic ideas had the effect of releasing new transforming energies. Ultimately the Humanists anticipated that preoccupation with learned matters would have a moralizing, improving, and ennobling influence on a person who engaged in learned studies.

To put it crudely, one could state that the ideal of the *gentiluomo* or the *gentleman* was a consequence of these humanistic ideas about the reasonable way to live. Elegance of manners, an all-round education, a more moral way of life, a readiness for public responsibility, and an aestheticizing self-presentation combined with a higher conception of morality all seemed very important. This was especially true for those who sought a position in the public service, and so it had to be taken into consideration in their education and the disciplines that prepared them for it; these had to conform to the ideal too. Although the pattern originated in Italy, it was transmitted to other European lands by the many travellers who came there from North of the Alps. Since it continued to be the case that the best understanding of what was meant by being a 'humanist' was to be found in Italy, *peregrinationes academicae* grew increasingly popular in the course of the late-fifteenth and sixteenth centuries, transcending confessional boundaries. Indeed, it was in fact only after the Reformation that the high tide of such academic pilgrimages was reached. Thus for anyone who coveted a position in a leading academic institution, it was more important to have visited a major European university town (initially in Italy or France, later in the Netherlands), than to have been educated at an institution with the right confessional affiliation. 'Mirrors for princes', *institutiones*, and educational treatises for rulers all gave expression to these ideals in their way. Aristocratic education frequently aimed to practise them, and persistently conveyed to the struggling academic the message that it could be highly beneficial to his career prospects if he modelled his behaviour on that of the noble.

Acquaintance with lands of other creeds was a great encouragement to civilized behaviour, broad-mindedness, and general worldly wisdom. In many places, and particularly in the smaller European courts of the Holy Roman Empire, in the states of Eastern, Central, and Northern Europe, and even in the rich city-states of the Netherlands and Flanders, this had a generally socializing effect that provided a great stimulus to the development of the Republic of Letters called for by Erasmus.[20] This was a society with a common spirit, a society that could not be found in the same form in the courts of England or France, and in its way it helped to shape ideals of appropriate education, elegant erudition, and the behaviour appropriate to a cultivated person.

It is certainly true, and I shall not be overlooking it here, that the confessionalisation that was the consequence of the Reformation and Counter-Reformation had a highly deleterious effect on the humanistic temper of this world, and was in many ways actually destructive. The optimism and the relatively carefree outlook evaporated, and both universities and sciences were increasingly reduced to being mere tools for confessional politics. But the fact is that this was not really so pronounced a phenomenon as scholars have liked to think in the past. There are adjustments to be made in the older view both in regard to the *peregrinationes* and in regard to the persistent strength of the *Res publica litteraria*. In fact the blockage of the development towards a more terrestrial orientation in views of man and the world was neither so negative nor so disastrous as the liberal nineteenth century imagined. There were important disciplines in which this situation gave rise to genuine humanistic-methodical approaches that were to be reliable and lasting, and that came to be seen as powerful models for imitation. This was reduced to a formula in the contemporary phrase *sapiens et eloquens pietas*.[21]

Of course the growth of confessionalism from the second half of the sixteenth century onwards prevented the unhindered evolution of humanistic ideas. Everywhere there was an intensification of political conflict, confessional wars broke out first in France and subsequently all over Europe in tandem with dynastic and constitutional struggles; and the result was that the growing problem of how men were to live together in peace came to predominate over all other issues. Every other question had to be put aside for a time. There was, moreover, a widespread awareness that proper solutions could not really be expected on the basis of the sort of methods that fitted in with the scientific ideals of the Humanists. The result was an increasing dissatisfaction with this philological-humanistic type of culture. It was felt to have been compromised by confessionalism and polemic. There is justification, then, in the common denomination of the period as an 'age of crisis',—problematic though such a term may be.[22]

At the time it was widely believed that a solution might be found in the study of *realia*, the 'useful facts' of the world, or experimentally verified truth—*res* instead of *verba*. To this end the sciences were to be taught in an improved and more easily comprehensible way, with the aim of freeing men from unbelief, insecurity, and obsessionality.[23] According to Comenius, Schottelius, Boecler, Bodin, Bacon, and Hobbes, relevant education and the direction of the sciences at the outset towards the practically useful seemed more important than general cultural ideals. Such ideas as these, then, were increasingly typical of the period after 1600. As a result, the academic life of the universities as it had previously been conceived now seemed in need of overhaul; it looked *passé* and out of date. In the course of the century this process was intensified. Some describe it as a crisis, others as the kind of inevitable change in attitudes to the disciplines that was seemingly required by new times; but the one thing we can say for sure is that there certainly was change.[24] The founding of institutions such as the Royal Society is a noteworthy outward sign of dissatisfaction with the academic life of the time. To the extent that these seemed to enjoy a measure of success, they clearly corresponded to a contemporary need. Hence it was that this pattern was quickly emulated in France and such societies grew in popularity on both sides of the Channel. They initially served the purpose of providing a forum where students of nature could indulge in the mutual exchange of opinions, and this sometimes enabled them to gain a new and more assured understanding of the nature of things. Such knowledge could be applied to the welfare of mankind.

These learned societies were different from the earlier Italian ones, and also from many that were to be found in Spain or the Empire, in that they no longer regarded as their true object the study of languages or ancient learning, but rather the dissemination of natural-scientific, medical, and cosmological knowledge. Consequently, they were a source of many of the impulses that were to give rise to the development of modern natural-scientific-medical research between then and the nineteenth century. At that time there could be no question of such impulses, even though they were a presupposition for subsequent successful developments.

The endeavour was one that again embraced the whole of Europe.[25] From the seventeenth century onwards a new or second Republic arose, a natural-scientific-learned one. Its members knew one another and maintained contacts that transcended both national boundaries and confessions, as is very clearly demonstrated in the recently published correspondence of the first secretary of the Royal Society.[26] Synonymous with this enterprise are names like those of Galileo, Mersenne, Descartes, Bacon, Newton, and Leibniz. It is what I called at the start of my article the 'scientific revolution of the seventeenth century'.

However, as far as the birth of modernity is concerned—and that is my main subject here—what I said at the start must not be forgotten; namely, that the importance of these scientific enterprises of the Academies and Learned Societies has been exaggerated. In Central and Eastern Europe at least, the truly reforming and innovative approaches came not from them, but from the supposedly antiquated universities. Of course this is not to say that no significance at all is to be attached to the work of all those students of nature whose numbers had multiplied since the Renaissance and who had to some extent successfully developed their disciplines. But the point I am wanting to emphasize is that in general they were not the real reformers or renewers of the university-based science of man. Within the circle of their *res publica scientifica* as one might call it, there was a constant forward march of knowledge in astronomy, botany, mathematics, physics, chemistry, and even in anatomy and so on. Their work certainly brought about many-sided practical improvements, useful insights, and application-orientated techniques. Without them scientific life and indeed life in general would have followed a very different course of evolution. But the question still remains; given the existence of these academies, the activity of these men of learning and of so many interested lay folk, including many Catholics and not least Jesuits, what sort of influence did they exercise on the development of the universities and their sciences or on the renewal of university instruction and teaching? Basically, the answer is that any such influence was minimal. It is only a little over-stating the case to assert that this natural-scientific-medical thought had an astoundingly small influence on the universities, and no real significance in the development of modern ideas about men's community life. This assertion is categorically true of conditions in the Holy Roman Empire, it is also true of many of the Catholic countries of Europe, and it is even true of the two English universities; such extra university research activity even where arts faculties or the higher faculties in general were transformed, was never the cause of any fundamental change in the actual ideas of the various disciplines.[27]

The Empire may serve as paradigm here. It needs to be remembered at this point that in the cultural life of the Germans the universities continued to play the same role they had always played, a role that was highly significant, prominent, successful, and somewhat unconventional.[28] This was something that in particular in the seventeenth century definitively set them apart from everywhere else in Europe. We can also say the same of the Netherlands universities at a slightly later period; and with the Enlightenment the universities of Spain, Scotland, and in some cases of Italy, also came to have this kind of outstanding importance for the development of a modern *Zeitgeist*. But this was much later on than in the Empire.

Many universities had already begun to respond to contemporary demands as early as the seventeenth century, and they were doing it in a manner that both ensured their viability and suggested plenty of promise for the future. However, the natural-scientific-medical disciplines were not prominently or decisively involved at this point. Other elements and other sciences were setting the pace, and it was these others that were chiefly responsible for the advance of the universities.

A look at the difficulties of the seventeenth century makes clear the nature of this phenomenon. The most pressing problems were associated with the issue of how to deconfessionalize the world and therefore also the sciences and the universities. The pressing need was to bring an end to a situation in which everything was dominated or seemed to be dominated by the question of confession and by religious and civil wars; any hope of a genuine future-orientated perspective depended on it. In other words, a solution had to be found, which could make a more this-worldly conception prevail and which could make it possible to transcend the narrow perspectives of confessionalism. The unambiguous domination enjoyed by theological imperatives in the universities over nearly all the sciences had to be destroyed. Beginnings had been made and precedents established for this, but they had not really had a chance to develop. It was perfectly obvious that the mere repetition of these earlier attempts could never serve the purpose—even supposing they had not been aborted or blocked. In the meantime, there had been a profound change in outward circumstances, ways of thinking, and the general mentality since the days around 1500 for example, when the high tide of Humanism and Renaissance had been reached.

To the 'modern' mind it would certainly seem that natural-scientific-medical knowledge was in the best position to lead people's minds away from these denominationally conditioned conceptions. There were already contemporaries who attempted to argue this way. The assumption was, as it still is, that 'science' was inherently detached from all non-natural-scientific connections. The problem is however not really quite so straightforward. Recent studies have rightly shown that there was nothing accidental about the way that more emphatic support was given to natural-scientific or medical research in certain particular politico-confessional contexts than in others; or that particular social and historico-political configurations offered a more favourable ground for such work than others.[29] At that time it was within the context of an overall religious world-view that men both conceived and at the same time tried to examine experimentally Nature, Man, the World, and the Cosmos. To this extent they shared that subjection to historical conditions which is the lot of the whole enterprise of learning.

This is still not however the most important issue; nor is it even crucial that only a comparatively small circle of *savants* was involved with these questions (for the circle was indeed a small one numerically, one that remained relatively limited especially by comparison with the numbers of scholars at universities, despite the fact that the scale of activity, correspondence, and communication was Europe-wide). The heart of the matter was, and is, that as far as the common life of men in society or in the state was concerned these sciences had no lasting insights to offer. They were prevented from offering any by their very nature. In this area they were, and are, fundamentally unproductive. There is nothing new in this. It was in calling for a more open, more equal society uninhibited by traditional religions and philosophical orthodoxies that natural scientists might have had a role to play; but in fact this was not to be, because they would have had to formulate insights that would have been premature for the times and for the contemporary state of European relations.

If we look at the universities of Central Europe it also becomes clear that the imposition of restraints on theology, still regarded as the first of the faculties and as one at least of the causes of confessionalism, could not have been accomplished by members of a faculty that was not only less highly regarded but that was actually viewed as the humblest of all. These researchers into nature were for the most part regarded as representatives of the 'quadrivium'; how could it ever happen that their knowledge should fundamentally change or even bring significantly into question theological or political ideas? This would have implied a revolution in the whole academic world-view; it would have presupposed that a decisive importance, indeed an ultimate meaningfulness, could for example be assigned to experiment, which would thus have priority over truth as laid down by theology. This might perhaps have applied in the case of the odd scholar here and there, but it was quite out of the question for the mass. Given that the disciplines in the arts faculties continued to be seen as playing a functional role which placed them firmly in the category of preparatory studies, they could not in any way be decisive for the higher disciplines. This was true for medicine too, which was customarily referred to as the last of the higher faculties.

From the purely external and numerical point of view medicine carried insufficient weight to have been able to give a lasting lead. This was true even of those universities where it played a dominant and internationally acknowledged role. Here too it kept its place within the hierarchy of the sciences in the cosmos. Moreover it continued for the most part to be pursued chiefly as a theoretical discipline. Where it did have practical goals, it aimed to heal individual patients, but not the whole body of the state. So that any enduring impulse for change in the structure and self-understanding of the universities and their sciences could not come from Medicine. Theology of course was under no compulsion to consider such a re-examination itself. It was still the case long after the Wars of Religion that most theologians started out from the basic position that it was sufficient to proclaim the true teaching energetically, logically, and successfully against all adversaries. Censorship, super-vision, and regimentation should and could, it was believed, ensure religious peace. This was one reason for the 'crisis-ridden' character of the seventeenth century, for the intransigence of theology did not really leave room for any possibility of appropriate and peaceable resolutions to changing problems. Consequently, many observers thought that the universities were doomed to decay, as in fact was the case if we follow the theories mentioned earlier, and as indeed did appear to happen to a greater or lesser extent in many countries in Europe.

Similar attitudes prevailed in the Empire at this time. Thus a Leibniz or a Pufendorf did not pursue his scientific activity at university but at Court, where he tried to give it a more permanent foothold. However, it very quickly became obvious that this way was not practicable.[30] This had partly to do with the excessive dependency of the science vis-à-vis the princely patrons of the day. It also became clear that the successful reform of the universities and their sciences on the territory of the Holy Roman Empire was inaugurating a new era in their history. At the same time the competition offered to the seemingly moribund universities by the growth of the knightly academies, special institutions for a noble-courtly education that had been targeted specifically at the needs of the aristocracy, quickly faded as they became redundant in the new order, falling away into insignificance.[31]

If the reinvigoration of the universities was in a certain sense a 'special case' of German development, and one characteristic of the Protestant territories at that, there was certainly a parallel phenom-enon in the Netherlands, in many Italian, and later even in Spanish and Scottish universities. Admittedly, it is true that the majority of the universities in these countries were in perceptible decline at the time: and this seems to confirm the general view that from natural-scientific-medical research alone could the necessary renewal of the sciences and their institutions arise. But it is open to dispute here what was the rule and what the exception. At all events it was the German universities (and this was of very special significance for the nineteenth century, as I said at the start), that underwent reform and took off into a new heady era of their history.

It was the Jurists to whom the credit for the revival of the German universities belongs. By a long familiar phenomenon, seen so often with the emergence of the early modern states, the Jurists were thrust into a markedly prominent role in community and university alike. Politico-confessional disputes had at least partly obscured the important role played by jurisprudence since the days of the reception of Roman Law in secularizing society.[32] The *Jurisperiti* were able in their persuasive way to order and pacify daily life and even to inject it with a certain element of industriousness. All that had vanished into obscurity during the 'wild' years of confessional dispute. Given that religion came before politics, disputed questions could no longer be settled by reference to general juridical rulings, rulings which were in essence worldly-rational. From now on, however, after the experiences of the Wars of Religion, those princely battles between 'brothers' which had raged all over Europe, there was a growing awareness that the interweaving of politics with religion was not going to contribute anything to human progress. This is so well known that it does not require any further comment. The result was a reversion to older patterns and a new interest in the experiences that had arisen from the European voyages of discovery. The latter had encouraged the development of theoretical models able to guarantee the stability of life even in communities of 'savages' and heathen. The earlier natural law of the schools of Salamanca and Coimbra did not in fact lead directly to the later natural law of Grotius, which was the one that first gave expression to modern conceptions of natural and human rights. But it does belong to the prehistory of these very crucial achievements.[33] There was also a great demand for a new and improved Public Law,[34] something that had been worked out only very unsatisfactorily in Roman Law. There was a call too either for a new art of politics, such as the one so pleasingly formulated for Europe by Justus Lipsius in the context of Neo-Stoicism,[35] or simply for an improved practical order of interhuman relations, like the one provided by the *usus modernus* or the Europe-wide *philosophia practica*.[36] The particular manifestation of this phenomenon in the Empire was grounded in the work of the Saxon school of jurists, which in the course of the seventeenth century and in common with many other parts of Europe developed an *instrumentarium* that was both juridical and political; it was well placed to find the much-desired solutions.[37]

Bodin, the Politiques, Lazarus Schwendi, Justus Lipsius, Hugo Grotius, Samuel von Pufendorf, Bacon, Gottfried Wilhelm Leibniz, John Locke, Milton—to name but a few—all belong to this background. What these men were all striving after was an adequate this-worldly basis for the common life of men, based on mutual tolerance. They were more and more successful as the seventeenth century wore on, as such concepts and techniques were increasingly adopted, usually in the teeth of considerable opposition from the theologians, by more and more reform-minded rulers, princely advisers, kings, and even princes of the Church. The same did not of course apply everywhere, but it certainly did throughout the more advanced countries or territories, and this gave it a base from which to bring round the laggards.

It is in fact the Empire that offers the best example of the phenomenon. Orthodoxy, intransigence, and polemic attained spectacular heights in all theological camps there. This had been a response to the Thirty Years' War, a response that had developed rather late on by general European standards. When war was declared on this orthodoxy from the second half of the seventeenth century onwards, it was at the impulse of men from the general background I have identified above. It cannot have been any accident that many of them were members of law faculties which were heading the revolt against subservience to theology. They initially had a tough time of it, and in the end in an age of absolutism they were of course self-evidently obliged to rely on the co-operation and support of the rulers. This is most easy to see in the case of the two universities where development was paradigmatic for the Empire of the eighteenth century: Halle and Göttingen.[38] Wherever theology faculties managed to hang on to their supremacy despite these underlying conflicts, the very decline of the universities in question was eloquent testimony to the primacy of the new juridical thought.

The success of the reinvigorated institutions meant increasingly that the law faculties were seen as the crucial and most important ones, and one crude external measure of this is the scale of the stipends that were paid the professors. In the new context of a less theological, more juridicalized and at the same time more historicist view of the sciences, relativism pervaded the general view of the word and of man, and a more tolerant politics and practice of public life became possible. At the same time a broader this-worldly vista opened up to the sciences themselves, a vista that from now on excluded theology. Of course in many parts of the Empire this went hand in hand with the rise of absolutism, and eventually led to what in Germany was called Enlightened Absolutism. And yet it would be a mistake to explain the origins of modernity in terms of the interests of absolute rulers and the inner necessities of absolutism. Certainly enlightened despots were modern men. They had a new confidence in the countability, the reasonableness, and the potential of the world, and they were convinced that man has responsibility for his actions and that human decisions can make a decisive effect on the way of things, within what seemed to be the legitimate limits of his calling. Nevertheless, it could be argued that in seventeenth-century England the natural-scientific orientation of many scholars corresponded in a sense to this new way of looking at the world, and yet the absolutist form of sovereignty failed to maintain a lasting hold there.

It was not so much the rulers themselves as their advisers, men with academic training, who ensured that an orientation that was truly conducive to peace was given to the education of the state's servants, an education that would guarantee order, self-awareness and self-discipline. Gerhard Oesterreich spoke of 'social disciplining' in this connection, and this term, though it does not cover all aspects of the process, nonetheless expresses the general tendency very well. It was then that the sciences and universities rid themselves of their 'monks' staffs', the rubbish of the old ideas was cleared out, and war was declared on *rabies theologica*. Consequently both professors and students divested themselves of their old garb, for they had to act out their parts in the new elegant and courtly style. Diligence, sophisticated learnedness, and composure had to overcome the boyish crudeness of the seventeenth century. In a sense these reformers were rediscovering ideals that had already been formed by Humanism. It was no accident that they placed such great emphasis on the learned person being helpful, elegant, well-bred, and thoroughly civilized. Everywhere in the days of the early Enlightenment it was felt to be appropriate that a well-bred person either should be a jurist himself or should possess at least a sufficiency of juridical knowledge.[39] It is certainly true that in France, Spain, and to some extent also in Italy, courts were at that time the places where such knowledge could be obtained, and where careers could be made and apprenticeships worked out. But one result of the juridical reforms in France under Louis XIV was that any possibility of a further evolution of these disciplines in the direction of a more enlightened content was destroyed. Opportunities for this were also limited by country-wide centralization and at many at least of the smaller courts by the lack of openings for public activity. The general tendency was however as described above. This is also true for Spain and Portugal, where the attempt was made in the eighteenth century to set in motion reforms corresponding to the North European pattern. On all sides it was those trained in the juridical mode who acted as councillors and reformers, while the previously all-powerful influence of the Jesuits was broken, until in the end the Order itself was a casualty of the whole process.

In England the court had a less dominant position, for here there was the City. In addition neither Oxford nor Cambridge had a law faculty of any importance, which meant that they lacked an element that was crucial to the process elsewhere. But in England too, as elsewhere in Europe, the search was on, albeit for the most part outside the confines of the universities, to find a way to subject the common life of men to a rationally-conceived and rationally-conducted system. This was most effective in 'Enlightened' circles of intellectuals, *salons*, and newspapers, and to some extent such circles set a style. All over Europe the trend was away from theological assumptions and towards more this-worldly ones.

In the places where it was the case that these reforming approaches could be adopted within the universities themselves along the lines of the traditional faculty and university structures, the institutions in question took on new life and vigour. This was true even for theology itself, which ultimately maintained a position within the university, while no longer clinging to its old dominance over the other disciplines.[40] This change of role for theology did not always happen without a struggle, for it often involved long-lasting rearguard actions, but in the end the inevitability of the process became obvious to all. Thus in the Empire, in the Netherlands, later in Scotland too, the universities could experience renewal, and in the end this was beneficial for theology too. In taking over many inspirations and methods from the renewed juridical and arts disciplines it tapped new sources for its own rejuvenation. Thus the university preserved for itself the whole cosmos of the science in all four faculties. This was as much a good thing for the university as it was for the individual scientific debates, since both thereby gained in alertness and vigour.

The way the reformers saw it, the arts men now had to dance to the tune of the jurists. Consequently the orientation of the contents of the arts curricula changed and to some extent their methods too. The result was an infusion of new life into the disciplines and this ensured that the universities remained important places for intellectual and scholarly self-discovery. Without the work of such universities and the sciences they taught, the Enlightened world of many parts of Europe simply cannot be understood. A this-worldly outlook and the models of a renewed jurisprudence and politics were in this connection more crucially significant than natural-scientific-medical theories. It is true that the latter were now no longer tied to theology's apron strings, and they certainly had much more scope for development than hitherto. But they were not the real driving force nor did they have prime importance in the reform of public life or the world of learning.

Everywhere where universities and their disciplines failed to embrace reform and the new ideas (and this applies in general to France, England, and initially in Spain and Italy too), the institutions fell back into mediocrity, or withered away into insignificance. In reality they merely continued to fulfil the function of pure and simple vocational training, and remained in existence solely on account of the capability they had and the necessity they were under of producing graduates. They were very far from providing intellectual leadership in their countries. In such places even natural-scientific-medical researches, learned societies, and academies were of little use!

In harmony with and as a consequence of the development of the Englightened scientific outlook it became fashionable in certain circles to argue that it would be better for the universities to be dissolved into appropriate separate institutions giving instruction in particular practical subjects. Thus doctors, veterinary surgeons, civil servants, clergy, teachers, city clerks, and the like were to be trained at specially adapted colleges. Such ideas were particularly favoured by Enlightened opinion in those areas where the universities had already degenerated into mere teaching and graduating institutions.

From time to time such projects did actually come to fruition. On the other hand the success of the reformed universities in a few countries guaranteed that ideas and suggestions like these were not generally followed in Europe. In fact the universities proved themselves to be so resilient that splitting-up or change involving radical dissolution was never taken seriously in many places as an option despite the examples that might have encouraged it. Ultimately, small, inefficient, and generally undistinguished universities could not weigh in the balance against a principle that was embodied in such powerful institutions as Göttingen, Leiden, Edinburgh, Ingolstadt, Mainz, or Leipzig. Here within the traditional establishments themselves specific subjects and interests were being researched with such encouragingly productive results that they also seemed to have the edge over the vocational colleges.

There was one further factor. During the second half of the eighteenth century a number of arts disciplines became self-contained and independent sciences. They belonged to a faculty that had for a long time categorized itself in the Empire as the philosophy faculty, and this it continued to do insistently. Both philological-historical and natural-scientific subjects could now be offered in a new guise and developed further. This faculty's claim no longer to be regarded merely as a handmaid had been heard frequently long before the foundation of the University of Berlin, even if it had never been embodied in practice. It was a claim which served as a signpost to the future evolution of the universities and their disciplines in nineteenth-century Germany. Within the inspired form given to the German universities and their disciplines by Humboldt, it was possible to give further development to the subjects that were both necessary for the times and that also had potential for the future. It is yet another proof of the connection I have alluded to that here again the crucial presuppositions and driving-forces for the university and its disciplines lay in ideals that were humanistic (or rather neo-humanistic, as they were now officially called).[41]

It is no accident that with this model the German universities were paradigmatic for many others in Europe. Of course it would be going too far to assert that these were also the really decisive factors in the subsequent scientization of the modern world. But the idea of the university, from now on customarily regarded as the *Universitas litterarum*, seemed convincing and successful enough to be a model and pattern. Throughout the nineteenth century it furthered, protected, and brought together essential viewpoints, viewpoints without which our modern universities are unimaginable. But the claim put forward in the seventeenth century to the effect that *realia* and not *verba* are the real sciences played a less important part in this process than has sometimes been suggested. Just as in the end it was with the development of industrialization that the natural sciences first attained outstanding importance in society at large, so likewise could it be said that it was in the course of the nineteenth century that they first attained great importance in a university context. That is why it seems to me that the above corrections to the prevailing picture of the development of the history of learning and the universities are called for.

Historisches Seminar
Johann-Wolfgang-Goethe Universität
Senckenberganlage 31
Postfach 11 19 32
D-6000 Frankfurt am Main
West Germany

REFERENCES

1. In this connection, see for example B. Croce, *Die Geschichte als Gedanke und als Tat* (Bern, 1944); O. Vossler, *Geschichte als Sinn* (Frankfurt am Main, 1979).
2. H. von Treitschke, *History of Germany in the Nineteenth Century*, tr. Eden and Cedar Paul (7 vols., London, 1915). All my quotations are taken from vol. 1, ch. 1, section 1.
3. Ibid.
4. See for example J. G. Gagliardo, *Reich and Nation. The Holy Roman Empire as Idea and Reality, 1763–1806* (Bloomington/London, 1980); R. Vierhaus, *Staaten und Stände, Vom Westfälischen bis zum Hubertusburger Frieden 1648–1763*, Propyläen Geschichte Deutschlands Vol. 5 (Berlin, 1984); B. Roeck, *Reichssystem und Reichsherkommen* (Stuttgart, 1984); see also the article 'Reich' in *Geschichtliche Grundbegriffe. Historisches Lexikon zur politisch-sozialen Sprache in Deutschland*, Vol. 5 (Stuttgart, 1984), pp. 456–86.
5. On the Scientific Revolution see e.g. the anthology edited by Charles Webster, *The Intellectual Revolution of the Seventeenth Century*, Past and Present Series (London/Boston, 1974).
6. Leonhard Bauer and Herbert Matis: *Die Geburt der Neuzeit* (München,

1987). According to the author science underwent a profound reorganization in the early-modern period; it was 'in the Academies—and therefore outside the universities—that a new production of meaning took place; this process passed by the old, church-dominated universities and later the national ones too' (p. 414).

7. Friedrich Ueberweg, *Grundriss der Geschichte der Philosophie*, Part III, *Die Philosophie der Neuzeit bis zum Ende des 18. Jahrhunderts*, revised by Max Frischeisen-Köhler and Willy Mogg, reprint of the 12th edition (Darmstadt, 1961), section 23ff.; *The New Cambridge Modern History*, vol. iv, *The Decline of Spain and the Thirty Years' War 1609–48/59*, ed. J. P. Cooper, Cambridge, 1970, ch. 1, iv; *Histoire Générale des Civilisations*, iv, ed. Roland Mousnier, *Les XVIe et XVIIe Siècles* (Paris, 1954), Book ii; *Histoire Générale des Sciences*, ed. René Taton, vol. ii, *La Science Moderne*, Paris, 1958, pp. 185ff.; Erwin Ackerknecht, *Kurze Geschichte der Medizin*, 2nd ed. (Stuttgart, 1975), pp. 100ff.; see also two older works: E. Norwitz, *Geschichte der Medicin* (Leipzig, 1848; reprint, Wiesbaden 1966), iv, 4, pp. 283ff.; Fielding H. Garrison, *An Introduction to the History of Medicine* (London, 1913); ('The 17th Century: The Age of Individual Scientific Endeavor').

8. Sir Eric Ashby, *Technology and the academics* (London, 1966), p. 4.

9. 'Kulturgeschichte der Naturwissenschaft', in E. du Bois-Reymond, *Reden*, vol. 1 (Leipzig, 1886), p. 271.

10. J. E. McClellan III, *Science Reorganized. Scientific Societies in the Eighteenth Century* (New York, 1985), pp. xixff. On the Academies in the seventeenth and eighteenth centuries see also F. Hartmann and R. Vierhaus (eds.), *Der Akademiegedanke im 17 und 18 Jahrhundert*, Wolfenbütteler Forschungen 3 (Bremen/Wolfenbüttel, 1977); L. Boehm and E. Raimondi, *Università, Academie e Società scientificne in Italia e Germania del Cinquecento al Settecento* (Bologna, 1981); and the older work by Frances A. Yates, *The French Academies of the Sixteenth Century* (London, 1947; reprint 1988).

11. Hans Werner Prahl, *Sozialgeschichte des Hochschulwesens*, München, 1978, pp. 156ff.

12. M. Crosland (ed.), *The Emergence of Science in Western Europe*, London, 1975, p. 7.

13. Paul Diepgen, *Geschichte der Medizin* I (Berlin, 1949), pp. 280ff.; Alexander Mette and Irena Winter, *Geschichte der Medizin* (East Berlin, 1968), pp. 196ff.; Th. Meyer-Steineg and K. Sudhoff, *Illustrierte Geschichte der Medizin*, 5th edition (Stuttgart, 1965), pp. 225ff.; a rather more discerning view is to be found in Charles Lichtentaler, *Geschichte der Medizin* (Köln, 1982), pp. 395ff.; Ch. Singer, *A Short History of Scientific Ideas to 1900* (Oxford, 1959), ch. viii, pp. 218ff.; A. Rupert Hall, *From Galileo to Newton, 1630–1720* (London, 1963); and the work of Webster, cited above, that has now become more or less paradigmatic.

14. Charles B. Schmitt, 'Science in the Italian Universities in the Sixteenth and Early Seventeenth Centuries', in Crosland (see note 12), pp. 35ff.
15. Joseph Ben-David, *The Scientist's Role in Society, A Comparative Study* (Prentice Hall, 1971).
16. L. Brockliss, *French Higher Education in the Seventeenth and Eighteenth Centuries. A Cultural History* (Oxford, 1987).
17. These ideas can be easily traced back to nineteenth-century believers in science and progress; cf. many of the works listed in notes 1 and 3. See also George Clark, *The Later Stuarts 1660–1714*, The Oxford History of England, 2nd ed. (Oxford, 1955), II.xvi.; Conrad Grau, *Berühmte Wissenschaftsakademien* (Leipzig, 1988), esp. pp. 34ff.; John D. Bernal, *Science in History*, 3rd ed. (London, 1965); H. S. Rose, *Science and Society*, Pelican Books (London, 1977), pp. 9ff.
18. Paul Joachimsen's treatment of this is still fundamental, and can now be followed in his *Gesammelte Aufsätze*, 2 vols., ed. Notker Hammerstein (Aalen, 1970/83); Stephan Skalweit, *Der Beginn der Neuzeit*, Erträge der Forschung, vol. 178 (Darmstadt, 1982).
19. A. Grafton and L. Jardine, *From Humanism to the Humanities* (London, 1986); W. Reinhard (ed.), *Humanismus im Bildungswesen des 15. und 16. Jahrhunderts* (Weinheim, 1984). G. Keil, B. Moeller, and W. Trusen (eds.), *Der Humanismus und die oberen Fakultäten* (Weinheim, 1987). It has been conclusively demonstrated with reference to certain particular universities by Anton Schindling in his *Humanistische Hochschule und Freie Reichsstadt. Gymnasium und Akademie in Strassburg 1538–1621* (Wiesbaden, 1977); Hans-Martin Decker-Hauff and Wilfried Setzler, *Die Universität Tübingen von 1477–1977 in Bildern und Dokumenten (500 Jahre Eberhard-Karls-Universität Tübingen)* (Tübingen, 1977); Erich Kleineidam, *Universitas Studii Erfordensis*, Erfurter Theologische Studien (4 vols., Leipzig, 1967 *et seq.*), esp. vol. II; Gustave Adolf Benrath, 'Die deutsche evangelische Universität der Reformationszeit' in H. Rössler and G. Franz (eds.), *Universität und Gelehrtenstand 1400–1800* (Limburg/Lahn, 1970), pp. 63ff.
20. Notker Hammerstein, 'Res Publica Litteraria—oder Asinus in Aula? Anmerkungen zur "Bürgerlichen Kultur" und zur "Adelswelt" ', in *Res Publica Guelpherbytana (Festschrift Paul Raabe)*, Chloe (Beihefte zum Daphnis), vol. 6 (Amsterdam, 1987), pp. 35ff.
21. The saying goes back to Johannes Sturm(ius) of Strasburg, but it applies—*grosso modo*—to Lutherans, Calvinists, and Jesuits alike, and holds for well into the seventeenth century; cf. among others Eric Cochrane (ed.), *The Late Italian Renaissance 1525–1630* (Glasgow, 1970); Notker Hammerstein, 'Universitätsgeschichte im Heiligen Römischen Reich Deutscher Nation am Ende der Renaissance', in August Buck and Tibor Klaniczay (eds.), *Das Ende der Renaissance: Europäische Kultur um 1600*, Wolfenbütteler Abhandlungen zur Renaissance-Forschung, 6 (Wiesbaden, 1987), pp. 109ff.

22. Hugh Trevor-Roper, *Religion, the Reformation, and Social Change, and other Essays* (London, 1967); Theodore K. Rabb, *The Struggle for Stability in early modern Europe* (New York, 1975); cf. my review of this in *Francia*, 5 (1977), 922ff.

23. Charles Webster, 'Introduction', in C. Webster (ed.), *Samuel Hartlib and the Advancement of Learning* (Cambridge, 1970).

24. Barbara J. Shapiro, *Probability and Certainty in 17th Century England* (Princeton, 1983).

25. A. Rupert Hall, *The Revolution in Science 1500–1780* (London, 1983).

26. A. Rupert Hall and Mary Boas Hall (ed.), *The Correspondence of Henry Oldenburg*, 14 vols. (Madison/Milwaukee, 1965 *et seq.*).

27. Trevor H. Aston, General Editor, *The History of the University of Oxford*, of which two volumes have so far been published that cover the modern era, vols. 3 and 5 (Oxford, 1986); these deal with the sixteenth and eighteenth centuries respectively.

28. Notker Hammerstein, 'Zur Geschichte und Bedeutung der Universitäten im Heiligen Römischen Reich deutscher Nation' in *Historische Zeitschrift*, 241 (1985) pp. 287ff.

29. The outstanding work for this subject is Charles Webster, *The Great Instauration, Science, Medicine, and Reform, 1626–60* (London, 1975).

30. *Samuel von Pufendorf 1632–1982* Rättshistoriska Studier, Serien II, Tolfte Banded, ed. Kjell A. Modéer (Lund, 1986); Wilhelm Totok and Carl Haase (eds.), *Leibniz. Sein Leben—sein Wirken—seine Welt* (Hanover, 1966); Notker Hammerstein, 'Leibniz und das Heilige Römische Reich deutscher Nation', *Nassauische Annalen* 85 (1974), 87ff.

31. N. Conrads, *Ritterakademien der frühen Neuzeit. Bildung als Standesprivileg im 16. und 17. Jahrhundert* (Göttingen, 1982).

32. The fundamental text is still Paul Koschacker, *Europa und das römische Recht* (München, 1947); also Franz Wieacker, *Privatrechtsgeschichte der Neuzeit*, 2nd ed. (Göttingen, 1967).

33. Ernst Reibstein, *Die Anfänge des neueren Natur- und Völkerrechts* (Bern, 1949); Richard Tuck, *Natural Rights Theories. Their Origin and Development* (Cambridge, 1979).

34. N. Hammerstein, 'Jus publicum Romano-Germanicum', in *Diritto e Potere nella Storia Europea*, Atti del Quarto Congresso Internazionale della Societá Italiana di Storia del Diritto (Florence, 1982), pp. 717ff.; M. Stolleis, *Geschichte des Öffentlichen Rechts in Deutschland*, I (München, 1988).

35. The work of Gerhard Oesterreich is still indispensable, see his *Geist und Gestalt des frümodernen Staates* (Berlin, 1969); also Günther Abel, *Stoizismus und frühe Neuzeit* (Berlin, 1977).

36. J. Brückner, *Staatswissenschaften, Cameralismus und Naturrecht* (München, 1977); H. Dreitzel, *Protestantischer Aristotelismus und absoluter Staat* (Wiesbaden, 1970).

37. F. Wieacker (see n. 32).
38. See generally N. Hammerstein, *Jus und Historie* (Göttingen, 1972), and also the same author's 'Die deutschen Universitäten im Zeitalter der Aufklärung', in *Zeitschrift für Historische Forschung* 10 (1983), pp. 73ff.
39. W. Schneiders, 'Leibniz—Thomasius—Wolff. Die Anfänge der Aufklärung in Deutschland', in *Akten des II. Internationalen Leibniz-Kongresses 1972* (Wiesbaden, 1972), pp. 105ff. N. Hammerstein, 'Thomasius und die Rechtsgelehrsamkeit' *Studia Leibnitiana* XI (1979), 22ff.
40. In this connection see also the treatment in Bernd Moeller (ed.), *Theologie in Göttingen* (Göttingen, 1987).
41. The indispensable text is : U. Muhlack, 'Die Universitäten im Zeichen von Neuhumanismus und Idealismus: Berlin', in *Beiträge zu Problemen deutscher Universitätsgründungen in der frühen Neuzeit*, ed. P. Baumgart and N. Hammerstein, Wolfenbütteler Forschungen 4 (Nendeln, 1978), pp. 299ff.; Thomas Nipperdey, *Deutsche Geschichte 1800–1866* (München, 1983), esp. pp. 57ff.

Evolution, Obstacles and Aims: the Writing of Oxford and Cambridge College Histories

John Twigg

In an article in the first volume of *History of Universities* in 1981, Mordechai Feingold looked at Oxford and Cambridge college histories both old and, principally, new and asked if they were not in fact 'an outdated genre' in their present form.[1] The raising of this question was timely, for there has been renewed interest in the subject in recent years: several new college histories have been published over the last decade or so, and others are in preparation.[2] The purpose of this short essay is to examine the genre again, partly in the light of Feingold's strictures, partly in view of these recent publications, and to look more generally at the difficulties which confront historians who work in this field. The arguments advanced here are based on the author's own findings during various research projects into the history of the two universities.[3] Although most of the illustrations used here are from Cambridge, owing to my greater familiarity with these sources, there are a number of illustrations from Oxford too, and the following remarks seem equally applicable to both universities and their colleges. These observations may also serve as a basis for comparison with histories of other colleges in the British Isles and on the continent.

Evolution

First, it is necessary to understand how the genre has evolved and the place of recent college histories in this scheme of evolution. In part this also affords some insights into the range and nature of the historian's source materials for the subject, and the effects these have had on its development. The first signs of serious antiquarian-historical interest in college or university history—and in the cases of Oxford and Cambridge, the two are intertwined throughout—

appear in the sixteenth century. It was an offshoot, no doubt, of the wider scholarly interest in the past that owed much to contemporary humanism and was a feature of the intellectual culture of early modern Britain. But it may also have reflected the growing national importance of the two universities in the Tudor and Stuart era. This was the period too in which the colleges grew substantially in number and size, and in influence within the universities. Just as this led visibly to a general—though uneven—expansion and improvement in college record-keeping, so it may well have contributed towards a greater self-consciousness or awareness of college identity.

One of the earliest of these early modern antiquarians with an interest in universities and colleges was John Caius, a humanist and an eminent physician who refounded Gonville Hall in Cambridge as Gonville and Caius College in 1558.[4] Caius' interest in record-keeping is shown in his decree that the college's admissions register should contain details of students' places of origin and parental occupations, which has made these registers a particularly valuable source of evidence for the social composition of the early modern student body.[5] Caius also wrote *Annals* of his college, which contained details of college worthies and benefactors.[6] His other works on the history and antiquity of Cambridge University are better known but less valuable, owing far more to mythology than history in places, especially when describing the university's origins,[7] although this was seemingly a common outlook in those times.[8]

When writing about their colleges and universities, the early modern antiquarians tended to concentrate on founders, benefactors and their works and in this they were echoing the interests of the educated public at large. This tradition has exerted an enduring and powerful influence on much subsequent research, which in its persistence into recent times can be regarded as restrictive; but antiquarian writings have also been invaluable in preserving material which would otherwise have been lost. For example, the vast collection of transcripts made by the late seventeenth-century Cambridge antiquarian Thomas Baker, who was ejected from his fellowship at St John's for refusing to swear allegiance to the succession of William and Mary, reproduces many documents from the 1640s and 1650s—the period of the English Revolution—which we do not have in any other source.[9] The collection of William Warren, an eighteenth-century fellow and bursar of Trinity Hall

Cambridge, compensates partly for the sparseness of the college's records from that time.[10] This kind of antiquarianism was more marked in the seventeenth century, with the work of men such as Anthony Wood at Oxford, and of Thomas Fuller and Thomas Baker at Cambridge,[11] than in the eighteenth, although the enthusiasm was by no means extinguished in the later period: Warren's Trinity Hall collection was paralleled elsewhere in Cambridge by work on the history of Corpus Christi College by Robert Masters and of Queens' College by Robert Plumptre.[12] But interest in university and college history began truly to flourish again in the nineteenth century, at first because there was a greater public interest in antiquarian research, and subsequently because of the new sense of collegiate identity— even mission—which the Victorian university reforms and the new generations of dons engendered. The modern college history has grown out of these twin developments, and they require closer inspection for this reason.

The antiquarianism of the nineteenth century was in many ways a straight descendant of earlier work: founders, benefactors and college worthies continued to receive their due. But it does seem to have been more extensive and perhaps more ambitious, and in some areas it has marked an evolutionary leap in the progress of historical studies. One particularly popular and influential field of study within the tradition has been that of biographical history, stemming from the traditional interest in the lives of famous *alumni*, but extending to massive, comprehensive biographical registers of university and college men. Foster's *Alumni Oxonienses* and especially the Venns' *Alumni Cantabrigienses*[13] have speeded and assisted the work of historians immeasurably, as have the handful of sometimes more detailed college registers.[14] More recently, Emden's exhaustively researched registers of Oxford and Cambridge men before 1540 and 1500 respectively[15] have greatly improved and extended previous biographical data, and facilitated significant advances in research into the medieval university.[16] Progress would have been slow indeed without such biographical information: the labour involved in even the simple identification of names would be considerable, even though the registers' very convenience as sources for historians can, and often does, perpetuate the biographical bias of the antiquarian tradition from which they are derived.

Another area in which antiquarian enthusiasm and expertise have assisted other historians greatly is that of architecture, a conveniently self-contained subject, reflecting an old interest in the details of university and college buildings. Willis and Clark's massive *Architectural History of the University of Cambridge*, based on a diligent trawl of all relevant references in college and university archives and marked by a fine attention to detail, and the more recent Royal Commission for Historical Monuments volumes,[17] represent a core source for any Cambridge college history: the historian need not become bogged down in the often obscure or confusing details of college fixtures and fittings, and is able to look at the buildings against this established background of collegiate architecture in general. This in turn can then be incorporated into a wider historical overview, the style and purpose of buildings helping us to understand better the society that erected them. Not that such writings should be accepted uncritically—they are neither infallible nor necessarily the latest word on the subject—and researchers need to pay careful attention to details of college fabric contained in primary sources, for these can often modify the picture substantially; but they supply a *context* in which to work.

But perhaps the most important effect which the nineteenth-century antiquarian revival had upon the writing of college histories was through the rage for printing historical documents of every kind. Personal materials from the past, such as sermons and treatises, diaries, letters, autobiographies, and contemporary biographies appeared in print in abundance during the century and cast much light on their own times. At Cambridge a number of compilations of documents relating to the history of the university and its colleges also appeared:[18] these too were the work of diligent antiquarians and although all were and remain valuable source books, perhaps the most significant was C. H. Cooper's massive collection of *Annals of Cambridge*, printed in five volumes over more than half a century from 1842 and covering both university and town matters from the earliest times with extracts from an extremely wide range of printed and unpublished sources.[19] Cooper's work may have acted as a catalyst for much of the subsequent research and writing—everyone who has written since on any aspect of Cambridge history is certainly deeply in his debt. An equally significant rôle has been played in Oxford by the extensive series of printed documents published over the years by the Oxford Historical Society.

The value of such publications in encouraging and expediting research is obvious enough, though there are evident dangers in over-reliance upon them: the books of documents are only selections, after all; and the individuals whose writings were printed were by no means a representative cross-section of the university community of their times (it was generally clergymen who were published rather than the often more numerous gentlemen, the latter being less prolific writers). Both types of publication were bound, too, to reflect the prevalent historical outlooks of the century in which they were printed. There was far more interest shown in events and personalities—the stuff of narrative history—than in structural analysis. W. G. Searle's lengthy antiquarian history of Queens' College Cambridge from 1446 to 1662, published in 1867–71 and an extremely valuable piece of research,[20] illustrates one of these blindspots: though he covered the college sources diligently, he had almost nothing to say about the college statutes, which provide much valuable evidence of its organisation and workings for this period. We know that this was not by chance: Searle did have access to copies of the statutes, and studied them carefully.

The expansion of antiquarian enthusiasm, together with the example and assistance of these publications which it inspired, led to the publication of many secondary works on university history from the mid-Victorian period onwards; it also led to the emergence of the college history as a recognizable genre. This found its expression in the 'college history series' published by F. E. Robinson Ltd. of London over several years around the turn of the century: the series comprised a volume on each of the Oxford and Cambridge colleges and one each on the University of Durham, Trinity College Dublin and the University of Wales. There had been other Cambridge college histories earlier in the nineteenth century: Searle's early history of Queens', weighty and antiquarian (1867–71); Lamb's edition of Masters' eighteenth-century story of Corpus Christi (1831); and Mayor's extensive edition of Thomas Baker's seventeenth-century history of St John's (1869).[21] All three were important and learned contributions, but the new 'series' aimed at a more popular market. Doubtless the publisher hoped to profit from the new sense of college identity and community which the Victorian reformers had created and which was expressed in the proliferation of college clubs and societies in the late Victorian and Edwardian periods, and the launch of college magazines. At the same time there was a rapid numerical expansion in the universities and hence a swelling market of old boys, more strongly attached to their colleges than ever before. The college authorities were probably no less enthusiastic about the idea—although it is not clear what agreements, if any, existed between the governing bodies and the publisher—for they shared, and had fostered, the new collegiate ideals.

The series' aims were unpretentious:[22] the books were largely narrative in style, relatively short, readable, and semi-scholarly (in other words, footnotes and references were avoided, and the range of sources was often relatively narrow). Heavy tomes and severe scholarship were unlikely to find favour with most students and alumni. The volumes are of variable quality, but the leading experts of the day in university history, several of whom published other works on aspects of the subject, appear in the list of authors[23] and ensured that the histories were respectable if not comprehensive. Contemporaries were quite aware of the limitations of the genre, as reviews of some individual volumes in *The Cambridge Review*, then an undergraduate weekly, indicate. The reviewer of J. B. Mullinger's history of St John's in 1901 observed that for the historian of a large and old college, 'it is hard to find room for more than a summary catalogue of persons and events'.[24] Subsequent reviews commented on the same tendency, E. S. Shuckburgh's history of Emmanuel being praised in 1905 for escaping the catalogue by concentrating on the college's early, Puritan, years.[25]

There is no reason to suppose that the authors were any less conscious of the aims and limits of the series—certainly not the expert scholars amongst them. For example, at the time of writing his history of St John's, Mullinger was also working on a massive scholarly history of the university from its origins to the end of the seventeenth century, a work which had already occupied him for some thirty years or so and which demonstrated just what he could achieve given sufficient space and time.[26] He surely made no great claims for his college history. At the other extreme, perhaps, was J. H. Gray, who wrote the volume on Queens' College for the series and was a classicist, not a historian, although he was a college man through and through[27] and he had Searle's history to draw on for the first two centuries of the college's existence. The preface to his book, published in 1898, is suitably modest about his achievement, explaining that 'a really adequate History of Queens' College . . . would require an amount of time, and also of knowledge, historical, antiquarian and architectural, which it is wholly out of my power to command'.[28]

It is instructive to compare this disclaimer with Macleane's utterance of an older, narrower view of the subject which had prefaced his history of Pembroke College Oxford (not in fact part of the same series) the previous year: Macleane wrote that it was difficult to learn much of a college's domestic life and that

'The chief interest then of an educational institution must always lie in the sons whom . . . it has given to serve God in Church and State'.[29]

Given the extent of knowledge at the time and the need to address a broad readership, little more could have been expected of the college history series than it achieved, and we cannot blame the volumes for embodying the fashionable historical prejudices of their period. For all its limitations, the series did mark an important evolutionary stage in the writing of college history: nothing like it had been attempted before, and it may be said to have put the subject firmly on the map. The books set a new model for further essays in the genre that later generations could use either by adapting or rejecting its forms: this would depend partly on subsequent developments in the researching and writing of university history and the new enthusiasms of historians.

An inevitable lull followed the conclusion of the series, and it is only in the last few years that new college histories have begun to appear again in significant numbers. The concern expressed in Feingold's 1981 article was that many of these recent volumes did not appear to have advanced much beyond the late Victorian model, despite substantial developments in historians' approaches to the history of the two universities in general: it was for this reason that they could be called 'an outdated genre'. The argument has much to commend it. Yet it is worth noting that A. B. Cobban, writing in 1969 from perhaps a more limited viewpoint, that of the medieval historian, argued that 'several well documented college histories', founded on the printing of documents and the more thorough sifting of college archives, had emerged in the twentieth century, 'which have had the effect of raising the subject from the antiquarian to a professional level'.[30] Furthermore, there is much more diversity among modern college histories than ever before and many of them are far more sophisticated than their predecessors: the genre is developing rapidly.

Obstacles

There are a variety of reasons for these differing approaches. The circumstances under which the histories are written is one factor. As Feingold observed,

'many of these college histories were commissioned by the governing bodies of the respective institutions for the "internal consumption" of their members.'[31]

Commercial considerations are certainly significant and can influence the style and scale of the publication; but within broad limits governing bodies are unlikely to interfere, and the choice of author(s) is likely to prove at least as decisive, if not more so. Indeed, colleges are able to keep costs down because they do not have the same overheads as publishing houses: college histories offered for 'internal consumption' therefore tend to be much less expensive than books of comparable size and substance elsewhere, and this has made it possible to publish substantial works at bargain prices.

More significant are the methodological difficulties facing the authors, which are not fully appreciated by those who have not worked in this field. At first sight, a college history must seem an easy enough commission: a small-scale topic with clearly defined boundaries, most of the source material within easy reach, and needing little knowledge of foreign languages (except Latin). In fact the subject is far more complex than this first glance might indicate, and the sources often give problems.

The first difficulty is that of definition. What is a college? This is a more complicated question than it seems.[32] A college has many different facets and a conscientious college historian should attend to them all. It has a physical aspect in its buildings and material possessions: the historian must therefore learn about architectural styles and techniques, fixtures and fittings, plate and paintings. It is an institution: organization and government are therefore important themes. There is a financial aspect: the historian needs to understand property-owning, accounts and economics. The college is a community and society—actually, more than one, since junior and senior members, and often fellows and masters, form distinct albeit interconnected sub-communities—and so the historian has to look at every aspect of its social history; this is made more difficult by the fact that colleges have a largely transient population. Its academic side must be explored, and this too is a more complicated task than is often supposed: the historian must learn about the history of many arts and sciences, and although the formal student curriculum can generally be established without too much difficulty, the informal academic life of college members is often unclear and intellectual links at this level are frequently elusive.[33] The history of Oxford and Cambridge until the nineteenth century is closely bound with that of the church, which means that the college historian must research into ecclesiastical and theological history. Especially in the early modern period, but at many other times too, the universities possessed political significance: political history must therefore be added to the list. As well as the college's national environment, its local background and relationship with the surrounding communities should also be explored: as Cobban puts it, 'the investigation should transcend the institution'.[34] Biographical history cannot be omitted, particularly in the study of relatively small communities. In addition, the history of any institution will contain many events of significance peculiar to itself—for example, its foundation, wars and other upheavals—and a host of miscellaneous aspects may require treatment in detail. On top of all this, the research will generally have to span several centuries.

The historian cannot hope honestly to become truly expert in every one of these fields. There will always be some imbalances even in the most thorough college history reflecting its author's particular strengths and weaknesses. The balance will also depend upon the extent and quality of background material available. The assistance given by certain developments within the antiquarian tradition has already been commented upon; there is also a considerable volume of secondary literature from the Victorian period onwards, and scholarly interest in university history has been particularly marked in the last three decades or so, which has provided a number of valuable secondary studies in the form of books, articles and dissertations. Where extensive secondary material is available—especially for the sixteenth/seventeenth and later nineteenth centuries—the college historian can easily establish a context for interpreting the college's development at a given time, and can more easily evaluate the evidence from primary sources. Where this background is deficient the problem can be acute: the eighteenth-century universities, for example, have only recently come under close scrutiny again;[35] hitherto it was necessary to rely largely on Victorian studies. The present century has scarcely been touched upon as yet, although work is in hand. In such cases the historian often has to be more tentative in drawing conclusions, more matter-of-fact in description.[36]

The quality and accessibility of the college's own sources are also vital factors. It may not be appreciated by many historians that Oxford and Cambridge college archives demonstrate wide variations in the range and usefulness of their archival materials. Record-keeping was often a haphazard business and the survival of documents owes much to chance. The college's needs and the historian's interests do not always coincide: archives tend to contain masses of evidence about landholding—title deeds, lease contracts and the like—but precious little about intellectual affairs and many aspects of social life. College order books, recording the formal decisions of governing bodies, which first appear in the late medieval period at some colleges, only come into general use during the sixteenth century, and not all were kept with equal diligence. College accounts, as several contributors to the *History of the University of Oxford* series have observed,[37] can sometimes defy interpretation. Entering recent times the researcher faces a very different problem: the sheer volume of paperwork generated by modern college administrations can be overwhelming. The quality of colleges' archival administration also varies, though they are well kept in the main: there is no guarantee that all the records will be fully catalogued, or held in the same place, and anyone who has worked in the field will be aware of how easily documents can be missed.

Other difficulties attend recent times in particular. The need for personal accounts and biographical material in addition to formal college documents is self-evident. At a college level, there may be little of this to choose from, and as with similar material from earlier periods there is a risk that such accounts may be unrepresentative: it is usually only the famous alumni who publish autobiographies, whose letters are printed, and whose lives are written. Relatively few of these are dons; and for the others, student years are unlikely to occupy much space in the account of an active life. The problem is compounded now by the marked tendency since the Victorian reforms for students to look back on college life through rose-tinted spectacles, focusing on its idyllic or sensational aspects instead of the routine or mundane; fortunately there are sometimes a few 'dissident' accounts to compensate for this,[38] though like any other personal view they cannot be accepted wholly at face value. There is a further obstacle in that such material is unlikely to be published until a good many years after the author or subject has left college; and in the case of biographies the time lag will be longer still. For this reason other unpublished, even unwritten sources of information must be pursued.

The undergraduate who reviewed J. H. Gray's history of Queens' College for the *Cambridge Review* in 1899 thought it

'a pity that college historians dare not write for posterity and tell what they know from personal experience'.[39]

It is in this area that governing bodies are likely to place restrictions, not on controversial events as such, but on speaking ill of the living, which is generally a legitimate handicap. Certainly the college historian ought to draw on the memories of fellows and old members, which can extend a long way. Sometimes old members write brief autobiographical reminiscences of their college days and send them to the colleges for their records. An appeal through college magazines for such material may be fruitful—probably much more so than a request merely for old diaries, letters, and other contemporary documents which their authors may wish to keep private; besides, undergraduate diarists are usually far more interested in themselves than in their surroundings. Elderly fellows tend to be happy to talk about the old days and answer questions but are more reluctant to write their reminiscences down. Modern techniques of oral history, applied to a large sample, would certainly yield a rich harvest, but the practical difficulties here in interviewing, and recording and compiling data on the scale required are considerable. The alternative method of selective interviewing is always open to challenge on the grounds of partiality. For recent history—and especially contentious happenings—it may be better, and safer too, to rely on documents alone, bolstered by questions to participants where the facts are unclear. An anthropologist, though, might find a contemporary college, with its distinctive hierarchies, rituals and sub-cultures, a worthwhile subject; and the results of such research could be used to good effect by the historian.

It is nonetheless imperative for the historian to write about recent changes, even though their long-term consequences cannot always be foreseen—a factor exacerbated by the rapidity of change since the Second World War. If nothing else, the historian can still perform a valuable rôle as the chronicler of developments, and such descriptions are in themselves historical documents in perceiving and expressing the currents of the author's own times.[40]

Aims

Enough has been said to demonstrate the potential for diversity among college histories; it is time to examine the different approaches adopted by some recent histories and to suggest some of the reasons for this. The simplest type of history is that which comes closest to Feingold's criticism that some histories were

'little more than sophisticated guides to the colleges, their sites and their most distinguished members'.[41]

G. M. Trevelyan's *Trinity College. An Historical Sketch*, first published in 1943, was a brief, but as one would expect, an intelligent, informed and literate survey.[42] C. W. Scott-Giles's history of Sidney Sussex College, first published seven years later,[43] similarly described itself as no more than 'a background sketch' giving students 'a swift survey of their college' and seeking to encourage them to study it more completely, by which the author seems principally to have meant going on to read G. M. Edwards's earlier contribution to the college history series.[44] Both Trevelyan and Scott-Giles were writing with strictly limited aims, and it would be unreasonable to complain that they did not go further, since in no sense were they seeking to block or pre-empt more substantial works.

Another method of dealing with the difficulties which the range of source materials poses has been to limit the scope of the study, by concentrating either on a particular theme or on a restricted historical period. Many of the former have been highly successful. One of the first essays in this field was John Venn's *Early Collegiate Life*, based on evidence of Caius College, which made good use among other material of information contained in an extensive collection of undergraduate letters from the early seventeenth century. A more recent work along similar lines is W. J. Harrison's *Life in Clare Hall Cambridge 1653–1713*, a precise study based on books of fellows' and students' accounts which give a remarkably complete picture of day-to-day life in the college, and many other details of its history. Though narrowly focused, the study has more general value, serving as a reference point for historians working on other colleges which lack such comprehensive information.[45] H. F. Howard's history of the finances of St John's from its foundation until the early twentieth century, also a thorough and expert study, is likewise of great value to all historians who struggle to comprehend college accounts.[46] A work such as Gaskell's study of the Trinity College library is of course relevant to broader work on the history of university, and college, teaching.[47] Largely pictorial or iconographic works dealing with aspects of college fabric may become more numerous in future, though as yet there have been few essays in this genre.[48] The visual record—drawings and paintings, photographs, and the fabric itself—is a source which deserves to be exploited more fully.

Studies limited to relatively short spans of time have tended to stick to the chronicler's method, revealing their closeness to the old antiquarian tradition. J. P. T. Bury's history of Corpus Christi College Cambridge between 1822 and 1952[49] professes to follow the approach adopted by the eighteenth- and nineteenth-century historians of the college, Masters and Lamb, continuing chronologically where Lamb's work left off: this was to relate the principal events during each mastership and to supply brief biographies of masters and fellows, together with lists of incumbents of college livings and college members. To a large extent, the book is a biographical register, but it is also a self-conscious 'chronicle'[50] of the college in the period. As one would expect in a chronicle, the research is intensive and full of details; analysis and context play a lesser rôle. It is a well-informed study, but what sets the book above many others of this kind is its use of letters of recollections imaginatively solicited from old members to illustrate college life in modern times.

Another work to adopt a detailed, mainly chronological approach over a short period of time—in this case, just one hundred years—is Grave's history of Fitzwilliam College Cambridge.[51] The extensive quotations of primary sources in full in this book also owe much to antiquarianism. The volume of material reproduced—reflecting the extent of modern sources—serves as a substitute for analysis and can appear a catalogue, but this is a large book and contains a great deal of information. The short timespan covered facilitates a narrative style, which is further assisted by the subject's ready-made theme: the struggle of a non-collegiate body to become a full college of the university. Eight of the thirteen chapters are on the history of Fitzwilliam, but the other five are thematic, covering student activities (principally their clubs and societies), the Fitzwilliam Society, the chapel, the library, and the all too often neglected subject of research students. Grave's method echoed that already seen in the historiography of more recent British universities: Arthur Chapman's history of the University of Sheffield of 1955 was also a large digest (over 500 pages), full of details, covering just fifty years.[52]

More concentrated still is E. H. F. Smith's *St. Peter's. The Founding of an Oxford College*[53] which covers fewer than twenty years, and is mostly focused on a period of less than half that time. It is therefore a deliberately detailed, almost blow-by-blow history, and forms a distinct category of college history on its own.

The only college history confined to a restricted period in time that breaks free of the traditional style is of a medieval college which is no longer in existence. Cobban's history of the King's Hall in Cambridge, which was absorbed into Trinity College in 1546,[54] is based on a substantial surviving body of medieval college documents, which enabled the author to conduct a full inquiry into the economic, constitutional, and administrative organization of the college in a thematic manner.[55] The book's seven chapters discuss: the hall's origins and royal significance (it was an arm of the chapel royal); educational significance; relations with university and ecclesiastical authorities; internal economy; constitutional organization; aspects of college life; and the careers of its wardens and some of its notable scholars. This approach was made easier too by the limited timespan—less than 250 years—which the documents covered. Cobban seems to have felt, with some justification, that his history was breaking new ground.

Histories of the older surviving colleges face, as we have seen, a different scale of difficulties. Charles Crawley's history of Trinity Hall Cambridge[56] had to cover over 600 years of history, relying on a relatively limited and uneven collection of college archives. The author's preface to the book explains the problems he faced with source material and the effects this had on the shape of the history, compelling some unevenness in its treatment. The approach is largely chronological, with two thematic chapters on the site and buildings, and the college's special connection with the civil law; both are subjects which respond well to this treatment. There is also a large number of appendices containing information not easily incorporated into the narrative account. Some of the uneven treatment is more from choice than necessity, as the preface acknowledges, but overall the book makes a good job of an awkward assignment, and where evidence is accessible its discussions are appropriately thorough, as well as perceptive.

Most of the college histories published since Crawley's work have also been of medieval foundations. In his history of Lincoln College Oxford,[57] V. H. H. Green overcame the genre's difficulties by producing a large scale history that was both comprehensive and scholarly. It was duly praised by Feingold on these counts.[58] The apparent lack of any constraints regarding length in the Lincoln history must have rendered great assistance to the author in his task; so too must his previous experience in the field as the author of several works on university and college history.[59] Most college histories to date have been written by college 'elders': senior figures who tend to be historians or long-serving college officers (and in many cases, both).

The history of New College Oxford, which also appeared in 1979,[60] adopted a different approach to the problems of college history writing, in particular that of finding a single person with the time and qualifications to produce a substantial and comprehensive study. Like the history of the University of Oxford, the New College history was a collaborative effort involving several expert authors, who could bring their respective expertise to bear on different aspects of the study. The idea was an imaginative one, though the book is rather unbalanced in its coverage. It is divided into three sections: in the first, there are some 140 pages on the college's history from 1379; in the second, almost 120 on its architecture; and nearly 100 on its music, plate, archives, library and memorials in the third.[61] Within the first section, there is no real investigation of the college's recent history: instead, in an ingenious attempt to escape some of the difficulties of writing about modern times, it prints six individual reminiscences of the inter-war years. The editors' justification for this method was that 'a more formal treatment of a period within living memory would have provoked dispute';

they hoped too that the reminiscences would provide material for later historians and perhaps prompt others to record their memories.[62] The New College volume did not set its sights too high: it was intended, wrote the editors, to be 'a worthy and accurate record' rather than 'a formal, learned history of the college',[63] and its multi-author method may have caused some logistical difficulties and contributed to the unbalanced coverage. Nonetheless, even if the idea did not quite come off, it may be worth pursuing in future by other colleges, providing that sufficiently broad expert coverage can be achieved.

Closely related to this branch of the genre is the collected essays format, which does not seek to provide a college history as such, but rather to illuminate its existence across the centuries through short separate studies by recognized experts of different aspects, personalities or events. The collection edited by E. E. Rich marking the 500th anniversary of the foundation of St Catharine's College Cambridge, and J. Prest's *Balliol Studies* collection,[64] suggest another direction which college history studies may choose to follow with profit, focusing on particular topics or themes. Like the single-theme college studies mentioned above, such work can be of use to broader histories of colleges and universities.

But the single-author approach to college histories has to date proved the most successful in combining range and depth of study. Christopher Brooke's fine history of Gonville and Caius College Cambridge (1985)[65] is comprehensive and scholarly, and its author is not afraid to tackle recent events. He also achieves the not inconsiderable feat of presenting over 600 years of history in digestible form.[66] Brooke's work and the other major contributions to the genre in the 1970s and 1980s demonstrate how far college histories have come in recent years and what can be achieved. There may be no single correct way to write a college history—several forms have emerged, as we have seen, and a number of future evolutionary patterns are possible—but these books have set a modern standard and are valuable models for other historians who may come to work in this field.

11 Hope Drive
The Park
Nottingham NG7 1DL

REFERENCES

* I am grateful to Dr G. H. R. Tillotson of Peterhouse, Cambridge, for his advice on a point of information in this article, and for kindly checking certain references for me.

1. M. Feingold, 'Oxford and Cambridge College Histories: An outdated genre?', *History of Universities* i (1981).
2. For example, C. Crawley, *Trinity Hall. The History of a Cambridge College 1350–1975* (Cambridge, 1976); V. H. H. Green, *The Commonwealth of Lincoln College, 1427–1977* (Oxford, 1979); J. Buxton and P. Williams (eds.), *New College Oxford 1379–1979* (Oxford, 1979); C. N. L. Brooke, *A History of Gonville and Caius College* (Woodbridge, 1985); J. H. Jones, *Balliol College. A History 1263–1939* (Oxford, 1988).
3. J. D. Twigg, 'The University of Cambridge and the English Revolution, 1625–1688' (University of Cambridge Ph.D. thesis, 1983; to be published shortly by the Boydell Press); 'The parliamentary visitation of the University of Cambridge, 1644–1645', *English Historical Review* xcviii (1983); 'The Limits of "Reform": Some Aspects of the Debate on University Education during the English Revolution', *History of Universities* iv (1984); *A History of Queens' College, Cambridge 1448–1986* (Woodbridge, 1987); 'College Finances, 1640–1660', in N. R. N. Tyacke (ed.), *Seventeenth-Century Oxford* (The History of the University of Oxford volume iv, Oxford, forthcoming); 'Royal Mandates for Degrees in the Reign of Charles II (1660–85): an Aspect of the Crown's Influence in the University of Cambridge', *Proceedings of the Cambridge Antiquarian Society* lxxxvi (1987).
4. For Caius and his foundation, see Brooke, *Gonville and Caius*, chapter 4.
5. ibid., pp. 80–4.
6. ibid., pp. 24–5, 56, 60, 63, 66.
7. ibid., pp. 74–5; and see pp. 10, 28–9, 144.
8. See for example G. W. Groos (ed. and transl.), *The Diary of Baron Waldstein. A Traveller in Elizabethan England* (London, 1981), pp. 88–9. For an Oxford illustration, see C. Fiennes, *The Journeys of Celia Fiennes*, ed. C. Morris (London, 1949), 38. I am not sure that all contemporaries were equally convinced, however: see for example Twigg, 'University of Cambridge', p. 22.
9. Most of the Baker Manuscripts are in the Cambridge University Library; a few volumes are in the British Library.
10. W. Warren, *Warren's Book*, ed. A. W. W. Dale (Cambridge, 1911); G. Storey, foreword to Crawley, *Trinity Hall*, p. x.
11. For example, Anthony Wood, *The History and Antiquities of the Colleges and Halls in the University of Oxford*, ed. J. Gutch (Oxford, 1786); *The History and Antiquities of the University of Oxford*, ed. J. Gutch (Oxford, 1792–6); *Athenae Oxonienses*, ed. P. Bliss (London,

History of Universities

1813–20); *Fasti Oxonienses*, ed. P. Bliss (London, 1815–20); Thomas
Fuller, *The History of the University of Cambridge* (1655); Thomas
Baker, *History of the College of St. John the Evangelist* ed. J. E. B.
Mayor (Cambridge, 1869).
12. Above, note 10; Robert Masters, *History of the College of Corpus
Christi*, ed. J. Lamb (Cambridge, 1831); Queens' College Library,
Books 72 and 73 (Robert Plumptre's history).
13. Joseph Foster, *Alumni Oxonienses* (Oxford and London, 1891–2); J.
and J. A. Venn, *Alumni Cantabrigienses* (Cambridge, 1922–7, 1940–54).
14. For example, J. Peile, *Biographical Register of Christ's College* (Cambridge, 1910); T. A. Walker, *Admissions to Peterhouse, 1615–1911*
(Cambridge, 1912); J. Venn, *Biographical History of Gonville and Caius
College* (Cambridge, 1901). The value of Venn's biographical history,
and of his other antiquarian researches, is acknowledged by Christopher Brooke, *History of Gonville and Caius*, pp. xiii–xiv.
15. A. B. Emden, *A Biographical Register of the University of Oxford to
1540* (Oxford, 1957–59, 1974); *A Biographical Register of the University
of Cambridge to 1500* (Cambridge, 1963).
16. For example, T. H. Aston, G. D. Duncan and T. A. R. Evans, 'The
Medieval Alumni of the University of Cambridge', *Past and Present* 86
(1980); A. B. Cobban, 'The Medieval Cambridge Colleges: a Quantitative Study of Higher Education to c. 1500', *History of Education* 9
(1980).
17. R. Willis and J. W. Clark, *The Architectural History of the University of
Cambridge* (Cambridge, 1886); Royal Commission on Historical
Monuments, *An Inventory of the Historical Monuments in the City of
Cambridge* (London, 1959).
18. For example, J. Lamb (ed.), *A Collection of Letters, Statutes, and other
Documents . . . illustrative of the History of the University of Cambridge
during the period of the Reformation* (London, 1838); J. Heywood (ed.),
Collection of Statutes for the University and the Colleges of Cambridge
(London, 1840); J. Heywood and T. Wright (eds.), *The Ancient Laws of
the Fifteenth Century for King's College, Cambridge* (London, 1850); J.
Heywood and T. Wright (eds.), *Cambridge University Transactions
during the Puritan Controversies of the Sixteenth and Seventeenth
Centuries* (London, 1854). Many documents were also printed by the
Cambridge Antiquarian Society in its *Communications*.
19. C. H. Cooper (ed.), *Annals of Cambridge* (Cambridge, 1842–1908).
Cooper's other antiquarian work includes 'Inventory of Plate sent to
King Charles I by Queens' College, Cambridge, and Receipt of moneys
advanced for his service by the President and Fellows, 1642', *Cambridge
Antiquarian Society Communications* i (1851); *Memorials of Cambridge*
(Cambridge, 1860–6); and (with T. Cooper), *Athenae Cantabrigienses*
(Cambridge, 1857–1913).
20. W. G. Searle, *The History of the Queens' College of St Margaret and St*

Bernard in the University of Cambridge. 1446–1662 (Cambridge, 1867–71).

21. Above, notes 11 (Baker/Mayor), 12 (Masters/Lamb), 20 (Searle).
22. T. H. Aston described it as 'unpretentious but none the less useful', in his prefatory note to J. I. Catto and R. Evans (eds.), *The Early Oxford Schools* (History of the University of Oxford volume i, Oxford, 1984), p. v.
23. At Cambridge they include W. W. Rouse Ball (Trinity), J. B. Mullinger (St John's), J. Peile (Christ's), E. S. Shuckburgh (Emmanuel), H. P. Stokes (Corpus Christi), J. Venn (Gonville and Caius), and T. A. Walker (Peterhouse).
24. *Cambridge Review*, 7 Mar. 1901, p. 226.
25. ibid., 4 Dec. 1902, p. 117; 16 Mar. 1905, pp. 262–3.
26. J. B. Mullinger, *The University of Cambridge* (Cambridge, 1873–1911).
27. Twigg, *Queens'*, pp. 228, 232, 257–9, 281, 299, 330–1. Gray did give college history lectures around the turn of the century in the days before it had a history fellow: ibid., p. 292, n.34.
28. J. H. Gray, *The Queens' College of St Margaret & St Bernard in the University of Cambridge* (Cambridge, revised edition 1926), p. viii.
29. D. Macleane, *A History of Pembroke College, Oxford* (Oxford Historical Society xxxiii 1897), p. vii. Macleane did contribute a volume on Pembroke to the college history series three years later: D. Macleane, *Pembroke College* (London, 1900).
30. A. B. Cobban, *The King's Hall within the University of Cambridge in the Later Middle Ages* (Cambridge, 1969), pp. 3–4. The examples cited by Cobban are A. H. Lloyd, *The Early History of Christ's College* (Cambridge, 1934); and J. R. Magrath, *The Queen's College* (Oxford, 1921).
31. Feingold, 'College Histories', p. 207. Many histories are published to mark anniversaries such as centenaries or jubilees.
32. The question is also discussed by Brooke, *Gonville and Caius*, p. xi.
33. Feingold commented that relatively little work has been done in this field: 'College Histories', p. 211. But he did not explore the reasons why.
34. A. B. Cobban, *The Medieval Universities: their development and organisation* (London, 1975), p. 158.
35. The principal recent works are L. S. Sutherland and L. G. Mitchell (eds.), *The Eighteenth Century* (History of the University of Oxford volume v, Oxford, 1986); J. Gascoigne, *Cambridge in the Age of the Enlightenment: Science, Religion and Politics from the Restoration to the French Revolution* (Cambridge, forthcoming).
36. Feingold chided Buxton and Williams for arguing that a full scholarly history of New College Oxford would have to await the completion of the History of the University of Oxford series: Feingold, 'College Histories', p. 209; Buxton and Williams (eds.), *New College*, p. viii. Perhaps the editors of the New College volume were ducking the issue

to an extent, but their remarks also point to the real difficulty of working without adequate background material.

37. For the difficulties of interpreting Oxford college accounts, see G. E. Aylmer, 'The Economics and Finances of the Colleges and University *c* 1530–1640', in J. McConica (ed.), *The Collegiate University* (History of the University of Oxford volume iii, Oxford, 1986), pp. 524–9, 532, 545; J. P. D. Dunbabin, 'College Estates and Wealth 1660–1815', in Sutherland and Mitchell (eds.), *The Eighteenth Century*, pp. 270–2; Twigg, 'College Finances' (forthcoming).

38. For example, the author's history of Queens' made use of three valuable 'dissident' accounts illuminating different periods: S. Atkinson, 'Struggles of a Poor Student through Cambridge', *The London Magazine and Review*, 1 April 1825; G. Harding, *Along My Line* (London, 1953); J. Vaizey, untitled essay in R. Hayman (ed.), *My Cambridge* (London, 1977). If personal accounts in general are likely to be thin on the ground at a college level, 'dissident' sources will of course be fewer still.

39. *Cambridge Review*, 16 Feb. 1899, p. 208.

40. The difficulties of writing about modern times are also discussed in Brooke, *Gonville and Caius*, pp. 259–60; Twigg, *Queens'*, p. 363.

41. 'College Histories', p. 207.

42. G. M. Trevelyan, *Trinity College. An Historical Sketch* (Cambridge, 1983 edition). The volume has been revised and brought up to date since Trevelyan's death.

43. C. W. Scott-Giles, *Sidney Sussex College. A Short History* (Cambridge, 1975 edition).

44. ibid., p. ix; G. M. Edwards, *Sidney Sussex College* (London, 1899).

45. J. Venn, *Early Collegiate Life* (Cambridge, 1913); W. J. Harrison, *Life in Clare Hall Cambridge 1653–1713* (Cambridge, 1958). Harrison's earlier *Notes on the Masters, Fellows, Scholars and Exhibitioners of Clare College, Cambridge* (Cambridge, 1953) is another useful book of this kind, though perhaps more limited in its general application.

46. H. F. Howard, *An Account of the Finances of the College of St John the Evangelist in the University of Cambridge 1511–1926* (Cambridge, 1935). Another useful work on a related subject from the same college is A. F. Torry, *Founders and Benefactors of St John's College, Cambridge* (Cambridge, 1888).

47. P. Gaskell, *Trinity College Library. The first 150 years* (Cambridge, 1980).

48. For example, A. D. Browne and C. T. Seltman, *A Pictorial History of the Queen's College of Saint Margaret and Saint Bernard commonly called Queens' College Cambridge 1448–1948* (Cambridge, 1951); A. F. Kersting and David Watkin, *Peterhouse, 1284–1984: an Architectural Record* (Cambridge, 1984).

49. J. P. T. Bury, *The College of Corpus Christi and of the Blessed Virgin Mary. A History from 1822 to 1952* (Cambridge, 1952).

50. ibid., pp. 113, 174.
51. W. W. Grave, *Fitzwilliam College Cambridge, 1869–1969* (Cambridge, 1983).
52. Arthur W. Chapman, *The Story of a Modern University. A History of the University of Sheffield* (Oxford, 1955).
53. E. H. F. Smith, *St. Peter's. The Founding of an Oxford College* (Gerrards Cross, 1958). The book was planned as the first in a series on the college: see Cairncross's foreword, ibid., p. 9.
54. See above, note 30.
55. Cobban, *King's Hall*, pp. 1–8 and *passim*.
56. See above, note 2.
57. See above, note 2.
58. Feingold, 'College Histories', pp. 210–11.
59. For example, V. H. H. Green, *Oxford Common Room: A Study of Lincoln College and Mark Pattison* (London, 1957); *The Young Mr Wesley: A Study of John Wesley and Oxford* (London, 1961); *Religion at Oxford and Cambridge* (London, 1964); *The Universities* (London, 1969); *A History of Oxford University* (London, 1974).
60. See above, note 2.
61. See also Feingold's comments on this: 'College Histories', pp. 208–9.
62. Buxton and Williams (eds.), *New College*, p. ix.
63. ibid., p. viii.
64. E. E. Rich (ed.), *St. Catharine's College, Cambridge, 1473–1973* (Cambridge, 1973); J. Prest (ed.), *Balliol Studies* (London, 1982).
65. See above, note 2.
66. The book is discussed more fully in this author's review in *History of Universities* vi (1987), pp. 155–6.

Sven Stelling-Michaud and the History of Universities

Jacques Verger

Sven Stelling-Michaud, Emeritus Professor at the University of Geneva, died in 1986 at the age of eighty. Although he remained active until his death, his passing has been largely overlooked, at any rate by scholars of medieval and modern university history. Perhaps it is not too late to correct this omission and to pay tribute to his work which, I believe, took a pioneering role in the field of study to which the *History of Universities* is dedicated.[1]

The history of universities was never S. Stelling-Michaud's sole area of interest. Indeed, his work on this subject accounts for barely a third of his scholarly output.[2] Led to history by the relatively well-worn paths of diplomatic history (his thesis of 1935 was on 'Saint-Saphorin et la politique de la Suisse pendant la guerre de succession d'Espagne (1700–1710)') and the history of ideas (to which he always remained loyal, as indicated by his numerous articles on J.-J. Rousseau, Burckhardt, D. Lubin, G. Ferrero, Romain Rolland, H. de Man, etc.) he was able gradually to widen his interests to encompass the history of law, of institutions and of society. 'L'examen du passé est le plus délicat qui soit. Il y faut, à côté de connaissances historiques étendues, le sens de la vie qui seul permet de comprendre. Car l'histoire envisagée comme une succession de faits est chose intolérable', he wrote as early as 1930.[3] This striking conception was contemporary with the creation of the *Annales* of M. Bloch and L. Febvre. Indeed, he was a friend of Fernand Braudel. And it was in this context that his interest in the history of universities was sparked and began to develop.

S. Stelling-Michaud was not, however, a pedantic scholar; nor was he desk-bound. As well as being professor of modern and medieval history at Geneva for thirty-two years, he was also a great traveller, journalist, translator, administrator, and writer of prefaces as well as, when he had to be, a crusader for democratic and humanitarian causes. An accomplished linguist, he readily presented himself as a European and child of the Enlightenment, a bearer of the intellectual tradition of his fellow countrymen J.-J. Rousseau and Sismondi, a living example of a cosmopolitan internationalist. In short, in his life as in his work, it can be seen that S. Stelling-Michaud consistently rejected narrow specialization, the separation of historical research from present-day concerns, the recourse to a narrowly nationalistic or political outlook. While not, of course, unaware of the demands of a rigorous methodology, he always managed to capture the flavour and essence of the ideas in question. Here lies, in part, the value of his contribution to the renewal of university history.

As S. Stelling-Michaud began to study the history of universities, a little before 1940,[4] a first phase of the historiography had clearly just passed its peak. Begun at the end of the nineteenth century, with obvious links with the rise of European nationalism and the contemporary renewal of the university institution, this was the era of the classic publications of sources (Denifle-Châtelain and M. Fournier for France, Sarti and Malagola in Bologna, Gloria in Padua) and of the first European (Denifle, Rashdall) or national syntheses (V. de la Fuente for Spain, M. Fournier for France, F. Paulsen for Germany, G. Manacorda for Italy, etc.). This movement began to run out of steam after 1918 and, after a few final publications like those of the last volumes of *Chartularium Studii Bononiensis*, the statutes of the theology faculty of Bologna by F. Ehrle or the *Statuta antiqua* of Oxford by S. Gibson, ground to a halt in the 1930s, leaving unfinished many projects launched a few decades earlier. What must be confessed to be the mediocrity of the few syntheses attempted in those years (one thinks of the two volumes of St. d'Irsay or that of Zaccagnini on Bologna, for example) bears testimony in its own way to this historiographical exhaustion.

This admittedly schematic account of the scholarship of that period helps us to see the innovative quality of the research which S. Stelling-Michaud then undertook on the relationship between the University of Bologna and medieval Switzerland. Spearheaded by a few preliminary articles, but delayed by the war, this would eventually culminate in the great work on *L'Université de Bologne et la Pénétration des Droits Romain et Canonique en Suisse aux XIIIe et XIVe Siècles* (Geneva, 1955) which was completed by the publication of the catalogues of manuscripts and registers of acts which had served as its documentary foundation.[5] Despite the rather unpromising title, this work was in every respect remarkable.

1. In boldly tackling the case of Bologna at its apogee as the most important university of the European Mediterranean region and model for all medieval law schools, rather than choosing a university of secondary importance, S. Stelling-Michaud was certainly confronting a particularly voluminous quantity of source material. But at least he could be sure that the historical problems raised would be of major interest, and that the methods and hypotheses used would give his work the inherent value of a reference work.

2. Whereas most previous publications of sources concerning the university of Bologna had concentrated either on the problem of the origins of the schools or else on the statutes and political history of the university, S. Stelling-Michaud conceived of his subject as one of social history. Who were the Swiss students of Bologna? How many were there? Where did they come from? How did they actually live during their stay at the university? What studies did they pursue, and for how long? What careers did they finally take up once they returned home? What cultural baggage had they acquired? To what extent was this a factor in the evolution of the society, *mentalités*, and institutions of a country which was, like Switzerland, fairly traditional in its legal customs and feudal structures?

3. He understood that this broadening of the historical problem demanded that new kinds of documents, beyond those of the university archives, be used. These included the notarial registers where so many of the actual details of student life are buried; the manuscripts, annotated in the margins, which were actually used in the schools, shedding light on the practice and content of the teaching far better than official syllabuses or the lists of *puncta taxata*; and finally the papal registers (letters and petitions) which partially make up for the paucity of matriculation registers in the thirteenth and fourteenth centuries.

4. S. Stelling-Michaud also had the insight to see, even before the publication of the monumental 'biographical registers' of Emden, that prosopography was the best tool for the social analysis of medieval student populations. And his prosopography was a university prosopography worthy of the name, which sacrificed neither a

knowledge of the time spent at university as seen from Bolognese sources, nor that concerning the origins and career destinations which he drew from local Swiss sources. Some of his imitators have not managed to piece together such a balanced picture and, by favouring one of the two aspects of the source material, have left themselves open to the charge of unfortunate misinterpretations, either of the relative importance of the standing and achievement of the universities, or the place of graduates in medieval societies.[6]

5. S. Stelling-Michaud managed, then, to keep the social history of student populations at the heart of his approach without neglecting either the classical history of university institutions or the courses of study actually followed. Indeed, the first part of his book (pp. 13–75) remains one of the best general treatments of the organization of the medieval university of Bologna and is both clear and vigorous. Essentially, he saw that this most traditional but indispensable approach could be thrown into sharper relief by an understanding of both the social and individual contexts. It is these which enable one to measure the always significant gap between plans and their practical application, between official programmes of study and the teaching which was actually given and received.

Today the problems which S. Stelling-Michaud faced seem all too familiar to us. One is, of course, tempted to reproach him for his still hesitant or impressionistic use of statistics, for his sometimes summary social classifications, and for certain imprecise concepts, such as that of the 'lay student' which he frequently draws upon. His investigations paid the price of any individual endeavour in that they did not really cover more than sixty-odd years (1265–1330) which is rather a short time span in which to trace profound changes.[7] And one would, of course, hesitate to generalize on the strength of observations which are primarily applicable to Swiss medieval society (although many subsequent studies of the rest of the Empire or even northern France do not point to very different conclusions).[8]

But none of this undermines the overall soundness and therefore the pioneering quality of his fundamental insights. Let us add to this that as far as Bologna itself is concerned, it is only very recently that S. Stelling-Michaud has found worthy successors. C. Piana and A. Perez Martin have delved in their turn into the legal archives and have published numerous extracts from them.[9] Other researchers led by G. P. Brizzi and A. I. Pini have extracted new findings on the student population, the daily life of the *scolares*, the book trade, and so forth from these same archives.[10] Their conclusions have tended to call into question some of S. Stelling-Michaud's hypotheses and in particular to lessen the global significance which he assigned to the university of the 'Ultramontanes'. But such revisions are to be expected of any innovative work.

S. Stelling-Michaud had himself hoped to continue to pursue his work on the University of Bologna, but in the form of a collective investigation. In the sixties he conceived of a project which he called the *Corpus scholarium (ultramontanorum) Bononiensium*. This would have consisted of publishing (along with biographical notes and other complementary series) the registers of all the acts of the *Memorialia Communis* relating to the Ultramontane students of Bologna in the Middle Ages.[11] The starting-point would have been provided by the gleanings which S. Stelling-Michaud had already brought out for the years 1300–1330, subsequently extended in both directions (1265–1300 and 1330–1500). S. Stelling-Michaud hoped to entrust this work to an international network of colleagues (a collaboration made essential by the need for research and identification in many local archives). The project was not seen through to the end and S. Stelling-Michaud had some regrets about this.

It must be admitted that, in the form in which he had presented it, the project was undoubtedly both too large in scope and too rigidly defined. It nevertheless pointed to a historiographical gap and will need to be taken up again one day in one form or another. For it is clear that so long as we do not have exact information on the attendance of Ultramontane students at Bologna from the thirteenth to the fifteenth centuries, all that one might otherwise say on the rapid growth and importance of other European law faculties will be based in part on an element of doubt.[12]

S. Stelling-Michaud had better luck with his other prosopographical project, admittedly more locally based, which he launched with the publication of the 'Livre du Recteur' of the Academy of Geneva and its accompanying five volumes of biographical entries contributed by various colleagues.[13] Despite the limitations of the sources, especially for the early period, this work with its 12,000 student names (as well as, for the nineteenth century, 3,000 'externals'), remains an invaluable source for studying the workings and influence of this intellectual centre of Protestantism from its foundation by Calvin in 1559 to its evolution into a fully-fledged university in 1878.

S. Stelling-Michaud, it seems, never envisaged the publication of a definitive work on the history of European Universities. In its stead, one must turn to the important paper which he delivered at Stockholm in 1960 to the International Congress of the Historical Sciences, a paper which was at once provocative and appraising, a bibliographical summary and a call to further research.[14] Thirty years later this text still merits attention, and not only for its bibliographical notes.

In it one can easily discern what I will call three historiographical layers. The oldest, still prevalent in many publications of about 1960, was that of studies into the institutions and privileges of the universities.[15] This classical historiography was also distinguished by an attention to the twin problems of the origins (conceived in rather legalistic terms) and decline (which often took the form of a debate on the humanistic-scholastic opposition and the difficulty of the introduction of new disciplines in the universities).

A more novel as well as heterogeneous second layer, reflecting renewed interest in the period, gathered together S. Stelling-Michaud's own work as well as that of some other historians who had remained active since the '30s. Some already noteworthy publications were brought to light concerning both the content of teaching (Parisian and Italian Aristotelianism of the thirteenth and fourteenth centuries with A. Birkenmajer, F. Van Steenberghen, A. Maier,—salernitan medicine with O. Kristeller—Bolognese law), and certain aspects, in particular economic ones, of university life (the resources of the universities, student revenues, the problem of 'poor students', the book trade, etc.).

Finally, at a third level, S. Stelling-Michaud called for new, and if possible quantitative, investigations into areas of research which still remained largely unexplored: the individual characters of the arts faculties, which were less well known than the others; the social origins of the students and geographical distribution of university recruits; the total number of students; the daily life of masters and pupils; the social and political functions assigned to the universities by both ecclesiastical or lay powers, and those which they effectively carried out, etc.

Although the problems raised sometimes proved to be more complex than was anticipated, it should be recognized that on the whole the perspectives opened by S. Stelling-Michaud in his 1960 text inspired many important works from this time.

Of course, other avenues of research, which S. Stelling-Michaud had not anticipated, opened up as well. The most noteworthy of these seems to me to be that of the actual 'rehabilitation' of the universities at the end of the Middle Ages, which are increasingly studied in their own right, and no longer merely in terms of decline and renewal. A few of the themes given prominence by the most recent findings and which were scarcely thought of thirty years ago are: the growth of the political and social position of the graduates; the dynamism of the university foundations; the ascendancy of the colleges; the intrinsic value of what was being taught, whether of Parisian physics, Oxford logic and mathematics, or the whole intricate area of philosophy and theology which is often conveniently labelled 'nominalism' and has been illuminated by the works of P. Vignaux, H. Oberman, G. Leff, and W. J. Courtenay.

It also becomes apparent, in re-reading S. Stelling-Michaud's text, how sparse knowledge of universities in the sixteenth century, which was hardly touched upon except in the context of Reformation and Counter-Reformation developments, still was.

To the advancement, whether planned or unforeseen, of research into the history of universities, S. Stelling-Michaud brought a further personal contribution in 1964 by seizing, along with some colleagues and friends, especially G. Cencetti, A. L. Gabriel, and J. Le Goff, the initiative to create, in the very heart of the International Committee of the Historical Sciences, an International Commission for the History of Universities. Presiding over this Commission until 1974, he was succeeded by A. L Gabriel and then, in 1985, by R. Feenstra.

S. Stelling-Michaud directly inspired one of the principal accomplishments of the Commission in the shape of the publication of a large, if not complete, international bibliography of the history of universities.[16]

This Commission may not have always enjoyed the influence which S. Stelling-Michaud would have hoped to give it. Developing out of a small group of medievalists, it tackled new problems which could not have been anticipated by its founders and which were demanded by the actual enlargement of the history of universities through to the present day and therefore to the whole world. Yet thanks to its activities, the international coordination of research, publication, and scholarly exchanges are guaranteed a secure place.

In this it remains true to the spirit of its creator and thus continues to help to keep his memory alive among all historians of universities.

Ecole Normale Supérieure
Paris

REFERENCES

1. Madame J. Buenzod furnished me with various documents and information which have helped me in preparing this paper and I offer her my warmest thanks.
2. S. Stelling-Michaud's works prior to 1975 have been catalogued in the volume of 'Mélanges' which was dedicated to him in that year (*Pour une histoire qualitative. Etudes offertes à Sven Stelling-Michaud*, Geneva, 1975), pp. 323–33.
3. Cited in the preface to *Pour une histoire qualitative*, op. cit., p. 10.
4. S. Stelling-Michaud, 'La Suisse et les universités européenes du XIIIe au XVIe siècle. Essai d'une statistique de fréquentation', *Revue universitaire suisse*, Sept. 1938, pp. 148–60, is his first work on the history of universities.
5. See in particular S. Stelling-Michaud, *Catalogue des manuscrits juridiques (droit canon et droit romain) de la fin du XIIe au XIVe siècle conservés Suisse* (Geneva, 1954), and (co-edited by Suzanne Stelling-Michaud), *Les juristes suisses à Bologne (1255–133)*. *Notes biographiques et regestes des actes bolognais* (Geneva, 1960). S. Stelling-Michaud returned to the subject more recently in vol. V/12 of the collection 'Ius Romanum MediiÆvi', *La diffusion du droit romain en Suisse* (Milan, 1977).
6. I am in agreement here with R. N. Swanson's comments (in 'Learning and livings: University Study and Clerical Careers in Later Medieval England', *History of Universities*, VI, 1986–7, pp. 81–103) on the importance of looking at the given statistics of medieval universities in conjunction with those concerning society as a whole in the same period.
7. This period corresponds to the 110 first volumes of the *Memorialia Communis* collection (Archivio di Stato di Bologna); these enormous registers, where the town notaries copied out by hand all transactions worth 20 Bolognese pounds or more, supplied S. Stelling-Michaud with the base of his documentary prosopography in the absence in this period of all registers or lists of graduates, as well as giving much information on the day-to-day lives of the students.
8. I am thinking in particular of those works, sometimes less reliable than those of S. Stelling-Michaud since they favour local sources at the

expense of the university documentation, of Chr. Renardy, *Le monde des maîtres universitaires du diocèse de Liège, 1140–1350. Recherches sur sa composition et ses activités* (Paris, 1979), and *Les maîtres universitaires dans le diocèse de Liège. Répertoire biographique (1140–1350)* (Paris, 1981).

9. C. Piana, *Ricerche su le università di Bologna e di Parma nel sec. XV* (Florence, 1963); *Nuove ricerche su le università di Bologna e di Parma* (Florence, 1966); *Chartularium Studii Bononiensis S. Francisci (saec. XIII–XVI)*, (Analecta Franciscana, II), (Florence, 1970); *Nuovi documenti sull'università di Bologna e sul Collegio di Spagna* (Bologna, 1976); *Il "Liber secretus iuris caesarei" dell'università di Bologna (1450–1500)* (Milan, 1984); A. Perez Martin, 'Büchergeschäfte in Bologneser Regesten aus den Jahren 1265–1330', *Ius Commune*, VII, 1978, pp. 7–49.

10. See in particular *Studenti e Università degli Studenti dal XII al XIX secolo*, a cura di G. P. Brizzi e A. I. Pini (Studi e Memorie per la Storia dell'Università di Bologna, n.s. VII, Bologna, 1988). Cf. also M. Bellomo, *Saggio sull'Università nell'età del diritto comune* (Catania, 1979).

11. See also A. Perez Martin's brief account, 'Il Corpus Scholarium Bononiensium', *Bolletino informativo dell'Istituto Giuridico Spagnolo in Roma*, XVII, 1969, pp. 7–11.

12. This is particularly true for the Midi of France, for example, cf. J. Verger, 'Les rapports entre universités italiennes et universites méridionales françaises (XIIe–XVe siècles)', *Università e società nei secoli XII–XVI* (Pistoia, 1982), pp. 145–76.

13. *Le Livre du Recteur de l'Académie de Genève (1559–1878)*, vol. I; *Le texte*, vols II to VI, *Notices biographiques des étudiants* (vols. I to III are under the direction of Sven Stelling-Michaud; vols IV to VI by Suzanne Stelling-Michaud, Geneva, 1959–80).

14. S. Stelling-Michaud, 'L'histoire des universités au Moyen Age et à la Renaissance au cours des vingt-cinq dernières années', *Rapports du XIe Congrès international des Sciences historiques*, vol. I (Stockholm, 1960), pp. 97–143. An Italian translation was given in *Le origini dell'Università*, a cura di G. Arnaldi (Bologna, 1974), pp. 153–217.

15. This phase of the historiography might be said to have reached its culmination in P. Kibre's *Scholarly Privileges in the Middle Ages. The Rights, Privileges, and Immunities of Scholars and Universities at Bologna, Padua, Paris, and Oxford* (London, 1961).

16. G. Steiger and M. Straube, 'Forschungen und Publikationen seit 1945 zur Geschichte der deutschen Universitäten und Hochschulen auf dem Territorium der DDR', *Zeitschrift für Geschichtswissenschaft*, VIII, 1960, Sonderheft, pp. 563–99, and M. Straube and W. Fläschendräger, 'Forschungen zur Geschichte der Universitäten, Hochschulen und Akademien der DDR [1960–1970]', *Zeitschrift für Geschichtswissenschaft*, XVIII, 1970, Sonderband, pp. 187–209; *Bibliographie inter-*

nationale de l'histoire des universités, vol. 1, *Espagne, Louvain, Copenhague, Prague*, by R. Gilbert, J. Paquet, S. Ellehój, F. Kavka, J. Havránek (Geneva, 1973), and vol. II, *Portugal, Leiden, Pècs, Franeker, Basel*, by A. Moreira de Sà, R. Ekkart, M. Fényes, A. de Kalbermatten, L. Haeberli (Geneva, 1976); E. Stark, *Bibliographie zur Universitätsgeschichte. Verzeichnis der im Gebiet der Bundesrepublik Deutschland 1945–1971 veröffentlichen Literatur*, ed. E. Hassinger (Munich, 1974); A. L. Gabriel, *Summary Bibliography of the History of the Universities of Great Britain and Ireland up to 1800, covering publications between 1900 and 1968* (Notre Dame, 1974); S. Guenée, *Bibliographie de l'histoire des Universités françaises des origines à la Révolution* (2 vols.; Paris, 1978–81).

Conference Reports

Summary of the Proceedings of the Workshop on 'Arab-Islamic Thought and the Evolution of Ideas at the Time of the First European Universities' held 18–20 July, 1988,as part of The Summer Euro-Arab University, Bologna

This workshop was organized by Professor Charles E. Butterworth of the University of Maryland. The title in the official documents is rather misleading, and the subject-matter is better described by the title used by Professor Butterworth in his correspondence before the conference: 'The First Appearance of Arabic Philosophy in European Universities.' There were two principal themes covered in this workshop:

1. The introduction of Arab science and philosophy into European universities. This centred on the rediscovery of Ancient Greek learning through the intermediary of the Arabic language and with the addition of Arabic commentaries. This 'Arabic' science and philosophy was known and read in translations into Latin, and these translations became part of the mainstream of learning in the Middle Ages, and beyond.

2. The awakening of interest in Arabic literature and philosophy in its own language from the Renaissance onwards. The focus here is on individual scholars who went to great efforts to learn Arabic and understand Islamic thought, and the establishment of teaching positions in Arabic in European universities.

Jamal al-Din al-Alawi of the University of Fez spoke of the relationship between the Arabs in al-Andalus and the Arabic writers in the Middle East, and the time-lapse between the composition of philosophical works and their reception in al-Andalus. This theme was developed and the story was continued by Josep Puig of the University of Madrid. He explored the historical situation in al-Andalus which was at certain periods more favourable towards transmitting Arabic learning to the Christian than at other times.

The apparent absence of translating activity during the eleventh century was due to the general poverty in cultural exchange between Arabs and Christians after the destruction of Barcelona by the caliph al-Mansur in 986. The translation of philosophical works began in the third decade of the twelfth century, soon after Arab scholars in al-Andalus first began to show interest and competence in Aristotelian philosophy. The stimulation to translate works came largely from French ecclesiastics who had been imported to restore the Church in the newly-conquered areas of Spain. The reception of Arabic translations must be seen in relation to the Christian philosophical outlook of the conquerors. Having listed the philosophical works translated in the twelfth century, mainly at Toledo, Puig considered how they were assimilated. He saw Daniel of Morley and Hermann of Carinthia as largely presenting a Western, Christian, world picture, to which Arabic thought was an embellishment. The first substantial assimilation of Arabic philosophy can be seen in the five original works of Dominicus Gundisalvus. Gundisalvus does not merely quote the Arabic texts he has translated, but adapts and changes them to suit his needs. For example he replaces Avicenna's *principia altissima* and active intellect by God, and he attempts to reconcile Avicebron and Avicenna in a Christian synthesis. Arabic learning largely displaced the native European ideas on cosmology and natural science. However, in the case of psychology and ontology, it did not fundamentally change Christian thought, but rather enhanced the native tradition and provided clear definitions. Puig ended his informative talk by considering whether Arabic philosophy had a particular influence on Christian Spain. It was outside Spain that the translations and the secondary works such as Gundisalvus' original texts were diffused. Spain probably failed to provide a nurturing ground because it had no lively schools or universities of its own.

One of these nurturing grounds was investigated by Charles Burnett of the Warburg Institute, London, who discussed 'The Introduction of Arabic Learning into English Schools'. He pointed out that the English had a predilection for mathematics and natural science; that, numerically, the majority of translators were British: and that the earliest manuscripts of translations are found in England, especially in cathedral libraries. British scholars with interests in mathematics and natural science were disappointed by the kind of study favoured in the schools of Paris and Northern

France, and they established links with Spain and Southern Italy
and Sicily. A thriving scientific tradition was established in several
English centres, and especially in Hereford and Worcester cathed-
rals. Moreover, the earliest use of both Avicenna's *Shifa* and
Averroes' commentaries appears in the works of English masters.
Avicenna was well known to Alexander Nequam who also received
texts from Salerno soon after they were written. A wide range of
commentaries by Averroes are used in writings by Robert Grosse-
teste soon after they were translated by Michael Scot in Sicily. Since
he procured Greek texts from Southern Italy, and learnt Greek from
a certain 'Nicholas Siculus', he might well have obtained manuscripts of Averroes directly from the kingdom of Frederick II.
Avicenna was taught by masters who established Oxford as a
university at the turn of the twelfth to thirteenth centuries. Averroes
in turn became the standard interpreter of Aristotle for Oxford
masters from the 1240s onwards.

The introduction of Avicenna and Averroes was also critical for
the development of the University of Paris, as pointed out by
Abdelali Elamrani-Jamal ('La reception de la philosophie arabe à
l'Université de Paris au xiiie siècle'). He showed how successive
condemnations of the works of Aristotle on natural philosophy and
of their commentators were responses to successive introductions of
Arabic philosophical works. The availability of the new Aristotle
and his commentators to masters of arts gave them more scope and
power vis-à-vis the masters of theology. The condemnations of 1210
and 1215 seem to include in the terms 'commenta' and 'summa' the
works of Avicenna, Alfarabi, and Algazel. The teaching of Aristotelian natural science was a point at issue in the general strike at the
university in 1229–31. Averroes at first seems to have been brought
in as a weapon against Avicennism. However, with the work of Siger
of Brabant Averroism itself began to be suspect, and the reaction led
to Aquinas' *De unitate intellectus contra Averroistas* (1270) and the
condemnation of 219 propositions allegedly taught by Parisian
masters of arts in 1277. The conflict does not seem to have been so
much between Christian and Muslim philosophy as between theology and philosophy. In fact, the 219 condemned propositions have
many elements in common with those condemned by al-Ghazali
(Algazel) and Ibn Taymiyya (d.1328) in an Arabic and Muslim
context.

In 1397 the University of Cracow was founded. Jerzy Korolec of the Warsaw Academy of Arts and Sciences pointed out how all-pervasive Arabic works were in the teaching of optics, medicine, and astrology in the university. He based his conclusions on the contents of the manuscripts of fifteenth-century students and masters which have survived in the Jagellonian Library of Cracow. Several Arabic works were commented upon by Cracow scholars, who had often spent part of the training in Prague or Bologna. Copernicus, who studied at Cracow from 1491 to 1495, cites a paraphrase of Ptolemy's *Almagest* by Averroes in speaking of the passage of Venus and Mercury in front of the solar disk. This citation may have come from Pico della Mirandola's *Disputatio adversus astrologiam divinatricem*, which was published in Bologna in 1495, and quotes from an abridgement of the *Almagest* by Averroes which has survived only in a Hebrew translation. The quantity of Arabic scientific texts in late fifteenth-century Cracow suggests that Copernicus could have read these works whilst a student there, rather than in Bologna where he continued his studies.

Yuri Kotchubey, Under-Director General at UNESCO, spoke of the use of Arabic philosophy in a still later foundation—the University of Kiev ('La philosophie de l'ouest et de l'est dans l'academie de Kiev-Mohyleana'). This institution was a 'grandchild' of the University of Padua and was born in 1632. Philosophy was a particularly prominent part of the syllabus in the seventeenth and eighteenth centuries and 'Latin Averroism' can be detected in writings on the soul

Most of the other papers of the conference were devoted to Arabic studies in European studies in more recent times.

Not before the age of humanism was the interest in oriental cultures developed into a systematic study of Islam. The history of this development was traced first by Hans Daiber of the Free University of Amsterdam in his lecture on 'The Reception of Islamic Philosophy at Oxford in the Seventeenth Century: the Pococks' (Father and Son) Contribution to the Understanding of Islamic Philosophy in Europe.' The first European books on Islam and Arabic literature depended on Arabic bio-bibliographical sources, such as the Latin work written by an Arab, Leo Africanus' *De viribus quibusdam illustribus apud Arabes* (1527). Edward Pocock (1604–91) spent six years in Aleppo, where he collected manuscripts for William Laud, chancellor of Oxford University and archbishop of Canterbury. Laud established a chair for Arabic at Oxford, which

Pocock was the first to occupy, but the survival of the chair was precarious and depended entirely on the whims of outside benefactors. Daiber described in detail the two works to which Pocock devoted most of his energies: an edition and translation of Barhebraeus' *Compendious History*, and an edition and translation of Ibn Tufail's *Hayy ibn Yaqzan*. From the first he published a small chapter accompanied by a commentary which cited a wide variety of Arabic sources, though these are still mainly bio-bibliographical. Pocock gives an account of the beginning of the study of philosophy among the Arabs which on the whole is accurate, but lays undue emphasis on the opposition to learning on religious grounds, a subject which concerned him deeply. The edition and translation of Ibn Tufail was completed by the younger Edward Pocock. The theme of the work seemed to match the spirit of the age of rationalism, replacing the narrow dogmaticism of a traditional religion with the rational ascent of the human mind, using its innate resources. However, this attitude was rather different from that of the elder Pocock's patron, Archbishop Laud, whose attempt to introduce a generally valid Anglican prayer book lead to strong opposition from liberal-minded people. Nevertheless, after the publication in 1671 the edition of Ibn Tufail was quickly seized by enlightenment minds, and soon translated into other languages.

Daiber wished to counter the general view that the early seventeenth century was a period in which orientalists spent all their time preparing lexicons and grammars. Pocock was concerned about Islamic thought and he believed in seeking out and making known original texts. In this way he continued a humanistic tradition of using literary-philological interests to discover a new ideal of life in the study of classical sources.

In 'The Teaching of Islamic Philosophy in Louvain' Thérèse-Anne Druart told an engaging story of three failed attempts, and one successful attempt at establishing Arabic philosophy in the curriculum of Louvain University. The three languages of the famous Collegium Trilingue (founded 1519) were Latin, Greek, and Hebrew. Soon after its foundation, a teacher at the Collegium Trilingue, Nicolas Cleonardus, wanted to learn Arabic, but could find neither a native speaker nor a grammar. Druart told us how he deciphered the Arabic languages, using a five-language psalter, how he learnt to read Avicenna from a deaf physician in Evora, and finally how he learnt to speak the language by living in the Hebrew community in Fez. Unfortunately, on his way back to Louvain he died. The tale was picked up a century later in the person of Abudacnus (alias Joseph Barbatus), a polyglot Jacobite from Cairo, who wandered through Europe teaching Hebrew and Arabic, until he was recommended for a post at the Collegium Trilingue. However, because of personal difficulties with the incumbent Hebrew professor, lack of Arabic students, and questionable morality, he was forced to leave. Serious study of Arabic began only with the foundation of the Higher Institute of Philosophy in 1893, and the appointment of Jacques Forget to teach the history of Arabic philosophy. But here too tensions arose between the factions wanting the Institute to be open to secular students and the teaching to be in French, and those who wanted the Institute to cater for theological students and instruction to be in Latin. In 1899 Forget was obliged to teach only Christian Arabic literature and the study of Avicenna and other Arabic philosophical texts lapsed. Only after the foundation of the Wulf-Mansion Centre within the Higher Institute of Philosophy (1956) and the appointment of Simone van Riet to prepare the critical edition of Avicenna's *De anima* in Latin (1962), was Arabic philosophy restored as an option.

At about the same time as Forget was active, Ignaz Goldziher was introducing Arabic philosophy into Budapest University. In 'The Reception of Arabic Philosophy at the University of Budapest' Miklos Maróth of the same university traced the background to the career of Ignaz Goldziher (1850–1921). The foundation of the University of Pest (1635) was due to Peter Pázmány (1570–1637), who, in his own philosophical writings, shows himself to be much indebted to the Arabic philosophers whose works had been translated into Latin in the Middle Ages. Goldziher's career began with four years of training under the best-known Arabists in Berlin, Leipzig, and Leiden, and a sojourn in Damascus and Cairo which left him, though a Jew, a close friend of Muslims. In Budapest, however, he encountered only difficulties. The climate was against Jews, the nationalist sentiment affected university appointments, and a new chair in Semitics, which had been promised to Goldziher, was instead given to a Hungarian heretical theologian. Goldziher refused to leave Hungary, but served the Jewish community and gave lectures without charge in the university. He believed strongly in the power of scholarship to break down barriers between religions and races, and was devastated by the outbreak of the first world war.

The two remaining lectures fell a little outside the two main themes of the workshop. The relevance of Yury Isayevich's paper on 'George Drohobych's Astronomical Tables and Their Arabic Sources' (read by Professor Kochubey), was that this Ukrainian scholar was professor at Bologna, and rector of the university from 1481–2. His works on current astronomical phenomena—especially eclipses—and their significance, depended on Arabic works in Latin translation. Scholars in the Ukraine drew their scholarship from the West, but one of the best descriptions of the Ukraine in the mid-seventeenth century was written down in Arabic, by Paul of Aleppo. Most of the papers were well-prepared and full of interest. They took the form of surveys of published work by the speakers or by others rather than fresh studies. They were the kind of papers that would contribute to two general volumes: the first on the introduction of Arabic science and philosophy into European Universities as part of the mainstream of philosophical and scientific teaching in the Middle Ages and Renaissance, the second on the establishment of the teaching of Arabic philosophy in the Arabic language in European universities. To make such volumes comprehensive both would have to include further surveys: e.g. articles on the introduction of Arabic philosophy into Italian universities, and the beginning of Arabic studies in Leiden, Florence, Paris, and Cambridge.

Charles Burnett
Warburg Institute
Woburn Square
London

The Seminar in the History of the Book to 1500, Conference 8–10 July 1988, St Edmund Hall, Oxford

This was the second international conference of the Seminar in the History of the Book to 1500, a Seminar (based in Oxford) which promotes the study of Western medieval manuscripts and incunables. The Conference took as its theme 'Medieval Book Production: Assessing the Evidence'. Three papers examined the book production associated with religious houses during the twelfth century: Yolanta Załuska discussed the products and working practices of the scriptorium at Citeaux, Aliza Cohen-Mushlin, those of the scriptorium of the Augustinian canons of Frankendal, and Teresa Webber, the books produced for the secular canons of Salisbury Cathedral. A second group of papers used layout and page design as evidence for the transmission of texts: Albinia de la Mare demonstrated the relationship between a group of copies of the *Chronicle* of Eusebius/Jerome, Alison Stones discussed the page design of thirteenth-century manuscripts of the French prose Launcelot, and Peter Jones discussed the manuscript evidence for stages in translating from Latin to Middle English the texts of a medical manuscript (British Library MSS Sloane 76 and Harley 3371). Another group of papers examined the ways in which layout and mise-en-page were adapted to suit the needs of texts accompanied by illustrations, or the needs of particular readers: Lucy Freeman Sandler gave an account of the compilation and design of a fourteenth-century English encyclopaedia, the *Omne bonum* (British Library, MS Royal 6 E vi, vii), Claire Baker traced the development of the design of the earliest Books of Hours, Adelaide Bennett examined the mise-en-page of an illustrated *Manuel des péchés* of the late thirteenth century, and Claudine Chavannes-Mazel, the mise-en-page of copies of the *Miroir historial*. A fourth group of papers was concerned with late medieval manuscript production: Ian Doyle discussed book production by and for English monastic houses, Lynda Dennison gave an account of a late-fourteenth-century Psalter (Exeter College MS 47) in order to demonstrate how a combination of codicological and stylistic evidence may be used to date and localize manuscripts, and Eberhard König examined the books and manuscripts associated with the Housebook Master. The final group of papers was devoted to the fifteenth-century printed books and their production: Lotte Hellinga presented evidence for the two-pull press, Margaret M. Smith examined patterns of incomplete rubrication in incunables as evidence for working methods, and Richard Rouse used the example of the Ripoli Press to illustrate the collaborative working practices of *cartolai*, illuminators and printers in fifteenth-century Italy. A number of the papers will be printed in the Conference Proceedings which are to be published jointly by the Seminar and the Black Gull Press. The Seminar's next conference will be held in 1990.

Teresa Webber
Department of History   University of Southampton

Essay Review

University Records, Social History, and the Creation of Large Databases

Armando F. Verde, O.P., *Lo Studio Fiorentino, 1473–1503. Ricerche e Documenti*, Vol. IV. *La Vita Universitaria*. Florence: Leo S. Olschki Editore, 1985. 3 Tomi, pp. 1546.

Premier Livre des Procurateurs de la Nation Germanique de l'Ancienne Université d'Orléans, 1444–1546:
I.I: *Texte des Rapports des Procurateurs*, ed. Cornelia M. Ridderikhoff with Hilde de Ridder-Symoens, Leiden: Brill, 1971. pp. 390.
I.II: *Biographies des Étudiants*, eds. Hilde de Ridder-Symoens, Detlef Illmer and Cornelia M. Ridderikhoff. Vol. I: *Introduction, Sources et bibliographie, Biographie des étudiants 1444–1515*, Leiden: Brill, 1978. pp. 354. Vol. II: *Biographie des étudiants 1516–1546*, Leiden: Brill, 1980. pp. 504. Vol. III: *Tables, Additions et corrections, Illustrations*, Leiden: Brill, 1985. pp. 204, 16 illustrations.

Les universités européennes du XVIe au XVIIIe siècle. Histoire sociale des populations étudiantes. Tome I. *Bohême, Espagne, États italiens, Pays germaniques, Pologne, Provinces-Unies*, eds. Dominique Julia, Jacques Revel and Robert Chartier. Paris: Éditions de l'École des Hautes Études en Sciences Sociales, 1986. pp. 260.

Schulen und Studium im Sozialen Wandel des hohen und späten Mittelalters, ed. Johannes Fried. (Vorträge und Forschungen XXX, herausgegeben vom Konstanzer Arbeitskreis für mittelalterliche Geschichte), Sigmaringen: Jan Thorbecke Verlag, 1986. pp. 656, 49 illustrations. DM. 158.—

Much research on university history today has logistical features that set it apart from other types of investigation. The 'big' project is still very much alive, partly because of a willingness on the part of the universities or their host cities or governments to fund publication on a scale usually denied to other researchers. The anniversary celebration often provides the excuse; the motive, however, is often not so much 'alma mater' devotion or hagiographic nostalgia of the kind that inspired so many earlier *monumenta*, but rather the practical competitive instincts that universities increasingly need to display as corporate bodies in a public-relations-driven world. Happily, though, the current sophistication of the world of sponsorship does not seek to impose distortions. By and large, university historians can organize their research as they consider most appropriate and most relevant to the perspectives of the time. The multi-volume serial publication of source material continues—university history has been unusually privileged here—but it has been joined by other forms of research publication: the joint multi-author project, the proceedings of conferences (themselves often aided by generous funding).

One of the most impressive recent publications, however, is the result not so much of sponsorship as of the remarkable and indefatigable efforts of a Dominican scholar, Father Armando Verde. The single-handed publication of the documents pertaining to the University of Florence between 1473 and 1503 has become more spectacular as it has unfolded. This is partly a consequence of Verde's unorthodox scheme of publication, which makes sense of the tremendous quantity of material and presents it in stimulating if tantalizing form. Volumes I–III were reviewed in Vol. II of this journal, but it will help to summarize briefly how the work has been planned.

Verde has eschewed the simple *ad annum* scheme, and organized some of his material chronologically only within thematic divisions. Volume I, published in 1973, contained (besides a most detailed *bibliographie raisonnée*) the lists of officials and the *rotuli* or annual lecture lists. Volume II (also 1973) consisted of an alphabetical register of teachers, with a chronological list of their contracts but also transcriptions of a wide range of documents relating to these individuals, not necessarily in the university context but invaluable as contributions to the whole portrait of university life. The volume also contained a tabular summary of degrees taken at Florence during the period. In Volume III (1977) Verde moved on to the students, and again produced a goldmine of biographical information, with appendices of correspondence or notes about humanists and other figures, reconstructed matriculation lists, and details of the 1035 children listed in the 1480 tax declarations as attending school.

With Volume IV (1985), published in three tomes, Verde has turned to 'La Vita Universitaria', and here the structure has changed again. After an edition of statutes, the material is organized by academic year, but within each year is subdivided into two sections, one presenting administrative documents, the other biographical and cultural information. Each year begins with a summary of officers, teachers and students featuring that year. For the most part these are given as cross-references to earlier volumes, but this is also the opportunity for additional material to be inserted.

The administrative documents are of great interest to university historians. In moving the bulk of the Florentine *studio* to Pisa, and thus necessitating a regular flow of correspondence between the university and its administrators, Lorenzo de' Medici ensured for posterity a quantity and quality of documentation perhaps only surpassed by his own celebrated correspondence. The letters—often exchanged almost daily—give a rich portrait of what it was like to try to run an Italian university in the late fifteenth century. Following them through one sees the major and perennial problems—hiring the teachers they want at prices they can afford, negotiating the terms of contract, allocating classrooms without offending the pride and jealousy of their teachers, administering the system of concurrent lectures in the same subject (a source of endless conflict). The disciplinary problems are also highlighted. At Pisa the main one was carnival: students not only went in for increasingly exuberant and violent behaviour as the years progressed, they were constantly trying to bring forward the starting date, in one year actually beginning before Christmas. For no Italian town has such a rich source been published.

The second section of each year's entry is more miscellaneous and arguably less central to university life. Here Verde has given us a wide variety of additional information about individual teachers, about books, legal and medical *consilia*, disputes and rivalries between humanists, and ultimately information about cultural or political figures whose relevance is to Florentine civic life rather than to the university. But it would perhaps be pedantic to discuss what is properly university history in this context. This approach is certainly preferable to that which regarded it as axiomatic that the universities and the humanists were confirmed enemies, and that consequently what the latter thought or wrote could not be of relevance to the former. Verde has published a vast amount of biographical information on Florentine cultural life; it will be for the users of these volumes to make the analysis. But that introduces the main problem. At nearly 4,000 pages (and a fifth volume, on finance, to come), this magisterial labour of love is inevitably unwieldy. That there are 48 pages of corrections and additions is in no way a criticism; it is inevitable given the rambling and haphazard sequence in which the documents have come to light and been published over decades of research. The index, promised as the sixth volume, will be quite indispensable if much of this material is not to languish in semi-hiding.

Much more compact in its presentation of information, but no less massive in its scope and effort, is the programme of publication of the series of *Livres des Procurateurs* of the German Nation of the University of Orléans, initiated ten years ago. The University of Orléans had by the sixteenth century not only substantially recovered its reputation as foremost law school of Northern Europe (a reputation won in the thirteenth century before it became a university), it had also established itself as a major centre for academic *peregrinationes*, above all in Germany and the Low Countries. Quantitatively speaking, the influx of law students from these areas to Orléans is matched only by that to those other traditional destinations of the northern law student, the universities of Italy. And the movement is in one respect better documented than that towards Italy; the undoubted continuity of the system of nations at Orléans—something that cannot be assumed for many Italian universities—has left us with earlier and more detailed records than is the case elsewhere. As the largest and most organized regional grouping of students on the move in early modern European universities, the German Nations appear always to be the most active and best organized. In Italy this often takes on the aspect of a sixteenth-century revival; in Orléans the surviving records of the nation date from the fifteenth century. Indeed, it is not fanciful to suppose that the German nation at Orléans provided a model for the organization of later German Nations elsewhere.

It was in recognition of the international importance of Orléans, and specifically of its German Nation, that the International Commission for the History of Universities initiated a programme of research into the Nation's history from 1444 to 1602. The first step in publication terms was an edition of the first *Liber Procuratorum*, covering the years 1444–1546. The procurator, the head of the nation, was a student elected for a three-month period. He was charged with representing the nation in the university (he was an *ex officio* member of the *collegium doctorum et procuratorum nationum*), with the summoning of the general assembly of the nations, with matriculating members and receiving their oaths, and, until 1485 (when a *receptor* took over the responsibility), with the administration of the nation's finances. In the *Liber* procurators kept a continuous record of the chief events of their period of office. They did so with varying conscientiousness and at varying lengths: some used it almost as a diary, others entered a brief summary only at the end of their period of office. Despite these inconsistencies the *Liber* is an invaluable source for the life of the nation. It chronicles collective decisions and matters of discipline, legislation imposed by it or on it, the feasts observed by the nation and the crises it faced (plague, quarrels of jurisdiction). It describes elections and degree ceremonies, deliberations regarding the weight and value of the seal, the aftermath of the deaths of members. These are all areas known through statutes to be the concern of nations; here is a source which details their working in practice.

For the social historian one of the most valuable features of the *Liber Procuratorum* is that the procurators recorded in it the names of those whom he matriculated. The book in effect doubles up as matriculation register, and provides the basis for the most substantial part of the research published to date in the series, summary biographies of the 1265 students who matriculated into the German Nation between 144 and 1546. For this task the work was divided into regions; biographies of students from the southern half of the Low Countries (516, the largest contingent) were prepared by Hilde de Ridder-Symoens, those for the northern half of the

Low Countries (375) by Cornelia Ridderikhoff, and those from the Empire proper (374, including those from Switzerland, Savoy, Alsace, Lorraine and some Polish dioceses) by Detlef Illmer. The documents of the German nation—the *Liber Procuratorum* plus several other series—are only the starting-point, however. Each entry presents first the university career of the individual—for which the records of other universities have been trawled—and then a concise but thorough and informative summary of what is known about the individual from other sources. It is here that the greatest achievement of the three contributors is evident. The scale of the project is best illustrated by the fact that the bibliography of archival and published material consulted, and referred to in abbreviated form in the entries, runs to almost 80 pages.

The standard of scholarship and presentation is impeccable and the work extremely easy to use once its conventions have been understood. The only matter for regret—expressed by the presenters themselves—is that the index has had to be compiled in two separate sections, reflecting the linguistic division in the work itself. But this is only a minor blemish on an outstanding contribution to the prosopography of the student population of Orléans, and of the educated of the Low Countries and the Empire, of the period.

Prosopographical analysis of the kind enabled by such painstaking research is an increasing concern of university historians. There is now a growing specialist literature on the subject, much of it dating back to Lawrence Stone's provocative thesis of 1964 that there was an educational revolution in England in the early seventeenth century, followed by a prolonged decline. Subsequent to this suggestion scholars have looked for similar trends elsewhere in Europe, with mixed results. But the growth of this enquiry has sent scholars back to certain kinds of source material—in particular matriculation records—with a new purpose, and with a new, quantitative, approach that, inevitably given the nature of historical prejudice, has not won universal approval.

No synthesis of this work has yet been attempted, and indeed it is far too early for one, However the recognition that the field is too unwieldy for individuals working in isolation has produced some important collaborative work and some interesting collaborative publications. Stone's own publication of essays by several seminar contributors as *The University in Society* (2 vols., Princeton, 1975) gave the enquiry new focus. Shortly after that the Centre de Recherches Historiques de l'École des Hautes Études en Sciences Sociales, Paris, initiated an enquiry into 'Universités et société dans l'Europe moderne', with a specific emphasis on student populations. The first result of this international collaborative effort is Volume I of *Histoire sociale des populations étudiantes*, studies collected by Dominique Julia, Jacques Revel and Roger Chartier. The scope of this first volume is the

universities of Europe outside France (the second volume will deal exclusively with France). It is of course not comprehensive: Portugal, Scandinavia, England and Scotland do not feature at all, while other areas are
covered superficially. But that merely emphasizes that the work is not
attempting an overall portrait. Rather, as its cover declares, the work
attempts to air a number of questions. What social role did the universities
play in Ancien Régime Europe? What caused the continued student
migration? What was the relationship of the growth of numbers of students
with the growing bureaucracies of church and state? What opportunities did
students leaving university have? Was there, from the later seventeenth
century onwards, an over-production of graduates, and if so what consequences did this have?

The studies in this volume fall into two categories. The majority try to
provide a sketch of the basic trends in a country. Irena Kaniewska provides
two chapters on Crakow, tracing first the students of 1433–1560 and then
those of the seventeenth and eighteenth centuries. These give a modest but
useful basic statistical profile of the heyday and then the decline of Crakow
as a major university centre. Mariano Peset and Maria Fernanda Mancero
give a similar, chiefly quantitative, profile of the situation in eighteenth-
century Spain, building particularly on Richard L. Kagan's major work on
the subject and on their own researches on Valencia. František Šmahel's
approach to the University of Prague, 1433–1622, is bolder; an informative
profile of who graduated is followed by a study of the career patterns of
those graduates, in which a strong feature to emerge is the transient and
unrespected character of schoolmastering. A high proportion of graduates
found their initial employment here, but very few remained for more than a
short period. This, and the confessional situation in Bohemia, colour the
geographical recruitment of Prague and mobility of Bohemian students, a
theme neatly taken up by Jiři Pešek and David Šaman in their chapter on
Bohemian students abroad, 1596–1620. The remaining profile article, by
Richard L. Kagan on the Italian universities in the sixteenth and seventeenth centuries, perhaps suffers from over-extension. The statistics presented are those available or calculable from (chiefly) published sources; but
they provide anecdotal evidence rather than an overall portrait. Kagan
skilfully traces the reasons for the decline of the Italian universities.
Comparing the situation of 1600 with that of 1500, he concludes that there
was no parallel to Stone's educational revolution here; but that must surely
be a question of the period examined. There is no shortage of evidence, both
anecdotal and quantitative, for substantial expansion in the fifteenth
century. In this as perhaps in many other respects the Italian experience may
have foreshadowed that of other parts of Europe.

The second category of contribution to this volume is the more ambiguous; substantial and thorough contributions to the historiographical

tradition on specific issues. The introduction by Dominique Julia and Jacques Revel spells out some of the dangers in the indiscriminate application of quantitative methods. The basis of most such study is matriculation records; but the great unevenness in the records makes this extremely precarious. Matriculation meant different things in different places; in some it was a once-for-all initial step, in others it was repeated each academic year or even more frequently than that. In practice by no means all students matriculated, while not all who did were *bona fide* students; and here too there are greater regional variations. Likewise the value of degrees as a measure of student presence or numbers is severely limited. The quantification of student populations is a very approximate art; the best practitioners are those who stress this constantly.

One such is Willem Frijhoff, who, in a chapter on 'Grandeur des nombres et misère des réalités: la courbe de Franz Eulenburg et le débat sur le nombre d'intellectuels en Allemagne, 1576–1815', makes an important contribution to the long-running debate about German student numbers and the overproduction of intellectuals (*Überfüllungsthese*). The statistics compiled by Eulenburg at the beginning of the century (and taken as a starting-point ever since) argued a growth in student numbers in the second half of the sixteenth century and the first quarter of the seventeenth, convulsions for the next fifty years during and after the Thirty Years' War, a smaller rise thereafter but a prolonged decline in the second half of the eighteenth century and beyond. Frijhoff shows that this picture, however attractive in terms of its fit with other events, is inaccurate. Its fundamental flaw lies in Eulenburg's treatment of matriculation. It is students, not number of matriculations, that must be counted, and if that count must nonetheless be based on matriculation records, short of a head count which matched up all the occasions on which students matriculate more than once (which, with over a million students, is 'irréalisable'), recourse must be had to a coefficient of matriculation. But this coefficient will vary considerably from period to period. After painstakingly constructing a moving coefficient (on the basis of extensive sampling and cross-reference to communities, such as Zutphen, for which there is a complete record of who studied), Frijhoff is able to redraw Eulenburg's graph, with less spectacular but subtler conclusions. The Thirty Years' War did not result in a dramatic decline of student numbers, only of student mobility, while the much-talked of decline of the late eighteenth century is more of a tailing off, leaving overall numbers still significantly higher than those two centuries previously.

What then of the *Überfüllungsthese*, and its consequences for government, the professions, the universities and the overproduced intellectuals? In a second chapter, a case study on university and employment in the United Provinces, Frijhoff shows this trend too to be more complex and less dramatic than is sometimes supposed, certainly than was often believed to be the case at the time. The number of graduates produced fluctuates because of several factors—the graph is here tested for correlation with a range of economic indicators, for example—as different channels of education and training evolve. Another indicator of this is the decline of Latin schools, still the passport to university education, but less relevant to occupations other than those requiring university degrees. Those professions, particularly medicine and law, are examined, and it is demonstrated that, at least in the case of medicine, overproduction, when it occurred, was not so dramatic as not to be absorbed again within a short time. In a concluding chapter Roger Chartier takes up the theme of 'alienated intellectuals', well known from M. H. Curtis' article (*Past and Present*, 1962), and pulls together many of the consequences of the disparity between university degrees and graduate opportunity. That there was such a disparity is not denied, nor is its effect on, for example, the quality of schoolmastering, the perennial resort of the otherwise unemployable graduate. But the main emphasis of the article is on the attitudes and government actions that ensued from the belief that the universities were overproducing. In France there were complaints about an excessive number of universities or about their lack of social 'use', and suggestions that some (particularly in small towns) should be closed; in Germany there was a preoccupation with statistics with which the universities could be monitored. These may raise a wry smile to historians who work in the beleaguered universities of today. Chartier also points to the darker side; the concern of an élite about the dangers of an excessive spread of learning and the possibility of true competition on a meritocratic basis for the jobs which it at present holds and transmits.

In the end this collection asks many more questions than it answers; and it is right that this should be so. In the process, the contributors have made important methodological points about the need for greater rigour, particularly in the definition of criteria of measurement. Most of the contributors are already practitioners of such rigour. The second volume is eagerly awaited.

A much broader scope of social issues is encompassed in *Schulen und Studium im sozialen Wandel des hohen und späten Mittelalters*. This comprises most of the proceedings of two conferences held at Constance in spring 1981 and 1982. The events were the inspiration of the late Peter Classen, who did not live to see them realized; his pupil Johannes Fried took over their organization and edited this book. Seventeen extensive papers are published (an eighteenth is to appear as a separate monograph). The resulting volume examines the intellectual history of the universities, and of learning generally, in its social context, and does so by ranging across many different and sometimes apparently unrelated aspects of university and cultural life.

The first half of the papers presented here concerns the period of the origin of the universities, and provides full and probing enquiries into those origins. Alfred Wendehorst gives a clear introductory survey of current work on literacy in the middle ages. Peter Johanek gives a polished and sensitive depiction of the relationship between the twelfth-century monasteries and the new university movement, with examples particularly from Germany. Jacques Verger discusses possible social approaches to the origins of the University of Paris, emphasizing the importance of the local, specific factors which produced the concentration on Paris as well as the general factors leading to the birth of a higher educational system on a new scale, while Helmut Walther provides an equally fine summary of the factors which in Bologna transformed the burgeoning law school into a *studium generale*. Joachim Ehlers gives an overview of the activity of German scholars in France in the twelfth century, and the editor, Johannes Fried, breaks new ground with an account of the Cathedral School of Bamberg and the *Rezeption* there of legal and scholastic culture until the mid-thirteenth century. The most substantial of these very solid pieces is Rolf Köhn's comprehensive survey of the teaching of the *trivium*, at school and at university level and in its social rather than just its intellectual context, a contribution which will undoubtedly become the standard point of departure for the subject.

With the thirteenth century the contributions begin to take the flavour of 'social history' in the sense more recognizable to students of the later period—heavier emphasis on prosopography and indeed, to a limited extent, on quantification. Jürgen Miethke, in his piece on the church and the university, looks at the church's attitude to the universities and the level of learning in the higher echelons of the church, and attempts a quantitative profile. Reinhard Schneider traces the reactions of the Cistercians to the growth of the universities, from the educational reform within the order under Abbot Stephen Lexington and the beginnings of the Collège des Bernardins in Paris, through to the growth of Cistercian *studia* in the later middle ages. Herman Diener introduces and assesses the value of four-teenth- and fifteenth-century papal registers as a source for university history, describing supplications of universities for bulls, corporate suppli-cations (*rotuli*) for students, and the possibility of tracing the growing significance of degrees, and of the universities themselves, through papal records. In a chapter on the impact of university training and careers in royal service in fifteenth-century France, Neithard Bulst gives a thorough and cautious introduction to the general problems of the prosopography of fifteenth-century French universities, while nonetheless arriving at justifiably bold conclusions about the socially conservative impact of university training on the career patterns of the Third Estate. Building around the theme of the law school of Orléans and the German students of the later middle ages, Detlef Illmer explores some unexpected aspects of corporate organization and legislative interference, and puts in a new and seductive form the theory that it was the relative freedom of French teaching in the pre- and early university days which gave France its pre-eminence in medieval education.

In an extensive chapter, Peter Moraw sheds new light on the first 70 years of the history of the University of Prague, concentrating on the jurists in the late fourteenth century. Prague's key role as the first focus of legal studies, and of the university movement, in the Empire is accepted: Moraw emphasizes in addition the extent to which it took from Bologna as constitutional model (and, to a lesser extent, as direct influence on legal studies). Klaus Wriedt examines the many complex social interrelations of university and town, church and court through case studies of graduate careers and office-holding in north German towns, while Rainer Christoph Schwinges studies the *Burse* or hall, the most common form of student accommodation in late medieval Germany, drawing especially on his work on Cologne and describing the varying social levels of its five *Bursen*. Hartmut Boockmann provides a valuable survey of the iconography of German universities, ranging over architecture, seals and sceptres, manuscript illuminations, tombs, epitaphs and altars. Arno Seifert concludes the volume with some stimulating reflections on higher education as a social system, assessing the tensions between the practitioners' aspirations to being a 'scientific community', and criteria of social utility, particularly through the perspective of the various methods of funding which underpinned their activity.

It is impossible in a short space to do justice to the richness of these studies. Intended as a collection of enquiries into social aspects of the medieval university, taken as a whole the volume provides an admirable survey of the current state of scholarship. As that, and as a penetrating contemplation of the social aspects of university history from very many angles, it will undoubtedly become a fundamental text.

No fewer than eight of these pieces are at least partly based on prosopographical and quantitative techniques. As with the other works under review here, records of individuals attending universities and their subsequent careers are the basic building-blocks on which our picture must be founded. The tremendous effort, and great expense, of performing such research and publishing the results prompts some general reflections. In prosopographical work there is often a tension—healthy in itself—between the wish to explore the records and amass information about individuals *per se* and the drive to analyse, extrapolate and arrive at conclusions about the significance of these records. Current fashion dictates that the latter should be the dominant requirement; and where the documentation and the statistical techniques permit it this is amply justified by the results—as, for example, in Rainer Christoph Schwinges' magisterial *Deutsche Universitäts-besucher im 14. und 15. Jahrhundert* (Stuttgart, 1986), to be reviewed in a subsequent volume of this journal. For the longer term, however, for successive historians of possibly different persuasions and different interests, we should never forget that it is the data itself that will be of more durable value. And here the growing phenomenon of collaborative undertakings— healthy in itself, and increasingly indispensable given the scale of prosopo-graphical investigation—prompts another observation. The technology already exists that enables such research to be conducted in a form readily available for further modification by subsequent scholars. It can also greatly reduce the cost of publication—or obviate the need for paper publication at all, by enabling on-line access—and can make possible the cross-consul-tation of different databases. In a field as resource-intensive, but at the same time as internationally interdependent, as university prosopography it should surely be a priority to explore the possibilities offered by computers beyond that, already widespread, of the individual project. Maybe the conference organized by *History of Universities* to be held in Glasgow in 1990 on 'University and Society' could provide an appropriate forum for such a discussion.

Peter Denley
Westfield College
University of London

Book Reviews

John H. Jones, *Balliol College. A History 1263–1939*. Oxford: Oxford University Press, 1988. xix + 323 pp. £35.00.

Balliol has been remarkably well served by its historians. The first history of the college was published in 1668, and many scholarly books and articles on its history have appeared in print during the last hundred years; there is also unpublished research. Dr Jones, the college's archivist, has played a significant part in this tradition, through a number of articles, a co-edition of the latest volume of the *Register* of the college's members, and a catalogue of its archives. His deep and detailed knowledge of the subject is evident throughout this new, meticulously researched, and thoughtful college history.

The 18 chapters cover every aspect of the college: its constitution and government, administrative and financial organization; college society at its several levels, its life and activities; intellectual life; benefactions; the fabric; the library; college staff; the impact of religious and political changes; and the main incidents and individuals in its history over nearly 700 years. We even learn about college slang, ghosts, and mulberry trees. As one would expect from the college's archivist, full use is made of documents from Balliol's own archives, and those of the university, but material has also been procured from more than thirty other collections outside Oxford; and extensive use has been made of secondary literature. A particularly interesting primary source from the college archives employed here is the diary of Jeremiah Milles, a fellow of Balliol at the beginning of the eighteenth century: this gives a fascinating insight into the day-to-day life of an Oxford college fellow in the period. Dr Jones has also, sensibly, sought one or two personal reminiscences of their student days from living alumni.

The book is full of information and detail, yet written with admirable conciseness; and a good balance of coverage is maintained across the ages despite the highly uneven distribution of archival material. He has extracted the utmost information from the college's rather meagre medieval records, and has tackled the thorny question of collegiate finances effectively. Quotations from original sources are employed to good effect, for conveying both information and period colour. Evidence and interpretation have been examined critically, and points of detail or uncertainty have been established by painstaking research and analysis; Dr Jones firmly eschews unsubstantiated claims.

There are times, though, when this caution is carried to extremes. John Jones has focused, deliberately, on what he calls 'parochial matters', with background matter serving mostly to 'put the College's fortunes into a rough context'. His book is, he writes, 'an archivist's account, rather than a historian's'. In fact, though he is a college tutor in science and has a peculiar theoretical notion of what constitutes 'proper history', he greatly underestimates his own abilities as a historian. The extent to which background material should be brought into an institutional history of this kind is open to debate, and this history of Balliol provides a rather better sense of context than its author's prefatory disclaimer might suggest; but there are occasions when greater use of such material would have enhanced the understanding of events or developments within the college considerably. For example, when a college is expanding or contracting, intellectually vibrant or dormant, when it becomes richer or poorer, papist or puritan, whig or tory, broad church or anglo-catholic, it is important to know whether this is following a more general trend elsewhere in the university, or if it is in advance of the trend, behind it, or even counter to it. These points of singularity or similarity are significant features of a college's particular history, and need to be explained more fully; in several places, this book might have profited from such comparisons and contrasts. (To take another small instance, a closer comparison with other colleges would have demonstrated that many of the disciplinary regulations for colleges enjoined by the university's parliamentary visitors in the later 1640s simply echoed the recurrent efforts of college authorities of various religious hues to tighten up their discipline in the early modern period, and were not necessarily specific to puritanism, as suggested here.)

A second point concerns the decision to halt the study at 1939, on the curious grounds that an objective appraisal of the last 50 years of Balliol's history 'will not be possible until at least another half-century has elapsed'. Has Dr Jones considered the implications of this remark for the study of contemporary history in general? Excessive diffidence—or perhaps the fear of giving offence—appears to have won out here, too. Yet it is possible to cover the period within living memory in a detached fashion; and indeed, if so necesary, too, for such accounts are in themselves a valuable historical source for future generations. Elsewhere in this book use is made of Henry Savage's account of his own times in his 1668 history of Balliol, and of an interpretation of a development in his own times by another historian of Balliol, H. W. C. Davis; and Dr Jones has put a few of his own personal memories of lesser issues into footnotes.

But there will always be grounds for disagreement over such matters of range and emphasis. There is no single correct way to write a college history: it is a difficult and complex subject—far more so than may appear at a first glance—and the decision on how to tackle it must in the last resort be an individual one. And John Jones has given us a most valuable book. It is informative and scholarly, and a worthy addition to the 'new wave' of college histories.

John Twigg
11 Hope Drive
The Park
Nottingham NG7 1DL

Jan Havránek, Josef Petráň, and Anna Skýbová, *Universitas Carolina, 1348–1984*. Prague: Univerzita Karlova, 1987. 87 pp. Kčs 21 (paper).

This is a sound sketch, with some telling illustrations, of the history of the Charles University of Prague, written in competent English. It is bland on recent developments (the fate of the German University is not even mentioned), and surprisingly thin on the nineteenth century. It will be found of most use for its up-to-date summary of the early history of the institution.

R. J. W. Evans
Brasenose College
Oxford

John Twigg, *A History of Queens' College, Cambridge, 1448–1986*. Woodbridge: Boydell & Brewer, 1987. xvi + 533 pp. £19.50.

John Twigg's history of Queens', achieved, remarkably in two years, avoids many of the pitfalls of the genre as outlined by Mordechai Feingold ('Oxford and Cambridge College histories—an outdated genre?', *History of Universities*, i (1981) 207–13). Ostensibly this history follows the usual pattern of such works: it is divided into five chronological parts entitled 'The outline history of the college in its times from the foundation until 1660'; 'The college and its society from the 15th to 17th centuries'; 'The 18th century and early 19th centuries'; 'The age of reform: the later 19th and early 20th centuries' and 'Modern Times'.

The size and composition of the student body is considered in the three central sections, and valuable appendices provide further data on this. These sections also address themselves usefully, albeit without startling revelations, to the curriculum and to the Presidents and Fellows. The dangers of the episodic and biographical approach are avoided, the more readily in that, as the author admits, Queens' does not claim a host of nationally distinguished alumni.

Queens' was fortunate in an earlier historian, W. G. Searle, and Twigg generously admits his debt to him, especially in the early sections dealing with the multiple foundations of the college. There is, indeed, a judicious use of secondary sources throughout the book, notably of John Morgan and John Gascoigne, and indeed of Twigg's own Ph.D. thesis, for the sixteenth and seventeenth centuries, and it is, perhaps, in these sections, and in the last, that most of the new material is to be found. Other topics, such as the workings of patronage, patterns of endowment and benefaction, and the religious tone of the college at different times, although not new in themselves, were not to be found in earlier college histories. It is good, too, to find a miscellaneous chapter in the section dealing with the fifteenth to seventeenth centuries embracing the topics of college servants and tradesmen, visits, and health and disease.

Throughout the first four sections in particular Dr Twigg is at pains to relate the development of Queens' to that of the university at large, both as a nationally regarded, or disregarded, institution and as an object of court or state intervention. In this respect, indeed, this book may be hailed as not only the first modern history of the university, at least since the mid-fifteenth century, but as the only history of Cambridge that is not dominated by the history of Trinity College.

The archives of Queens' are particularly rich and voluminous for most of its history and one cannot but regret that the terms on which this work was undertaken clearly prohibited as full a use of them as Dr Twigg is well equipped to carry out. He has, however, indicated a number of avenues for future research and in his final chapters, dealing with the commotions of the late 1960s and early '70s he has drawn almost exclusively on college minutes, both of the Governing Body and of the student representative bodies struggling into existence. His account is perceptive, dispassionate, and judicious and as such was bound to appeal equally to all members of the college. It should do much to correct the image of the college disseminated by the television series of 1985.

The book is furnished with extremely useful bibliographies, especially of printed sources, and with numerous illuminating appendices, including a list of subjects of student debate from 1886 to 1914. It is also lavishly illustrated.

E. S. Leedham-Green
Cambridge University Archives
The University Library
West Road
Cambridge CB3 9DR

J. S. G. Blair, *History of Medicine in St Andrews University*. Edinburgh: Scottish Academic Press, 1987. xi + 416 pp. £25.00.

In recent times historians of medicine in Scotland have concentrated almost exclusively on the attainments of Edinburgh and, to a lesser extent, of Glasgow. John Blair, a distinguished surgeon with no professional training as a historian, is to be congratulated on his achievement in chronicling the hitherto neglected story of the frequently denigrated St Andrews medical degrees and the largely disappointed efforts to create a lasting school of medicine.

As Scotland's most ancient university, founded in 1411, it was fitting that St Andrews should have been the first to award an MD degree, probably in the year 1696. This was, however, virtually the last occasion on which St Andrews could claim priority in medical education in Scotland. The establishment of the Chandos Chair of Medicine in 1722, preceded by the purchase of a skeleton fifteen years earlier, heralded a false dawn, speedily eclipsed by the contemporaneous foundation of the Edinburgh School of Medicine, soon to be the premier centre in the English-speaking world.

The Chandos incumbents of the eighteenth and early nineteenth centuries made only a token contribution to medical education, apparently doing little more than process MD applications as a source of income for the impoverished university. Mid-century attempts to improve the position, charted here in precise detail, fared little better.

During the 1870s some formal medical education was initiated in Dundee which, unlike its neighbour on the south side of the river, did possess a large infirmary capable of providing the essential clinical instruction. The establishment of a Conjoint School in 1889 was an uneasy alliance which lasted until Dundee's elevation to independent university status in 1967. Dr Blair's unusually full and frank account of this period paints a fascinating, if occasionally confusing, picture of the tensions and personalities which bedevilled and hampered the proper development of this medical school. External and frequently malign influences—notably that of the *Dundee Advertiser* and its autocratic proprietor, D. C. Thomson—clearly had much to do with this failure.

The final separation was hastened by the impact of the 1963 Robbins Report with its call for a rapid expansion of higher education. Deprived of the Dundee clinical facilities and faced with a range of choices, including the total abandonment of medical education, St Andrews opted to introduce a pre-clinical BSc in medical science, with graduates proceeding to the University of Manchester for clinical training under the terms of an exclusive arrangement drawn up between the two bodies in 1967. Since 1977 there have been two attempts to propose a re-amalgamation between Dundee and St Andrews, so far without success.

As the author readily acknowledges, St Andrews was never in the first rank of British medical schools but it did make an important contribution over the centuries. Mr Blair's pride in his *Alma Mater* sometimes colours his judgment, particularly in his disdain for D. G. Southgate's centenary history of university education in Dundee. This is more than balanced, however, by his intimate knowledge of St Andrews medicine in the twentieth century, seen to best effect in the excellent (if not always complimentary) biographical sketches of the major actors on the stage. Unfortunately, the interpolation of these and other ephemera too often hinders the thread of the narrative.

Some of the confusion experienced by this reader would have been alleviated by the inclusion of appendices of the main *dramatis personae* and chronological tables of academic and clinical teachers, particularly during the period when there were parallel appointments in both St Andrews and Dundee. Considerable space is devoted to the analysis of student and graduate numbers—never large by comparison with the other Scottish schools—and it would again have been helpful to have these gathered in tabular form. The bibliography and index are somewhat erratic in compilation and do not do justice to the author's endeavours.

Most, if not all, of these defects could have been rectified by a minimum of judicious pruning and editing of what is a very long book—some 200,000 words in total—and it is unfortunate that such a reputable publisher as the Scottish Academic Press apparently did not see fit to undertake this task. It is perhaps indicative of their efforts that the title page bears the inscription 'History of Medicine in the University of St Andrews' while the dustjacket and spine are inscribed 'History of Medicine in St Andrews University'.

Despite such reservations this is a valuable and scholarly work and Mr Blair merits high praise for his industry and painstaking devotion to what, of necessity, has been a labour of love executed during the infrequent leisure hours of a demanding professional life.

Derek A. Dow
University of Glasgow

F.-B. Lickteig, *The German Carmelites at the Medieval Universities.* Rome: Institutum Carmelitanum, 1981. 608 pp.

The Carmelites provide us with a useful example of the changing character of the attitude of the religious orders to higher education. From being in their early days fervent opponents of such studies, the Carmelites had by the close of the Middle Ages been forced to establish their own network of training facilities and were sending their qualified members to universities in some numbers. Indeed, the order frequently took the lead in promoting the organization of a faculty of theology in several German universities.

This detailed, comprehensive, and thorough study, based mainly on material preserved in the archives of Frankfurt and Dresden, describes the development of the friaries of the German provinces and their growing provision for the education of their students. The allocation of members to universities within and outside the Empire is traced and evidence for the life and achievement of these students is discussed. The value of the text is increased by the provision of tables illustrating the numbers of known Carmelites at the various institutions. It is unlikely that anything of substance will be added to this careful work.

Students of German history will find much of value in these pages, but for those interested in the development of European universities as a whole, two important conclusions emerge from Dr Lickteig's work. First, it is evident that the impact of the Great Schism seriously altered the character of the German Carmelites' provision of university education. An early dependence on Paris for many of their instructors in theology suddenly ceased when the French gave their allegiance to a Pope rejected by the Germans. Excluded from France, the German Carmelites turned to strengthen the movement to establish faculties of theology in the Empire and in Italy. The ending of the Schism did not mean a complete return to France. Students were now found in a great variety of universities in all European countries except Spain. Secondly, it is clear that the progress of the Reformation virtually destroyed the Carmelite educational network in Germany. The Upper German Province disintegrated and the Lower lost many of its houses. The Carmelites survived, with a nucleus of theologians especially at Louvain and Cologne, but their great days as an educational force were ended.

Dr Lickteig tells this story in an interesting and informative style. He is able to introduce personal details from the central province records and trace the careers of some of those who were sent to universities. Although the order found it difficult to combine its pastoral and priestly duties with the requirements of the various university faculties, a serious and successful effort was made to provide trained manpower for the German provinces.

John M. Fletcher
Department of Modern Languages
Aston University
Birmingham B4 7ET

D. Poirion (ed.), *Milieux universitaires et mentalité urbaine au Moyen Age*. Colloque du Département d'Etudes Médiévales de Paris-Sorbonne et de l'Université de Bonn (Cultures et civilisations médiévales VI). Paris: Presses de l'Université de Paris-Sorbonne, 1987. 172 pp. 100F.

Relations between town and gown have been for a long time the subject of research and scholarly discussion. In June 1986 a colloquium was devoted to the impact of the academic milieu on urban life. The proceedings of this colloquium show a variety of themes and approaches. Nevertheless, we can discern certain clusters of topics, some of them new and original.

Two refreshing contributions were given on regions without universities, the Islamic countries,[1] or even without towns, Iceland.[2] It is interesting to read how these countries could attain high intellectual levels in a period when universities in England and on the Continent were acquiring a monopoly of higher education. The 'Icelanders' Sagas' and some scholarly works are products of a highly educated people. If transmission of knowledge was mainly a family question in Iceland, in the Islamic world, on the contrary, religious and juridical education was a school concern. The *madrasa* was a centre of higher learning and its teachers can be considered as the intellectual elite of their country. Analogies between the *madrasas* and the European universities are clear. Both institutions provided an answer to specific educational and intellectual demands.

A second cluster of papers deals more with universities and literature than with town and gown. Nevertheless these give interesting examples of the relation between the academic and non-academic worlds. On the other hand C. Cormeau[3] explains how a university—Vienna—became a centre for the popularization of academic learning. The treatises on moral theology of Henry of Langenstein and some of his colleagues were translated into German or were propagated by Langenstein's pupils in writings which originated outside the university. There is evidence that these works reached people without a Latin education. On the other hand, Rutebeuf lets us hear the voice of popular opinion in academic matters.[4] In his poems he describes the quarrels of the Mendicant Orders in Paris as foreshadowing the Last Judgment and the denunciation of antichrist. Striking in French goliard literature is the love-hate relation of the poet with the studium. Many of these poets had followed academic courses; they exhibit their classical and philosophical knowledge and their association with the university world. But they are mainly conservatives polemizing intellectual and didactic innovations and academic quarrels. M. Zink[5] compares this type of literature with such present-day novels ridiculing university teachers as those by C. Rihoit, S. Doubrovsky or D. Lodge. M. Stanesco goes further.[6] He explores the rational world of the university and the irrational world of fiction, both dealing with magic. Around 1200 novels and scholarly works do not represent different spheres even when contacts are not direct. Both enjoy the capacity to delight and a belief in mystery. Two contributions pose some problems. They do not fit in the theme of the colloquium and they only indirectly deal with universities. J. Cl. Mühlethaler[7] describes the 'régime des princes' and analogous treatises written for the French court, and therefore associated with the Parisian intellectual milieu, and M. Mentré[8] explains the iconographical importance of the initials of thirteenth century Bibles originating from the Sorbonne. The last group of papers effectively deals with relations between university and city. For several regions we get information of the place of the studium in the medieval town and of the integration of academics with city government and urban life. Very welcome is the overview of the Castilian situation,[9] which in fact deals only with Salamanca and Valladolid. Desportes[10] also concentrates on two towns in Northern France, Amiens and Reims. Verger, on the other hand, tries to cover the whole of Southern France.[11] The examples are well chosen, even when it would be preferable to introduce also a purely commercial town. Salamanca symbolizes the big and important university town, Valladolid the government capital with a regional university, Reims a city dominated by the church, and Amiens, capital of the 'baillage royal', had a mainly administrative function. It is a pity that the paper by M. Ditsche on the financial support German cities and citizens gave to poor students is published only as a summary.[12] M. Ditsche is familiar with this subject. K. Wriedt also dealt with urban financial support in the large volume *Schulen und Studium im Sozialen Wandel des hohen und späten Mittelalters*, ed. J. Fried (Sigmaringen 1986). Both volumes complement each other well. For large parts of Europe we get now a much better picture of the quantitative and qualitative integration of academics into urban life. From Salamanca to Lübeck the similiarities are striking in spite of chronological differences. For the Middle Ages we hardly know how academic learning was popularized and how academic matters were received by the common man. The contributions of Cormeau, Stanesco, and Zink can show the way.

Hilde de Ridder-Symeons
University of Ghent and Free University
of Amsterdam

REFERENCES

1. D. Sourdel, *Universitaires sans université dans les villes des pays d'Islam*, pp. 119–28.
2. R. Boyer, *Des "intellectuels" sans villes ni universités*, pp. 23–34.

3. C. Cormeau, *Wiens Universitäts und die deutschen Prosatexte im Umkreis Heinrichs von Langenstein*, pp. 35–48. With a French summary.
4. J.-P. Bordier, *L'Antéchrist au Quartier latin selon Rutebeuf*, pp. 9–21.
5. M. Zink, *De Jean Le Teinturier à Jean Bras-de-Fer: Le Triomphe des cuistres*, pp. 157–70.
6. M. Stanesco, *Nigromance et université: scolastique du merveilleux dans le roman français du Moyen Age*, pp. 129–44.
7. J.-C. Mühlethaler, *Le poète face au pouvoir de Geffroy de Paris à Eustache Deschamps*, pp. 83–101.
8. M. Mentré, *L'iconographie des Bibles universitaires parisiennes du XIIIe siècle*, pp. 69–81.
9. A. Rucquoi, *Sociétés urbaines et universités en Castille au Moyen Age*, pp. 103–17.
10. P. Desportes, *Les gradués d'université dans la société urbaine de la France du Nord à la fin du Moyen Age*, pp. 49–67.
11. J. Verger, *Les gradués en droit dans les sociétés urbaines du midi de la France à la fin du Moyen Age*, pp. 145–56.
12. M. Ditsche, *Studienstiftungen (bursae volantes) für scholares pauperes in Spätmittelalterlichen deutschen Städten*, pp. 171–2.

Nancy G. Siraisi, *Avicenna in Renaissance Italy. The Canon and Medical Teaching in Italian Universities after 1500*. Princeton: Princeton University Press, 1987. xii + 410 pp. £31.40.

This work explores the history of Avicenna's *Canon* as a university textbook in the period *c.* 1500 to *c.* 1630. In the late middle ages the *Canon* in its twelfth century Latin translation by Gerard of Cremona had been the authoritative medical textbook prescribed in faculty statutes. At the turn of the sixteenth century its utility began to be questioned by humanists, such as Leoniceno and Symphorien Champier, who claimed that the text was riddled with terminological errors and that students would do better to return to the Greek, essentially Galenic, originals on which it was based. As a result, in the course of the sixteenth century the *Canon* ceased to be a prescribed authority in many universities north of the Alps. This was not the case in Italy, however, where it retained an important position in the curriculum in two of the most innovative medical faculties of the period, Padua and Bologna. Indeed, at Bologna the *Canon* was still a prescribed work in 1800, although from the end of the seventeenth century, professors, such as Morgagni, simply used the text as a peg on which to hang a modern course in physiology.

Siraisi's study is divided into four parts. She first traces the history of the *Canon* as a Latin medical book and introduces the reader to the complex structure of the work. Next she surveys the fortunes of the work in the medieval and Renaissance university, before, in part iii, tracing its history as a printed Latin book in the sixteenth and seventeenth centuries. The text of the *Canon*, she reveals, was amended rather than retranslated in the sixteenth century, for few medical scholars had any knowledge of Arabic. Textual revision was frequently the result of comparing the Latin with the extant Hebrew version. Finally, Professor Siraisi discusses the way in which one section of the *Canon* (the first *doctrina* of the first *fen*) was actually 'read' in the Renaissance classroom. *Canon* i.i. was not chosen at random. This was the one part of the work which retained its appeal in an age anxious to promote the study of the original Galenic texts. *Canon* i.i. was a succinct and accurate, if somewhat pedestrian, introduction to Artistotelo-Galenic medical theory. It was a good way of introducing the tyro to medical science (even if it appears that many students at Padua skipped theoretical lectures and proceeded directly to the practical part of the course).

Professor Siraisi's book is a mine of information for the historian of medicine as a university discipline. Her erudition is immense and the reader cannot but be impressed by the way she brings the *Canon* to life. The book, however, has an appeal beyond the specialist reader and will become a standard work of reference for anyone working on Renaissance thought. Her study of the commentaries (both MS and printed) of *Canon* i.i. are a model of their kind. At Renaissance Padua and Bologna, it seems, the professor/commentator departed from the medieval custom of attempting to reconcile one part of the text or one authority with another. Instead, where there was inconsistency or disagreement this was carefully pointed out and the professor made his preferences known to his students. As a result, Avicenna could be handled quite roughly, especially in the mid-sixteenth century, when commentators such as Da Monte were emphasizing where the *Canon* had misconstrued the Galenic original. The commentary, however, did continue to be a method for introducing extraneous material and informing the student in greater depth about classical and contemporary philosophical and physiological debates. For instance, the section in the work devoted to Aristotle's theory of the elements (actually in *Canon* i.ii) provided an opportunity to discuss atomism and, at the turn of the seventeenth century, even the Copernican theory. Some of the professors, notably Da Monte, showed an enthusiasm for the strict Aristotelian naturalism of Pompanazzi, but in general the professors were hostile to new and unorthodox ideas. Santorio in the 1610s, although very conversant with Galilean astronomy, continued to reject heliocentricity in the name of tradition, while also rejecting Colombo's account of the pulmonary circulation (the latter had also taught at Padua). The professors' real contribution to the new science, argues Siraisi, was to place a greater emphasis on the need to square theory with observation. Santorio remained a believer in the Galenic theory of temperaments (unlike his predecessor, Cardano) but he wanted the doctrine validated through experimentation with the help of the many instruments which he himself had developed (such as the thermometer).

Siraisi's study is an important contribution to a genre of Renaissance studies which the original editor of this journal, the late Charles Schmitt, did so much to promote: the history of classroom philosophy and science (in this case medical science). In the last twenty years a great deal has been done to map this history and as a result the Renaissance university has become for the first time a subject of serious study. Nonetheless, Professor Siraisi's work is unique. The chief foci of interest have been the classroom fortunes of the Aristotelian and to a lesser degree the Galenic corpus. Professor Siraisi is the first to look at the history of the *Canon*. This is a significant departure. Humanist critics might carp at the obscurantism of scholastic philosophy but they could not replace Aristotle by Plato. Avicenna, in contrast, was definitely expendable in an age that wanted to return to the purest source of medical knowledge. The *Canon* was the one medieval authority which did suffer mixed fortunes in the era. It is therefore extremely interesting to see how the text was actually handled. What emerges from the study is that in some way it was treated no differently from Aristotle or indeed any other scientific text read in the Renaissance classroom. There was one highly flexible form of commentary which was deployed in all circumstances. There again the way in which the content of the *Canon* could be criticized and the degree to which it became a peg on which to hang extraneous material does suggest that flexibility in this case was taken to an extreme. Commentaries on Aristotle were primarily discourses on a text whose content was deemed fundamentally sound. To some sixteenth-century commentators of the *Canon*, it would seem that the text was already little more than the structural prop it would be to Morgagni. Siraisi (like Schmitt before her) is keen to emphasize the unity of the period 1300–1600, an age in which scientific discourse was dominated by the scholastic and very elastic textual commentary. It was only after 1600, and really not before 1650, that the commentary began to be replaced by the textbook (and then of course only very slowly). This is a fair point and historians in the past have been mistaken in dividing the late middle ages from the Renaissance. Nevertheless, Siraisi's own work would tend to suggest that the Renaissance also saw the beginning of the end of the commentary as a satisfactory pedagogical device. In the case of Avicenna, text and commentary were already becoming divorced as early as 1550 as they would be increasingly in the case of Aristotle and Galen a century later once their fundamental principles were challenged by the proponents of the mechanical philosophy. Perhaps Siraisi's conclusion to her extremely worthy volume could be slightly revised. The history of the *Canon* in the Renaissance is certainly one of continuity with the medieval past but it is one of discontinuity, too. The *Canon*, where it survived as a classroom text, was already becoming an emaciated skeletal remains.

Laurence Brockliss
Magdalen College
Oxford OX1 4AU

E. S. Leedham-Green, *Books in Cambridge Inventories: Book-Lists from Vice-Chancellor's Court Probate Inventories in the Tudor and Stuart Periods* (2 vols.). Cambridge: Cambridge University Press, 1986.

I was fortunate enough to be introduced to the Cambridge University book inventories in the early 1970s, when I was learning my way around the University Library archives under the able tutelage of the late Tim Munby, librarian of King's College. I have found them, ever since, a fascinating and valuable source for the study of intellectual life in Tudor and Stuart Cambridge, and they have retained, for me, the excitement which Tim Munby managed to generate, as we opened each packet, and pored over its contents.

Dr Leedham-Green's long-awaited printed edition of the book-lists lives up to the promise of those early, happy encounters. She is infectiously and unabashedly enthusiastic about her project. She introduces the reader to her topic with humour and an engaging modesty; her alert introduction, raising as it does searching intellectual questions about her material, make the inevitably rather austere transcriptions of the lists themselves accessible and attractive from the outset. And as an aid to further scholarship the contribution she has made is invaluable. Her carefully researched and produced volumes are a rich resource which scholars of the period are bound to receive with gratitude—relieving them as it does of the need any longer to puzzle over the fading secretary hand, the lacunae, cryptic abbreviations, and ambiguous and incomplete attributions of the originals.

Volume I consists of a transcription of all the surviving book-lists included in inventories presented for probate in the Vice-Chancellor's Court at Cambridge (the period covered is 1535/6 to 1600, with a scattering of lists beyond that date, up to 1760). In addition, Dr Leedham-Green gives us two inventories of booksellers' stock (Reignold Bridges and William Hammond), which are not probate inventories, but which make useful comparison with the five booksellers' inventories within the probate records. For similar reasons, she also prints a Peterhouse Library Catalogue, MS 405, for comparison with the important 1589 inventory of Andrew Perne's books, since nearly nine hundred of Perne's titles can be identified in the library to which he bequeathed them. Volume II contains an author/title catalogue for the nearly twenty thousand titles which occur in the inventories, and a subject catalogue 'on 16th century lines'—actually a sort of hybrid between the subject headings in Gesner's *Pandectae* and the subject headings of the sixteenth century curriculum. This last, is, I think a mistake: unlike all the other ingenious collations with which Leedham-Green provides us, the subject-catalogue is not self-evidently particularly useful, even as a basic guide to determine the specialist bias in a particular inventory. Suppose we wanted to know whether the presence in an inventory of a work by Lorenzo Valla indicated a particular set of intellectual interests. Since Valla's *Elegantiae* spans the whole trivium, he is classified in the subject-index under 'grammar', 'dialectic' and 'rhetoric';[1] he also of course, appears under 'theology' for his annotations on the New Testament (but why not, then, under 'moral philosophy' for the *De vero bono*?). So we are no further forward. And since we are given only authors, not titles of works, in this compilation, major classical authors appear all over the place, somewhat inexplicably (why is Xenophon under 'economics' and 'history', but not under 'politics'; why (by analogy) is Virgil under 'poetry', but not under 'moral philosophy or 'useful arts' (for the *Georgics*?)). But this is to cavill.

Book inventories, like student notebooks, manuscript lecture notes, marginalia, and other contemporary ephemera, are increasingly recognized by scholars to be a mine of helpful information for research on the intellectual life of the past.[2] Dr Leedham-Green's volumes allow us to use the Cambridge book inventories to piece together a picture of sixteenth-century habits of reading. Comparison of the Perne inventory with Peter-house 405, for instance, shows us how a simple entry in the inventory 'vigetius de re militare fo. ij s' (Perne 1913) is in fact an edition of collected, related works: 'Vegetius de re militari; Frontini strategemata; Aelianus de instruendis aciebus; Modestus. de vocabulis rei militaris' (Classis 8a, item 15; Ad.331). By contrast, '[Demosthenis Olinthiacae] per Carrum 4o vj d' (Perne 115) is a composite volume (either put together by Perne himself, or purchased already bound together), consisting of the following: '[i] Demosthen: Olynth: & Philipp: Orat: lat. per Carrum; Dodington de vita & obitu Carri & Carm; in eius mortem; [ii] Humfred: de vita & obitu Joh: Juelli. & defens: eius verae doctr: contra Harding:; Sanderi Epistolae' (Classis XVII, item 24; (i) STC 6577; (ii) STC 13963). In both cases the complete set of titles within the volume, concealed behind the recorded first title, reminds the scholar working with the inventories alone that the reader of 'Demosthenis Olinthiacae' had his attention focused by the volume on doctrinal issues debated amongst Carr, Jewell, Harding, and others; the reader of the Vegetius volume had his focused on the modern use to be made of ancient observations on the practicalities of warfare.

In some cases such complications suggest that the sixteenth-century reader approached his academic disciplines in a manner distinctively different from the modern specialist. 'Vitruvius cum alijs fo. x s' (Perne 1811) is made up of '[i] Vitruvius Architectura cum comment: Daniel Barbari; [ii] Delphinus de fluxu & refluxu maris & de Motu 8ae Sphaerae; [iii] Capella de nuptiis Philologiae & Mercurii, & de 7 artib: liberalibus; [iv] Schoneri Gnomonic: & Mechanic: Gnomonic: & Inventio linea meridia & Compos: Astrolab:' Peterhouse 405, Classis 8a, item 14;(i) Ad.909; (ii) Ad.232; (iii) Ad.585; (iv) Ad.677). Here we can see that 'Vitruvius' is treated as a work in geometry/astronomy, alongside texts conventionally used as part of mathematics instruction. As it happens in this case we can find corroborating evidence that this is the habitual way of grouping Vitruvius with other contemporary texts. In the inventory of the books donated to Sidney Sussex College (c.1616) by Lucy, Countess of Bedford and Lady Ann Harrington, in the Sidney Sussex Donors' Book (Sidney Sussex MS 91), under 'Libri Mathemat: in Folio' we find 'Vitruvius de Architect: cu[m] com[m]ent: Dan. Barbari', together with 'Delphinus de fluxu & refluxu maris' and a number of other astronomical, optical, and geometrical works, including 'Theodosij Sphaerica' [Ad.548–9], 'Tychon. Brah. Astron. nova de Stella Martis', 'Plan. Sphaeric. Theorica' [Purbach, Ad. 2272A–2281] and 'Nic. Copernici Revolutiones' [Ad. 2602–3] (23–4).[3] As for the Martianus Capella—we need only note that unlike such influential ancient authors as Augustine, Capella makes astronomy one of the seven liberal arts which are the foundation of education, replacing philosophy.[4]

Inevitably, individual specialist readers will take pleasure in spotting anomalies which in the grand sweep of the inventories' coverage, Dr Leedham-Green (on her own admission) was bound to miss. 'Politian in englishe' (1559 Bateman 259) is surely a mishearing by one appraiser, as the title was called out by the other (introduction, xii), of 'angeli politiani' as 'anglii politiani'? 'Dr Harvy' (1588 Walters 88) is more likely to be John Harvey than Gabriel. Noting the presence of 15 'Catos' in the inventory of the bookseller Pilgrim (1546), Dr Leedham-Green comments that he 'clearly catered also for the more elementary level of education' (introduction xviii). But the *Disticha* are only the first items in a much-read Erasmus volume of his own minor works which also includes Rudolph Agricola's Latin translation of a standard curriculum item, Isocrates' *Paraenesis ad demonicum*. Thus the twenty-three 'Catos' in the inventories may be added to the seventy-one copies of Agricola's *De inventione dialecta*, the twenty-two Aphthonius's (in Agricola's translation) and various *opuscula*, as well as to the seventeen pages of Erasmus works found in the inventories (I, 305–22), to confirm the strong hold of the two Dutch humanists on the sixteenth-century Cambridge curriculum—a hold beautifully illustrated by the contents of the Pilgrim list itself.[5]

As I worked with the book inventories for this review, my one regret was that I did not have the material on computer disk, to ease the still arduous process of searching, retrieving, and collating the information the volumes contain. Dr Leedham-Green is now working on a further book-inventory project, which will provide us with more welcome archival evidence about Tudor and Stuart reading: *Private Libraries in Renaissance England: A Collection and Catalogue of Tudor and Early Stuart Book-Lists* (general editor Prof. R. J. Fehrenbach). And in this case the material *will* be made available as a computerized catalogue. For the time being, the only pay-off for the reader of the modern technology Dr Leedham-Green uses is the appalling typeface and print-quality of the volumes, and the odd moment of serendipity like item 65 in Chekyn 1535/6: 'opus pandect***Service stopping in 5 minutes, please logoff-orum ⟨Sylvaticus⟩'. The *Opus pandectarum medicinae* will never be the same again!

Lisa Jardine
Jesus College
Cambridge

REFERENCES

1. I doubt very much that Anderson 66 (1589), 'Logica' is Valla's *Dialecticae disputationes*, which never, to my knowledge, bore the title 'logic' in a printed edition.
2. See, most recently, M. Feingold, *The Mathematicians' Apprenticeship: Science, Universities and Society in England 1560–1640* (Cambridge, 1984), especially pp. 86–121; J. McConica (ed.), *The History of the University of Oxford*, volume III, *The Collegiate University* (Oxford, 1986), especially pp. 441–519; 693–721.
3. My thanks to Warren Boutcher for bringing this list to my attention.
4. See R. R. Bolgar, *The Classical Heritage and its Beneficiaries from the Carolingian Age to the End of the Renaissance* (Cambridge, 1954; 1964 edn.), p. 36.
5. See L. Jardine, 'Humanism and the sixteenth century Cambridge arts course', *History of Education* iv (1977), 16–31; and for comparable observations concerning Oxford, see J. McConica, 'Elizabethan Oxford: the collegiate society', in McConica (ed.), *History of the University of Oxford* III, 645–732; 701–2.

Ivana Čornejová and Anna Fechtnerová: *Životopisný slovník Pražské Univerzity, filozofická a teologická fakulta 1654–1773*. Univerzita Karlova: Prague 1986. liv + 597 pp. Kčs 54.

This biographical dictionary gives data about the teachers of the philosphical and the theological faculty of the Charles-Ferdinand-University of Prague for the period from 1654 to 1773. The period is limited by the fusion of the old university, founded by Emperor Charles IV, with the Jesuit academy, which occurred after long quarrels in 1654, and the general suppression of the Jesuit Order in 1773, when almost all of the former Jesuits had to leave academic teaching. The formation of the Carolo-Ferdinandea marked a late and small success in the Jesuit university policy because it was possible only by arrangement with the archbishop whose college was a strong concurrent to the Jesuit college of St Clement, and who became the chancellor of the university despite the rule that Jesuits were always subject only to the government of their General (p. v). On the other hand the Prague University was the only complete four faculty university in Bohemia while Olomouc (Olmutz) and Vratislav (Breslau in Silesia) were pure 'Jesuit Universities'. The authors call the philosophical and the theological faculties the 'spiritual faculties' (duchovní fakulty) evidencing thus the strong interrelation of both in a Jesuit curriculum. And since it happened quite regularly that a professor moved from one faculty of one university to one of another Bohemian university this handbook documents more or less all the personnel of Boheminan universities at that time.

The core of the dictionary is an alphabetical list of all professors with precise information about their forms of names and academic titles, dates of life, and professional career, and finally bibliographical data on their writings not only in theology and philosophy. References to the secondary sources conclude each article.

First of all this list is a tool for biographical research on Czech Jesuits of the period. The most common handbooks, such as de Backer/Sommervogel's *Bibliothèque de la Compagnie de Jésus*, and the special bio-bibliographical lists by Kalckbrenner and Welss,[1] are combined and completed by unpublished archival information accessible only to specialists, such as several archives at Prague, Brno (Brünn), and Olomouc. One would have preferred to see complete bibliographical data of the works of each author including format and number of pages, but this would have considerably increased the size of this volume, and mainly with book titles of comparatively minor importance, e.g. dissertation titles. One of the co-authors published in 1984 a four volume catalogue/edition of illuminated doctoral theses.[2]

Among the professors listed here one could mention Rodericus de Arriaga (pp. 4–6) who taught for more than forty years at the Clementinum and the university, and was author of two authoritative *cursus* of pholosophy and of theology; the Czech historian Bohuslav Balbin (pp. 13–15); the biographer of missionaries Emmanuel de Boye (pp. 35–7); the baroque poet Bartholomaeus Christelius (pp. 49–51); Joseph Conradi who commented on the Holy Scripture (pp. 55–6); Caspar Knittel, one of the last followers of A. Kircher (pp. 209–10); the mathematicians Adam Kochansky (pp. 213–14) who spent some years at the court of John III King of Poland, and Jacobus

Kresa (pp. 237–9) who taught at Madrid; the naturalist Joseph Stepling who published several meteorological studies; Franciscus Zeno (pp. 540–2) author of eighteenth century praises on St. Mary.

But handbooks like this always lead to quantitative questions, and therefore the authors show in two lists (pp. xxv and xxvi) that most of the academic staff were of Bohemian and Moravian origin with a tendency towards nationalization of the faculties. Most of them came from Prague (46 out of 150; p. xxvii). It would be interesting to see how many of them were of German, Czech, or any other mother language, a research not easily undertaken nowadays. It goes without saying that most of the writings are in Latin. As for geographical relationships one can say that most of the professors stayed within the borders of the Bohemian kingdom, moving between Prague, Olomouc, Brno, and minor colleges. On p. xv the authors show the 'ideal career' of a Jesuit teacher, starting with courses in the *humaniora*, including ethics, teaching the threefold philosophy course (logic, physics, metaphysics), changing to the theology department, where moral theology (*casus conscientiae*) was the minor topic, and via the teaching of Scripture or religious controversy arriving finally at speculative theology: for those professors who expected further engagements this career could be made within seven years' time, three years of philosophy and four years of theology, as the *ratio studiorum* of the Jesuits planned. A further question which arises is how many of the publications were connected with university teaching in the strict sense: I already mentioned Arriaga; Johannes Korzinek and Johannes Senftleben published philosophy textbooks in 1658 and 1685 respectively, but were there more? And which were the textbooks used in both faculties during the time period? One has to take into account that the reforms of Maria Theresia affected even Jesuit studies. Already in 1747 Jesuits introduced *physica experimentalis* in addition to *physica speculativa* in their teaching (p. xx) and from 1752 faculty directors were established and the teaching system changed completely: natural theology as well as history were introduced in a two year course. Along with these changes non-Jesuits entered the spiritual faculties (see list p. xix) and Jesuits lost influence.

These events are explained in an introduction (pp. iv–ix) with a German summary (pp. l–liv). The dictionary is completed by five appendices, concerning Latin-Czech academic terminology, a chronology of Czech Jesuit residences (including the four towns of Prague, i.e. Old Town, New Town, Small Side or 'Kleinseite', and the Castle, and Litoměřice, Brno, Vratislav, and others), a Czech-German glossary of names of places outside of the present ČSR, a very complete bibliography including many items difficult to find in western libraries today (pp. 566–85), and a list of archival sources (pp. 586–93). The only misprints are few and unimportant, so we can only admire the diligence and accuracy with which the authors, librarians to the State Library at Prague, provided this useful research tool.

Paul Richard Blum
Freie Universität Berlin
FB Philosophie U.
Sozialwissenschaften 1 (WE 1),
Königin-Luise-Straße 34,
1000 Berlin 33.

REFERENCES

1. E. Kalckbrenner, 'Personalbibliographien der Professoren der philosophischen Fakultät der Karl-Ferdinands-Universität in Prag im Zeitraum von 1654–1720'. (Med. Diss. Erlangen 1972). G. Welss, 'Personalbibliographien der Professoren und Dozenten der philosophischen Fakultät der Karl-Ferdinands-Universität in Prag im ungefähren Zeitraum von 1700–1773 mit kurzen biographischen Angaben über die Sachgebiete'. (Med. Diss. Erlangen 1971).
2. A. Fechtnerová: *Katalog grafických listu univerzitních tesí uložených ve Státní Knihovně ČSR v Praze* (4 vols.; Prague, 1984)

E. G.W. Bill, *Education at Christ Church Oxford 1660–1800*. Oxford: Clarendon Press, 1988. xi + 367 pp. £35.

The late Dame Lucy Sutherland began the rehabilitation of Oxford's eighteenth-century reputation, and the recent publication of the volume in *The History of the University of Oxford* which she edited with L. G. Mitchell carried the work forward weightily (see the review in *History of Universities* (1988), pp. 344–9). *Education at Christ Church* complements the university history, and gives a generally flattering account of Oxford's then most flourishing college. The constitution of the college, which was a cathedral as well as a college, is carefully explained, and there are sympathetic portraits of the Deans, from John Fell (1660–86) to Cyril Jackson (1783–1809)—the two who did most to advance the standing of their college. The work of other college officials and tutors is covered, and Appendix II gives sources for identifying the tutors, lists of whose names were not preserved since, though appointed by the Dean, they were private employees of their pupils. Similarly, there are lists of Vernon Students (p. 348) and Faculty Students (pp. 350–2). The methods by which undergraduates were attracted to Christ Church are demonstrated, and the particular links between the college and Westminster School are examined. There were two main categories of

Students of the college: the Westminster Students selected from the School by the Dean, and the Canoneer Students elected by the Dean and Chapter on the nomination of individual Canons of Christ Church. Though a few lesser men got an education at Christ Church, Dean Fell 'believed that the education of the ruling classes was of crucial importance, and he strove with unremitting vigour to attract the aristocracy and gentry to Christ Church' (p. 30); while Dean Jackson—different from his predecessor in so many ways—equally 'sought to ensure that through the education received at Christ Church the country was governed and administered by men of character and ability' (p. 80). Materially and educationally, this corner of Oxford was far from decayed.

In exploring the educational system at Christ Church, this book (like *The History of Oxford*, vol. V) relies heavily on the unique source material provided by the college's Collections books. Enough of these survive to show what undergraduates read throughout this period. E. G. W. Bill analyses the changing curriculum, with its growing emphasis on Greek, and shows how the classically-based 'liberal education', which was to be such a powerful influence in the nineteenth century, was built up. Whereas in the Scottish universities logic, ethics, and physics held their place in the undergraduate curriculum, and the science taught was modernized, in Oxford, though mathematics and the philosophies were studied, classics became increasingly predominant. Of Christ Church, the author concludes that 'the vacuum caused by the demise of Aristotelian science was filled by classical and not by scientific studies owing partly to the nature of the tutorial system but perhaps pre-eminently owing to the assumptions of liberal education, which were inimical to the practical application of science. ... Stripped of its originally comprehensive character, liberal education became synonymous with classical education' (p. 326).

Jennifer Carter
Department of History
University of Aberdeen
Old Aberdeen AB9 2UB

Marina Roggero: *Il Sapere e la Virtù: Stato Università e Professioni nel Piemonte tra Settecento ed Ottocento*. Università di Torino: Centro di Studi per la storio dell'Università: Studi e Fonti I.: Deputazione Subalpina di Storia Patria & Università degli Studi di Torino: Turin, 1987.

Professor Roggero has chosen to devote this thoughtful and thoroughly researched volume to situating the Collegio delle Provincie, nucleus of the modern University of Turin, in its social, intellectual, and political context. Founded by the king of Sardinia in 1729 as part of the reforming projects of one of the minor monarchs of Enlightenment Europe, it had, by the time of the Napoleonic occupation eighty years later, educated the majority of the academic, social, and political elite of Piedmont.

Although this study terminates in 1815, it clearly has, as the author points out, considerable implications for the study of the Piedmontese Risorgimento, led by men of the generation which had passed through the Collegio during the French occupation period. Attitudes formed and relationships made at the Collegio also shaped the reactions of the Piedmontese ruling class to the revolutions of the 1820s and 1830s. In providing these insights, this book adds greatly to the surprisingly sparse material in this area. Increasingly too, it is being realized that the history of university institutions only becomes significant in the context of the surrounding society and political culture.

This work grew originally out of team projects co-ordinated by Egle Becchi on the group history of educators in Piedmont and the pedagogy applied by them to Italian ruling elites, and by the well-known historian of the *Triennio*, Mario Mirri, on the diffusion of projects of reform during the Italian Enlightenment. Such projects, many of whose findings are reflected in this volume, enable us to gain considerable insight into the political culture internalized through the educational institution, through role-modelling on the respected educators described in chapters 1–3 of the present work, and through the peer-group pressures characteristic of, by present day standards, small, elite, institutions such as the Collegio delle Provincie. This study, however, does more than enable us to assess the means by which plans of reform might be internalized by an existing elite.

Its discussion of the allocation of sponsored places in the Collegio not only allows us to assess the play of political patronage and cultural values between central government and the provinces; it also allows us to place a purchase on the problem of social mobility through education in a pre-modern society. Here again, most importantly, the history of education provides a jumping-off-point for the consideration of the extent to which old-regime elites were permeable or permitted themselves to ally with newly emergent social forces. Through the study of the scholarships awarded to the Collegio may also be assessed the success of the Piedmontese monarchy itself in creating and controlling the emergence of new professional groups, which while not, as yet, in competition with existing elites, yet paved the way for the diversification of social power which marks the transition from aristocratic to 'mixed' society. For all these reasons, this study is a landmark both in the history of the Italian Enlightenment, of its educational practice, and of the history of European elites in general.

Dorinda Outram
University College,
Cork, Republic of Ireland.

Atlas de la Révolution française. 2. L'Enseignement 1760–1815.
Direction scientifique Dominique Julia; *conception graphique*
Huguette Bertrand, Serge Bonin and Alexandra Laclau (Editions de
l'Ecole des Hautes Etudes en Sciences Sociales, Paris, 1987). 105 pp.
FF90.

This work is part of a series devoted to a statistical study of the sociology of
French culture in the Revolutionary era. Each volume brings together a
team of researchers and illustrators. The former provide the statistical data
which the latter transform into a visual format by a clever use of maps and
histograms. The present volume, under the direction of Dominique Julia, is
the result of the combined efforts of sixteen educational historians, many of
whom like the *directeur scientifique* are well-established *érudits*. A part of the
statistical data has already appeared in learned monographs and these are
carefully listed in the bibliography. Much of the data, however, is presented
here for the first time and the volume contains a very useful guide to the
sources deployed (see *Sources des cartes et graphiques*). The *Atlas* is divided
into four chapters that deal with (i) elementary education, (ii) the colleges,
the *écoles centrales* and the *lycées*, (iii) *pensionnats*, and (iv) technical schools
and the university faculties of theology, law, and medicine. The division is
deliberate. In France both before and after 1789 educational institutions
were broadly divisible into three types: elementary schools that taught a
proportion of the lower orders to read and write, secondary schools which
prepared the sons of the elite to be gentlemen either as day-boys or
boarders, and professional schools which trained young gentlemen for a
career. To have devoted a single chapter to the university in a work on
education during the French revolution would have made no sense. Before
1789 the twenty-four French universities were umbrella institutions. On the
one hand, they played a role in the creation of gentlemen as their affiliated
colleges and seminaries provided a generalist education in the humanities
and philosophy; on the other, they offered a training for the Church, bar,
and medicine in the three higher faculties. In the course of the 1790s,
however, the French revolutionaries created a very different system of
education which made a modern distinction between secondary and tertiary
institutions. The universities were abolished in 1793; a generalist education
was entrusted to the new departmental *écoles centrales* in 1795 (later the
lycées); and the higher faculties eventually became professional schools.
Napoleon revived the concept of the university in 1808 but now in a
completely new guise. There was henceforth only one university, the
Université impériale, and it was a purely administrative organization watch-
ing over the *lycées* and the old professional faculties (but not the new
technical schools).
      The fullness of the sociological data presented in the *Atlas* is inevitably

determined by the quality of the surviving sources. Information about patterns of attendance at primary schools is extremely scanty, so the contributors have understandably focused their attention on simply mapping the provision of elementary education. This in itself is extremely valuable, for they are able to show that the 1790s was not a period of declining provision as has often been thought. The revolutionaries may not have achieved their aim of establishing elementary education for all but the era was not a disaster. The accompanying details about literacy, based primarily on the study of wills and marriage contracts, are less exciting. The broad pattern of literacy in eighteenth and early-nineteenth century France has been known for some time and the new work only confirms existing understanding. The same could be said for much of the work on the colleges and the *pensionnats* which repeats in greater detail much of the information to be found in R. Chartier, M. M. Compère and D. Julia, *L'Education en France du XVIᵉ au XVIIIᵉ siècle* (Paris, 1976). The really novel parts of chs. 2 and 3 concern the information on the *écoles centrales* and the *lycées*. These have never before been subjected to a close sociological analysis and the results (although as yet limited to the short-lived *écoles centrales* and one or two top *pensionnats*) are very interesting. If the Revolution did not adversely affect primary provision, it certainly reduced opportunities at the secondary level. The number of students attending the *écoles centrales* was only a quarter of the number in the colleges and the social intake always quite exclusive became even more so. On the other hand, the *pensionnats* became more socially open or at least the nobility was replaced by sons of the mercantile bourgeoisie. The most novel chapter is that devoted to the technical schools and the faculties. There are some highly interesting details about the geographical origins of students at the new *grandes écoles* and for the first time an attempt has been made to chart the pattern of faculty matriculations. In the past researchers (including this reviewer) have been content with studying total student numbers and it has been impossible to tell what proportion of students took a degree.

There can be no doubt that this is a very useful volume and that it will become a standard work of reference for historians of the sociology of education. As the editor himself admits, however, it is only an interim study. As far as the faculties and technical schools are concerned there is clearly much more work to be done on the social origin of students during the Revolutionary epoch, although this will be a difficult and laborious task given the sources (there is seldom any mention of social status in the school or faculty records). Also there is a crying need for a detailed study of the career orientation of school and faculty graduates. Some work has been done for the pre-1789 period by Ferté[1] and Kagan[2] but the Revolutionary epoch as such remains largely unexplored (the *Atlas* only refers to the graduates of the *Ecole polytechnique*). Only once this has been achieved will it be possible to draw useful conclusions about the social role of the institutions of higher education in the Revolutionary period. Criticisms that can be levelled against the volume as such are few. The illustrations are highly ingenious (over the last twenty years the French *Annalistes* have developed the histogram into an art form). Nevertheless they are not always easy to follow and the data they provide does not always gel with the text. The maps only make sense if the reader has a good knowledge of the geography of France for there is no topographical key supplied. A lot of the information presented as histograms could be more easily read in tabular form; there is an irritating habit of switching from total numbers to percentages; and it will be extremely difficult for historians to extract precise data from the diagrams. At the same time, the volume will be of more use to the informed reader then the tyro for the textual apparatus, while extremely succinct, leaves a lot unsaid. The data on graduates in medicine before and after the Revolution, for instance, will be wrongly appraised by the reader if he does not realize the profound change that took place in the medical profession in the course of the 1790s. Before 1789 physicians and surgeons belonged to two distinctive professions, and only the physicians were trained in the faculties of medicine. From 1802, however, the two professions were fused and the *écoles*/faculties educated henceforth all legitimate medical practitioners; only apothecaries continued to be educated separately. The section on the faculties of medicine, then, would have been more informative had the pre-1789 data contained information about patterns of attendance at the surgical colleges (which can be collated from existing records).

Nevertheless, it would be churlish to end this review on a sour note. In general, this is an extremely well-produced and informative work. Above all, in the study of the history of education, it is unique, and the director of the enterprise is to be commended for bringing such a difficult task to a successful conclusion.

Laurence Brockliss
Magdalen College
Oxford OX1 4AU

REFERENCES

1. P. Ferté, 'L'Université de Toulouse au XVIIᵉ et XVIIIᵉ siècles: étude quantitative de ses trois facultés supérieures de 1679 à la Révolution' *thèse de troisième cycle* (2 vols.; Toulouse: Le Mirail, 1978).
2. R. Kagan, 'Law Students and Legal Careers in Eighteenth-Century France', *Past and Present* 68 (1975), 38–72.

James T. Flynn, *The University Reform of Tsar Alexander I 1802–1835*. Washington, D.C.: The Catholic University of America Press, 1988. xvi + 283 pp. No price given.

This book and Cynthia H. Whittaker's *The Origins of Modern Russian Education: An Intellectual Biography of Count Sergei Uvarov, 1786–1855* (DeKalb, 1984) may transform the historiography of Russia's universities in the first half of the nineteenth century. Professor Flynn points out that the arguments of the two books are 'congruent' (p. 69, n. 61), but if he is right to claim that Uvarov, in 1835, completed what Alexander I set in train thirty years earlier, newcomers to the field should read his book first. It deals not just with the 'reform' of Russian universities, not just with universities, and not just with Russia. In respect of four of the institutions covered (Kazan, Kharkov, St. Petersburg, Kiev), Flynn is dealing with the foundation as well as the reform of a university. Because the legislation of 1803–4, to which the book's first chapter is devoted, imposed upon universities the duty to oversee the rest of the state educational network, the author is often speaking of Russian education as a whole. Because at least two of the universities discussed, Vilna (Vilnius) and Dorpat (Tartu), were Russian only in the sense that they took their orders from St. Petersburg, and because the inspiration for setting up universities in the early nineteenth-century Russian Empire came from abroad, Flynn frequently addresses himself to developments in the West. The book, then, is wide-ranging. It is the product of more than twenty-five years' work and is based on literature in Russian (published and unpublished), Polish, Lithuanian, German, French, and English. There are six chapters. After describing the sources and content of the early nineteenth-century legislation, Flynn goes on to the difficulties which the universities experienced on the ground in the first ten years of their life; the tsar's misguided enthusiasm for amalgamating education and religion in the ten years after that (a phenomenon which is taken too seriously and awarded two chapters); two rather weak ministers' attempts to correct the deficiencies of the original legislation in the decade 1824–34; and the success of Uvarov in this endeavour within two years of becoming Minister of Education in 1833, as indicated by the foundation of Kiev University (along new lines) in 1834 and the general university statute of 1835. Flynn is at his best in the second part of Chapter VI, in effect the conclusion (pp. 241–59). Contrary to received opinion, he holds that Alexander I's legislation eventually bore fruit. It did not do so until ten years into the reign of his brother, but thereafter the Russian university system remained more or less as the early nineteenth-century reformers conceived it. Imperial Russian universities, in other words, were far from being blind servants of the autocrat. Their autonomy was much greater than previous authors (e.g. Patrick Alston) have allowed. They never closed their doors to students from the taxable estates. Apparent derogations from their dignity between 1803–4 and 1835 (loss of responsibility for lesser educational establishments, reduction of academic involvement in many financial and disciplinary questions) were pluses not minuses. Why then did universities not have a greater civilizing effect in late imperial Russia? Because only small numbers of students could gain admission to them as long as the state failed to invest heavily in primary and secondary education. Why did students join the revolutionary intelligentsia? Because the authorities moved to the right, not because the universities became hotbeds of radicalism. The thesis is a controversial one, and implies a greater than usual respect for the makers of the 1803–4 legislation and for Uvarov. With the help of Cynthia Whittaker's book, however, Professor Flynn may establish a new orthodoxy.

David Saunders
Department of History
The University
Newcastle upon Tyne NE1 7RU

Robin S. Harris, *A History of Higher Education in Canada 1663–1960*. Toronto: University of Toronto Press, 1976. xxv + 715 pp. n.p.

It is an axiom of Canadian historiography that national unity and a distinctive identity have been created in the teeth of obstacles suffered by few other societies. Stretched between oceans three thousand miles apart and bisected by some of the world's highest mountains, Canada was difficult to cross before mass air travel, and it remains at least costly to do so today. Though its area is vast the terrain and weather of most of it is unwelcoming, and dense human settlement is confined to a narrow strip north of the 49th parallel; Canada's economy and culture have always owed a lot to the alluring monster to the south, and have had good reason to fear a friendly bear-hug that would squeeze the vestiges of independent life from both. Assimilation into the USA has been hindered by Canada's British and French legacies, but the competition between these has also made national unity harder to achieve. Colonial societies are naturally influenced from outside, but Canada has experienced a greater range of inputs than others. Her higher education system has always reflected this diversity.

Robin Harris has not chosen to write the customary or expected sort of university history. His book says very little about the daily life of professors or students, or the conditions of freedom or tenure they have enjoyed, or the ways universities have been governed and financed. It concentrates on course-content, sometimes in considerable detail—giving us, for example, the titles of the books set for the B.A. examination in Trinity College, Toronto, in 1860. This information is instructive and fascinating, though it is not organized in a narrative, or in any manner that makes academic evolution very clear. The greater part of the book comprises five cross sections of the higher-education scene, at 1860, 1890, 1920, 1940, and 1960, the details of degree programmes at these dates being drawn from institutional calendars. Few scholars can have disturbed the ancient calendars of Acadia, Laval, or Waterloo before Robin Harris undertook his herculean task of disinterment in the bookstacks of the University of Toronto library back in the 1960s.

Apparent from his very dense pages is the separateness of the French-language universities. Until very recent times they drew on the academic traditions of metropolitan France and were little touched by Anglophone patterns. Similarly, McGill, a British implant in the heart of Montreal, was until the victory of the Parti Quebecois in the 1960s largely unaffected by the Gallic culture around it. Founded in 1821, McGill reflected in its curriculum the tastes of the large Scots merchant community in Lower Canada, and offered in its early decades a four-year B.A. course that ranged broadly across humanities, mathematics, and natural sciences, just as in Edinburgh or Aberdeen. There were borrowings from Scotland elsewhere in 'British' colleges in Canada, but a stronger influence was the traditional Oxford three-year degree course. For example in 1860 Trinity College, Toronto, prescribed for its B.A. large chunks of Latin and Greek, Old and New Testament history, mathematics, and Paley's *Evidences*; it even used the Oxford phrase 'Previous Examination' for its first-year test. Oxford's Anglican and classical focus naturally appealed to the Tory gentlemen in power in Upper Canada's early days, and they tried to use university instruction as a means of retaining it. (By contrast, Cambridge's intense mathematical bias won no friends in Canada nor for that matter elsewhere—the lack of export demand for Cantabrigian ways being indeed a lasting conundrum.)

In 1860 Canada's economy was colonial and agricultural. The largest groups it needed to educate were clergy, schoolmasters, and administrators. For this task the liberal models of Scotland and Oxford seemed most appropriate, and the universities' spirit, at least in British Canada, appears to have been best expressed by a writer Harris does not mention, John Henry Newman, the prophet of non-vocational instruction. In the later nineteenth century, as economies developed everywhere, technical and professional courses were added to the university repertory and traditional learning itself became more specialized. America was the pioneer in these developments, and the largest Canadian institutions followed its lead, introducing the Ph.D. degree and building up technological and professional schools. 'Americanisation' was sometimes lamented by Canadian academic conservatives, but the continuing pull of British exemplars is remarkable in retrospect; it may be traced in the detail Harris offers, though he rarely analyses it sufficiently. Just as British history dominated the syllabus in Ontario schools, so it was usual right down to the 1950s for Ontario historians to take Oxford D.Phils, often on British topics. When a century ago Anglophone Canadian universities were developing honours degrees to meet the demand for specialists it was natural to turn for guidance to Oxford, which was then increasing its own honours courses. Harris avers that the changes Canadians made in the Oxford recipe— broadening single-subject specialisms with subsidiary options—established a distinctive menu, something that he is eager to claim. But this assessment is mistaken, as comparison between Canada and what has happened elsewhere reveals. England's provincial universities also turned to Oxford for inspiration, yet also modified its honours format in just the same way as British Canada, and for the same reasons—the inadequate general education of their matriculants. (A less complacent Oxford would have come to the same conclusion.) Canada's honours degrees are part of a much wider family.

Robin Harris began with the intention of studying the American and British universities as well as the Canadian, 1,000 institutions altogether. One realizes why he abandoned this task, as unfinishable as Robinson Crusoe's boat, in favour of his more restricted purpose that itself took fifteen years to complete. But the lack of a comparative dimension is very noticeable; Harris frequently fails to record that in the last two centuries universities have become interconnected, units in an international community that have been facing similar pressures. Though their responses have sometimes been divergent, universities have inevitably grown more alike, at all events in the liberal western world. This has been especially true in the last forty years, when for example the old inflexible curricula of the French Canadian universities have been rendered more diverse and vocational, as they too have become assimilated to the formula of the transatlantic multiversity. The forty years have been hectic, for all our universities including Canada's. In the 1950s the hope grew that higher education could transform advanced industrial economies, and a decade of optimistic expansion followed. Canada founded universities as blithely as any nation, and then suffered the inevitable reaction of disillusionment as the transformation failed to occur. Harris closes his survey at the threshold of the great boom, though his writing reveals awareness of the vast changes that were to come. An eventual second volume is promised, to extend his account into the last thirty years.

Peter Searby
Department of Education
University of Cambridge

M. Anne Crowther & Brenda White, *On Soul and Conscience. The Medical Expert and Crime. 150 Years of Forensic Medicine in Glasgow.* Aberdeen: Aberdeen University Press, 1988. 169 pp. £14.90 (hbk.), £7.95 (pbk.).

To some degree the study of medical education in Scotland is a victim of Catch-22—without histories of the individual academic departments there is no sound basis for the interpretation of its development as a whole, yet without the framework of a more general account of the subject it is infinitely more difficult to produce departmental or subject histories which fit convincingly into the overall picture. In their stirring tale of the transition from the solitary medical detective beloved of fiction to the era of modern forensic science, with its rigorous demands upon doctors, scientists and technicians, Anne Crowther and Brenda White have made a valuable and lasting contribution to the history of one of the UK's leading medical schools.

After a brief but lucid outline of the early nineteenth century Scottish commitment to the continental philosophy and practice of 'medical police', the authors turn their attention to the expression of these concepts in Glasgow itself. The foundation of the Regius Chair of Medical Jurisprudence at the University of Glasgow in 1839 occurred at a time of intense political rivalry reaching into the very heart of university life. The complications of this period are admirably dealt with before the reader's attention is focused on the role of the successive professors.

The first three incumbents—Robert Cowan, Harry Rainy, and P. A. Simpson—apparently made few lasting contributions with the exception of Rainy's work on the still partly unresolved question of the cooling time of dead bodies, and Edinburgh retained a virtual monopoly in the supply of Crown witnesses in criminal proceedings until the end of the nineteenth century. This imbalance was irrevocably changed with the appointment of the elder John Glaister to the Glasgow Chair in 1898. Succeeded by his son—'Young John'—in 1931, these two men dominated forensic medicine in Scotland for more than four decades and there can be few Scottish medical graduates or diplomates of this century who are not familiar with the Glaisters' *Textbook of Medical Jurisprudence*, first published in 1902.

Much of the book is devoted to a lively but never sensationalist analysis of the changing role of the expert witness as demonstrated in the careers of the Glaisters, who appeared in almost every major murder trial (Slater, Merret, Buck Ruxton *et al.*) in Scotland in the first half of this century, a time during which forensic science began to replace the older tradition of the medical detective. The latter part of the story of forensic medicine in Glasgow is devoted to the changing nature of the university development in the subject in the post-Glaister era, from 1962 onwards.

From a period of decline during which the academic future of the discipline was under threat and the number of chairs in the UK fell from eight in 1945 to the current figure of three, the department's lateral expansion to meet the new challenges of the 1970s and 1980s is recorded in careful and occasionally humorous detail. The eight specialized laboratories of the present department, occupied only since 1987, are a far cry from the early 1960s experimental work on drink-driving, where volunteers were sought to consume a staggering 10 fluid ounces of whisky in periods ranging from 5–15 minutes before subjecting themselves to scientific measurement!

Despite the obvious merits and impressive grasp of difficult concepts there are some disappointing omissions from this work. The description of the city's extra-mural schools and their relationship to university teaching, especially in the nineteenth century when they often served as a training ground for men who later rose to eminence in University circles, is far from clear even to a reader with some knowledge of Glasgow medicine. No explanation is offered for the fact that no fewer than three of the extramural teachers subsequently (or in one case simultaneously) held lectureships in midwifery: neither is there any reference to the fact that one of these men, Professor J. M. Pagan, even published a textbook on *Medical Jurisprudence and Insanity* in 1840, the year in which he succeeded to the Regius Chair of Midwifery.

All in all, this is a fine example of historical detection and expert testimony, appropriate to the subject matter. The joint authors are currently engaged on the production of a history of forensic medicine in Scotland as a whole. Our appetites should be whetted by this preview of what is yet to come.

Derek A. Dow
University of Glasgow

David R. Jones, *The Origins of Civic Universities: Manchester, Leeds and Liverpool*. London: Routledge. 231 pp.

All of the civic universities founded in England before 1914 have their historian. All that is, except one: the Victoria University. And there are two good reasons for this.

First, many histories of education institutions have been celebratory. With some recent notable exceptions, most were written to clean up the past, sanitize it, and lay it out as a monument to the glory of the present. The Victoria University never quite fitted the bill. Founded in 1880, it survived just 24 years. Furthermore, during its short life the federal university was never a cause for celebration, even by its three member colleges. For varying reasons, the Owens College Manchester, University College Liverpool, and the Yorkshire College Leeds, viewed their overarching body as a bureaucratic means to an end—chartered status—rather than as an end in itself. When the federation was dissolved in 1904 all three new civic universities looked forward, and when their respective historians looked back, their teleological foreshortening all but ignored a federal structure, which, without buildings, professors, or students lacked the heart or soul to make an effective link between humble origins and high-powered chartered status.

Second, fashions change. Revisionists have dragged the history of education into mainstream academic respectability. Institutions are now the context for historical analysis of professional association, social mobility and social control, intellectual growth and cultural change, rather than the agents of historical change, and the vehicle for historical narrative. While the former genre is well stocked by histories of the civics, the latter had tended to pass them by. Despite Armytage's success, as far back as 1955, in opening up a new subject for deep historical study, no historian has yet offered a convincing and scholarly explanation of the rise of civic universities. Attracted perhaps by a longer past, more obvious traditions, a more self contained world, richer, more accessible records, and longer lunch breaks, historians of higher education tend still to be obsessed with Oxbridge.

David Jones is therefore treading welcome ground. And there is much to admire in his book. Jones challenges strongly, and in my view rightly, the long established generalization that civic colleges were founded by industrialists to teach science and technology to their future workforce. Like Armytage before him, Jones shows clearly that every civic college was multi-functional, but unlike Armytage, goes on to show that every civic college was different. While all offered the focus for a whole range of activities, from medicine to evening classes; for a broad-ranging clientele, men, women, professional, skilled and manual, to meet a wide range of needs, vocational and intellectual, cultural and social, the balance struck by every institution was distinctive. It was only in the 1890s when a clear consensus model for chartered status began to emerge which successfully balanced the needs and wants of liberal, vocational, and research camps that colleges began to form a clearly recognizable central shape.

But the daringly ambitious scope of the book is also its central weakness. Quite simply, for whatever reason, Jones has tried to fit a quart into a pint pot. At 174 pages of text the book does not tackle most of the issues it raises in sufficient depth to further our knowledge or aid our understanding. The book's layout highlights the problem. The seven chapters are broken down into 51 textual sub-headings. Every sub-heading addresses a substantial issue in its own right, and in most cases does so by considering it from the separate standpoint of every one of the three institutions. Chapter 4, for instance, covers the relationship in the three universities between the demands of a strictly local clientele and the growth of the curriculum. It is just 28 pages long, and has 12 sub-headings, each of which covers a single discipline. Typical of much of the rest of the book, it reads like a check list of points rather than a coherent and sustained thesis.

This is a great pity. The format does not allow Jones's considerable efforts in the archives to show through, or give rein to any proper amplification of his important insights. He has fallen victim to two problems. First, every issue he has touched on needs detailed specialist work. It has not been done. As a result, we are left with a summary of ideas for further work. There are, after all, clear scholarly reasons for the multi-volume, multi-contributor approach adopted by Oxford and Aberdeen. Second, the book misses the obvious focus that might have pulled it together. The Victoria University, dismissed in just 3 pages, holds the key to the real growth of civic universities and their impact, real and perceived, in Victorian society. The archives *are* there. And contrary to Dr Jones's views, they do contain the background to student origins, as well as the protracted story of the university's demise. The Victoria University awaits its historian. Is there anybody out there?

Peter Slee
University of Durham

Henry Tudor, *St Cuthbert's Society 1888–1988*. Durham: St Cuthbert's Society. 236 pp. £7.95.

St Cuthbert's Society is Durham's non-collegiate institution, a focus for the 'unattached' for over a century. It is indeed, as the book's subtitle suggests, 'a modest but exciting institution', and one well worthy of study. Readers expecting insight into the composition of the student body, the growth of the University curriculum, or the relationship between Durham and the world outside must, however, wait a while longer. This study takes its place firmly among the commemorative canon of the genre. But, based on thorough and patient research in the archives, the book provides a brisk narrative record of the Society's growth, and throws much new and interesting light on a hitherto neglected corner of academic history.

Peter Slee
University of Durham

J. Gwynn Williams, *The University College of North Wales: Foundations 1884–1927*. Cardiff: University of Wales Press, 1985. xii + 499 pp.

The history of the University College at Bangor, by a former Vice-Principal and Head of the Department of Welsh History, draws on a wealth of published and unpublished sources, fully acknowledged, including private correspondence and papers, college archives, and the oral evidence and recollections of former staff and students. It owes something to an abandoned work, by a different author, which had been intended to celebrate the college's centenary. The present volume, however, is restricted to the years 1884–1927, the period in office of the first Principal, H. R. Reichel. He was only 28 years old when appointed. An Anglican and a Conservative he was chosen partly because those favouring Welsh applicants could not agree on a candidate.

The chapter on Bangor's first decade, before the University of Wales itself was established, shows Reichel contending with financial problems, the teaching of Welsh at a time when students took London degrees and, above all, with what is described as a crisis of unprecedented dimensions concerning the running of the University Hall for Women, an affair involving Parliamentary exchanges, Lloyd George, libel suits, and resignations from Court and Council.

Subsequent chapters deal with Academic Advance 1894–1914, College, Community and Nation, the New Building, opened in 1911, Student Life 1884–1914, and War and Reconstruction. A final chapter summarizes and assesses the record up to 1927, when Reichel retired. In a sense, then, it is the history of a reign, but one which ranges widely, making clear that the central figure exercised limited authority over a constituent part of a federal structure.

In what remains largely a celebration of a particular college there is naturally material dealing with the minutiae of finances, appointments, degree courses, student societies, sporting achievements, and the like. Of interest to students of educational administration, they do not perhaps concentrate the mind in quite the same way as the Women's Hall affair. Nevertheless, they throw light on the influence of Victorian and Edwardian social attitudes and educational values. These intramural concerns are accompanied by broader considerations linking the college's evolution to nationalism, the local economy, particularly agriculture and quarrying, working class and female access to university, and relationships with other sectors of education.

The chapter on Reconstruction highlights some of the administrative and managerial complexities of the University's federal organization, with its inevitable inter-collegial tensions. It also indicates the increasing involvement of the state in university affairs. The Royal Commission on University Education in Wales, originating in a request for Treasury funding of a medical school, headed by Lord Haldane, reported in 1918. Federalism survived its scrutiny especially as Lloyd George was convinced that a single university was a necessary bulwark of national identity, threatened by the particularism of colleges like Cardiff, which showed interest in independence. Federal organization, however, offered no protection against a future in which the fate of Bangor would depend less on its Principal than on central government policy. As the Prime Minister commented, cash and control are inseparable.

George T. Popham
School of Management
University of Aston
Birmingham B4 7ET

Stephen Parks, *The Elizabethan Club of Yale University and Its Library*, with Introduction by Alan Bell. New Haven and London: Yale University Press, 1986. 280 pp.

The Elizabethan Club of Yale University was a product of the gilded age of American universities. Its benefactor, Alexander S. Cochran (Yale '96), was a multimillionaire carpet manufacturer and a playboy of the era as well. About a decade after leaving Yale, an atavistic impulse, originating from a course in Elizabethan Drama, prompted him to begin collecting rare books from the sixteenth and seventeenth centuries. In 1910 he offered his holdings to Yale with the proviso that they become the centrepiece for a sodality that would bring together students and faculty for polite conversation about books. Cochran assured the acceptance of this notion by first donating a building to house the collection, and then purchasing in its entirety an outstanding collection of Shakespearean folios. Although Yale at this juncture was best known for the brutality and efficiency of its football team, the 'Lizzie' as it came to be known soon became a campus fixture. Cochran's improbable conception became central to a literary renaissance on the campus, and its purchased gentility fit well with the growing exclusiveness of social relations at Yale. During a generation when literary concerns dominated the intellectual life of Yale College, the Lizzie became the meeting place for the arbiters of taste. As for Cochran, he soon lost interest in books and in the institution he launched, and devoted himself determinedly to serious yachting.

The volume under review has been published to honour the seventy-fifth anniversary of the founding of the Elizabethan Club. It emphasizes the bibliophilic roots of the Club rather than its unusual role in the history of the Yale extracurriculum. The introduction by Alan Bell presents the basic facts of Cochran's brief career as a book collector, but then devotes most attention to the provenance of the Club's holdings. Indeed, recounting the ownership of these volumes provides a brief excursion into the history of British book collecting. The bulk of this volume consists of Stephan Park's meticulous catalogue of the holdings of the Club's library. This volume aims at a select audience: viz. former members of the Elizabethan Club, perhaps, but chiefly bibliophiles with a special interest in the Elizabethan and Stuart materials in its fine collection.

Roger L. Geiger
Pennsylvania State University

Mario Lanczik, *Der Breslauer Psychiater Carl Wernicke. Werkanalyse und Wirkungsgeschichte als Beitrag zur Medizingeschichte Schlesiens.* Jan Throbecke Verlag, Sigmaringen 1988. 97 pp. no price given.

Carl Wernicke (1848–1905), an important psychiatrist and neurologist best remembered for his work on the brain localization of aphasia (speech disorders) has received little historical attention. This Würzburg University thesis is therefore welcome. It was written with a view to stressing the historical importance for Germany of Breslau University where Wernicke taught—today Breslau is Polish. The book is part of a series on the culture and history of Silesia.

Mario Lanczik opens with a short biography of Wernicke based on printed sources. Unfortunately, as the author points out in his introduction, the Breslau archives 'have not been able to give any information'. Subsequent chapters deal with the history of the localization theory and Wernicke's scientific work. They draw on range of Wernicke's writings in addition to his *Lehrbuch der Gehirnkrankheiten* (1881–3, 3 vols.) and complex neurological models of the latter are very competently summarized. The main part of the book discusses Wernicke's historical influence. This includes terms such as 'autochtone Idee' or 'Halluzinose' attributed to Wernicke. We then get an assessment of Wernicke by his most important disciples such as Hugo Liepmann, Karl Bonhoeffer, and Karl Kleist. Wernicke's ultimate legacy was in the 'anatomo-neurological-localistic method' which, Lanczik asserts, has lost none of its significance particularly for the neuro-surgeon.

English readers should be warned that this book is written within a German tradition by an author with a sound knowledge of neurology and psychiatry but—apparently—little historical training. It lacks any wider historical and historiographical context: characteristically there is no mention of Foucault or Doerner. The author establishes some interesting-sounding links without following them up: for example, Wernicke's view that any classification of psychiatric diseases was a premature project was contradicted by Emil Kraepelin. Kraepelin's classification was then on its way to becoming the leading model of understanding psychiatric diseases.

We also learn that Kraepelin and Wernicke met, at least once, in summer 1890 at a meeting of the 'ostdeutsche Irrenärzte' but hardly exchanged a word (p. 42). Similarly Lanczik briefly mentions (p. 11) that Wernicke was Sigmund Freud's main opponent (in what sense?) suggesting that Wernicke has increased in historical importance over the last few years as Freud has decreased. These are both huge and challenging claims and it is disappointing that they are not substantiated.

Notwithstanding these criticisms there is much useful information brought together here. The full bibliography of Wernicke's work will prove valuable to all future research on Wernicke and indeed on German-speaking neurology of the nineteenth century.

Renate Hauser
Wellcome Institute for the History of Medicine
Euston Road
London

R. Clogg, *Politics and the Academy: Arnold Toynbee and the Koraes Chair.* London: Frank Cass, 1986. x + 117 pp. No price.

Richard Clogg tells a fascinating story, reconstructed largely from correspondence and from committee minutes. It sounds premonitory alarm bells about the endowment of academic posts with strings attached and more broadly about academic freedom.

Ronald Burrows, Principal of King's College, London from 1913 to 1920, an ardent philhellene, was so keen to have a chair of modern Greek studies endowed by wealthy Greeks in Britain that, while freeing the money from several other strings, he let through a 'Subscribers' Committee' with limited rights. This fact was not revealed to Arnold Toynbee when he was appointed in 1919 (at the age of 29), nor was it made known to Burrows' successor as Principal, Ernest Barker.

During the terrible conflicts in Asia Minor in 1921–2 Toynbee became a partisan of the Turkish case rather than the Greek. He made his views clear in reports to the *Manchester Guardian*, in public lectures, and in his book *The Western Question in Greece and Turkey*. My only regret about Dr Clogg's book (apart from the over-reaction of omitting even aspiration marks ('breathings') from ancient Greek quotations) is that he gives little idea of Toynbee's polemics, and makes no attempt to assess the justification or intellectual quality of his views. In any case, the Subscribers' Committee kicked up a stink, and, though they could not actually dismiss their Professor, they succeeded, with the help of numerous sympathizers in King's and in the University Senate, in giving him little choice 'as a gentleman' but to resign. Indeed, before the next appointment in 1926 their official influence was strengthened.

It was far from a black and white issue. In principle, however, it raised the question of how far donors may or should be allowed to influence the research and teaching enabled by their money. The Toynbee affair might seem particularly pertinent because the money came from foreign donors (including at first an annual contribution by the Greek Government), and because it was caught up in a contemporary and *overtly* political conflict. It seems to me, however, that when there are statutory sanctions which can be invoked if teaching or research does not meet with the approval of the 'donor' on grounds other than quality, whether the source is foreign or local, private or public, then there is a real inhibition on academic freedom. And is this not what we have in the Education Reform Bill of 1988?

O. Taplin
Magdalen College
Oxford OX1 4AU

Wolfgang Weiss, *Der anglo-amerikanische Universitätsroman.* Erträge der Forschung Volume 260. Darmstadt: Wissenschaftliche Buchgesellschaft, 1988. x + 178 pp.

It is a strange fact that whenever someone powerful wants to vilify universities in general and the Humanities in particular for their irrelevance to today's world, he or she is very likely to support the accusations by appeal to a work of fiction. Thus, Dr Graham Hills, a scientist and the Principal of Strathclyde University, later to be knighted for his services to Education, claimed, when speaking to a conference of Scottish businessmen in May 1988, that Sharpe's *Porterhouse Blue* 'was extremely funny because it was largely true'. And it is another strange fact that the only two books on British fictional texts involving academics—a tradition, incidentally, which goes back to Chaucer at least—have stemmed from non-British pens.

Professor Weiss's extremely illuminating study suggests that our two 'strange facts' may be linked. Not only do the British cling tenaciously to their very negative fantasies about academics, they also show no great desire to have those fantasies revealed for what they are: the perspectival products of the continuing interaction between a multi-dimensional higher education system and a stratified, traditionalist society. Proctor's earlier study of the subject (1957) tended to see the development of the British university novel as a function of the internal history of that system. Weiss goes two steps further: not only is he much more attuned to the relationship between university fiction and the dialectic described above (pp. 5 and 19), he also, building on Lyons's pioneering study of the American college novel (1962), realizes that dialectic takes different forms in Britain and the USA. The result of this twofold advance is a series of penetrating explanations—for the negative depiction of academics in British texts around 1600 (pp. 31–3); the up-grading of British fictional universities in the mid-nineteenth century (p. 46); the origins of the educational ideal which is set against academic education in so many nineteenth-century and early twentieth-century American novels (p. 101); the changing perspective and subject-matter of American campus fiction during the 1930s (pp. 113–6); the up-grading of American fictional academics during the McCarthyite era (p. 140); and the changing picture of the university during the 1970s (p. 154).

Because the book is fairly short and written by an author who, though a recognized expert on Anglo-American literature, is not an insider, it is not hard to find gaps. Neither J. B. Priestly's *Out of Town* (1968) (the first fictional attack on the expansion of higher education in Britain) nor Howard Jacobson's *Coming from Behind* (the only British academic novel to be set in a Poly) are discussed. Weiss does not seem to realize that the up-grading of fictional Oxbridge and the institutionalization of the Arnoldian ideal there in the second half of the nineteenth century were related to the need to provide a growing imperial elite with a culturo-moral justification for their rôle: conversely, he does not relate the down-grading which began in earnest in the 1950s to the loss of Empire and the redundancy of the earlier need. Although Weiss repeatedly identifies disillusion with the Humanities as a motif in and a motivation behind academic novels, he does not quite see that the extreme disillusion that marks so many British texts, especially those written by former or practising teachers of English Literature, derives from a loss of faith in the quasi-religious ideal of Criticism as that was set out by Leavis and, before him, Eliot. And although Weiss sees with great clarity the *differences* between the British and the American traditions of university novel-writing up to about 1950, he blurs his differential picture thereafter. After all, the cuts which Weiss mentions (p. 158) are a feature of the British, not the American situation—though Allan Bloom's *The Closing of the American Mind* (1987) may mark a shift in the latter context—and an investigation of the popular media would, I think, indicate that at the precise juncture when the stock of the fictional British academic began to fall (*Lucky Jim*, 1954), that of his transatlantic counterpart began, for a variety of reasons, to rise.

Not only is Weiss's book a real contribution to the subject which a specialist can read with profit, it also shows how the study of literature has genuine relevance to live, socio-cultural problems. And it will also provide the beleaguered scholar with a certain amount of reassurance inasmuch as Weiss not only shows explicitly how popular images can change for the better, but also demonstrates implicitly the ability of the ideal of humane scholarship to survive assaults by moralistic puritans, vilification by Scottish utilitarians, and persecution by the politically extreme. For that reason alone, it deserves to be translated into English.

Richard Sheppard
Magdalen College
Oxford OX1 4AU

Historical Research, Volume 60, No. 142, June 1987. Annual subscription £10.00/institutions £19.50.

This issue of what used to be the *Bulletin of the Institute of Historical Research* is largely devoted to papers delivered at the Institute's Anglo-American Historian's Conference, held in July 1987, which had as its theme the history of higher education. No indication is given at the beginning of the issue as to whether any particular area of debate connects the two medieval essays and three nineteenth-century ones, but a unifying dialectic does seem to emerge: the university as culture-centre as opposed to the university as career-factory. In his 'The changing role of universities in medieval Europe' R. W. Southern explains how ambitious scholars turned to canon and civil law as the unity of medieval Christendom broke up in ways which required—and rewarded—a sophisticated blend of theology and jurisprudence. Paul Brand's 'Courtroom and schoolroom: the education of lawyers in England prior to 1400' argues that, at roughly the same time, the early fourteenth century, the teaching of common law had become fairly elaborate, and such professional instruction had reached out to the universities, or at least to Oxford.

Both essays accord with Hastings Rashdall's contention in *The Universities of Europe in the Middle Ages* (1895) that the original purposes of higher education were professional rather than cultural: an historical contribution to a major contemporary debate. This forms the backbone to the remaining three papers. Reba Soffer, in 'The modern university and national values, 1850–1930' concentrates on the universities as the providers of the cultural pabulum of the British governing elite, and sees this increasingly coming from historical teaching of a narrow nationalistic curriculum—adapted in part to the resources and restrictions of college tuition. There are two problems here. Prof. Soffer's paper pre-dates Peter Slee's *Learning and a Liberal Education* (Manchester U.P., 1986) which examines in detail policy and curriculum among the historians of Oxford, Cambridge, and Manchester in the nineteenth century. Slee doesn't deny the primarily gymnastic element in Oxbridge history, but argues that this was little different in effect from what Greats students had to go through. He also sees a change in the direction of research and a wider conspectus of studies setting in around 1885—a point at which the older universities had politically become, in Prof. Soffer's terms, more conservative. The other problem is a tendency to the sweeping generalization: 'Outside the universities, few historians survived and those only marginally. Hardly any flourished'. In the period of Acton, the Webbs, the Hammonds, not to speak of those awkward, invisible nationalities, the Scots, Welsh, and Irish?

Prof. Soffer is right, however, to imply that it was at the margin of university life that the fricative contact with contemporary reality occurred, although this also brought its penalties, in that many of the groups which were eager to make contact with higher education were impelled by social factors which made that contact difficult to sustain. Two such groups are handled by A. Kadish in 'University extension and the working classes: the case of the Northumberland miners', and Janet Howarth and Mark Curthoys in 'The political economy of women's higher education in late nineteenth and early twentieth century Britain'. The miners made contact with the Cambridge extensionists in the mid-1870s and for a decade there was a remarkable growth in local classes—a type of proto-Open university. But this was largely based on a mineowner-labour consensus enabled by prosperous conditions; when depression set in, around 1885–7, the initiative crumbled. The women's situation was more ironic, as their colleges benefitted from no substantial endowments, and had to operate along orthodox economic lines. As a result of a remarkable exercise in number-crunching, Janet Howarth and Mark Curthoys, show that a 'dual market' developed for women's higher education, summed up by the Lady Margaret Hall student who recollected being asked in the 1890s: 'Are you going to teach when you go down or be a Home Sunbeam?' The combination of the two made raising endowment or state finance very tricky. Why subsidize poor clergy daughters to get degree-equivalents when the kudos or cash they would, in the long term, yield would not be up to much? And why subsidize Home Sunbeams at all? It took a long time, the vote, and a world war to— only partly—sort that one out.

Christopher Harvie
University of Tübingen

History of Education Quarterly, Volume 7, Nos. 3 and 4. Bloomington, Indiana: History of Education Society, 1987. $25 per year.

Students of university history will be interested in two recent articles in *History of Education Quarterly*, relating to liberal education in the nineteenth-century American university. Jack C. Lane contributes to a body of recent reinterpretations of the Yale Report. This report, in which Yale defended its classical curriculum against advocates of vocationalism, is coming to be seen as a cautiously progressive, rather than a reactionary, document. It is Lane's thesis that the report redefined the purpose of a liberal education for a competitive era, promoting it as a system of mental training suitable for success in any enterprise and superseding the older ideal of training for a life of civic virtue. This compromise temporarily saved the classical curriculum but weakened it fatally by dissociating it from the moral ends it was designed to serve.

In an account of early teaching at Johns Hopkins, Charles C. Bishop challenges the belief that the pioneering system of instruction through research and emphasis on graduate education contributed to the decline of undergraduate teaching in the American university. He surveys the earliest members of the Johns Hopkins teaching staff, demonstrating their widely divergent abilities and pedagogical theories, concluding that the institution was committed to the formation of a 'teacher corps' to balance its research side.

Elizabeth J. Morse
Center for Studies in Higher Education
University of California, Berkeley
USA 94720

Publications on University History since 1977: A Continuing Bibliography

Edited by
John M. Fletcher
With the assistance of
Christopher A. Upton

Produced with the co-operation of the international
Commission for the History of Universities

Preface

With the production of the following details, lists of publication are now available from 1977 until 1988 for these areas: British Isles, France, Hungary, Switzerland and the United States. Future issues of *History of Universities* will add to these lists and attempt to bring up to date also information supplied for other regions. We regret that problems in Birmingham, after fires in the local post office sorting department, have hampered our contact with some areas abroad. Certain lists have reached us incomplete or too late to be included among the material printed below. Readers are reminded that lists for the period 1977–81 were published annually as *History of European Universities, Work in Progress and Publications*, and that these five volumes may be purchased from the address below. The first list of further publications was produced for *History of Universities*, 7(1988): 371–472.

The following scholars have contributed reports for this issue: membership of the International Commission for the History of Universities is indicated by an asterix: H. de Ridder-Symoens* and J. Paquet* (Belgium and the Netherlands), C. A. Upton (British Isles), J. Verger* (France), W. Fläschendräger (DDR), L. Szögi (Hungary), A. García y García* and A. M. Carabias Torres (Spain and Portugal), W. Rother (Switzerland) and N. G. Siraisi (USA). We are most grateful for their help.

Copy for this issue has been prepared by Pauline A. Fletcher and Françoise Bannister for whose assistance we are deeply grateful.

Additions to these published lists and contributions to the preparation of future lists are always most welcome at the address below.

Dr John M. Fletcher,
Dept of Modern Languages,
Aston University,
Aston Triangle,
Birmingham B4 7ET
England

Belgium and the Netherlands

Additions to Earlier Lists

For 1984

Delannoy, Y.: Des finances de la ville d'Enghien au milieu du 16e s., du gouverneur Charles de Carondelet et de sa fond. au profit du coll. de Standonck, *Annales du cercle archéol. d'Enghien*, 21: 305–22.

For 1985

Antoine, R. and Hennebert, G.: La fac. des scs agron. de l'univ. cath. de Louvain 1878–1985, *Louvain. Rev. trimestrielle des amis de l'univ. de Louvain*, 2: 3–66.

Bouwen voor Utrechts universiteit. Architectuur en stedebouw binnen de stad (Bldg for U.'s univ. Architect. and urbanisation within the city), Utrecht.

Jensma, G. T. ed.: Betinking 400 jier stifting univ. yn Frjentsjer. Lezingen balden op it kongres fan 28 sept. 1985 yn Frjentsjer (Commemoration of the 400th anniv of the fnding of the univ. of F. Lectures given at the congress of 28 Sept. 1985 in F.), *It beaken* (special section), 47: 149–237.

Keyser, M.: Het intekenboek van Benjamin Bosma, Natuurwetenschappelijk en wijsgerig onderwijs te Amsterdam 1752–90. Een verkenning (The subscription book of B.B. The teaching of nat. science and phil. at A. 1752–90), *Jaarverslagen van het koninklijk genootschap*, 124–27 (1981–85): 65–77. (Considers higher educ. in the private colleges).

Lehr, J. P. W.: De Groninger academiebiblioth. en haar hist. boeken 1615–19 (The acad. library of G. and its hist. books 1615–19), *Groniek*, 19: 1–12.

Lieburg, M. J. van and F. A. van: *Album Promotorum van de Rijksuniversiteit Leiden 1813–1900* (The A.P. of the univ. of L. 1813–1900), Amsterdam/Rotterdam.

Luyendijk-Elshout, A. M.: The beginning of the univ. of Leiden, *Koroth*, 33: 101–111.

Martens, P.: 125 ans d'existence de la fac. des scs agron. de l'état à Gembloux, in *Les cent dernières années de l'histoire de l'ingénieur en Belgique*, Brussels: 1–8.

Neef, G. de: *De eerste vrouwelijke studenten aan de universiteit te Leuven 1920–40* (The first female students at the univ. of L.), Louvain.

Rooden, P. T. van: *Constantijn l'Empereur 1591–1648 professor Hebreeuws en theologie te Leiden. Theologie, bijbelwetenschap en Rabbijnse studiën in de 17e eeuw* (C. l'E. 1591–1648 prof. of Hebrew and theol. at L. Theol., biblical scholarship and rabbinical studies in the 17th cent.), Leyden.

Wittop Koning, D. A.: *Harderwijker boekdrukkers* (Printers in H.), Nieuwkoop. (Considers their relation with university).

Publications 1986

Aerts, R. and Hoogkamp, L.: *De Gelderse Pallas, Gymnasium Illustre, Gelderse universiteit, Rijksathenaeum te Harderwijk 1600–1818* (The Gelderland P., G.I., Gelderland univ., state Atheneum at H. 1600–1818), Barneveld.

Ahsmann, M.: *De jurid. fac. te Franeker 1585–1635. Een studie over de prof. en hun onderwijs met lijsten van verdedigde disputaties* (The fac. of law at F. 1585–1635. A study of the profs and their teaching with lists of disputations defended), *Tijdsch. voor rechtsgesch.*, 54: 3–72.

Art, J.: 'Les rapports triennaux sur l'état de l'enseignement sup.': un arrière-fond pour des recherches ultérieures sur l'hist. des élites belges entre 1814 et 1914, *Rev. belge d'hist. contemp.*, 17: 187–224.

Bergh, G. C. J. J. van den, Spruit, J. E. and Vrugt, M. van de eds: *Rechtsgeleerd Utrecht, Levensschetsen van elf hoogleraren uit driehonderdvijftig jaar faculteit der rechtsgeleerdheid in Utrecht* (U. learned in law. Sketches of the lives of 11 lecturers from 350 yrs of the fac. of law at U.), Zutphen.

Beukens, H.: *Aan bed geleerd. 350 jaar medisch klinisch onderwijs* (Learning at the bedside. 350 yrs of med.-clinical teaching (at Leyden), Leyden. (Record of exhib. at Leyden).

Blankenberg, H. M. etc.: *Het Utrechts studentencorps 1936–86* (The U. student corporation 1936–86), Utrecht.

Bots, J. A. H.: *De Noordbrabantse intelligentsia 1550–1750 nader beschouwd: soc. positie en cult. ontwikkeling* (The N. Brabant intelligentsia 1550–1750 more closely considered: soc. position and cult. devel.), in *Bewogen en Bewegen. Album Amicorum aangeboden aan Prof. Dr H. F. J. M. van de Eerenbeem ter gelegenheid van het 25-jarig professoraat*, Tilburg (henceforth noted as *Bewogen en Bewegen*): 365–77.

Breugelmans, R. etc. eds: *Erasmus en Leiden. Catalogus van de tentoonstelling . . . 23 oktober tot 19 december 1986* (E. in L. Cat. of an exhib. . . . 23 Oct.–19 Dec. 1986), Leyden.

Bruylants, A.: *Louis Henry 1834–1913 en de scheikunde te Leuven* (L. H.

1834–1913 and chem. at L.), *Meded. van de konink. acad. voor weten-schappen, letteren en schone kunsten van België. Klasse der wetenschappen*, 48(4): 101–112.

Ceyssens, W.: Over Limburgse studiebeursstichtingen (On L.'s scholarships for students), *De Vlaamse Stam*, 22(10): 427–30.

Clerck, K. de and Langendries, E.: De oprichting van de 'Vlaamsche Hogeschool' tijdens de eerste wereldoorlog (The fndation of the 'Flemish Univ.' during World War I), *Pedagog. tijdsch.*, 11: 195–200.

Colignon, A.: A l'origine des grands instits univ. liégeois: Le vieux 'Quartier de Bêche', *Rev. médicale de Liège*, 41: 755–75.

Collin, L.: Maurice de Baets en het hoger instit. voor fil. te Leuven (M. de B. and the higher instit. for phil. at L.), *Collationes*, 16: 429–67. (M. de B., 1863–1931).

Commémoration du 100e anniv. de l'inaug. des instits Edouard van Beneden, August Swaen, Léon Frédéricq, *Rev. médicale de Liège*, 41: 753–54.

Coppens, C. etc.: Erasmiana Lovaniensia. Cat. van de Erasmus-tentoon-stelling . . . Leuven nov.–dec. 1986 (E. at L. Cat. of the E. exhib. Louvain Nov–Dec. 1986). Supplement to *Humanistica Lovaniensia*, 4.

Deelstra, H.: Het scheikunde-onderwijs aan de RUG. tijdens de 19de eeuw (The teaching of chem. at the RUG during the 19th cent.), *Acad. analecta: Meded.-wetenschappen*, 48: 113–28.

Despy-Meyer, A.: Les étudiantes dans les univs belges de 1880 à 1941, *Perspectives univ*, 3(1–2): 17–49.

—— L'instit. géog. de l'univ. nouvelle, *Colloque Elisée Reclus. Rev. belge de géog.*, 110: 53–70.

De universiteit te Leuven 1425–1985, Louvain.

Devos, G.: Bijd. tot het tech. onderricht in de Oostenrijkse Ned.: de hydrografische schl (Contribs to tech. instruction in N. Neths. The schl of hydrography), in *Cultuurgeschiedenis in de Nederlanden van de Renais-sance naar de Romantiek. Liber Amicorum J. Andriessen etc.*, Louvain/Amersfoort: 167–78.

Duerloo, L.: Een Leuvens studentenwapenboek (A book of the arms of L. students), *Ex officina*, 3: 66–73. (Concerned with 18th century).

Dunk, H. W. von der, Heere, W. P. and Reinink, A. W. eds: *Tussen ivoren toren en grootbedrijf. De Utrechtse universiteit 1936–86* (Between ivory tower and big business. Utrecht univ. 1936–86), Maarssen.

Etambala Zana, A.: De Leuvense alma mater en Kongo 1885–1914 (Alma mater L. and the Congo 1885–1914), *Onze alma mater*, 40(3): 187–210.

Feenstra, R.: 'Legum doctor', 'legum professor' et 'magister' comme termes pour désigner des juristes au moyen âge, in O. Weijers ed.: *Terminologie de la vie intellectuelle au moyen âge* (henceforth noted as *Terminologie*), The Hague: 71–76.

Felix, A.: Les débuts et les titulaires de la chaire de chimie à la fac. de médecine de l'ancienne univ. de Louvain, *Rev. belge de philol. et d'hist.*, 64: 234–55.

Fletcher, J. M.: Some problems of collecting terms used in medieval acad. life as illustrated by the evidence for certain exercises in the fac. of arts at Oxford in the later middle ages, in *Terminologie*: 43–50.

Frijhoff, W.: Hoger onderwijs als inzet van stedelijke naijver in de vroegmoderne tijd (Higher educ. as motivated by town jealousy in early modern times), in P. B. M. Blaas and J. van Herwaarden eds: *Stedelijke naijver. De betekenis van interstedelijke conflicten in de geschiedenis. Enige beschouwingen en case-studies*, The Hague: 82–127.

—— Modèles éduc. et circulation des hommes: les ambigüités du second refuge, in *La révocation de l'Edit de Nantes et les Provinces-Unies 1685. Colloque international*, Amsterdam/Maarssen: 51–75.

—— Univ. en religie, staat en natie in de 16de eeuw (Univ. and relig., state and nat. in the 16th cent.), in W. P. Blockmans and H. van Nuffel eds: *Staat en religie in de 15de en de 16de eeuw. Handelingen van het colloquium te Brussel*, Brussels: 121–42.

Gabriel, A. L.: The acad. career of Gervasius Wain, abbot *in commendam* of Cuissy, *Analecta Praemonstratensia*, 63: 35–53.

Gabriel, G.: L'extension de l'univ. sur la rive droite à la fin du 19e s., *Rev. médicale de Liège*, 41: 776–78.

García y García, A.: La terminología en las facs juridicas ibéricas, in *Terminologie*: 63–70.

Geurts, P. A. M.: 'Teneamus confessionem'. Nieuwe gegevens omtrent de eerste kath. studentenvereniging in Ned. ('T.c.' New inform. concerning the 1st cath. student soc. in the Neths), *Arch. voor de gesch. van de kath. kerk in Ned.*, 28: 14–22.

Gilles, R.: L'éc. liégeoise de physiol. et de biol. comparées. Hist. et développement, *Rev. médicale de Liège*, 41: 802–811.

Groen, M.: *Het wetenschappelijk onderwiis in Nederland van 1815–1980. Een onderwijskundig overzicht. 7 Wis- en natuurkunde: 8 Letteren* (Scholarly teaching in the Neths 1815–1980. 7 Maths and Physics. 8 Letters), Eindhoven.

Grosheide, D., Monna, A. D. A. and Pesch, P. N. G.: *Vier eeuwen universiteitsbibliotheek Utrecht. 1 De eerste drie eeuwen* (4 cents of the univ. library of Utrecht. 1 The first 3 cents), Utrecht.

Hamesse, J.: '*Collatio*' et '*reportatio*': deux vocables spécifiques de la vie intellect. au moyen âge, in *Terminologie*: 77–86.

Hees, P. van: Een opzienbarende rede. De toespraak van de rect. magnificus prof. dr C. W. Vollgraff ... op 23 juni 1936 in de Domkerk (A sensational speech. The rect.'s address ... 23 June 1936 in the cathedral), *Jb. oud-Utrecht*: 114–37.

Heesakkers, C. L.: Ned. studenten stichten een biblioth. in Frankrijk (Neths students found a library in France (Orléans 1566)), in *Boek, bibliotheek en geesteswetenschappen. Opstellen door vrienden en collaga's van dr Reedijk ... van de koninklijke bibliotheek te 's-Gravenhage*, Hilversum: 137–50.

—— and Thomassen, K.: Inventarisetie van Alba Amicorum uit de Ned.

voor 1800 (An inventory of A.A. from the Neths before 1800), _Batavia acad._, 4(2): 38–42.

Het Pand (The Pand), Ghent. (Former Dominican friary, then cultural centre for the RUG. A hist. 1201–1986).

150 jaar ingenieursopleiding aan de RUG 1835–1985 (150 yrs of engineering educ. at the RUG 1835–1985), Ghent.

Houbrechts, H.: Leuven in de herinnering van de historici. De historische Kring 1935–61 (L. in the hists' memory. The hists' club). Thesis. Louvain.

Jensma, G. T.: Twee adviseurs, een stadhouder en een koning. Over de benoeming van William Ames tot hoogleraar in de theol. te Franeker 1622 (2 advisers, a town official and a king. The nomination of W. A. as lect. in theol. at F. 1622), _De Vrije Fries_, 66: 59–70.

Jeuniaux, C.: Essai d'un panorama de cent ans de recherche zoolog. à l'instit. zoolog., _Rev. médicale de Liège_, 41: 790–801.

Jongeneel, J. A. B. and Klootwijk, E.: _Nederlandse faculteiten der godgeleerdheid. Theologische hogescholen en de derde wereld. Algemene inleiding en overzichten vanaf 1876_ (Neths facs of theol. Theol. high schls and the third world. General introd. and a survey from 1876), Leyde/Utrecht.

Joset, C.: _Facultés Notre-Dame de la Paix. Rénovation de 1929 à 1965_, Namur.

Labrie, A.: 'Bildung' en politiek 1770–1830. De 'Bildungsphilosophie' van Wilhelm von Humboldt bezien in haar politieke en sociale context ('B.' and pols 1770–1830. The 'B.' of W. von H. seen in its pol. and soc. context), Thesis. Amsterdam.

Meensel, J. van: _Berkven. 100 jaar Vlaamse studentenbeweging. 50 jaar Katholieke Vlaamse Berkvenbond. 25 jaar Oud-Berkvenbond te Geel_ (B. 100 years of the Flemish student movt. 50 yrs of the cath. Flemish B. 25 yrs of the O.-B. at Geel), Geel.

Mey, J. de and Hoonacker, M. van: _Moeder Brugse 1885–1985_ (Mother B. 1885–1985), Bruges. (Hist. of a club for Bruges students at Louvain).

Neef, M. de: De faculteit wijsbegeerte en letteren aan de rijksuniversiteit te Leuven 1817–35 (The fac. of phil. and lit. at the univ. of L. 1817–35). Thesis. Louvain.

Ossieur, E. G. R.: Promoti uit de zuidelijke Ned. en het Prinsbisdom Luik aan de noordned. univ. (Graduations from south Neths and the bishopric of Liège at univs of the north Neths), _De Vlaamse Stam_, 22: 317–35.

Otten, A.: Laurens de Keizer en het coll. van de Duitse Orde te Leuven (L. de K. and the coll. of the German Order at L.), _Gemerts heem_, 2: 37–46. (An early 17th cent. fndation).

Overdiep, G. ed.: _Acht Groningse juristen en hun genootschap. 225 jaren 'Pro Excolendo Iure Patrio'_ (8 lawyers of Groningen and their soc. 225 yrs of the P.E.I.P.), Groningen.

Renterghem, V. van: De Brugse seminaristen 1817–1914 (The seminarists of B. 1817–1914), _De Leiegouw_, 28: 427–34.

—— *Het belang van Gent voor de universiteits—en studiekeuze van de Brugse studenten 1817–1914* (The importance of Ghent for Bruges students choosing their univ. and studies), Ghent.

Ridderikhoff, C. M.: De Germaanse natie en het onderwijs aan de univ. van Orléans in de 16de eeuw (The German nat. and teaching at the univ. of O. in the 16th cent.), in *Handelingen van het 9e Nederlands-Belgisch rechtshistorisch congres—Rondom Feenstra—2 nov. 1985*, Leyden (henceforth noted as *Rondom Feenstra*): 47–56.

Ridder-Symoens, H. de: De univ. van Dowaai en Rijsel, centra van cult. in de franse Ned. (The univs of D. and R., cult. centres of the French Neths), *De franse Ned.—Les Pays-Bas fr.*, 11: 11–30.

—— Enkele gegevens over Joos Balbiaens univ. studies (Some inform. concerning J.B.'s univ. studies), *Handelingen van de maatschappij voor gesch. en oudheidkunde te Gent*, 40: 97–100.

Roegiers, J.: Anima Acad. Biblioth. 350 jaar Centrale Biblioth. (A.A.B. 350 yrs of the Central Library), *Ex officina*, 3: 66–73.

Roelevink, J.: Gedicteerd verleden. Het onderwijs in de algemene geschiedenis aan de universiteit te Utrecht 1735–1839 (The past dictated. The teaching of universal hist. at the univ. of Utrecht 1735–1839). Thesis. Amsterdam.

—— 'Gepromoveerde ezels'. Enkele kanttekeningen bij de origine en de originaliteit van dissertaties en disputaties ('Graduating donkeys'. Some observations on the origin and originality of dissertations and disputations), *Batavia acad.*, 4(2): 25–37.

—— Hist. Gentium. P. W. van Heusde and the teaching of hist. at the univ. of Utrecht in the 1st decade of the 19th cent., *Lias*, 13(1): 123–38.

Schutte, O.: Alba van studenten aan de acad. te Franeker (Albums of students of the F. acad.), *De Ned. Leeuw*, 103(9): 339–52.

Schuur, J. A.: Bouwen voor Utrechts univ. Tentoonstelling en boek ter gelegenheid van het 350-jarig bestaan (Bldgs for U. univ. An exhib. to mark the 350th anniv. of its erection), *Maandblad oud- Utrecht*, 59(1): 7–8.

Snelders, H. A. M.: Chem. at the Dutch univs 1669–1900, *Acad. analecta Meded. . . . wetenschappen*, 48(4): 59–75.

Soete, L.: *De rol van de Gentse universiteit in de afschaffing van de 'Ecole normale des sciences' 1870–90* (The role of the univ. of G. in the abol. of the 'Ec. norm. des scs' 1870–90), Ghent.

Soetermeer, F.: Doctorshoed en doctorskus (The doctor's cap and the doctor's kiss), *Ned. juristenblad*: 380–81.

—— La terminologie de la librairie à Bologne aux ·13e et 14e s., in *Terminologie*: 87–95.

—— The origin of MS d'Ablaing 14 and the transmission of the Clementines to the univs, *Tijdsch. voor rechtsgesch.*, 54: 101–112.

Stevens, F. : Het rechtsonderwijs in België in de 19de eeuw (The teaching of law in B. in the 19th cent.), in *Rondom Feenstra*: 57–70.

Struick, J. E. A. L. etc.: *Goede buur of verre vriend. De relatie tussen de universiteit en de stad Utrecht* (Good neighbour or distant friend. Relations between the univ. and the city of U.), Utrecht.

Toye, M. and Steenkiste, L. van: '*En kendet gii de tewaers niet, dit liedje zal 't u leren* . . .', Courtrai. (Hist. of the oldest Flemish student club. 'Moeder Kortrijkse', fnded 1884–85 for Courtrai students at Louvain).

Vandermeersch, P. A.: Bruggelingen aan de Leuvense univ. in de 16de eeuw. Soc. universiteitsgesch. op basis van prosopograf. onderzoek (The intake from B. to the univ. of L. in the 16th cent. The soc. hist of the univ. on the basis of a prosopograph. enquiry), *Handelingen der konink. zuidned. maatschappij voor taal- en letterkunde en gesch.*, 40: 159–73.

——— Univ. en maatschappij. Bronnen, methode en resultaten van een onderzoek naar de studie en levensloop van Brugse academici (Univ. and soc. Sources, methods and results of an enquiry into the studies and careers of B. scholars), *De Leiegouw*, 28: 401–410.

——— The reconstruction of the Liber Quintus Intitulatorum Universitatis Lovaniensis 1569–1616. 2. The theologians 1579–1605, *Lias*, 13(1): 1–67.

Vanpaemel, G.: Cartesianism in the south. Neths: the role of the Louvain fac. of arts, *Bull. de la soc. royale des scs de Liège*, 55: 221–30.

——— *Echo's van een wetenschappelijke revolutie. De mechanistische natuurwetenschap aan de Leuvense Artesfaculteit 1656–1797* (Echoes of a scientif. revoln. The mechanistic nat. science of the L. fac. of arts 1656–1797), Brussels.

——— 'Terra autem in aeternum stat'. Het kosmologiedebat te Leuven ('T. autem in aet. stat'. The debate on cosmology at L.), *De zeventiende eeuw*, 2(2): 101–117.

——— J. B. van Mons 1765–1842 en scheidkunde-onderwijs aan de rijksuniv. Leuven (J. B. van M. 1765–1842) and the teaching of chem. at the univ. of L.), *Acad. analecta. Meded . . . wetenschappen*, 48(4): 87–100.

Verbeeck, M.: De 18de-eeuwse aardewerkvondsten van het Van Dale-Coll. te Leuven (The discovery of the 18th cent. pottery of V. D. coll. at L.), *Brabantse folklore*, 249: 17–27.

Verwilghen, M.: L'enseignement du droit notarial à l'univ. cath. de Louvain de 1836 à 1986, in *Le notariat en roman pays de Brabant et l'enseignement du notariat à l'université catholique de Louvain. Catalogue de l'exposition organisée à Louvain-la-Neuve du 13 au 28 mars 1986*, Brussels: 149–75.

Vos, L.: Die nieuwe studentenbeweging. Welvaart en mentaliteit in de jaren zestig (The new student movt. Prosperity and attitudes in the 60s), in *Bewogen en Bewegen*: 393–409.

Weijers, O.: La spécificité du vocabulaire univ. du 13e s., in *Terminologie*: 35–41.

Publications 1987

Berkel, K. van: Eigentijdse universiteitsgesch. De Rijksuniv. te Utrecht van 1936 tot 1986 (A personal univ. hist. The univ. of U. 1936–86), *Spiegel hist.*, 22: 217–20, 352–54.

Boekholt, P. T. F. M. and Booy, E. P. de: *Geschiedenis van de school in Nederland vanaf de middeleeuwen tot aan de huidige tijd* (Hist. of the schls in the Neths from the middle ages to the present), Assen/Maastricht. (Some observations about univ. education).

Bots, H.: Constantijn Huygens een wetenschapsbeoefenaar? (C. H. A scholar in science?), *De zeventiende eeuw*, 3: 149–60.

Braive, G.: Les premières étudiantes à la Fac. Saint-Louis en 1925, *Facs univ. Saint-Louis* (Brussels). *Bull. d'inform.*, 25: 15–20.

Bruin, R. E. de: *Revolutie in Utrecht. Studenten, burgers en regenten in de patriottentijd 1780–87* (Revoln in U. Students, citizens and town council in the age of patriotism), Utrecht.

Clerck, K. de: En toen werd de lerarenopleiding aan de univ. toevertrouwd (And then teachers' training in the univ. was entrusted to him), in M. Depaepe and M. D'hoker eds: *Onderwijs en opvoeding en Maatschappij in de 19de en de 20ste eeuw. Liber Amicorum Prof. Dr M. de Vroede*, Louvain/Amersfoort: 191–98.

Couderé, G.: De studenten aan de Rijksuniv. Leuven (Students of the univ. of L.), in *Liber Amicorum Dr J. Scheerder*, Louvain (henceforth noted as *Liber Scheerder*): 241–62.

Courtois, L.: *L'introduction des étudiantes à l'université de Louvain. Les tractations préliminaires 1890–1920. Etude statistique 1920–40*, Louvain-la-Neuve.

Dehon, G.: Quelques règlements et statuts à l'univ. de Douai au 18e s., in G. Macours ed.: *Cornua legum. Actes des journées internationales d'histoire du droit et des institutions*, Antwerp: 61–70.

Derez, M.: Hollandia Lovaniensis. De Ned, aanwezigheid aan de Leuvense univ. in de 19de en de 20ste eeuw (The attendance of Dutchmen at L. univ. in the 19th and 20th cent.), *Onze alma mater*, 41: 81–104.

Feenstra, R.: Het juridisch onderwijs aan de univ. van Leuven in de 15de eeuw (The teaching of law at L. univ. in the 15th cent.), *Batavia acad.*, 5: 50–51.

Felix, A.: La vie scientif., in *La Belgique autrichienne 1713–94. Les Pays-Bas méridionaux sous les Habsbourgs d'Autriche*, Brussels: 405–35. (Considers univ. of Louvain).

Frijhoff, W.: *Keuzepatronen van de universiteit in historisch perspectief* (The choice of support for the univ. in its hist. perspective), Rotterdam.

—— Opleiding en wetenschappelijke belangstelling van het Ned. regenten-patriciaat tijdens de repub.: uitgangspunten, kenmerken, ontwikkelingen (Educ. and an interest in science among the governing class of the Neths during the time of the repub.: origins, characteristics, devel.), *Bull. werkgroep 'Elites'*, 8: 6–20.

Gevers, L.: *Bewogen Jeugd* (Disturbed youth), Louvain. (19th cent. student movt in Flanders).

Goeyse, M. de: *O Vrij—Studentenheerlijkheid. Historisch—Studentikose schetsen* (O the pleasures of the free student life! Sketches of historic student life), Louvain.

282   Bibliography

Graffart, A.: La matricule de l'univ. de Louvain 1817–35, in *Album C. Wyffels*, Brussels: 177–88.

Groen, M.: *Het wetenschappelijk onderwijs in Nederland van 1815–1980. Een onderwijskundig overzicht. 9: Technische Wetenschappen* (Scholarly teaching in the Neths 1815–1980. A survey of teaching skills. 9. Tech. science), Eindhoven.

—— *Het wetenschappelijk onderwijs in Nederland van 1815–1980. Een onderwijskundig overzicht. I. Wetgeving. Civiel Effect. Godgeleerdheid. Rechtsgeleerdheid. Indologie. Geneeskunde* (Scholarly teaching in the Neths 1815–1980. A survey of teaching skills. I. Legislation. Impact on soc. Theol. Law. Med.), Eindhoven.

Jansen, C. J. H.: Over de 18de-eeuwse docenten natuurrecht aan de Ned. univ. en de door hen gebruikte leerboeken (The 18th cent. teachers of nat. law in Dutch univs and the text-books they used), *Tijdsch. voor rechtsgesch.*, 55: 103–115.

Kingma, J.: De universiteitsbiblioth., haar collecties vroeger en nu (The univ. library (of Groningen), its collection in earlier times and now), *Open. vaktijdsch. voor bibliothecarissen*, 19: 348–55.

Koops, R. H.: De huisvesting van de universiteitsbiblioth. 1615–1985 (Accommodation for the univ. library (of Groningen) 1615–1985, *Open. vaktijdsch. voor bibliothecarissen*, 19: 265–74.

Kubbinga, H. H.: Christiaan Huygens' wetenschappelijke opleiding (C.H's scholarly educ.), *De zeventiende eeuw*, 3: 161–70.

Lamberts, E.: De Leuvense univ. tijdens het rectoraat van P. de Somer (The univ. of L. during the rectorat of P. de S.), *Onderwijs en opvoeding*, 15: 227–39.

Lieburg, M. J. van: De betekenis van het Rijksatheneum te Franeker 1815–44 voor de medische en farmaceutische beroepsopleiding (The significance of the F. Atheneum 1815–44 for med. and pharmaceutical professional educ.), *Tijdsch. voor de gesch. der geneeskunde, natuurwetenschappen, wiskunde en tech.*, 10: 20–36.

—— De medische promoties aan de Ned. univ. 1815–99 (Med. degrees in Dutch univs. 1815–99), *Batavia acad.*, 5: 1–17.

Maesschalck, E. de: Tuchtproblemen met rechtsstudenten in het 15de-eeuwse Leuven. Pogingen tot oplossing (Problems of disciplining students of law in 15th-cent. L. Attempts towards a solution), in *Liber Scheerder*: 165–88.

Massaux, E.: *Pour l'université catholique de Louvain. Dialogue avec Omer Marchal*, Brussels. (O.M. 1st rect. of L.la.N.).

Otterspeer, W.: Rondom Steinmetz en het eerste lectoraat in de soc. aan de Leidse univ. (R.S. and the 1st lectureship in soc. at L. univ.), *Leids jaarboekje*, 79: 139–60.

Poelgeest, L. van: Mr Bavius Voorda 1729–99 een rechtlijnig Fries jurist aan de Leidse univ. (B.V. 1729–99 a Friesland jurist at L. univ.), *Leids jaarboekje*, 79: 96–123.

Raes, R.: *'Ons Verbond', historiek van een studententijdschrift 1945–76* ('Ons Verbond'. The hist. of a student magazine 1945–76), Ghent.

Ridder-Symoens, H. de: Intellect. and pol. backgrounds of the witch-craze in Europe, in M.-S. Dupont-Bouchat ed.: *Sorcellerie aux anciens Pays-Bas—Hekserij in de Nederlanden*, Heule-Kortrijk: 37–64. (Discusses role of the univs).

——*Tot nut of onnut van 't algemeen. De functie van de universiteit in de middeleeuwen* (To the benefit or disadvantage of all. The function of the univ. in the middle ages), Amsterdam.

Roegiers, J.: Professorencarrières aan de oude univ. Leuven 1425–1797 (The careers of profs at the old univ. of L. 1425–1797), in *Liber Scheerder*: 227–40.

Smeyers, P.: L'astron. à la 'Kath. Univ. Leuven', *Quelques étapes*, 54: 35–47.

Snelders, H. A. M.: De bemoeienissen van Lorentz en Einstein met de Utrechtse Leerstoel voor theoret. fysica 1911–14 (The concern of L. and E. with the chair of theoret. physics at U. 1911–14), *Tijdsch. voor de gesch. der geneeskunde, natuurwetenschappen, wiskunde en tech.*, 10: 57–71.

Spaamer-Buursink, H. and Terken, L.: Het nieuwe *theatrum physicum* 1768. De oranjerie aan de Eligensteeg te Utrecht (The new *t.p.* 1768. The orangery on the E. at U.), *Maandblad oud-Utrecht*, 60: 69–75.

Struyker-Boudier, H. A. J.: Tien jaar RL. Een uitdaging of een gemiste kans (10 yrs of the univ. of Limburg. A challenge or a missed opportunity), in *Universiteit en maatschappelijke betekenis*, Maastricht: 26–34.

Uytterhoeven, R.: *Leuven weleer. 3. Langs de oude universiteit naar het Begijnhof* (L. in olden times. 3. Near the old univ. by the B.), Louvain. (Illustrated description).

Vandenghoer, C. : Criminaliteit en ordehandhaving binnen de *civitas academica*: de promotorrekeningen van Johannes Wolffs 1644–70 (Crime and the maintenance of order in the *c.a.*: the account of the promotor J.W. 1644–70), in *Liber Scheerder*: 203–26.

——Historiografie in functie van tentoonstellingen: een overzicht van 300 jaar chemie te Leuven (Historiography functioning as an exhibition. A survey of 300 yrs of chem. at L.), *Onze alma mater*, 41: 41–56.

Vanderheyden, J. F.: Het herstel van de Leuvense universiteitsbibliotheek 1940–41 (The restoration of the L. univ. library 1940–41), *Onze alma mater*, 41: 119–39.

Vos, L.: Twee Leuvense studentenrevolties 1924–25, 1968. Een vergelijking (2 student uprisings at L. 1924–5, 1968. A comparative study), in *Liber Scheerder*: 291–309.

Vries, H. de: transformatie van de Ned. univ. van 1815 tot 1940: een onderzoeksproject (The transformation of Neths univs 1815–1940: a research project), *Batavia acad*, 5: 31–42.

Welten, R.: Utrechtse hoogleraren in de rechten 1636–1815. Enkele aspecten van de gesch. van de rechtenfac. te Utrecht (Legal lecturers at U. 1639–

1815. Some aspects of the hist. of the fac. of law at U.), *Tijdsch. voor rechtsgesch.*, 55: 67–101.

The British Isles

Additions to Earlier lists

For 1982

Cohen, A.: An hist. overview of the state of higher educ. in the Neths, *Europ. jnl of educ.*, 17(3): 271–81.

For 1983

Field, A.: The *Studium Florentinum* controversy 1455, *Hist. of univs*, 3: 31–59.
Gaskell, P.: An early inventory of Trinity Coll. books, *Trans of the Cambridge bibliog. soc.*, 8(3): 374–41. (From *c.* 1550).
Kren, C.: Astron. teaching at the late medieval univ. of Vienna, *Hist. of univs*, 3: 15–30.
McCuaig, W.: Andreas Patricius, Carlo Sigonio, Onofrio Panvino and the Polish nat. of the univ. of Padua, *Hist. of univs*, 3: 87–100.
Rosa, S. de: Studi sull' univ. di Pisa. 2. La riforma e il paradosso. Girolamo da Sommaja, provved. dello studio Pisano 1614–36, *Hist. of univs*, 3: 101–25.

For 1984

Leader, D. R.: Philos. at Oxford and Cambridge in the 15th cent., *Hist. of univs*, 4: 25–46.
Siraisi, N. G.: Renaissance commentaries on Avicenna's *Canon*, Book 1, Part 1, and the teaching of med. *Theoria* in the Italian univs, *Hist. of univs*, 4: 47–97.
Trio, P.: Financing of univ. students in the middle ages a new orientation. *Hist. of univs*, 4: 1–24.
Twigg, J.: The limits of 'reform'. Some aspects of the debate on univ. educ. during the Eng. Revoln., *Hist. of univs*, 4: 99–114.

For 1985

Black, R.: The *Studio Aretino* in the 15th and early 16th cents, *Hist. of univs*, 5: 55–82.
Bush, S., Jr and Rasmussen, C. J.: Emmanuel Coll. library's first inventory, *Trans of the Cambridge bibliog. soc.*, 8(5): 514–56. (Of *c.*1597).

Carpenter, H.: *OUDS. A centenary history of the Oxford University Dramatic Society 1665–1985*, Oxford.

Corona, S. C.: The fnding of the royal and pontifical univ. of Mexico in the 16th cent., *Hist. of univs*, 5: 83–99.

Ferruolo, S. C.: The Paris statutes of 1215 reconsidered, *Hist. of univs*, 5: 1–14.

Freedman, J. S.: Philos. instruction within the inst. framework of central Europ. schls and univs during the Refn era, *Hist. of univs*, 5: 117–66.

Lyall, R. J.: Scottish students and masters at the univs of Cologne and Louvain in the 15th cent., *Innes rev.*, 36: 55–73.

Trio, P.: A medieval students' confraternity at Ypres. The Notre Dame confraternity of Paris students, *Hist. of univs*, 5: 15–53.

Welch, E. ed.: *Records of university adult education 1886–1939. A calendar*, Portsmouth. (Efforts of univ. of Cambridge and univ. of Southampton to encourage adult educ. in Portsmouth).

For 1986

Carley, J. P.: John Leland and the contents of the Eng. pre-Dissolution libraries: the Cambridge Friars, *Trans of the Cambridge bibliog. soc.*, 9(1): 76–100.

Feenstra, R.: Scottish-Dutch legal relations in the 17th and 18th cents, in T. C. Smout ed.: *Scotland and Europe 1200–1850*, Edinburgh: 128–42.

Hudson, A.: Wycliffism in Oxford 1381–1411, in A Kenny ed.: *Wyclif in his times*, Oxford: 67–84.

McConica, J. ed.: *The history of the university of Oxford 3. The collegiate university*, Oxford.

Pearson, D. P.: The books of Peter Shaw in Trinity Coll. Cambridge, *Trans of the Cambridge bibliog. soc.*, 9(1): 76–89. (A donation of 1603).

Sutherland, L. S. and Mitchell, L. G. eds: *The history of the university of Oxford. 5. The eighteenth century*, Oxford.

Publications 1987

Avi-Yonah, R.: Career trends of Parisian masters of theol. 1200–1320, *Hist. of univs*, 6: 47–64.

Beinart, J.: *A history of the Nuffield Department of Anaesthetics, Oxford 1937–87*, Oxford.

Bill, E. G. W.: *Education at Christ Church, Oxford 1660–1800*, Oxford.

Bingham, C.: *The history of the Royal Holloway College 1886–1986*, London.

Cheney, C. R.: A reg. of MSS borrowed from a coll. library 1440–1517. Corpus Christi Coll. Cambridge MS 232, *Trans. of the Cambridge bibliog. soc.*, 9(2): 103–29.

Childress. B.: Library hist., univ. hist. and photographic hist.: some considerations for research, *Jnl of library hist.*, 22: 70–84.

Clement, R. W.: Thomas James's Ecloga Oxonio-Cantabrigiensis. An early printed union catalog, *Jnl of library hist.*, 22: 1–22.

Cross, A.: *Cambridge—some Russian connections*, Cambridge.

Etzkorn, G. J.: Codex Merton 284. Evidence of Ockham's early influence in Oxford, in A. Hudson and M. Wilks eds: *From Ockham to Wyclif*, Oxford (henceforth noted as *Ockham to Wyclif*): 31–42.

Fletcher, J. M.: Inter-fac. disputes in late medieval Oxford, in *Ockham to Wyclif*: 331–42.

——and Upton, C. A.: 'Monastic enclave' or 'open soc.'? A consideration of the role of women in the life of an Oxford coll. community in the early Tudor period, *Hist. of educ.*, 16: 1–9.

Gingerich, O. and M.: Matriculation ages in 16th-cent. Wittenberg, *Hist. of univs*, 6: 135–41.

Hammerstein, N.: The univ. of Heidelberg in the early modern period: Aspects of its hist. as a contrib. to its sexcentenary, *Hist. of univs*, 6: 105–33.

Hiddinga, A.: Obstetrical research in the Neths in the 19th cent., *Med. hist.*, 31: 281–304.

Keats-Rohan, K. S. B.: John of Salisbury and educ. in 12th cent. Paris from the account of his *Metalogicon, Hist. of univs*, 6: 1–45.

Leedham-Green, E. S.: *Books in Cambridge inventories*, 2 vols, Cambridge. (List of contents of 200 private libraries 1535–1760).

Lytle, G. F.: John Wyclif, Martin Luther and Edward Powell: Heresy and the Oxford theol. fac. at the beginning of the Refn, in *Ockham to Wyclif*: 465–79.

McGrade, A. S.: Enjoyment at Oxford after Ockham: philos., psychol. and the love of God, in *Ockham to Wyclif*: 63–88.

Morton, V.: *Oxford rebels: the life and friends of Nevil Story Maskelyne 1823–1911: pioneer Oxford scientist, photographer and politician*, Gloucester.

O'Connor, T. F.: Collection devel. in the Yale univ. library 1865–1931, *Jnl of library hist.*, 22: 164–89.

Paulin, R.: Julius Hare's German books in Trinity Coll. library, Cambridge, *Trans of the Cambridge bibliog. soc.*, 9(2): 174–93. (Hare died 1855).

Raedts, P.: *Richard Rufus of Cornwall and the tradition of Oxford theology*, Oxford. (Considers postion in 13th century).

Rietbergen, P. J. A. N.: Fnding a new library: Pope Alexander VII 1655–67 and the Alessandrina, *Jnl of library hist.*, 22: 190–205.

Roberts, P. B.: Univ. masters and Thomas Becket. Sermons preached on St Thomas of Canterbury at Paris and Oxford in the 13th and 14th cents, *Hist. of univs*, 6: 65–79.

Roche. D.: Acads et pol. au s. des lumières. Les enjeux pratiques de l'immortalité, in K. Baker ed.: *The French Revolution and the creation of modern political culture. 1. The political culture of the old regime*, Oxford: 331–43.

Sarnowsky, J.: Nat. philos. at Oxford and Paris in the mid-14th cent., in *Ockham to Wyclif*: 125–34.

Southern, R. W.: The changing role of the univs in medieval Europe, *Hist. research*, 60: 133–46.

Sutherland, G.: The movt for the higher educ. of women: its soc. and intellect. context in England *c*.1840–80, in P. J. Waller ed.: *Politics and social change in modern Britain*, Brighton: 91–116.

Swanson, R. N.: Learning and livings: univ. study and clerical careers in later medieval England, *Hist. of univs*, 6: 81–103.

Sylla, E. D.: Math. physics and imagination in the work of the Oxford Calculators: Roger Swineshead's 'On Natural Motion', in E. Grant and J. E. Murdoch eds: *Mathematics and its applications to science and natural philosophy in the middle ages*, Cambridge: 69–101.

Tachau, K. H.: The influence of Richard Campsall on 14th-cent. Oxford thought, in *Ockham to Wyclif*: 109–23.

Publications 1988

Allen, M.: *The goals of universities*, Milton Keynes. (Inform. about devel. of univs in Britain and U.S.A. in 20th century).

Anderson, R. D.: *The student community at Aberdeen 1860–1939*, Aberdeen.

Azad, Y.: The limits of univ.: the study of language in some Br. univs and acads 1750–1800, *Hist. of univs*, 7: 117–47.

Brooke, C. and Highfield, R.: *Oxford and Cambridge*, Cambridge. (Scholarly text with many illustrations).

Cobban, A. B.: *The medieval English universities: Oxford and Cambridge to c.1500*, Aldershot.

Colvin, H.: *The Canterbury Quadrangle, St John's College Oxford*, Oxford.
—— and Simmons, J. S. G.: *All Souls. An Oxford college and its buildings*, Oxford.

Corsi, P.: *Science and religion. Baden Powell and the Anglican debate 1800–60*, Cambridge. (Considers position at univ. of Oxford).

Dow, D. and Moss, M.: The med. curriculum at Glasgow in the early 19th cent., *Hist. of univs*, 7: 227–57.

Fletcher, J. M.: Welcome stranger or resented intruder? A reconstruction of the fndation of the univ. of Aberdeen in the context of Europ. univ. devel. in the later middle ages, *Aberdeen univ. rev.*, 180: 298–313.
—— and Upton, C. A.: The end of short cuts. The use of abbreviated Eng. by the fellows of Merton Coll., Oxford 1483–1660, *Jnl of the simplified spelling soc.*, 2: 13–16.

Flynn, J. T.: Russia's 'univ. question': origins to Great Reforms 1802–63, *Hist. of univs*, 7: 1–35.

Gillam, S.: *The Divinity School and Duke Humfrey's Library at Oxford*, Oxford.

Gratton-Guinness, I.: Grandes Ecs, Petite Univ. Some puzzled remarks on higher educ. in maths in Fr. 1795–1840, *Hist. of univs*, 7: 197–225.

Herbst, J.: American higher educ. in the age of the coll., *Hist. of univs*, 7: 37–59.

Hibbert, C. ed.: *The encyclopaedia of Oxford*, London. (Many articles on devel. of univ. and colleges).

Ives, E. W.: *Image of a university. The Great Hall at Edgbaston 1900–1909*. Birmingham. (Early hist. of Birmingham university).

Jenkins, Lord, of Hillhead: *An Oxford view of Cambridge*, Cambridge.

Jones, D. R.: *The origins of civic universities. Manchester, Leeds and Liverpool*, London.

Jones, J.: *Balliol College. A history: 1263–1939*, Oxford.

La Vopa, A. J.: *Grace, talent and merit. Poor students, clerical careers and professional ideology in 18th-century Germany*, Cambridge.

Lawrence, C.: The Edinburgh med. schl and the end of the 'Old Thing' 1790–1830, *Hist. of univs*, 7: 259–86.

Meinel, C.: *Artibus acad. inserenda*: Chem's place in 18th and early 19th cent. univs, *Hist. of univs*, 7: 89–115.

Moore, M. ed.: *Royal Holloway and Bedford New College: centenary lectures 1886–1986*, London.

Morrish, P. S.: *Dr Higgs and Merton College library: a study in 17th-century book-collecting and librarianship*, Leeds.

Outram, D.: Military empire, pol. collab. and cult. consensus. The *Univ. Impériale* reappraised: the case of the univ. of Turin, *Hist. of univs*, 7: 287–303.

Roelevink, J.: *Lux veritatis, magistra vitae*. The teaching of hist. at the univ. of Utrecht in the 18th and the early 19th cents, *Hist. of univs*, 7: 149–74.

Schrecker, E. W.: *No ivory tower. McCarthyism and the universities*, Oxford.

Shepperson, G. and Guild, J. R.: *The Library as I knew it*, Edinburgh. (Concerns Edinburgh univ. library).

Slee, P.: The Oxford idea of a liberal educ. 1800–60: the invention of tradit. and the manufacture of practice, *Hist. of univs*, 7: 61–87.

Springer, H. W.: *The Commonwealth of Universities. The Story of the Association of Commonwealth Universities 1963–88*, London.

Thomson, R. M. ed.: *Alexander Nequam: Speculum Speculationum*, Oxford. (Refs to A. N.'s lects at Oxford in 1190s).

Vanpaemel, G.: Experimental physics and the nat. science curriculum in 18th-cent. Louvain, *Hist. of univs*, 7: 175–96.

Wallace, S.: *War and the image of Germany. British academics 1914–18*, Edinburgh.

Yates, F. A.: *The French academie of the 16th century*, London.

Young, A. P.: *Higher education in American life 1636–1986. A bibliography of dissertations and theses*, London.

France

Additions to Earlier Lists

For 1985

Hadas-Lebel, M.: Les études hébraïques en France au 18e s. et la création de la première chaire d'Ecriture sainte en Sorbonne, *Rev. des études juives*, 144: 93–126.

Paqué, R.: *Le statut parisien des nominalistes*, Paris. (Trans. from German of statute of Dec. 1340 condemning 'nominalists').

For 1986

Chartier, R.: Espace soc. et imaginaire soc.; Les intellects frustrés au 17e s., in D. Julia, J. Revel and R. Chartier: *Les universités européennes du 16e au 18e siècle. Histoire sociale des populations étudiantes*, Paris (henceforth noted as *Univs européennes*): 245–60.

Chêne, C.: Les facs de droit fr. du 17e s. à la Révn. Eléments de bibliog. Fac. de droit de Douai, *Annales d'hist. des facs de droit*, 3: 221–22.

Frijhoff, W.: Grandeur des nombres et misères des réalités: La courbe de Franz Eulenburg et le débat sur le nombre d'intellects en Allemagne 1576–1815, in *Univs européennes*: 23–63.

—— Univ. et marché de l'emploi dans la Répub. des Provinces-Unies, in *Univs européennes*: 205–43.

Kagan, R. L.: Univs in Italy 1500–1700, in *Univs européennes*: 153–86.

Kaniewska, I.: La conjoncture étudiante de l'univ. de Cracovie aux 17e et 18e s., in *Univs européennes*: 135–51.

—— Les étudiants de l'univ. de Cracovie aux 15e et 16e s. 1433–1560, in *Univs européennes*: 113–33.

Livesey, S. T.: Proportions in late medieval univs: an examination of two treatises, *Rev. d'hist. des textes*, 16: 284–310. (Considers versions of Bradwardine's *De proportionibus*).

Motte, O.: Le voyage d'Allemagne. Lettres inéd. sur les missions d'univs fr. dans les univs allemandes au 19e s., *Francia*, 14: 561–66.

Pešek, J. and Šaman, D.: Les étudiants de Bohême dans les univs et les acads d'Europ. centrale et occidentale entre 1596 et 1620, in *Univs européennes*: 89–111.

Peset, M. and Mancebo, M. F.: La population des univs espagnoles au 18e s., in *Univs européennes*: 187–204.

Šmahel, F.: L'univ. de Prague de 1433 à 1622: recrutement géog., carrières et mobilité soc. des étudiants gradués, in *Univs européennes*: 65–88.

Publications 1987

Bellone, E.: Les étudiants fr. de l'univ. de Turin aux 15e et 16e s., in B.

Grosperrin and E. Kanceff eds: *L'enseignement dans les Etats de Savoie*. *L'insegnamento negli stati Sabaudi, Cahiers de civilisation alpine*, 6 (henceforth noted as *Les Etats de Savoie*): 47–63.

Bériou, N.: *La prédication de Ranulphe de la Houblonnière. Sermons aux clercs et aux simples gens à Paris au 13e siècle*, Paris. (R. H. of univ. of Paris). Bibliog. d'hist. de l'éduc. fr. Titres parus au cours de l'année 1984 et supplément des années antérieures, *Hist. de l'éduc.*, 35–36: 1–180.

Bordier, J.-P.: L'Antéchrist au quartier latin selon Rutebeuf, in D. Poirion ed.: *Milieux universitaires et mentalité urbaine au moyen âge*, Paris (henceforth noted as *Milieux universitaires*): 9–21.

Bouchet, A. ed.: *La médecine à Lyon des origines à nos jours*, Lyons/Paris.

Bourdieu, P. and Saint-Martin, M. de: Agrégation et ségrégation. Le champ des Grandes Ecs et le champ du pouvoir, *Actes de la recherche en scs soc.*, 69: 2–50.

Boyer, R.: Des 'intellectuels' sans villes ni univs, in *Milieux universitaires*: 23–32. (Considers Iceland).

Bruneel, C.: Le *primus* de Louvain au 18e s., *Rev. du Nord*, 69(274): 575–89.

Charle, C.: *Les élites de la République 1880–1900*, Paris. (Discusses higher educ. of elite).

—— and Delangle, C.: La campagne électorale de Lucien Febvre au Coll. de France 1929–32. Lettres à Edmond Faral, *Hist. de l'éduc.*, 34: 49–69.

Cormeau, C.: Wiens Univ. u. d. deutschen Prosatexte im Umkreis Heinrichs von Langenstein, in *Milieux universitaires*: 35–48. (Summary in French).

Desportes, P.: Les gradués d'univ. dans la soc. urbaine de la France du Nord à la fin du moyen âge, in *Milieux universitaires*: 49–67.

Devaux, D.: Recherches sur les maîtres et étudiants en droit de Bourges aux 16e et 17e s., *Ec. nat. des chartes. Position des thèses*: 71–76.

Ditsche, M.: Studienstiftungen (bursae volantes) f. *scholares pauperes* in spätmittelalterlischen deutschen Städten, in *Milieux universitaires*: 171–72. (A summary in French only).

Fourcy, A.: *Histoire de l'Ecole polytechnique*, Paris. (New ed. of the 1828 vol. with introd. and further sections by J. Dhombres).

Guenée, B.: *Entre l'Eglise et l'Etat. Quatre vies de prélats français à la fin du moyen âge*, Paris. (On pp. 125–213 discussion of career of Pierre d'Ailly of univ. of Paris).

Kalmár, J.: L'univ. hongroise au temps des réformes, *Etudes Danubiennes* 3(2): 99–113.

Langins, J.: Sur l'enseignement et les examens à l'Ec. polytechnique sous le Directoire: à propos d'une lettre inédite de Laplace, *Rev. d'hist. des scs*, 87: 145–77.

—— *La République avait besoin de savants: Les débuts de l'Ecole polytechnique: l'Ecole centrale des travaux publics et les cours révolutionnaires de l'an 3*, Paris.

Lançon, S.: La fondation de l'Ec. des scs pol. en 1871. 4 textes d'E. Boutmy, F. Guizot, E. de Laboulaye, H. Taine, *Commentaires*, 37: 149–61.

Bibliography 291

Leguay, J.-P.: Ecs et enseignement dans la Savoie médiévale, in *Les Etats de Savoie*: 9–45.

Marichal, R. ed.: *Le livre des prieurs de Sorbonne 1431–85*, Paris.

Mentré, M.: L'iconographie des Bibles univ. parisiennes du 13e s., in *Milieux universitaires*: 69–81.

Mühlethaler, J.-C.: Le poète face au pouvoir, de Geffroy de Paris à Eustache Deschamps, in *Milieux universitaires*: 83–101.

Neveu, B.: Le palais de la Sorbonne, *Commentaires*, 37: 597—610. (Considers the prestige and authority of univ. of Paris).

Neveux, F.: *L'évêque Pierre Cauchon*, Paris. (Pp. 27–41 discusses his career as student and teacher at Paris 1385–1407).

Poirion, D. ed.: *Milieux universitaires et mentalité urbaine au moyen âge*, Paris. (Individual items noted separately).

Prélot, P.-H.: *Naissance de l'enseignement supérieur libre. La loi du 12 juillet 1875*, Paris. (Discusses the creation of Cath. faculties).

Rivé, P. ed.: *La Sorbonne et sa reconstruction*, Lyons. (Considers the new Sorbonne of the late 19th century).

Roggero, M.: Il Coll. delle Prov. all'Univ. di Torino, in *Les Etats de Savoie*: 87–123.

Rucquoi, A.: Socs urbaines et univ. en Castille au moyen âge, in *Milieux universitaires*: 103–117.

Sourdel, D.: Universitaires sans univ. dans les villes des pays d'islam, in *Milieux universitaires*: 119–28.

Stanesco, M.: Nigromance et univ.: scolastique du merveilleux dans le roman fr. du moyen âge, in *Milieux universitaires*: 129–44.

Verger, J.: Les gradués en droit dans les socs urbaines du midi de la France à la fin du moyen âge, in *Milieux universitaires*: 145–56.

—— Les libertés univ. en France au moyen âge, in *Les libertés au moyen âge*, Montbrison: 419–32.

—— L'univ. de Paris au moyen âge, *Commentaires*, 36: 759–69.

—— Pour une hist. de la maîtrise ès-arts au moyen âge: quelques jalons, *Médiévales*, 13: 117–30.

Voisin, J.-P.: *L'histoire rapportée et inachevée d'Edouard Massaux, prêtre et recteur*, Paris/Brussels. (E.M. prof., pro-rect. of Fr. section of univ. of Louvain and 1968–86 rect. of univ. of Louvain-la-Neuve).

Vörös, K.: Le défi du développement moderne. La réponse par les univs. L'organisation des univs en Hongrie, *Etudes Danubiennes*, 3(2): 147–56.

Zink, M.: De Jean le Teinturier à Jean Bras-de-Fer: le triomphe des cuistres, in *Milieux universitaires*: 157–70.

Publications 1988

Bataillon, L. J., Guyot, B. G. and Rouse, R. H. eds: *La production du livre universitaire au Moyen Age. Exemplar et pecia*, Paris.

Bibliog. d'hist. de l'educ. fr. Titres parus au cours de l'année 1985 et suppléments des années anterieurs, *Hist. de l'éduc.* (Special issue): 39–40.

Charle, C. and Telkes, E.: *Les professeurs du Collège de France. Dictionnaire biographique 1901–39*, Paris.

Jolly, C.: *Histoire des Bibliothèques françaises. 2. Les Bibliothèques sous l'Ancien Régime 1570–1789*, Paris. (Ch. on univ. and coll. libraries). *Rev. d'hist. et de philos. relig.*, 68. Special issue devoted to hist. of fac. of theol at univ. of Strasbourg.

Verger, J.: Dépenses univ. à Avignon au 15e s. 1455–56, in *Avignon au Moyen Age. Textes et documents*, Avignon: 207–218.

German Democratic Republic

Additions to Earlier Lists

For 1981

Breunig, W. and Spaar, D. eds: *Festschrift anlässlich der 100. Wiederkehr des Gründungsjahres der Landwirtschaftlichen Hochschule Berlin und des 30 jährigen Bestehens der Akademie der Landwirtschaftswissenschaften der DDR*, Berlin.

For 1982

Franke, M.: 75 Jahre Karl-Sudhoff-Inst. f. Gesch. d. Medizin u. d. Naturwiss. Leipzig, *NTM*, 19(1): 104–105.

Heyde, W. etc.: *Zur Geschichte der Sektion Sozialistische Betriebswirtschaft (an der TU Dresden)*, Dresden.

Klein, H. ed.: *Ehrung Einsteins an der Humboldt-Universität zu Berlin anlässlich seines 100. Geburtstages am 14.3.1979*, Berlin.

Schwartze, P.: Georg Schiltel u. d. Anfänge d. Physiol. an d. Univ. Leipzig, *Wiss. Z. d. Karl-Marx-Univ. Leipzig, mathem.-naturwiss. Reihe*, 31(3): 272–76.

Wandt, B.: Die geplante Berufung von Johannes Kepler an d. Univ. Rostock 1629–30, *NTM*, 19(1): 77–84.

Wissenschaftliches Kolloquium 25 Jahre Hochschulausbildung in der Fachrichtung Kartographie (der Sektion Geodäsie und Kartografie der TU Dresden), Dresden.

Wussing, H.: Wissenschaftsgesch. am Karl-Sudhoff-Inst. (d. Karl-Marx-Univ. Leipzig)—Rückblick u. Aussicht, *NTM*, 19(1): 1–5.

Zeil, W.: Die Sorabistik im wiss. Wirken Reinhold Trautmanns 1883–1951 (an d. Univ. Leipzig u. Jena), *Lětopis, Bautzen*, B29(2): 200–222.

For 1983

Blaschick, K.-D.: Zur jugendpolitischen Führungstätigkeit der SED bei der Herausbildung, Entwicklung und weiterer Ausprägung des Stils des studentischen Lebens an einer lehrerbildenden Hochschuleinrichtung. Thesis. Halle/Saale.

Bursian, H., Hübner, H. and Würpel, H.: 30 Jahre TH 'Otto von Guericke'. Ein Abriss ihrer Entwicklung, *Wiss. Z. d. TH Magdeburg*, 27(3): 1–29.

Falk, G.: Die Univ. Frankfurt (Oder) als Patron über d. Kirchen u. Schulen ihrer Grundherrschaft, *Frankfurter Beitr. zur Gesch.*, 12: 41–49.

Friedrich, C.: Zur Entwicklung der pharmazeutischen Wissenschaft an der Ernst-Moritz-Arndt-Universität Greifswald von 1903 bis 1968. Thesis. Griefswald.

Hübner, H. and Thaler B. eds: *Die Universität Halle-Wittenberg in Vergangenheit und Gegenwart*, Halle/Saale.

Ladanyi, S.: Ungarische Studenten an d. Univ. Frankfurt (Oder), *Frankfurter Beitr. zur Gesch.*, 12: 27–32.

Meischner, W. and Metge, A.: *Zur Geschichte der Psychologie an der Universität Leipzig*, Leipzig.

Oehme, B.: *Die Medaillen der Friedrich-Schiller-Universität Jena 1945–83*, Jena.

Pfefferling, U.: Grundlegende Entwicklungsrichtungen der FDJ-Grundorganisation 'Bruno Kühn' der Pädagogischen Hochschule 'Karl Friedrich Wilhelm Wander' Dresden von ihrer Gründung bis 1971. Thesis. Dresden.

Schlenzig, P.: Rechtsgeschichtliche Aspekte der Neugestaltung der wissenschaftlichen Einrichtungen in der Sowjetischen Besatzungszone Deutschlands in den Jahren 1945–49, dargestellt am Beispiel der Sächsischen Akademie der Wissenschaften zu Leipzig. Thesis. Freiberg. (Considerable inform. about higher education).

Schneider, R.: Die Entwicklung der Fakultät/Sektion für Journalistik der Karl-Marx-Universität Leipzig. Ein geschichtlicher Abriss. Thesis. Leipzig.

For 1984

Arndt, H.: Über Versuche, an d. Univ. Leipzig in d. Jahren d. Weimarer Repub. d. Marxismus zu propagieren, *Beitr. zum marxistisch-leninistischen Grundlagenstudium f. Hoch-u. Fachschullehrer*, 23(3): 35–45.

Baranowski, G. and Tautz, G.: Tradition u. Verpflichtung d. Sektion Rechtswiss. d. Karl-Marx-Univ. Leipzig, *Staat u. Recht*, 33(12): 997–1004.

Bielfeldt, H.-H. and Zeil, W.: Forschungen in d. DDR zur Gesch. d. Slawistik, *Z. f. Slawistik*, 29(5): 777–81.

Feige, H.-U.: Das gesellschaftswiss. Grundstudium an d. Karl-Marx-Univ. Leipzig in d. Jahren 1956 u. 1957, *Beitr. zum marxistisch-leninistischen Grundlagenstudium f. Hoch-u. Fachschullehrer*, 23(2): 50–65.

——Der Aufbau d. SED-Betriebsgruppe an d. Univ. Leipzig 1945–48, *Beitr. zur Gesch. d. Arbeiterbewegung*, 26(2): 247–56.

Fiedler, H.: Die Strategie d. SED zur Entwicklung von Wiss. u. Tech. in d. zweiten Hälfte d. 50er Jahre, *Jb. f. Wirtschaftsgesch.*, 3/84: 30–57.

Girnus, W. and Zott, R.: *Beiträge zur Geschichte der Chemie in Deutschland, insbesondere in Berlin (Universität, Technische Hochschule) im 19. und 20. Jahrhundert*, Berlin. *Hochschule für Musik 'Felix Mendelssohn Bartholdy' Leipzig 1843–1983*, Leipzig.

Ittig, S.: Die Geschichte des gesellschaftswissenschaftlichen Grundstudiums, dargestellt an den Technischen Hochschulen Ilmenau, Karl-Marx-Stadt und Magdeburg in den Jahren 1953–1960/61. Thesis. Ilmenau.

Jackstel, K. and Roger, G.: Das progressive hochschulpädagog. Erbe— wesentlicher Bestandteil d. theoret. Fundus d. soz. Hochschulpädagog., *Wiss. Z. d. Wilhelm-Pieck-Univ., Rostock, gesellsch.-u. sprachwiss. Reihe*, 33(6): 1–7.

Königliche Gewerbeschule Chemnitz—Technische Hochschule Karl-Marx-Stadt. Ein Überblick in Daten 1796–1980, Karl-Marx-Stadt.

Mohrmann, U.: 30 Jahre Ethnographie an d. Humboldt-Univ. zu Berlin, *Jb. f. Volkskunde u. Kulturgesch.*, 27/84: 154–56.

Pawlow, V.: Aus d. Gesch. d. Berliner Orthopädie. Julius Wolff 1844– 1902—d. erste Prof. f. orthopädische Chirurgie d. Berliner Univ., *Orthopädie-tech. Inform.*, 4(16): 189–92.

Pfefferling, U.: Zu Aufgaben u. Problemen bei d. Erforschung d. Gesch. d. FDJ-Grundorganisation 'Bruno Kühn' d. PH 'Karl Friedrich Wilhelm Wander', Dresden, *Wiss. Z. d. PH Dresden, gesellsch.-u sprachwiss. Reihe*, 18(1): 33–45.

Preuss, D.: Zur Vorgeschichte und Entstehung der Hochschule für Verkehrswesen 'Friedrich List' Dresden und zu ihrer Entwicklung zur sozialistischen Lehr-, Erziehungs- und Forschungsstätte 1919/52–1961. Thesis. Dresden.

——and Rehbein, G.: Chronik d. Hochschule f. Verkehrswesen 'Friedrich List', 1: 1952–61, *Wiss. Z. d. Hochschule f. Verkehrswesen Dresden, Sonderheft 5*; 2: 1961–71, *Sonderheft 16*.

Schenkel, S.: Zur Entwicklung des Zahnärztlichen Instituts der Universität Leipzig und der deutschen Zahnheilkunde in der Zeit der faschistischen Diktatur 1933–1945. Thesis. Leipzig.

Spading, K.: Niederländer an d. Greifswalder Univ. Ein Beitr. zur Gesch. d. geistig-kult. Beziehungen in d. Zeit d. Hanse, in K. Fritze, E. Müller-Mertens and W. Stark eds: *Autonomie, Wirtschaft und Kultur der Hansestädte*, Weimar: 190–204.

Trigesimo anno. Festschrift der Medizinischen Akademie 'Carl Gustav Carus' anlässlich ihres 30 jährigen Bestehens, Dresden.

Publications 1985

Abe, H. R.: Der Anteil d. Adels u. d. Geistlichkeit an d. Promotionen d. Erfurter Artistenfak. im Mittelalter 1392–1521, *Beitr. zur Hochschul- u. Wissenschaftsgesch. Erfurts*, 20: 7–14.

—— Angehörige d. ehemaligen 'Akad. nützlicher (gemeinnütziger) Wiss.' zu Erfurt 1794–1945 als Mitglieder d. späteren 'Akad. d. Wissen. d. DDR', *Beitr. zur Hochschul- u. Wissenschaftsgesch. Erfurts*, 20: 59–78.

—— Zum 25 jährigen Bestehen d. Abteilung f. Gesch. d. Medizin an d. Medizin. Akad. Erfurt 1960–85, *Beitr. zur Hochschul- u. Wissenschaftsgesch. Erfurts*, 20: 209–214.

—— Gedenkkalender d. Med. Akad. Erfurt f. d. Jahre 1986–90, *Beitr. zur Hochschul- u. Wissenschaftsgesch. Erfurts*, 20: 215–22.

—— Die Univ. Erfurt im Spiegel d. Neuerscheinungen anlässlich d. Martin-Luther-Ehrung 1983 d. DDR. Eine Auswahl-Sammelbesprechung, *Beitr. zur Hochschul- u. Wissenschaftsgesch. Erfurts*, 20: 223–34.

Albrecht, K., Herud, H. and Nerlich, B. P.: *Zur Entwicklung der Weiterbildung und des Fernstudiums an der Humboldt-Universität zu Berlin. Ein Überblick*, Berlin.

Barnikol, I.: Otto Hartwig 1830–1903 als Student in Halle 1852–53, *Wiss. Z. d. Martin-Luther-Univ. Halle-Wittenberg, gesellsch.-u. sprachwiss. Reihe*, 34(3): 94–110. (O.H. keeper of univ. library 1876–98).

Beiträge zur Geschichte der Hochschulwesens der DDR, 2, Berlin.

Beiträge zur Geschichte der Mathematik und ihrer Entwicklung an der Universität Rostock, Rostock.

Blumenthal, E.: Die Leipziger Ägyptologie, *Wiss. Z. d. Karl-Marx-Univ. Leipzig, G-Reihe*, B4(6): 585–91.

Bohmüller, L.: Die Universitätsbibliothek Jena während d. Faschismus, *Wiss. Z. d. Friedrich-Schiller-Univ. Jena*, 34(5–6): 781–90.

Brauer, W.: Zum hochschulpol. Wirken von Rudolf Schick an d. Univ. Rostock, in *Rudolf Schick 80 Jahre*, Rostock: 1–22.

Buchholz, E. and Tack, F.: 25 Jahre Landtech. Hochschulausbildung an d. Univ. Rostock, *Beitr. zur Gesch. d. Wilhelm-Pieck-Univ. Rostock*, 7: 1–83.

Buder, M.: Die Entwicklung der FDJ-Organisation (der Studenten) an der Leipziger Universität 1955–61. Thesis. Leipzig.

Debes, D.: Die Akte Lindner, *Leipziger Blätter*, 5: 21. (L. prof. of theol. who stole from the univ. library).

Die kleinste Hochschule d. Welt: Das Inst. f. Literatur 'Johannes R. Becher' Leipzig, *Leipziger Blätter*, 7: 49–53.

Duparre, M.: Die Entwicklung der Wirtschaftswissenschaftlichen Fakultät der Humboldt-Universität zu Berlin . . . bis zum Ende der 50er Jahre (des 20. Jh.). Thesis. Berlin.

Fink, H. etc.: Beitr. zur Gesch. d. Theol. Fak. Berlins. Zum 175. Jahrestag d. Gründung d. Berliner Univ., *Wiss. Z. d. Humboldt-Univ. zu Berlin*, GR, 34(7): 517–628.

Fläschendräger, W.: 'Die univ. dorfften auch wol einer gutten starken reformation'. Zu Luthers Tätigkeit als Universitätslehrer u. als Universitätsreformer, *Wiss. Z. d. Martin-Luther-Univ. Halle-Wittenberg, mathem.-naturwiss Reihe*, 34(2): 17–22.

Fliess, G. etc.: *Lebendiges Erbe. Arbeiter-und Bauernfakultät der Friedrich-Schiller-Universität Jena. Zum 40. Jahrestag der Neueröffnung der Alma mater Jenensis*, Jena.

Franke, M. etc.: Die Leipziger Physik-Prof. seit 1835, *Wiss. Z. d. Karl-Marx-Univ. Leipzig, mathem.-naturwiss. Reihe*, 34(1): 82–87.

Fünfundzwanzig Jahre Landtech. Ausbildung an d. Univ. Rostock, *Beitr. zur Gesch. d. Univ. Rostock*, 7: 1–84.

Gandert, K.-D.: *Vom Prinzenpalais zur Humboldt-Universität. Die historische Entwicklung des Universitätsgebäudes in Berlin mit seinen Gartenanlagen und Denkmälern*, Berlin.

Germann, D.: Gründung u. Anfänge d. seismologischen Station d. Univ. Jena 1897–1906, *Wiss. Z. d. Friedrich-Schiller-Univ. Jena, gesellsch.-u. sprachwiss. Reihe*, 34(5–6): 749–61.

Göthner, K.-C.: 25 Jahre Lateinamerikawiss. an d. Wilhelm-Pieck-Univ. Rostock, *Z. Asien, Afrika, Lateinamerika*, 13(2): 299–307.

Güthert, H.: Pathologie einst u. jetzt, *Beitr. zur Hochschul- u. Wissenschaftsgesch. Erfurts*, 20: 149–66.

Guntau, M.: Doppelentdeckungen in d. Gesch. d. Wiss., *Rostocker Wissenschaftshist. Manuskripte*, 11: 61–67.

—— Gedanken zu 100 Jahren Geologie als Universitätsfach in Deutschland 1770–1870, in H. Prescher ed.: *Leben und Wirken deutscher Geologen im 18. und 19. Jahrhundert*, Leipzig (henceforth noted as *Leben u. Wirken*): 9–17.

—— Gedanken zur Kulturgesch. Mecklenburgs u. d. Univ. Rostock aus d. Sicht von Wiss. u. Tech., *Rostocker Wissenschaftshist. Manuskripte*, 12: 7–16.

—— and Kirschner, E.: Zur Bedeutung d. Wissenschaftsgesch. f. d. Ausbildung von Geolog. während d. Studiums, *Wiss. Z. d. Wilhelm-Pieck-Univ. Rostock*, GR, 34(3): 42–44.

Guntau, M. and Wirth, U.: Ernst Beyrich 1815–96 u. Wilhelm Hauchecorne 1828–1900 . . . u. d. Entwicklung d. Geolog. in Berlin während d. zweiten Hälfte d. 19. Jh., in *Leben u. Wirken*: 291–310.

Hölzel, H.: Die neuen Denkmäler d. Friedrich-Schiller-Univ. Jena 1953–85, *Wiss. Z. d. Friedrich-Schiller-Univ. Jena, gesellsch.-u. sprachwiss. Reihe*, 34(5–6): 709–20.

Hoffmann, E.: Rudolf Kötzschke u. d. Ur- u. Frühgeschichtsforschung an d. Univ. Leipzig, *Z. f. Archäolog.*, 19: 271–83.

Kaiser, W.: Bei Durchsicht d. Wittenberger Matrikel, *Wiss. Z. d. Martin-Luther-Univ. Halle-Wittenberg, mathem.-naturwiss. Reihe*, 34(2): 57–59.

—— Der Lehrkörper d. Medizinischen Fak. in d. halleschen Amtszeit von Georg Ernst Stahl, *Wiss. Beitr. d. Martin-Luther-Univ. Halle-Wittenberg*, 66 (E73): 59–66.

—— Georg Forsters Promotion (21.9.1785) in Halle, *Wiss. Beitr. d. Martin-Luther-Univ. Halle-Wittenberg*, 55 (E77): 224–30.

—— Die halleschen Kinderkrankenhäuser von 1708 u. 1722 u. d. Entwicklung d. klinischen Pädiatrie, *Wiss. Beitr. d. Martin-Luther-Univ. Halle-Wittenberg*, 66 (E73): 283–310.

—— and Völker, A.: August Schaarschmid 1720–91 als Anatom an d. Univ. Bützow, *Rostocker Wissenschaftshist. Manuskripte*, 12: 56–63.

—— Praemii loco: die hallesche Promotion von Georg Forster 1754–94 u. sein hallescher Kontaktkreis, *Z. f. d. gesamte innere Medizin u. ihre Grenzgebiete*, 40: 269–76.

—— Orientalisten u. Altertumsforscher d. Nordhäuser Raumes an d. Univ. Halle, *Beitr. zur Heimatkunde (von) Stadt u. Kreis Nordhausen*, 10: 55–73.

Kantel, L.: Auf d. Weg zu marxistisch-leninistischen Gesellschaftswiss. Erfahrungen d. Friedrich-Schiller-Univ. Jena 1949–62/63, *Alma mater Jenensis. Studien zur Hochschul- u. Wissenschaftsgesch*, 2: 7–25.

Keller, D.: Laudatio f. eine Jubilarin, *Leipziger Blätter*, 5: 7–10. (Celebration of 575 yrs of univ. of Leipzig).

Kibbel, H.-U.: 150 Jahre Chem. Laboratorium an d. Univ. Rostock, *Wiss. Z. d. Wilhelm-Pieck-Univ. Rostock, mathem.-naturwiss. Reihe*, 34(9): 5–11.

Kiefer, J.: Übersicht über d. Schriftgut d. ehemaligen 'Akad. nützlicher (gemeinnütziger) Wiss. zu Erfurt' 1754–1945, *Beitr. zur Hochschul- u. Wissenschaftsgesch. Erfurts*, 20: 27–57. (Inform. about the hist. of the 'Hierana' at E.).

Klare, H.: *Geschichte der Chemiefaserforschung*, Berlin. (Discussion of hist. of THs in Germany).

Klaus, W.: Zur Gründung d. naturkundlichen Gesellsch. 'Isis' im Zeichen d. Vormärz (u. d. Beziehungen zum Dresdner Polytech.), *Dresdner Hefte*, 3 (*Beitr. zur Kulturgesch.*, 6): 50–54.

Klein, A.: Wie Erich Kästner Erich Kästner wurde, *Leipziger Blätter*, 5: 54–55. (E.K. student and dr of univ. of Leipzig).

Klein, H. ed.: *Humboldt-Universität zu Berlin. Überblick 1810–1985*, Berlin.

Kleine-Natrop, H.-E.: Medizin in Dresden zwischen Tradition u. Fortschritt, *Dresdner Hefte*, 3 (*Beitr. zur Kulturgesch.*, 6): 73–80.

Kobuch, A.: Aspekte d. Frühaufklärung in Sachsen, besonders auf theol. Gebiet, *Jb. f. Regionalgesch.*, 12: 99–115. (Inform. about hist. of univs of Leipzig and Wittenberg).

Köhler, R., Rey, M. and Syniatowa, A.: Freundschaft u. Zusammenarbeit zwischen d. UdSSR u. d. DDR im Hochschulwesen: Zum 40. Jahrestag d. Sieges über d. Hitlerfaschismus u. d. Befreiung d. deutschen Volkes vom Faschismus, *Das Hochschulwesen*, 33(5): 133–37.

Köhler, R.: Die Zusammenarbeit der SED mit der SMAD bei der antifaschistisch-demokratischen Erneuerung des Hochschulwesens 1945–49. Thesis. Berlin.

—— Schritte zur weiteren Gestaltung d. sozialistischen-Hochschule in d.

DDR in d. sechziger Jahren, *Beitr. zur Gesch. d. Hochschulwesens d. DDR*, 2: 5–21.

Kossack, H., Beck, F. and Schmid, G.: *Humboldt-Universität zu Berlin. Dokumente 1810–1985*, Berlin.

Köster, U.: Zur Entwicklung d. wiss. Ausbildung von Chemikern im 19. Jh. in Deutschland, *Wiss. Z. d. Wilhelm-Pieck-Univ. Rostock, mathem.-naturwiss. Reihe*, 34(3): 45–49.

Kück, G. and Klien, E.: Zur Entwicklung d. marxistisch-leninistischen Afrika-, Nahost- u. Asienwiss. an d. Karl-Marx-Univ. Leipzig, *Wiss. Z. d. Karl-Marx-Univ. Leipzig*, GR, 34(6): 500–512.

Lange, P.: Die Institutionalisierung d. Silikattechnik an d. Hochschulen, *NTM*, 22(2): 61–67.

Langer, G.: Die Greifswalder Studentenschaft während der antifaschistisch-demokratischen Umgestaltung des Hochschulwesens 1945–49. Thesis. Greifswald.

Lippold, M.: Zur Entwicklungsgesch. d. marxistisch-leninistischen Ästhetik u. Kulturtheorie an d. Karl-Marx-Univ. Leipzig, *Wiss. Z. d. Karl-Marx-Univ. Leipzig*, GR, 34(5): 420–23.

Lösche, A.: Neubeginn u. Wiederaufstieg d. Physik in Leipzig nach 1945, *Wiss. Z. d. Karl-Marx-Univ. Leipzig, mathem.-naturwiss. Reihe*, 34(1): 43–59.

Lück, H.: Die Spruchtätigkeit d. Juristenfak. u. d. Schöffenstühls in Wittenberg, *Jb. f. Regionalgesch.*, 12: 77–98.

Mägdefrau, W.: Martin Luther u. d. Univ. Jena, *Wiss. Z. d. Friedrich-Schiller-Univ. Jena, mathem.-naturwiss. Reihe*, 34(5–6): 609–33.

Mährdel, C. and Krause, A.: Die Gründung u. Entwicklung eines Lehr-u. Forschungsbereichs zu Grundfragen d. Nationalen Befreiungsbewegung, *Wiss. Z. d. Karl-Marx-Univ. Leipzig*, GR, 34(5): 568–74.

Mahnke, R.: Ludwig Matthiesen, d. erste ordentliche Prof. d. Physik an d. Univ. Rostock 1874–1905, *Wiss. Z. d. Wilhelm-Pieck-Univ. Rostock, mathem.-naturwiss. Reihe*, 34(1): 74–86.

—— Rostocker Promotionen zur Physik 1908–45, *Wiss. Z. d. Wilhelm-Pieck-Univ. Rostock, mathem.-naturwiss. Reihe*, 34(1): 87–92.

Mokrzecki, L.: Das Bildungswesen in Gdańsk u. seine Beziehungen zur Rostocker Univ. vom 16. bis zum 18. Jh., *Wiss. Z. d. Wilhelm-Pieck-Univ. Rostock*, GR, 34(7): 53–57.

Mühlpfordt, G.: Georg Ernst Stahls Grundlegung d. neueren Chemie u. d. Weltwirkung d. Halleschen Aufklärung, *Wiss. Beitr. d. Martin-Luther-Univ. Halle-Wittenberg*, 66(E73): 117–60.

Müller, G.: Die Lebensmitteltech. an d. Humboldt-Univ. zu Berlin—ein Beitr. zur Gesch. dieses Wissenschaftsgebietes, *Wiss. Z. d. Humboldt-Univ. zu Berlin, mathem.-naturwiss. Reihe*, 34(10): 913–919.

Noack, H.-J. and Kirste, J.: Die Entwicklung d. Studentensports an d. Univ. Leipzig von ihrer Neueröffnung bis zur Gegenwart, *Wiss. Z. d. Karl-Marx-Univ. Leipzig*, GR, 34(4): 397–404.

Oehme, B.: Univ. Jena u. Denkmalpflege 1971–85, *Wiss. Z. d. Friedrich-Schiller-Univ. Jena*, GR, 34(5–6): 695–708.

Oehme, J.: Friedrich Gottlob Schulze—sein Wirken f. d. Herausbildung d. Landwirtschaftswiss., *Alma mater Jenensis. Studien zur Hochschul-u. Wissenschaftsgesch.*, 2: 85–98.

Pasemann, D.: Zur Faschisierungstendenz in d. 'Deutschen Gesellsch. f. Soz.' 1922–34. Untersuchungen an d. Nachlässen von Werner Sombart u. Ferdinand Tönnies, *Arbeitsblätter zur Wissenschaftsgesch.*, 15: 5–79.

Richter, E. etc.: Asienwiss. Forschung u. Lehre in Leipzig, *Wiss. Z. d. Karl-Marx-Univ. Leipzig*, GR, 34: 549–67.

Richter, I.: Karl-Marx-Univ. Leipzig—ein Zentrum. d. Nordafrika- u. Nahostwiss., *Wiss. Z. d. Karl-Marx-Univ. Leipzig*, GR, 34: 513–29.

Schädlich, C.: *Die Hochschule für Architektur und Bauwesen Weimar. Ein geschichtlicher Abriss*, Weimar.

Schilfert, B.-J.: Die Berliner Handelshochschule—Faktoren ihrer historischen Herausbildung . . . und Entwicklung. Thesis. Berlin.

Schmidt, H.: Zur Bedeutung d. Natur- u. Gesellsch. an einer medizin. Hochschule, *Beitr. zur Hochschul- u. Wissenschaftsgesch. Erfurts*, 20: 137–47.

Schmidt, S.: Revol. u. Universitätsreform. Reformbestrebungen d. Hochschullehrer in d. deutschen bürgerlich-demokrat. Revol. von 1848–49, *Alma mater Jenensis. Studien zur Hochschul- u. Wissenschaftsgesch.*, 2: 26–39.

Scholtz, H.-J. and Pries, D.: 100 Jahre Otolaryngologie als Lehrgebiet an d. Univ. Rostock. Zum Gedenken an Christian Lemcke, *Wiss. Z. d. Wilhelm-Pieck-Univ. Rostock*, NR, 34(7): 70–72.

Schrammek, W.: *Musikinstrumente aus dem Musikinstrumenten-Museum der Karl-Marx-Universität Leipzig*, Leipzig.

Schreier, W.: Die Physik an d. Leipziger Univ. bis zum Ende d. 19. Jh., *Wiss. Z. d. Karl-Marx-Univ. Leipzig, mathem.-naturwiss. Reihe*, 34(1): 5–19.

Schwabe, H.: 'Halam tendis, aut pietista aut atheista mox reversurus', *Wiss. Beitr. d. Martin-Luther-Univ. Halle-Wittenberg*, 66(E 73): 49–58.

Seiffert, M.: Rudolf Schick als Hochschullehrer an d. Landwirtschaftlichen Fak., in *Rudolf Schick—80 Jahre*, Gross Lüsewitz/Rostock: 5–35.

Steiger, G.: Das Jenaer Goethe-Denkmal d. Jahres 1821, wiederrichtet durch d. Friedrich-Schiller Univ. 1973–74, *Wiss. Z. d. Friedrich-Schiller-Univ. Jena*, GR, 34(5–6): 667–82.

—— *Goethe, die Universität Jena und die Naturwissenschaften*, Jena.

Steiner, G.: *Freimaurer und Rosenkreuzer. Georg Forsters Weg durch Geheimbünde. Ein Beitrag zur Studentengeschichte der Spätaufklärung*, Berlin.

Stodolka, E.: Die Entwicklung der FDJ-Organisation der Leipziger Universität 1945–55. Thesis. Leipzig.

Stolz, R.: Die Bemühungen von Johann Theodor Neukranz um d. Entwicklung d. Chemie an d. Univ. Wittenberg, *Wiss. Beitr. d. Martin-Luther-Univ. Halle-Wittenberg*, 66(E 73): 207–214.

Szeskus, R.: Die Bachforschung an d. Karl-Marx-Univ. Leipzig, *Wiss. Z. d. Karl-Marx-Univ. Leipzig*, GR, 34(4): 207–214.

—— 75 Jahre Leipziger Musikwiss., *Wiss. Z. d. Karl-Marx-Univ. Leipzig*, GR, 34(4): 405–406.

Treide, D.: Der Lehr- u. Forschungsbereich f. Ethnographie 'Julius Lips' and d. Univ. Leipzig (seit 1899), *Wiss. Z. d. Karl-Marx-Univ. Leipzig*, GR, 34(6): 575–84.

Tutzke, D. etc.: *Universität Berlin 1810–1985—Charité 1710–1985*, Berlin.

Uhle, K.: Zur Gesch. d. 'Seminargebäudes' auf d. Hof d. Hauptgebäudes d. Wilhelm-Pieck-Univ. Rostock, *Wiss. Z. d. Wilhelm-Pieck-Univ. Rostock*, GR, 34(9): 12–14.

Usbeck, W., Topf, B. and Usbeck, B.: Die Entwicklung d. Chirurgie in Erfurt bis zum Jahre 1983, *Beitr. zur Hochschul- u. Wissenschaftsgesch. Erfurts*, 20: 167–202.

Usbeck, W., Hikisch, K. and Pohl, M.: 30 Jahre Medizin. Akad. Erfurt. Daten u. Bemerkenswertes aus d. ersten drei Jahrzehnten ihres Bestehens, *Beitr. zur Hochschul- u. Wissenschaftsgesch. Erfurts*, 20: 129–136.

Usbeck, W.: 20 Jahre freundschaftliche Beziehungen zwischen d. Medizin. Akad. Erfurt u. d. Medizin. Univ. Pécs 1963–83, *Beitr. zur Hochschul-u. Wissenschaftsgesch. Erfurts*, 20: 203–208.

Völker, A.: Bei Durchsicht d. Stahlschen Disputationslisten, *Wiss. Beitr. d. Martin-Luther-Univ. Halle-Wittenberg*, 66(E73): 235–58.

—— Die medizin. u. pharmazeut. Einrichtungen d. Franckeschen Stiftungen während d. halleschen Amtsphase von Georg Ernst Stahl, *Wiss. Beitr. d. Martin-Luther-Univ. Halle-Wittenberg*, 66 (E73): 67–88.

—— Georg Forsters Promotor, d. 'hallesche Vetter' Philipp Adolph Böhmer, *Wiss, Beitr. d. Martin-Luther-Univ. Halle-Wittenberg*, 55 (E77): 230–34.

Wahl, V.: Das 'Collegium Jenense'—die Gründungsstätte d. Univ. Jena in d. ersten Jahren ihres Bestehens, *Wiss. Z. d. Friedrich-Schiller-Univ. Jena*, GR, 34(5–6): 635–66.

Wappler, K. and Zylka, C.: Physik u. Physiker an d. Leipziger Univ. im 1. Quartal d. 20. Jh., *Wiss. Z. d. Karl-Marx-Univ. Leipzig, mathem.-naturwiss. Reihe*, 34(1): 20–29.

Wenzel, J.: Die älteste Univ. d. DDR—575 Jahre Alma mater Lipsiensis, *Leipziger Blätter*, 5: 4–6.

Windsch, W. and Franke, M.: 1927–45: Blütezeit u. Niedergang d. Leipziger Physikal. Inst., *Wiss. Z. d. Karl-Marx-Univ. Leipzig, mathem.-naturwiss. Reihe*, 34(1): 30–42.

Wirth, G.: Friedrich Siegmund-Schultze als Berliner Hochschullehrer, *Standpunkt*, 6: 164–67.

Zeil, L.: August Ludwig Schlözer u. d. Berliner Akad. d. Wiss. Neues zur Wirkungsgesch. d. Göttinger Gelehrten, *Z. f. Geschichtswiss.*, 33(7): 605–21.

Zinserling, A.: Das Jenaer Universitätshauptgebäude von 1908 u. sein
Verhältnis zur architektonischen Tradition von Jena, *Wiss. Z. d. Friedrich-Schiller-Univ. Jena*, 34(5–6): 683–94.

Zur Gesch. d. Klassischen Archäol. in Jena u. in Kraków, *Wiss. Beitr. d.
Friedrich-Schiller-Univ. Jena*, Jena.

Zwanzig Jahre Rechenzentrum/Sektion Informationsverarbeitung an d.
Wilhelm-Pieck-Univ. Rostock, *Rostocker Inform. u. Berichte*, 1: 1–96.

Hungary

Additions to Earlier Lists

For 1985

Klaniczay, T.: Egyetem és pol. a magyar középkorban (Univ. and pols in
the Hungarian middle ages), in *Pallas magyar ivadékai*, Budapest (henceforth noted as Pallas): 67–76.

—— Értelmiség egyetem nélküli országban (The intellect. class in a land
without a univ.), in *Pallas*: 77–85.

—— Nicasius Ellebodius leuveni és római tanulmányai (The studies of N.E.
at Louvain and Rome), in *Pallas*: 86–95.

For 1986

Bakos, I.: Régió—Tudomány—Egyetem Debrecen, Pécs és Szeged városá-
ban (Region—Science—Univ. in the towns of D., P. and S.), *Tiszatáj*, 4:
51–66.

Petőcz, P.: Az egyetemi és főiskolai hallgatók második világháborús történetéhez (Contribs to the hist. of students of univs and high schls during
the 2nd world war), *Századok*, 2: 301–44.

Publications 1987

Bakonyi, F. and Gábor, I. eds: *Dokumentumok a magyar állatorvosi oktatás
történetéhez, 1. 1786–1816* (Docs for the hist. of the Veterinary Inst., 1.
1786–1816), Budapest.

Hamza, G.: Vécsey Tamás és a jogi szemináriumok (T.V. and the legal
seminars), in G. Hamza ed.: *Studia dedicata centenario fundationis
seminariorum universitatis Budapestinensis*, Budapest (henceforth noted
as *Studia dedicata*): 11–39.

Holló, F. ed.: *200 éves a magyar állatorvosi felsőoktatás 1787–1987* (200 yrs
of veterinary higher educ. 1787–1987), Budapest.

Horváth, P.: Magyar tanszabadság és a jogi szemináriumok (The freedom
of teaching and the legal seminars in Hungary), in *Studia dedicata*: 41–
83.

Köte, S.: A dualizmuskori felsőoktatás (Higher educ. in the age of the Dual Monarchy), in *Studia dedicata*: 99–113.

Mann, M. ed.: *Oktatáspolitikai koncepciók a dualizmus korából* (Conceptions of educ. pol. in the age of the Dual Monarchy), Budapest.

—— Trefort felsőoktatás-pol. (T's pol. for higher educ.), in *Studia dedicata*: 115–32.

Szögi, L.: Quellen zur Gesch. d. Univ. in Ungarn, *Acta hist. acad. scientiarum Hungaricae*, 33(1): 107–111.

—— 100 éves a pesti egyetemi történelmi szeminárium (100 yrs of the hist. seminar of Pest univ.), in *Studia dedicata*: 85–98.

Végh, F.: A korai magyar mérnökképzés és Beszédes József (Early Hungarian engineering educ. and J.B.), *Hidrológiai Közlöny*, 5–6: 327–32.

Publications 1988

Balás, G., Forrai, S. and Sándorfy, F.: Irás, könyvek, felső*fokú oktatás (Writing, books, higher educ.), in G. Balás ed.: A székely művelődés évszázadai*, Budapest: 139–61.

Kiss, J. M., Szögi, L. and Ujváry, G.: *Az Eötvös Loránd tudományegyetem levéltára 1635–1975. Repertórium* (Archives of the L.E. univ. 1635–1975. A repertory), Budapest.

Ólmosi, Z. and Urbán, K. eds: *Tanulmányok a magyar egyetemi ifjúsági mozgalom történetéből 1948–60* (Studies in the hist. of the univ. youth movt in Hungary 1948–60), Budapest.

Pétervári, A. ed.: *University of Agriculture. Faculty of Agricultural Sciences, Keszthely*, Keszthely.

Vargha, D. and Kanyó, S.: '. . . *csillagkoronák éjféli barátja'. Tittel Pál. A csillagászat professzora a pesti egyetemen. Élete és működése* (Life and work of P.T., prof of astron. at the univ. of Pest), Budapest.

Spain and Portugal

Additions to Earlier Lists

For 1979

Muñoz Delgado, V.: El convento de la Merced y la Univ. de Valladolid, *El norte de Castilla*, 12 June: 48.

For 1981

Muñoz Delgado, V.: La Univ. de Salamanca y los *Elementa recentioris philosophiae* (México 1774) de J. B. Diaz Gamarra y Alvalos, *Cuadernos salmantinos de filos.*, 8: 149–74.

For 1984

Muñoz Delgado, V.: El general fr. Francisco Maldonado y el col. merce-
dario de la Veracruz de Salamanca. Un documento para nuestra hist.,
Bol. de la prov. de Castilla de la Orden de la Merced, 22(74): 36–39.
—— Fr. Martín de Acevedo (+1658), comendador de Conjo, prof. y
obispo. Otros mercedarios catedráticos de la univ. Compostelana, *Bol.
de la prov. de Castella de la Orden de la Merced,* 22(77): 56–66.
—— La Veracruz de Salamanca y sus dos primeros profs en la univ., *Bol. de
la prov. de Castilla de la Orden de la Merced,* 22(75): 27–42.

For 1985

Muñoz Delgado, V.: Fray Juan García Rodriguez (+1649) y la cátedra de
Súmulas de Lógica en Salamanca, *Cuadernos salmantinos de filos.,* 12:
253–76.

Publications 1987

Echeverria, L. de: *Nuevas páginas universitarias salmantinas,* Salamanca.
Muñoz Delgado, V.: Fr. Ignacio de Andrade y Rioboo 1675–1723, comen-
dador de la Merced de Conjo y prof. de la univ. Compostelana, *Bol. de la
prov. de Castilla de la Orden de la Merced,* 25(86): 35–44.
Rodríguez—San Pedro Bezares, L. E.: *Vida, aspiraciones y fracasos de un
estudiante de Salamanca. El diario de Gaspar Ramos Ortiz 1558–69,*
Salamanca.
Ruiz Asencio, J. M., Herrero de la Fuente, M. and Albi Romero, G.:
Documentos reales medievales de la Universidad de Valladolid, Valladolid.
Sánchez y Sánchez, D.: *Un alumno mejicano rector de Salamanca en el siglo
de oro,* Salamanca.
Santamaría, A.: Consideraciones sobre la Univ. Luliana de Mallorca, in
Homanaje al Prof. Juan Torres Fontes, Murcia, 2: 1547–62.
Wagner, K.: *Impresos de los siglos 15, 16 y 17. Biblioteca de las facultades de
filologia, geografia e historia,* Seville.
Zamora, G.: La reforma de los estudios filos. en España bajo Carlos III,
Naturaleza y Gracia, 34: 7–26.

Publications 1988

Carabias Torres, A. M.: El 'poder' de las letras. Cols mayores salmantinos
en la administración Americana, *Rev. estudios de hist. soc. y econ. de
América,* 3–4 (1987–88): 2–28.
Robles Carcedo, L.: Catedráticos de la Univ. de Salamanca (s.17) y su
proyección en América, *Rev. estudios de hist. soc. y econ. de América,* 3–4
(1987–88): 77–93.
Rodriguez Cruz, A. M.: Profs salmantinos en América, *Rev. estudios de hist.
soc. y econ. de América,* 3–4 (1987–88): 42–66.

Switzerland

Additions to Earlier Lists

For 1977

Barahona-Fernandes, H. J.: L'univ. portugaise en mouvement, *CRE-Inform.*, 37: 5–10.
Bornewasser, J. A.: From schl of econs to univ. of soc. sciences and humanities, *CRE-Inform.*, 39: 42–53. (The univ. of Tilburg).
Bredow, W. von: Ut discipuli sub praeceptoribus sint . . . , *CRE-Inform.*, 40: 53–61. (The univ. of Marburg).
Delacrétaz, J.: *L'université et le pouvoir*, Lausanne.
Endress, P. K.: Das Inst. f. Systemat. Botanik an d. Univ. Zürich, *Vierteljahrsschrift d. Naturforschenden Gesellsch. in Zürich*, 122: 143–50.
Ferrari da Grado, H.-M.: *Une chaire de médecine au 15e siècle. Un professeur à l'Université de Pavie de 1432 à 1472*, Geneva.
Hellinga, F.: Landbouwhogeschl Wageningen, an agricult. univ., *CRE-Inform.*, 40: 63–71. (The univ. of Wageningen).
Hoppe, G.: The birth of a univ. of a capital city, *CRE-Inform.*, 39: 20–25. (The univ. of Stockholm).
Jankovic, D.: L'univ. de Belgrade après la deuxiéme guerre mondiale, *CRE-Inform.*, 37: 57–62.
Luchaire, F.: L'autonomie de l'univ. de Paris á l'époque de Philippe Auguste, *CRE-Inform.*, 39: 4–8.
Massaux, G.: L'univ. de Louvain dans la soc. et dans l'église d'hier et de demain, *CRE-Inform.*, 39: 27–40.
Segerstedt, T. T.: Autonomy and soc. relevance, *CRE-Inform.*, 39: 10–18. (The univ. of Uppsala).
Slottved, E.: Teaching at the univ. of Copenhagen over 5 cents. Organ. and econ., *CRE-Inform.*, 39: 69–86.
Wandel, U. J.: La contestation étudiante, hier et aujourd'hui, *CRE-Inform.*, 39: 55–67. (The univ. of Tübingen).
Wanner, H.: 135 Jahre Allg. Botanik an d. Univ. Zürich, *Vierteljahrsschrift d. Naturforschenden Gesellsch. in Zürich*, 122: 150–58.

For 1978

Andrey, G. etc. eds: *Roland Ruffieux. Vingt ans d'enseignement à l'Université de Fribourg 1958–78*, Freiburg i. Ü.
Centenaire de la Faculté de médecine de l'Université de Genève 1876–1976, Geneva.
Ecole polytechnique fédérale de Lausanne 125 ans, Lausanne.
Galliker, H. J.: *Die Geschichte des Gymnasiums und der philosophischen Abteilung des Lyzeums in Luzern 1830–47*, Berne.

Ganz, P. L.: Die Basler Professorengalerie in d. Aula d. Museums an d. Augustinergasse, *Basler Z. f. Gesch. u. Altertumskunde*, 78: 31–162.

Im Hof, U.: Die Gründung d. Hohen Schule zu Bern 1528, *Berner Z. f. Gesch. u. Heimatkunde*, 40: 249–59.

Koller, T.: *Professor Dr med. Christoph Aebi-Ramser 1835–85, Professor der anatomischen Wissenschaften in Bern-Prag. Ein Lebensbild*, Riehen.

Leisibach, D.: Die Aufhebung des Luzerner Jesuitenkollegiums 1774. Die Anfänge der Staatsschule 1774–1814. Thesis. Freiburg i. Ü.

Richter, M.: *Auf die Mensur! Geschichte der schlagenden Korporationen der Schweiz. Beiträge zum schweizerischen akademischen Leben und zum Waffenstudententum des Auslandes*, Zurich/Lucerne.

Sealy, R. J.: The Palace Acad. of Henry III, *Biblioth. d'humanisme et renaissance*, 40: 61–83.

Secret, F.: La première acad. fr. de musique, selon les témoignages de Genebrard et de Jean Bodin, *Biblioth. d'humanisme et renaissance*, 40: 119–20.

For 1979

Backus, I.: L'enseignement de la logique à l'Acad. de Genève entre 1559 et 1565, *Rev. de théol. et de philos.*, 111: 153–63.

Bargmann, V.: Erinnerungen eines Assistenten Einsteins, *Vierteljahrsschrift d. Naturforschenden Gesellsch. in Zürich*, 124: 39–44.

Baumgartner, C.: *Der Anatom Walter Felix 1860–1930*, Zurich. (Inform. about the teaching of anatomy at Zurich).

Bezel. R.: *Der Physiologe Adolf Fick 1829–1901. Seine Zürcher Jahre 1852–68*, Zurich.

Courvoisier, J.: La haute éc. de Genève au 16e s. d'après le discours de Théodore de Bèze à l'inaug. du Coll. et Acad. de Genève, *Theol. Z.*, 35: 169–76.

Hürlimann, U.: *Otto Haab 1850–1931. Ein Schweizer Ophthalmologe*, Zurich. (Inform. about the teaching of ophthalmology at Zurich).

Jokela, H.: Hist. de l'enseignement sup. en Finlande, *CRE-Inform.*, 45: 4–13.

Jost, R.: Einstein u. Zürich, *Vierteljahrsschrift d. Naturforschenden Gesellsch. in Zürich*, 124: 7–23. (E. as student and prof. at Zurich).

Koch, F.: *Der Anatom Georg Hermann von Meyer 1815–92*, Zurich. (Inform. about the teaching of anatomy at Zurich).

Rasche, G. and Staub, H. H.: Physik u. Physiker an d. Univ. Zürich 1833–1948, *Vierteljahrsschrift d. Naturforschenden Gesellsch. in Zürich*, 124: 205–20.

Schmid, M. A.: Karlstadt als Theol. u. Prediger in Basel, *Theol. Z.*, 35: 155–68.

Schnyder, B. etc.: *L'Université de Fribourg a 90 ans — quatre facultés au fil du temps. 90 Jahre Universität Freiburg — vier Fakultäten im Wandel der Zeit*, Freiburg i. Ü.

Steiner, J.: *Erich Hugo Ebstein 1880–1913. Biographie und wissenschaftliches Werk*, Zurich. (Inform. about the teaching of med. at Zurich).

Université de Genève, Section de chimie, ed.: *Centenaire de l'Ecole de chimie de l'Université de Genève 1879–1979*, Geneva.

For 1980

Aeschlimann, J.: *Rudolph Brun 1885–1969. Leben und Werk des Zürcher Neurologen, Psychoanalytikers und Entomologen*, Zurich.

Baumberger, H.-R.: *Carl Liebermeister 1833–1901*, Zurich. (Inform. about the teaching of med. at Zurich).

Grob, H., Bergier, J.-F. and Tobler, H. W. eds: *Eidgenössisch Technische Hochschule Zürich 1955–80*, Zurich.

Kuhn-Schnyder, E.: *Lorenz Oken 1779–1851. Erster Rektor der Universität Zürich*, Zurich.

Maissen, F.: Westschweizer Studenten an d. Univ. Innsbruck 1671–1900, *Freiburger Geschichtsblätter*, 62: 177–98.

Ott, E.: *Friedrich Horner 1831–86. Leben und Werk*, Zurich. (Inform. about the teaching of ophthalmology at Zurich).

Rintelen, F.: *Geschichte der Medizinischen Fakultät in Basel 1900–45*, Basle.

Robey, D.: Humanism and educ. in the early Quattrocento. The 'De ingenuis moribus' of P. P. Vergerio, *Biblioth. d'humanisme et renaissance*, 42: 27–58.

Rother, W.: Die Philosophie an der Universität Basel im 17. Jahrhundert. Quellen und Analyse. Thesis. Zurich.

Stelling-Michaud, S. ed.: *Le Livre du Recteur de l'Académie de Genève 1559–1878, 6: Notices biographiques des étudiants, T-Z*, Geneva.

Triet, M., Marrer, P. and Rindlisbacher, H. eds: *Die Matrikel der Universität Basel, 5: 1726/27–1817/18*, Basle.

For 1981

Bezel, E.: *Johann Jakob Steger 1798–1857. Beispiel eines Medizinstudiums im frühen 19. Jahrhundert nach den Briefen an seine Eltern*, Zurich.

Dolder, E. J. and Freihofer, H. H.: *120 Jahre zahnärztlicher Unterricht an der Universität Zürich 1861–1981*, Zurich.

Gyr, P.: *Josef Wolfgang von Deschwanden 1819–66, erster Direktor des Eidgenössischen Polytechnikums in Zürich*, Zurich.

Hamilton, A.: Lazare Marcquis' Leiden Years, *Biblioth. d'humanisme et renaissance*, 43: 567–71. (Inform. about the teaching of med. at 17th-cent. Leyden).

Picco, C.: *Das Biochemische Institut der Universität Zürich 1931–81*, Aarau.

Prahl, H.-W. and Schmidt-Harzbach, I.: *Die Universität. Eine Kultur- und Sozialgeschichte*, Lucerne.

Senn, C.: Die Entwicklung der Zürcher Tierarzneischule in den Jahren 1856 bis 1882. Thesis. Zurich.

Steffen, W.: *Die studentische Autonomie im mittelalterlichen Bologna. Eine Untersuchung über die Stellung der Studenten and ihrer Universitas gegenüber Professoren und Stadtregierung im 13./14. Jahrhundert*, Berne.

For 1986

Bishop, R. E. D.: Brunel univ., *CRE-Inform.*, 73: 13–19.
Bonke, F.: Creating a univ. The Rijksuniv. Limburg, *CRE-Inform.*, 73: 65–88.
Caspersen, S.: Dialoguer avec la soc. L'Univ. d'Aalborg, *CRE-Inform.*, 73: 121–41.
Mannerkoski, M.: The univ. of Oulu, *CRE-Inform.*, 73: 31–36.
Pollock, K.-H.: L'univ. de Passau, *CRE-Inform.*, 73: 39–50.
Schutter, B. de: L'univ. néerlandophone libre de Bruxelles—VUB 1970–85, *CRE-Inform.*, 73: 21–29.
Stalsberg, H.: The univ. of Tromso, *CRE-Inform.*, 73: 53–61.
Wolff, K. D.: Establishing an identity. The univ. of Bayreuth, *CRE-Inform.*, 73: 91–117.
Yim, H.-S.: Germanistik in Korea, *Jb. f. internat. Germanistik*, 18/2: 108–25.

Publications 1982

Carlen, L. etc.: *Hundert Jahre Rechts- und Wirtschaftsgeschichte an der Rechts-, Wirtschafts- und Sozialwissenschaftlichen Fakultät der Universität Freiburg*, Freiburg i. Ü.
Carruba, R. W.: The Latin document confirming the date and instit. of Wilhelm ten Rhyne's M.D., *Gesnerus*, 39: 473–76.
Chêne, C.: *L'enseignement du droit français en pays de droit écrit 1679–1793*, Geneva.
Hofmann, B.: Ein Geburtshelfer und Hebammenlehrer des 18. Jahrhunderts. Leben und Werk des Johann Philipp Hagen 1734–92, Hebammenlehrer und Professor für Entbindungskunst in Berlin. Thesis. Berne.
Hörning, B. and Fankhauser, R. eds: *Lehr- und Wanderzeit eines Studenten der Berner Tierarzneischule in den sechziger Jahren des vergangenen Jahrhunderts. David von Niederhäuserns 'Summarischer Generalbericht' über seine Studien, niedergeschrieben im Jahre 1869*, Berne.
Kaiser, W.: *Leben und Werk des Basler Psychiaters und Psychoanalytikers Hans Christoffel 1888–1959*, Zurich.
Kis, J.: *Der Knochenpathologe Emil Looser 1877–1936*, Zurich. (Inform. about the teaching of surgery at Zurich).
Leisibach, M.: *Das Medizinisch-chirurgische Institut in Zürich 1782–1833. Vorläufer der Medizinischen Fakultät der Universität Zürich*, Zurich.
Lorenz, S.: *Aktenversendung und Hexenprozess, dargestellt am Beispiel der Juristenfakultät Rostock und Greifswald 1570/82–1630*, Berne.

Marti, H.: Philosophische Dissertationen deutscher Universitäten 1660–1750. Eine Auswahlbibliographie. Thesis. Basle.

Rintelen, F.: Von d. Augenheilanstalt zur Universitätsaugenklinik Basel, *Gesnerus*, 39: 79–83.

—— Zur Persönlichkeit Karl Gustav Jungs, *Gesnerus*, 39: 237–42. (Inform. about the teaching of med. at Basle).

Schläpfer, H.: Die Entwicklung der Tierarzneischule Zürich von 1882 bis 1902. Thesis. Zurich.

Sutter, H.: Die Ed. d. Basler Universitätsmaktrikel, *Basler Stadtbuch 1981*, 102: 185–88.

Universität Zürich, Slavisches Seminar, ed.: *Slavisches Seminar der Universität Zürich 1961–81*, Zurich.

Publications 1983

Balmer, H.: Aus d. Gesch. d. Univ. Zürich, *Zürcher Chronik*, 51: 6–7.

Boehm, L.: Wilhelm von Humboldt 1767–1835 and the univ.: idea and implementation, *CRE-Inform.*, 62: 89–105.

Boschung, U., Muralt, A. de and Töndury, G.: *Johannes von Muralt 1645–1733. Arzt, Chirurg, Anatom, Naturforscher, Philosoph*, Zurich. (Inform. about the teaching of med. at Zurich).

Burke, P.: The reform of European univs in the 16th and 17th cents, *CRE-Inform.*, 62: 59–67.

Denley, P.: The soc. function of Italian Renaissance univs: prospects for research, *CRE-Inform.*, 62: 47–58.

Dufek, W. M.: *Der Internist Otto Naegeli 1871–1938*, Zurich. (Inform. about the teaching of internal med. at Zurich).

Fasol, E.: *Der Internist Hermann Eichhorst 1849–1921*, Zurich. (Inform. about the teaching of internal med. at Zurich).

Hammerstein, N.: Univ. devel. in the 17th and 18th cents: a comparative study, *CRE-Inform.*, 62: 81–88.

Histoire de l'Administration de l'enseignement en France 1789–1981, Geneva.

Lobkowicz, N.: Soc. et univ. de masse au 20e s.: une perspective europ., *CRE-Inform.*, 62: 133–53.

Perkin, H.: The changing soc. function of the univ.: a hist. retrospect, *CRE-Inform.*, 62: 117–31.

Pfarrwaller-Stieve, A.: *Friedrich von Müller 1858–1941 und seine Stoffwechseluntersuchungen*, Zurich. (Inform. about the teaching of med. at Zurich).

Pilleri, G. and Schnyder, J. J.: *Josef Breuer 1842–1925*, Waldau-Berne. (Inform. about the teaching of cerebral anatomy at Berne).

Portmann, M.-L.: Der Basler Medizinprof. Johann Jacob Harder 1656–1711 als Geburtshelfer, *Gesnerus*, 40: 139–47.

Ridder-Symoens, H. de: La migration acad. des hommes et des idées en Europe, 13e–18e s., *CRE-Inform.*, 62: 69–79.

Rintelen, F.: Der Basler Chirurg u. Rebell Johannes Fatio 1649–91, *Gesnerus*, 40: 149–58.

Rohr, A. von: Die Medizinische Poliklinik der Universität Zürich 1835–1983. Thesis. Zurich.

Rüttimann, B.: *Wilhelm Schulthess 1855–1917 und die Schweizer Orthopädie seiner Zeit*, Zurich. (Inform. about the teaching of orthopedy at Zurich).

Schmutz, H.-K.: Die Gründung d. Zürcher Lehrstuhles f. Anthropologie, *Gesnerus*, 40: 167–73.

Späth, H.-U.: *Der Hämatologe Albert Adler 1888–1980*, Zurich. (Inform. about the teaching of med. at Zurich).

Stadler, P. ed.: *Die Universität Zürich 1933–83*, Zurich.

Verger, J.: Univ. et communauté au Moyen Age, *CRE-Inform.*, 62: 21–44.

Vinay, V.: Die Arbeit einiger franz. Studenten f. d. Verbreitung d. Ref. in Turin u. ihre Beziehungen zu Farel 1523–30, *Cahiers de la Rev. de théol. et de philos.*, 9/1: 73–81. (With French summary).

Vossers, G.: The devel. of educ. for technol. both within and outside the univ., and its relation to scientif. research, *CRE-Inform.*, 62: 107–116.

Zahnd, C.: ETH-Habilitationsschriften. Verzeichnis der seit 1926 (– 1983) an der Eidgenössischen Technischen Hochschule Zürich eingereichten und angenommenen Habilitationsschriften nebst einem Verzeichnis der Privatdozenten, die von der Einreichung einer besonderen Habilitationsschrift an der ETH befreit worden sind, Zurich.

Publications 1984

Birchler, R.: Die Lehrer der Chirurgie an der Tierarzneischule Zürich 1820–1943. Thesis. Zurich.

Dibon, P. and Waquet, F.: *Johannes Fridericus Gronovius, pèlerin de la République des Lettres. Recherche sur le voyage savant au 17e siècle*, Geneva. (J.F.G a student at Paris and Angers, and prof. at Deventer).

Gavroglu, K.: Univ. reform laws in Greece. An hist. overview 1911–81, *CRE-Inform.*, 68: 19–30.

Heller, S.: *Boerhaaves Schweizer Studenten. Ein Beitrag zur Geschichte des Medizinstudiums*, Zurich.

Jilek, L.: *Historical compendium of European Universities. Répertoire historique des universités européennes*, Geneva.

Louros, N. C.: L'univ. nat. d'Athènes 1837–1937. Repères d'hist., *CRE-Inform.*, 68: 13–18.

Premuda, L.: Schweizer Medizinstudenten u. Ärzte im Gebiet zwischen Padua u. Triest, *Gesnerus*, 41: 299–321.

Ringeling, H. and Svilar, M. eds: *Die Universität Bern. Geschichte und Entwicklung*, Berne.

Scandola, P. ed: *Hochschulgeschichte Berns 1528–1984*, Berne.

—— *Die Dozenten der bernischen Hochschule*, Berne.

Sphiroéras, B.: La présence de l'univ. d'Athènes dans l'hist. de l'état grec, *CRE-Inform.*, 68: 5–11.

Publications 1985

Batllori, M.: Les univs et les colls jésuites du 16e au 18e s., *CRE-Inform.*, 72: 61–73.

Borgolte, M.: Die Rolle d. Stifters bei d. Gründung mittelalterl. Univ., erörtert am Beispiel Freiburgs u. Basels, *Basler Z. f. Gesch. u. Altertums-kunde*, 85: 85–119.

Boschung, U. ed.: *Johannes Gessners Tagebuch 1727*, Berne. (Inform. about the teaching of med. at Paris).

Charlton, K.: Univs in England 1500–1800, *CRE-Inform.*, 69: 45–59.

Chodakowska, J.: L'époque contemp., *CRE-Inform.*, 69: 171–80. (Inform. about the hist. of Polish universities).

Dutkowa, R. and Bartnicka, K.: Le 19e s., *CRE-Inform.*, 69: 139–56. (Inform. about the hist. of Polish universities).

Dybiec, J.: L'Entre-deux-guerres, *CRE-Inform.*, 69: 157–67. (Inform. about the hist. of Polish universities).

Egloff, C.: *Der Chirurg Emil Dagobert Schumacher 1880–1914*, Zurich. (Inform. about the teaching of surgery at Zurich).

Esch, A.: Die Anfänge d. Univ. im Mittelalter, in Universität Bern ed.: *Berner Rektoratsreden*, Berne: 7–29.

Frängsmyr, T.: Sweden, *CRE-Inform.*, 69: 205–214. (Inform. about the hist. of Swedish universities).

García y García, A.: Medieval univs in the Iberian peninsula, *CRE-Inform.*, 69: 181–86.

Gerbod, P.: La France depuis 1789, *CRE-Inform.*, 69: 85–93. (Inform. about the hist. of Fr. universities).

Gilissen, J.: L'enseignement du droit romain à l'Ec., puis Fac. de droit de Bruxelles 1806–17, in J. A. Ankum, J. E. Spruit and F. B. J. Wubbe eds: *Satura Roberto Feenstra*, Freiburg i. Ü. (henceforth noted as *Satura R.F.*): 659–77.

Hadjdukiewicz, L.: Du Moyen Age aux Lumières, *CRE-Inform.*, 69: 119–37. (Inform. about the hist. of Polish universities).

Hammerstein, N.: Allemagne. Des origines à Humboldt, *CRE-Inform.*, 69: 13–21. (Inform. about the hist. of German universities).

Im Hof, U.: *Die Berner Universität im Jubiläumsjahr. Kleine Chronik*, Berne.

Jong, O. J. de: States, churches and univs during the Refn, *CRE-Inform.*, 72: 47–60.

Klingenstein, G.: Austria, *CRE-Inform.*, 69: 23–31. (Inform. about the hist. of Austrian universities).

Krobot, A.: *Zur Geschichte der medizinischen Ausbildung an der Prager Karlsuniversität von 1650 bis 1800*, Zurich.

Langholm, S.: Norway, *CRE-Inform.*, 69: 95–111. (Inform. about the hist. of Norwegian universities).

Michel, H. A.: Das wiss. Bibliothekswesen Berns vom Mittelalter bis zur Gegenwart. Zum Jubiläum 450 Jahre Stadt- u. Universitätsbilioth. Bern 1535–1985, *Berner Z. f. Gesch. u. Heimatkunde*, 47: 167–234.

Moorman van Kappen, O.: Blick auf d. Werdegang einer Harderwijker Dissertation vom Jahre 1758, in *Satura R.F.*: 631–47.

Mrozowska, K.: Pologne, introd. et bibliog., *CRE-Inform.*, 69: 113–117. (Inform. about the hist. of Polish universities).

—— La Seconde Guerre mondiale, *CRE-Inform.*, 69: 168–70. (Inform. about the hist. of Polish universities).

Müller, E.: Die Entwicklung des Unterrichts in Kinderzahnmedizin am Zahnärztlichen Institut der Universität Zürich. Thesis. Zurich.

Neiger, R.: *Jakob Wyrsch 1892–1980*, Aarau. (Inform. about the teaching of med. at Zurich).

Peset, M.: Les univs hispaniques de la période mod. et contemp., *CRE-Inform.*, 69: 187–204.

—— La monarchie absolue et les univs espagn., *CRE-Inform.*, 72: 75–104.

Reeves, M.: Medieval Oxford, *CRE-Inform.*, 69: 33–44.

Schwöbel-Schrafl, E.: *Was verdankt die Medizinische Fakultät Zürich ihren ausländischen Dozenten? 1833–63*, Zurich.

Tremp-Utz, K.: *Das Kollegiatstift St Vinzenz in Bern von der Gründung 1484/85 bis zur Aufhebung 1528*, Berne.

Vautrey, L.: *Histoire du Collège de Porrentruy 1590–1865*, Porrentruy.

Verger, J.: La France sous l'Ancien Régime, *CRE-Inform.*, 69: 61–82. (Inform. about the hist. of Fr. universities).

Yushu, Z.: Die Germanistik in China. Vergangenheit u. Gegenwart, *Jb. f. internat. Germanistik*, 17/1: 168–84.

Publications 1987

Andenmatten, B.: Les 'Studia' des ordres mendiants à Lausanne 13e–16e s., in A. Paravicini ed.: *Ecoles et vie intellectuelle à Lausanne au Moyen Age*, Lausanne (henceforth noted as *Ecoles à Lausanne*): 73–93.

Belperrin, F. and Schaefer, P.: *Les portraits professoraux de la Salle du Sénat, Palais de Rumine*, Lausanne.

Bielman, A.: *Histoire de l'histoire ancienne et de l'archéologie à l'Université de Lausanne 1537–1987*, Lausanne.

Borle, J.-P.: *Le latin à l'Académie de Lausanne du 16e au 20e siècle*, Lausanne.

Büchi, A.: *Gründung und Anfänge der Universität Freiburg i. Ü. Erinnerungen und Dokumente*, Freiburg i. Ü.

Busino, G. and Bridel, P.: *L'Ecole de Lausanne. De Léon Walras à Pasquale Boninsegni*, Lausanne.

Christoff, D. etc.: *La philosophie dans la Haute Ecole de Lausanne 1542–1955*, Lausanne.

Cunha, A., Delapierre, C. and Lambelet, J.-C.: *L'Université dans la cité. Essai d'évaluation des apports de l'Université de Lausanne à la collectivité*, Lausanne.

De l'Académie à l'Université de Lausanne 1537–1987. 450 ans d'histoire. Catalogue de l'exposition----du 18 juin au 13 septembre 1987, Lausanne.

Gardiol, N.: _Le coup d'état académique du 2 décembre 1846_, Lausanne.

Künzle, A.: Die Entwicklung der Veterinär-medizinischen Fakultät der Universität Zürich von 1900 bis 1930. Thesis. Zurich.

Maehle, A.-H.: _Johann-Jakob Wepfer 1620–95 als Toxikologe_, Aarau. (Inform. about the teaching of med. at Zurich).

Marcacci, M.: _Histoire de l'Université de Genève 1559–1986_, Geneva.

Meuwly, O.: _Histoire des sociétés d'étudiants à Lausanne_, Lausanne.

Morerod, J.: Le Pays de Vaud et les univs aux 12e et 13e s., in _Ecoles à Lausanne_: 25–71.

Neumann, D.: _Studentinnen aus dem Russischen Reich in der Schweiz 1867–1914_, Zurich.

Policlinique médicale universitaire, ed.: _Policlinique médicale universitaire— 100 ans 1887–1987_, Lausanne.

Poudret, J.-F. etc.: _L'enseignement du droit à l'Académie de Lausanne aux 18e et 19e siècles_, Lausanne.

Pradervand-Amiet, B.: _L'Ancienne Académie de Lausanne. Innovation et tradition dans l'architecture scolaire du 16e siècle_, Lausanne.

Robert, O. ed.: _Matériaux pour servir à l'histoire du doctorat h. c. décerné à Benito Mussolini en 1937_, Lausanne.

Saudan, G. ed.: _L'éveil médical vaudois 1750–1850. Auguste Tissot, Jean-André Venel, Mathias Mayor_, Lausanne.

Saugy, C.: _L'Ecole de français moderne de l'Université de Lausanne 1892–1987_, Lausanne.

Schaefer, P.: _L'aula du Palais de Rumine. Le décor de Louis Rivier_, Lausanne.

Siegrist, W. and Labhardt, F.: 100 Jahre Psychiatr. Universitätsklinik, _Basler Stadtbuch 1986_, 107: 125–37.

Verger, J.: Géog. univ. et mobilité étudiante au Moyen Age. Quelques remarques, in _Ecoles à Lausanne_: 9–23.

Zupan, P.: _Der Physiologe Carl Ludwig in Zürich 1849–55_, Zurich.

Publications 1988

Andrzejewski, M.: Die Polen auf d. Hochschulen in d. Schweiz 1870–1945. Forschungsstand u. Forschungsbedürfnis, _Schweiz. Z. f. Gesch._, 38: 403–408.

Belser, K. etc. eds: _Ebenso neu als kühn. 100 Jahre Frauenstudium an der Universität Zürich_, Zurich.

Ducrey, P.: Le 900e anniv. de l'univ. de Bologne, _CRE-Action_, 84: 51–54.

Hobi, B. A.: Die methodisch-klinische Forschung des Internisten Theodor Juergensen 1840–1907. Thesis. Basle. (Inform. about the teaching of internal med. at Basle).

Köppel-Hefti, A.: _Der Gynäkologe Theodor Wyder 1853–1926_, Zurich. (Inform. about the teaching of gynaecology at Zurich).

Loretan, M.: _William Silberschmidt 1869–1947. Hygieniker und Bakteriologe_, Zurich. (Inform. about the teaching of med. at Zurich).

L'université en question. Actes du colloque du 450e anniversaire de la fondation de l'Académie de Lausanne, suivis du recueil des discours du 450e anniversaire, 13–18 juin 1987, Lausanne.

Piangger-Vavra, M.: *Die Anatomin Hedwig Frey 1877–1938. Erste Professorin der Universität Zürich*, Zurich.

Schobinger, J.-P. ed.: *Grundriss der Geschichte der Philosophie. Begründet von Friedrich Ueberweg. Die Philosophie des 17. Jahrhunderts, 3: England*, Basle. (Contains contribs on 17th-cent. teaching of philos. at univs in England, Scotland, Ireland and New England).

Thorens, J.: Bologne, Alma Mater des univs, *CRE-Action*, 84: 43–50.

Uebelhart, A.: *Richard Scherb 1880–1955, Orthopäde und Muskelphysiologe*, Zurich. (Inform. about the teaching of med. at Zurich).

The United States

Additions to Earlier Lists

For 1980

Courtenay, W. J.: The effect of the Black Death on Eng. higher educ., *Speculum*, 55: 696–714.

Hudson, W. S.: *The Cambridge connection and the Elizabethan settlement of 1559*, Durham, N.C.

For 1982

Meskill, J.: *Academies in Ming China*, Tucson, Ariz.

For 1984

Hunter, J. M.: Christopher St German's 'Doctor and Student'. The scholastic heritage of a Tudor dialogue. Thesis. Univ. of Colorado at Boulder.

Kiermayr, R.: On the educ. of the pre-Refn clergy, *Church hist.*, 53: 7–16.

Petersen, P. L.: *A place called Dana. The centennial history of Trinity Seminary and Dana College*, Omaha, Nebr.

Wallace, W. A.: *Galileo and his sources. Heritage of the Collegio Romano in Galileo's science*, Princeton, N.J.

For 1985

Bezilla, M.: *Penn State: An illustrated history*, University Park, Pa.

Ferruolo, S. C.: *The origins of the university. The schools of Paris and their critics 1100–1215*, Stanford, Calif.

Le Breton, M. M.: *Northwestern State University of Louisiana 1884–1984. A history*, Natchitoches, La.

Oren, D. A.: *Joining the club: A history of Jews and Yale*, New Haven, Conn.

For 1986

Christy, E. E.: The influence of the Soviet Union on Chinese higher educational and scientific development 1920–50. Thesis. Univ. of Oregon.

Clark, W.: From the medieval *universitas scholarium* to the German research university. A sociogenesis of the German academic. Thesis. Univ. of California, Los Angeles.

Luptrecht, M.: 'What people call pessimism'. The impact of the medical faculty of the university of Vienna on the world-views of Sigmund Freud and Arthur Schnitzler. Thesis. Florida State University.

Ridder-Symoens, H. de: Possibilités de carrière et de mobilité soc. des intellects-univ. au moyen âge, in H. Bulst and J.-P. Genet: *Medieval lives and the historian. Studies in medieval prosopography*, Kalamazoo: 343–57.

Solomon, B. M.: *In the company of educated women. A history of women and higher education in America*, New Haven/London.

Publications 1987

Bishop, C. C.: Teaching at Johns Hopkins: The first generation, *Hist. of educ. quarterly*, 27: 499–515.

Broman, T. H.: The transformation of academic medicine in Germany 1780–1920. Thesis. Princeton University.

Burney, J. M.: *Training the Bourgeoisie: the university of Toulouse in the 19th century-faculties and students in provincial France*, New York.

Campbell, R. F. etc.: *A history of thought and practice in educational administration*, New York.

Clark, B. R.: *The academic life: small worlds, different worlds*, Princeton, N.J.

Courtenay, W. J.: *Schools and scholars in 14th-century England*, Princeton, N.J.

Handy, R. T.: *A history of Union Theological Seminary in New York*, New York.

Harcleroad, F. F. and Ostar, A. W.: *Colleges and universities for change; America's comprehensive public state colleges and universities*, Washington, D.C.

Higuero, F. J.: The crisis of the univ. in the writings of Ortega y Gasset, *Jnl of general educ.*, 39: 36–53. (Spanish criticisms of univs of 1930s).

Hohner, R. A.: Southern educ. in transition: William Waugh Smith, the Carnegie fndation and the Methodist Church, *Hist. of educ. quarterly*, 27: 181–203.

Horowitz, H. L.: *Campus life; undergraduate cultures from the end of the 18th century to the present*, Chicago, Ill.

Johnson, E. L.: The 'other Jeffersons' and the State Univ. Idea, *Jnl of higher educ.*, 58: 151–80.

Koelsch, W. A.: *Clark university 1887–1987: a narrative history*, Worcester, Mass.

Mathers, C. J.: Students from Burgos at the Spanish Coll. at Bologna 1500–60, *16th-cent. jnl*, 18: 545–56.

Shaffer, R.: Jews, reds and violets. Anti-semitism and anti-radicalism at New York univ. 1916–29, *Jnl of ethnic studies*, 15: 47–83.

Siraisi, N. G.: *Avicenna in renaissance Italy. The Canon and medical teaching in Italian universities after 1500*, Princeton, N.J.

Stewart-Robertson, C.: The pneumatics and Georgics of the Scottish mind, *18th-cent. studies*, 20: 296–312. (Considers Thomas Reid at univ. of Glasgow).

Thelin, J. R.: Southern exposure. House hists with room for a view, *Rev. of higher educ.*, 10: 357–68. (Rev. of recent studies of hist. of southern universities).

Turner, P. V.: *Campus; an American planning tradition*, New York.

Williams, L. H.: *Black higher education in Kentucky 1879–1930; the history of Simmons University*, Lewiston, New York.

Wright, W. J.: Evaluating the results of 16th-cent. educ. pol.: some Hessian data, *16th-cent. jnl*, 18: 411–26.

Publications 1988

Adams, P. K.: James P. Wickersham and higher educ. in 19th-cent. Pennsylvania, *Soc. studies jnl*, 17: 13–18.

Albisetti, J. C.: *Schooling German girls and women; secondary and higher education in the 19th century*, Princeton, N.J.

Beauregard, E. E.: *History of academic freedom in Ohio; case studies in higher education 1808–1976*, New York.

Bender, T. ed.: *The university and the city; from medieval origins to the present*, New York.

Clifford, G. J. and Guthrie, J. W.: *Ed school: a brief for professional education*, Chicago, Ill.

Ferruolo, S. C.: 'Quid dant artes nisi luctum?' Learning, ambition and careers in the medieval univ., *Hist. of educ. quarterly*, 28: 1–22.

Flynn, J. T.: *The university reforms of Tsar Alexander 1 1802–35*, Washington, D.C.

Grobman, A. B.: *Urban state universities; an unfinished national agenda*, New York.

Hayhoe, R.: *China's universities and the open door*, New York.

Levine, D. O.: *The American college and the culture of aspiration 1915–40*, Ithaca, N.Y.

Malpass, L. F.: *What's past is prologue; the Board of Governors of State Colleges and Universities in Illinois 1965–87*, Macomb, Ill.

McConagha, G. L. etc.: *Blackburn College 1837–1987. An anecdotal and analytical history of the private college*, Carlinville, Ill.

Mujal-Leon, E.: *The Cuban university under the revolution*, Washington, D.C.

Myers, S. L. ed.: *Desegregation in higher education*, Lanham, M.D.

Potts, D. B.: *Baptist colleges in the development of American society 1821–61*, New York.

Shank, M. H.: *'Unless you believe, you shall not understand'. Logic, university and society in late medieval Vienna*, Princeton, N.J.

Shinnerf, J. R.: Univ. study licenses and clerical educ. in the diocese of Norwich 1325–35, *Hist. of educ. quarterly*, 28: 387–410.

Tent, J. F.: *The Free University of Berlin. A political history*, Bloomington, Ind.

Topping, R. W. etc.: *A century and beyond. The history of Purdue University*, West Lafayette, Ind.

Publications 1989

Brint, S.: *The diverted dream; community colleges and the promise of educational opportunity in America 1900–85*, New York.

Feldman, J.: *Universities in the business of repression; the academic-military-industrial complex and Central America*, Boston, Mass.

Knight, D. M.: *Street of dreams; the nature and legacy of the 1960s*, Durham, N.C. (Aftermath of 1960s at Duke University).

Index of Continents, Towns and Institutions